D1518103

BEST
JEWISH
WRITING
2002

BEST
JEWISH
WRITING
2002

MICHAEL LERNER

EDITOR

JOSSEY-BASS
A Wiley Company
www.josseybass.com

Published by

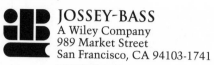

JOSSEY-BASS
A Wiley Company
989 Market Street
San Francisco, CA 94103-1741

www.josseybass.com

Copyright © 2002 by Michael Lerner

Jossey-Bass is a registered trademark of John Wiley & Sons, Inc.

Jossey-Bass books and products are available through most bookstores. To contact Jossey-Bass directly, call (888) 378–2537, fax to (800) 605–2665, or visit our website at www.josseybass.com.

Substantial discounts on bulk quantities of Jossey-Bass books are available to corporations, professional associations, and other organizations. For details and discount information, contact the special sales department at Jossey-Bass.

We at Jossey-Bass strive to use the most environmentally sensitive paper stocks available to us. Our publications are printed on acid-free recycled stock whenever possible, and our paper always meets or exceeds minimum GPO and EPA requirements.

Jossey-Bass also publishes its books in a variety of electronic formats. Some content that appears in print may not be available in electronic books.

Library of Congress Cataloging Card Number

ISBN 0-7879-6210-4

FIRST EDITION
PB Printing   10 9 8 7 6 5 4 3 2 1

CONTENTS

RECLAIMING THE SPIRIT IN JUDAISM

*To Trish Vradenburg, my brilliant,
talented, and creative sister*

PREFACE

Susannah Heschel

BEST JEWISH WRITING 2002 will be scrutinized for generations to come, to see how we responded to the traumas of a terrible year. We witnessed the onset of the second Intifada, the corruption of the electoral process in Florida, the growing economic recession in the United States that exploded into the Enron scandal, the collapse of the Argentinian economy, and the horrifying attacks on the World Trade Center, followed by the war in Afghanistan. During this, one of the most frightening periods in recent history, Jews did not draw together, but became more and more polarized. Passionate political opinions drew us apart, but so did feelings of frustration and apathy, as the rate of Jews abandoning the community through intermarriage kept on increasing. Throughout, Jewish intellectual life continued its vibrancy, but in the immediacy of the political horrors it became difficult to hear messages of messianic anticipation, of *tikkun olam,* the prophetic vision of repairing the world. By the end of the year, a new Tikkun Community emerged, under the leadership of Michael Lerner.

Lerner has gathered the key moments of our written expression of the past year, with a broad range of political viewpoints and religious concerns. Uniting them are the emotions: there is agony over the bombings in Israel and on September 11, outrage at U.S. and Israeli foreign policies, indignation at aspects of Jewish life that are perceived as sexist, racist, or homophobic. The dimensions of political debate during the past year have grown enormously and have taken on a new, graver significance. Israel may have won the 1967 war in six days, but seems unlikely to win the war it is waging against terrorism in a century, if ever. For many writers, the fruitlessness of current Israeli government policies and the shock over the utterly unanticipated September 11 attacks have prompted a reconsideration of traditional political ideas and modes of analysis. In the writings of others, the stench of arrogance pervades, an insistence of commentators across the political spectrum that they know the motivations of Al Qaida—although those motivations turn out to be nothing more than projections of the commentators' own views, a politics of the self-justifying mirror. Emerging occasionally in the tumult are the still, small eloquent voices of inspiration, reminding us that our significance lies not in who we are as Jews, but what we stand for.

Uniting the writings in this volume is an important struggle over what it means to articulate a Jewish sensibility. In whose voice does a Jewish writer speak: the voice of the collective Jewish community? Or of Judaism and its teachings? Is Jewishness defined by the historical experience of the Jewish people or by the messianic vision of the future for all people that has inspired us since biblical days?

The writings in this book give clear expression to those conflicts. The appeal from writers such as Jonathan Rosen is to the collective Jewish history of anti-Semitism, persecution, pogrom, and the holocaust. By contrast, Letty Cottin Pogrebin, Arthur Waskow, Danya Ruttenberg, and Galina Vromen, among others, speak in Judaism's prophetic voice, which often rubs against the grain of Jewish popular consensus.

Both groups would undoubtedly agree with Abraham Joshua Heschel's dictum that "the opposite of good is not evil, the opposite of good is indifference," but they differ in defining the scope of their highest loyalties: the greatest good of the Jewish people or the highest moral values taught by Judaism?

Jonathan Rosen, for example, voices his fear of rising anti-Semitism, with the looming specter of the Holocaust that engulfed his family. After September 11, he suggests, Jews have something to teach Americans: we Jews live in the shadow of the Holocaust, and with the daily terrorism in Israel. We can show Americans how to live with terror, and how to keep on with their normal lives. All Americans have been forced to become Jews, Rosen suggests; they are all experiencing the unique terror that stamps Jewish history. From the beginning and until recent years, American Jewish writers have fashioned Jews in their own image: characters who are marginalized, knowing little or nothing of their Jewish heritage, estranged from their communities, embarrassed by their families, yet not fitting into the Christian world that masquerades as secular. To be Jewish was always to be the odd figure, the one who doesn't fit in anywhere.

With the writers included in this book, we see a new kind of Jewish writer. One who is engaged with Judaism, not just with being Jewish. The depth of learning evidenced by these writers goes beyond what anyone could have imagined a generation ago. Think about well-known American Jewish writers—Ludwig Lewisohn, Saul Bellow, Philip Roth, Bernard Malamud—discussing Talmud, Kabbalah, or Midrash! A generation ago, our intellectuals believed assimilation was the golden path and assumed religious observance would die out within a few years; modernity was supposed to bring about secularization, the end of religion.

Instead, religious faith is very much alive, not only in ritual practice, but as a way of viewing the world and understanding our role as human beings in it. For example, Arthur Waskow, in his response to September 11, compares the United States to a *sukkah,* a temporary booth erected for the week-long autumn holiday, a booth that is fragile both for its impermanence and its openness to the elements: "What is the lesson, when we learn that we—all of us—live in a sukkah? How do we make such a vulnerable house into a place of shalom, of peace and security and harmony and wholeness?"

Other writers, too, insist that we Jews are defined not simply by our experience at the hands of the Gentile world. Rather, we are entrusted with a sacred mission: to convey Judaism's teachings of the holiness of life, the preciousness of every person, and the core belief that the destruction of human beings is an assault on God. Judaism insists that our world is held up by pillars of respect, compassion, dignity, and sanctity. Those writers are warning us not to abandon our soul out of worry in a desperate scramble for physical security. Jews are here not just to demonstrate to the world how we survive in the face of anti-Semitism, but to teach the world the purpose of survival, the messianic dream of a world permeated by peace.

That prophetic voice comes through clearly in several important essays. Writing about the current Israeli government, Letty Cottin Pogrebin warns, "Israel's heartless or sadistic treatment of the 'Other' seems to be proliferating. In response, right-wing apologists would probably say, 'these people' deserve it, all of them, because every Arab would destroy us if he could. But at this point in history—given Israel's unquestionable military superiority—I believe we should be less worried about external enemies than about the internal existential threat to the very essence and meaning of Judaism and the Jewish State. In short, if we stop acting Jewish, are we still Jews?"

Living with the conviction that "every Arab would destroy us if he could" is one of the most self-destructive elements of modern Jewish identity. The lachrymose view of Jewish history was first developed most fully by the German-Jewish historian of the nineteenth century, Heinrich Graetz, and while numerous historians since then have attacked the validity of Graetz's version of Jewish history, his model remains as sturdy as a mighty fortress. Indeed, the myth of Jewish suffering and misery has played a crucial role in modern Jewish political movements and in the creation, for better and worse, of the modern Jewish psyche. Appeals to a long history of persecution buttress everything from right-wing secular Zionism to haredi Orthodoxy. How better to justify the exceptional quality of Jewish rights than as reparation for centuries of anti-Semitism? Indeed, at the 1994 UN Conference on Population and Development, convened to coordinate strategies to lower the earth's population growth, several Jewish representatives argued that Jews were exempt from a worldwide decrease in family size, because Jewish numbers had been decimated by the Holocaust. Such exemption of Jews from the collective moral responsibilities of the world's population is frequently reiterated in relation to Israeli political and military policies as well.

Yet many Jews today speak in a different voice. They implore us to recognize that if the Jewish soul is destroyed, the coroner's report will declare the violence committed in the name of gaining security to have been one of the major causes of death. The fruitless military efforts to prevent terrorist attacks will bring us spiritual devastation. There are important voices in this volume that insist that the values of Judaism be translated into actual policy. What is at stake in Israeli politics is not mere survival of the Jews, but putting into action the moral principles that Jews have brought into the world. Michael Gross writes, "Israel has an opportunity to show how a Jewish war might be just—how humanitarian law might apply in the kind of wars now in vogue, not international armed conflict but local hostilities confounded by an asymmetry of arms, terrorism, incongruent cultures, and the general indifference of most of the world. The tragedies of Jewish history were instrumental in bringing humanitarian law to the fore; it would be ironic if the Jews were the agents of its demise."

Those who have identified with the Tikkun Community are Jews appalled by what they claim is a moral corruption in the organizations representing Jews in America. They point to Operation Birthright's decision to honor the felon Marc Rich, motivated apparently by his philanthropy to that organization, and by the invitation extended by the Rabbinical Assembly of America, the organization of Conservative rabbis, to Elliot Abrams, a felon convicted of lying to the U.S. Congress, to lecture about Jewish ethics to the rabbis. Many are disturbed by the continuing opposition of most large American Jewish organizations to affirmative action. All are horrified by the state of Israel's policy of collective punishment of Palestinians. Many say they would rather leave the Jewish community than be part of a people who claim their survival depends upon a "defensive" strategy of demolishing Palestinian homes.

Such protests stem not from a disaffection with Jewish life, but from a radical insistence on Judaism's integrity. Commitment to Jewish life entails sacrifice, but sacrifice cannot be one-sided: the sacrifice of the individual for the sake of the community. The community, too, must make its sacrifices, including the repudiation of corrupt leaders and tainted monies.

The critics of Jewish life call for changes, particularly in the treatment of women, and their demands evoke clamors of admonition. We are often cautioned that only Orthodox Judaism will prevent intermarriage and assimilation, and that radical change in Jewish religious practice is inauthentic and destructive to Jewish unity. The fear of change and the insistence on maintaining older forms of Jewish religiosity are sometimes used as disciplinary tools against those who insist that reform is a moral and spiritual necessity. Nostalgia may be intrinsic to religion, but it should not be glorified as a guide to the future.

Very few have offered a theological rationale for the necessity of change; Abraham Heschel, whose work serves as a profound source of inspiration for the Tikkun movement, writes, "A vibrant Jew does not dwell in the shadow of old ideas conceived by prophets and rabbis centuries ago, living off an inherited estate of laws and customs, convictions and interpretations. In the realm of the spirit only he who is a pioneer is able to be an heir. The wages of spiritual plagiarism is the loss of integrity; self-aggrandizement is self-betrayal. Authentic faith is more than an echo of a tradition. It is a creative situation, an event" (*Man Is Not Alone*, p. 164).

If adherence to older forms of Jewish expression constitutes spiritual plagiarism, as Heschel writes, then it is those bringing change who are the true heirs of the tradition. In recent decades, Jewish feminists have brought about the most significant transformations of Judaism since the destruction of the Jerusalem Temple in the first century C.E. Those changes began as efforts at egalitarian worship, but soon expanded to imagining new theological methods that would be rooted in the experiences of women and not just men. Increasingly, Jewish feminists have articulated their views through the voices of classical texts. Indeed, the crucial component of the radical change that has occurred in recent decades is the passionate devotion to Judaism that lies behind it. For example, Bonna Haberman proposes viewing the biblical Book of Esther as a significant tool for unmasking and destroying sexual oppression. Elsewhere, a short story by Galina Vromen, "The Secret Diary of a Bat Mitzva Girl," articulates the voice of innocence that finds a moral challenge within the Bible to the conventions of Jewish life today. In Vromen's story, a bat mitzvah girl holds up the biblical account of Miriam being punished by God for criticizing Moses' marriage to a Cushite woman and uses it to challenge her parents' hostility to her brother's exogamous marriage. For those appalled by the sexism inherent in Judaism, Danya Ruttenberg offers a theological interpretation based on kabbalistic teachings that wholeness occurs when the heart is broken: "And these words which I command you this day shall be upon your heart. The Baal Shem Tov asked, why are they upon your heart instead of in your heart? So that when your heart breaks, the words fall in. It's not about 'healing' from our wounds so that we can move forward into the Sacred—it's about using our wounds to encounter the Sacred. . . . Our broken bits and our divine spark are one and the same."

Jewish life at the start of the twenty-first century comes to us shattered, in many respects. The Holocaust brought an end to the great Judaisms of Europe, and the dream of a state of Israel, as a cultural and political homeland, stands under threat as well. If Tikkun is to arise, it will come about when the brokenness of Jewish life is viewed not as a threat to our continued existence, but as a potential source of the Sacred that makes possible our continuing presence on this earth.

INTRODUCTION

Michael Lerner

I WAS DELIGHTED AT THE ENTHUSIASTIC RESPONSE this new annual series of *Best Jewish Writing* received in its maiden voyage last year. For the purposes of this series, I use "best" to mean "most significant," that is, writing that shapes or has the capacity to reveal the underlying issues facing Jews today.

My selections address Jews who have been estranged from their Jewishness or Jews who have been struggling with what place if any they have in the Jewish people, as much as they address those who feel secure in their Jewishness and are using this series to stay in touch with the latest and most creative Jewish thinking and writing. Because there is so much talent and wisdom in the Jewish world, any selection is bound to exclude wonderful and creative work. In picking the material for this volume covering the period 2000 and 2001, I've focused on writing that had a Jewish sensibility—that is, an involvement in the healing and transformation of the world (the Hebrew word for this is *tikkun*).

I don't mean to suggest that the writers I've chosen share my perspective on how to accomplish that transformation. On the contrary, I take strong exception to many of the works I've selected for this volume—I think some of them are wrong-headed in their politics or their approach to how to accomplish *tikkun*. But this collection is not about my views; it's about presenting what is significant in the Jewish writing of the current period. I guarantee you that the writing here will at various times stimulate, provoke, challenge, excite, or delight you and will give you a sense of the creativity and brilliance that characterizes Jewish writing in the early twenty-first century.

As we enter a period in which our society validates multicultural identities and in which a globalized consciousness often contends with the calls of particularistic cultures, it is no surprise that Jews find ourselves in confusing and sometimes conflicting circumstances. On the one hand, there is a strong desire on the part of many Jews to remain loyal to the generations of the past, to acknowledge the incredible tragedy that recently faced anyone born Jewish as madmen sought to destroy us all, and to acknowledge also that there is something powerful in the Jewish experience that has sustained this people for some three thousand years or more. Yet on the other hand, many contemporary Jews grew up in a Jewish world that did not address their own deepest yearnings for spiritual fulfillment, a sense of meaning and purpose, or a connection to the sacred. Without that mooring, these Jews often wonder why they need to keep their Jewish identity, or how that identity can be reconciled with conflicting moral, social, political, and economic pulls that draw them to a more universal identity that gives no special place to Jewishness.

Perhaps the most powerful event of the past year was the tragedy at the World Trade Center and the Pentagon on September 11, 2001, so it is no surprise that Jews were deeply involved in trying to understand the meaning of those events. Nor is it a surprise that the range of responses go from those like Sylvia Barack Fishman, who warns that one should avoid blaming America for the craziness of the Taliban, to others who feel that the post–September 11 world will be better off if we do in fact try to rectify some of the conditions that lie in the background of worldwide rage at the United States. In this section I've included Jonathan Mark's moving account of "E-Mails from the End of the World" and Michael Bader's analysis of "Posttraumatic Love Syndrome." Arthur Waskow helps us to think in spiritual terms. And because my own article on September 11 has been so widely quoted after a version of it was printed in *Time* magazine and I was interviewed on the *Lehrer News Hour*, I've decided to include some of my own thinking, though with the disclaimer that I am not maintaining that it otherwise deserves acknowledgment as "best Jewish writing."

This has been a moment when many people have turned back to their own spiritual traditions for solace and support. Yet for many Jews, a return to Judaism also provokes new conflicts and reawakens old ambivalences. So, in this collection I present some of the inner struggles that continue to challenge many Jews. For many Jews, the conflict addressed in the section entitled "The Many Identities of a Jew" comes to fullest expression in the decision to circumcise their male children. Why should we stick to an ancient rite that seems to inflict unnecessary pain and whose only upside is to connect us to the cultural or religious history of the tribe to which we belong? Michael Kimmel, an activist who has helped reclaim "men's consciousness," argues that it is time to abandon circumcision. David Zaslow responds by pointing out some of the conflicts that emerged in his life when he and his wife decided not to circumcise, and why he has now changed his mind on this issue. That this is starting to be a debate at all is indicative of how deep the questioning of Jewish identity can go even among people who subjectively feel very committed to their Jewishness.

But for many, that commitment is not easy to come by. Young people confront this when they are asked at age twelve (for many girls) or thirteen (for many boys) to make a decision and commitment to Jewishness after having been exposed to nothing more than a culinary identity, while experiencing daily life in the Jewish world as intolerant, materialistic, and inherently selfish. Bar and bat mitzvah can provoke the kind of questioning that leads many young Jews to be afraid to acknowledge that their Jewishness is important to them. In Galina Vromen's "The Secret Diary of a Bat Mitzva Girl" we relive bizarre bat mitzvah stories that feel all too familiar. By the time they reach teen years, many young Jews face identity issues in a different form: Should they date and form sexual relationships with non-Jews? The selection from Binnie Kirshenbaum's novel *Pure Poetry* captures some of the tensions that inevitably result, while our selection from Allan Appel highlights the difficulty nonreligious Jews have in providing a reason for why not to convert to another religion in order to make such relationships smoother. How permeable should the boundaries be? This issue is raised explicitly by Aryeh Cohen's article and by the selection from Wendy Wasserstein's *Shik'sa Goddess*. But the deeper issue is whether American Jews have not already converted to the dominant religion of American society: its worship of money and power and its one-dimensional "realism" (as in "be realistic and stop going for old-fashioned ideals that have no reality and won't help advance you or help you make it in the competitive market economy") as the ultimate mantra of the established religion.

Yet against the dominant religion there continues to be a renewal of Jewish values and Jewish spirituality that is growing deeper year by year. Its thinkers write in magazines like *TIKKUN: A Bimonthly Jewish Critique of Politics, Culture and Society* (www.tikkun.org), *Lilith* (www.lilith. com), *Shm'a* (www.shma.org), *New Menorah* (www.ShalomCtr.org), and *Clal* (www.clal.org), or teach at retreat centers like Elat Chayyim in Accord, New York, and present a striking contrast to the boringly predictable establishment versions of Judaism that you will find in a magazine like *Moment* or the mainstream Jewish newspapers or at the functions of the UJA/ Federation world. Just visit the Website www.tikkun.org to get a feel for the new energies that are bubbling up in the Jewish world!

In this volume I have assembled a section called "Reclaiming the Spirit in Judaism," which presents some of the most exciting spiritual thinkers. Judith Plaskow's groundbreaking work in Jewish feminism is represented here in her "Authority, Resistance, and Transformation." David Cooper and Rami Shapiro, both pathfinders in the renewal of Jewish spirituality, present powerful new ideas that are as controversial as they are deep. Eric Yoffie, the creative leader of the Reform movement in Judaism, recognizes some of the problems in making prayer alive in Reform temples, while Leonard Felder shows us how we can personally unpack the spiritual practice of prayer and bring it alive in our daily lives.

Yet no matter how exciting some aspects of Jewish thought become, the reality of Israel as the dominant image of contemporary Jewishness continues to haunt many Jews. Letty Cottin Pogrebin, one of the founders of *Ms.* magazine before she became a Jewish feminist activist, puts the question powerfully, looking at Israeli human rights abuses in "How Could a Jew Do That?" Think she is exaggerating? Then check out Haifa University professor Michael Gross' article on "Just and Jewish Warfare." Yossi Klein Halevi, a former follower of Jewish Defense League leader Meir Kahane, raises some objections to the Palestinians—and reminds us that there really is an adversary who is often unpredictable and hurtful. Tanya Reinhart and Uri Avnery, on the other hand, teach us new ways to view the history and present reality of the struggle, and Jerome Segal helps us see that even the most seemingly intractable problem, the "right of return," can be solved if there is a basic framework of goodwill and desire for reconciliation.

In fact, many young Jews are trying to find a path toward social justice, peace, and reconciliation with Israel. They have become involved in a host of organizations, including the Shalom Center, New Israel Fund, Americans for Peace Now, Junity, Women in Black, B'tselem, Yesh Gvul, and most recently the creation of the Tikkun Community. But Jewish activism doesn't remain confined to Israeli issues. In the section "On Being a Mensch and Healing a Troubled World" I present several examples of work being done by Jews who are deeply embedded in their Jewishness but who are giving primary focus to acting on their values in the larger world. David Abram, one of the most creative thinkers of contemporary environmentalism, writes about "learning humility through nature." Roger Gottlieb discusses the ways that a spiritual understanding helped deepen his engagement with his developmentally disabled child. And Paul Wapner, an assistant district attorney, encourages us to give a new look at environmental ethics.

Finally, as in each volume in this annual series, I include a series of articles, poetry, and fiction that demonstrate the beauty and power of contemporary Jewish writing, even if they do not necessarily contribute in some more obvious way to the healing or transformation of the world.

This collection is filled with gems, brilliant insights, wonderful use of language, and important new directions in thought and Jewish practice. Share it with your friends and let them know how alive the Jewish world can be.

Enjoy!

P.S. Let me know your reactions, and send me (at RabbiLerner@Tikkun. org) the "snail-mail" and e-mail addresses of other authors whose poetry, fiction, or essays I should consider in the future.

This volume was possible only because of the tireless work, competence, and intelligence of Rachel Davidman, who played a major role in every detail of putting this collection together. Joshua Shapiro gave me advice on poetry, Thane Rosenbaum on fiction, and Sandee Brawarsky introduced me to many writers whom I did not previously know in this and the first volume of this series. Joshua Shapiro and Sandra Gambetti helped read and select manuscripts for consideration. I also appreciate the guidance and hard work from the people at Jossey-Bass/Wiley, particularly from my editor Alan Rinzler, Chandrika Madhavan, Mark Kerr, Jeff Penque, and Jessica Egbert. The time to do this was made possible by the cooperation and tireless work of the *TIKKUN* staff, and it is only because I could rely on their wisdom and competence to take care of matters there that I could devote energies to this project—in particular, managing editor Deb Kory, Tikkun Community coordinator Liat Weingart, design and production director David Van Ness, and editorial consultant JoEllen Green Kaiser.

BEST
JEWISH
WRITING
2002

JEWISH RESPONSE
TO SEPTEMBER 11

THE SUKKAH AND THE TOWERS

Arthur Waskow

WHEN THE JEWISH COMMUNITY CELEBRATES the harvest festival, we build *sukkot.*

What is a *sukkah?* Just a fragile hut with a leafy roof, the most vulnerable of houses. Vulnerable in time, where it lasts for only a week each year. Vulnerable in space, where its roof must be not only leafy but leaky—letting in the starlight, and gusts of wind and rain.

In the evening prayers, we plead with God: "Ufros alenu sukkat shlomekha." "Spread over all of us Your *sukkah* of shalom."

Why a *sukkah?* Why does the prayer plead to God for a "*sukkah* of shalom" rather than God's "tent" or "house" or "palace" of peace? Surely a palace, a house, even a tent, would be more safe, more secure, than a *sukkah?*

Precisely because the *sukkah* is so vulnerable.

For much of our lives we try to achieve peace and safety by building with steel and concrete and toughness:

> Pyramids,
> air raid shelters,
> Pentagons,
> World Trade Centers.

Hardening what might be targets and, like Pharaoh, hardening our hearts against what is foreign to us.

3

But the *sukkah* comes to remind us: we are in truth all vulnerable. If as the prophet Dylan sang, "A hard rain gonna fall," it will fall on all of us.

Americans have felt invulnerable. The oceans, our wealth, our military power have made up what seemed an invulnerable shield. We may have begun feeling uncomfortable in the nuclear age, but no harm came to us. Yet yesterday the ancient truth came home: we all live in a *sukkah*.

Not only the targets of attack but also the instruments of attack were among our proudest possessions: the sleek transcontinental airliners. They availed us nothing. Worse than nothing.

Even the greatest oceans do not shield us; even the mightiest buildings do not shield us; even the wealthiest balance sheets and the most powerful weapons do not shield us.

There are only wispy walls and leaky roofs between us. The planet is in fact one interwoven web of life. The command to love my neighbor as I do myself is not an admonition to be nice: it is a statement of truth like the law of gravity. For my neighbor and myself are interwoven. However much and in whatever way I love my neighbor, that will turn out to be the way I love myself. If I pour contempt upon my neighbor, hatred will recoil upon me.

What is the lesson, when we learn that we—all of us—live in a *sukkah?* How do we make such a vulnerable house into a place of shalom, of peace and security and harmony and wholeness?

The lesson is that only a world where we all recognize our vulnerability can become a world where all communities feel responsible to all other communities. And only such a world can prevent such acts of rage and mass murder.

If I treat my neighbor's pain and grief as foreign, I will end up suffering when my neighbor's pain and grief curdle into rage.

But if I realize that in simple fact the walls between us are full of holes, I can reach through them in compassion and connection.

The perpetrators of this act of infamy seem to espouse a tortured version of Islam. Responding to them requires two different, though related, forms of action:

1. Their violence must be halted. They must be found and brought to trial, without killing still more innocents and wrecking still more the fragile "sukkot" of lawfulness. There are in fact mechanisms of international law and politics that can bring them to justice.

2. At the same time, America must open its heart and mind to the pain and grief of those in the Arab and Muslim worlds who feel excluded, denied, unheard, disempowered, defeated.

We must reach beyond the terrorists—to calm the rage that gave them birth by addressing the pain from which they sprouted.

From festering pools of pain and rage sprout the plague of terrorism. Some people think we must choose between addressing the plague or addressing the pools that give it birth. But we can do both—if we focus our attention on these two distinct tasks.

Let us imagine that the United States were to support, instead of opposing, the creation of an International Criminal Court. Suppose that in a case like the 9/11 attacks, the United States had asked the UN Security Council to sit as a grand jury. Suppose the U.S. had submitted evidence that would have justified issuing a warrant for arrests of the Al Qaeda leadership, to stand trial for specific criminal acts before the International Criminal Court and for the arrest of anyone who forcibly tried to prevent those arrests.

If the warrant had been forcibly resisted, force might have been necessary to execute it. But it would have been much more in the mode of police using the minimum force necessary to get the job done than in the military mode of using maximum force to shatter the enemy.

The level of legitimacy of the U.S. action would have been far greater than the invasion of Afghanistan. The preponderant ethical judgment of those in the world who have preponderant political power would have been crystallized into transnational law. (All law is a dance between justice and power.) The next terrorist atrocity would have been made less likely.

The fabric of shared human responsibility, so badly ripped by the attacks of 9/11, would have been repaired and strengthened. The vision of an interwoven world would have grown stronger.

Going to war against whole nations—Afghanistan or perhaps Iraq or perhaps mobs in the streets of Pakistan or Egypt—may weave together temporary elite alliances, but it leaves out the suffering people who ultimately in despair can topple regimes. It will damage whole cities and countrysides. It makes war even against the future because it leaves behind weapons that for decades to come will maim and kill civilians—often children. It may kill those alleged to be guilty without ever building the legitimacy of showing that they were guilty. Only from that sense of legitimacy come threads of trust we can weave into fabrics of community.

The response of arming the walls that we build between us ends up by making war as well on those within the walls. The process begins by holding for detention without trial hundreds of people defined by race or religion; it continues by planning to try alleged terrorists in drumhead kangaroo courts; it proceeds by snarling at those who oppose such measures for giving aid and comfort to the enemy.

War will not drain the pools of pain and rage on which feed the plague of terrorism; it is far more likely to add to them.

What would it mean instead to recognize that both the United States and Islam live in vulnerable *sukkot?*

For example: What do we need to do to recover our knowledge of the history of two centuries of Western colonization and neocolonial support for oppressive regimes in much of the Muslim world?

How do we welcome Muslim societies fully into the planetary community?

What does the United States need to do to encourage grass-roots support for those elements of Islam that seek to renew the tradition?

How do we encourage not top-down regimes that make alliances with our own global corporations to despoil the planet, but grassroots religious and cultural and political communities that seek to control their own resources in ways that nurture the earth?

How do we establish the goal and encourage the emergence of a peaceful relationship between Israel and a viable, peaceful Palestine?

How do we ensure that Iraq is not preparing weapons of mass destruction, while also ensuring that Iraqi families are not devastated by the means we use?

Of course, not every demand put forward by the poor and desperate and disempowered becomes legitimate, just because it is an expression of pain. But we must open the ears of our hearts to ask: Have we ourselves had a hand in creating the pain? Can we act to lighten it without increasing the overall amount of pain in the world?

The choice we face is deeper than politics, broader than charity. It is whether we see the world chiefly as property to be controlled, defined by walls and fences that must be built ever higher, ever thicker, ever tougher; or made up chiefly of an open weave of compassion and connection, open *sukkah* next to open *sukkah*.

The choice is one of Spirit.

Instead of entering upon a "war of civilizations," we must pursue a planetary community. We must spread over all of us the *sukkah* of shalom.

FLAWS IN "BLAME AMERICA" ARGUMENTS

Sylvia Barack Fishman

ONE OF THE MORE DISTRESSING ASPECTS of the September 11 attacks is that certain groups of American intellectuals, and as a result many college students, are filled with an implacable anger at America, not her attackers. Among the propeace agitators are many who assert that America herself is responsible for, and guilty of causing, the violence of the terrorists.

Just hours after the World Trade Center had imploded and collapsed, while smoke and fires were still smoldering in New York and Washington, teach-ins on college campuses featured professors explaining to confused and frightened students that the real villains were America and the American government. Striking back would be the worst possible response, they suggested. Instead of continuing the cycle of violence, the United States should solve its problems with Islamic fundamentalists through diplomacy.

Among the prominent American writers who lambasted the United States was Barbara Ehrenreich, who was sorry that the attack on America—in her eyes justifiable—was implemented by persons with problematic social values. "What is so heartbreaking to me as a feminist," she wrote in the *Village Voice,* "is that the strongest response to corporate globalization and U.S. military domination is based on such a violent and misogynist ideology."

Vivian Gornick in the same issue agreed that America was in the wrong: "Force will get us nowhere. It is reparations that are owing, not retribution."

One advocate for a no-violence response was prominent novelist Alice Walker *(The Color Purple)*, who insisted that Osama bin Laden could be gently persuaded to live up to his own best self, "if he could be reminded of all the good, nonviolent things he has done. Further, what would happen to him if he could be brought to understand the preciousness of the lives he has destroyed?" "I firmly believe," wrote Walker in the *Voice*, "the only punishment that works is love."

Some postmodernists and postcolonialists assert that the United States is a greedy imperialist state responsible for much suffering around the world. Recent articles in *The Nation* assert that the September 11 terrorist attacks "were a result of injustices caused by the West" and that "our own government, through much of the past fifty years, has been the world's leading rogue state, having been responsible for killing hundreds of thousands, if not millions, of innocents."

This "blame America" mentality has persisted, and it colors reactions to America's military response. The day the United States launched its retaliatory strikes on bin Laden, thousands of protesters were marching in New York, singing antiwar songs and expressing opposition to military action.

It is not that I believe the government of the United States (or Israel for that matter) is free of guilt, but it is clear to me—I hold these truths to be self-evident—that the fundamentalist extremist attacks of September 11 constituted an unmitigated, premeditated, and unprovoked evil, and an act of war.

The Islamic fundamentalist suicide pilots of September 11 were well-educated, middle-class men who had not led particularly difficult lives. Most of them came from countries such as Saudi Arabia that are neither impoverished nor oppressed by the United States. Their hatred of America was fueled not by privation or misery but by radical extremist Islamic hatred of Christian, capitalist America.

Despotic rulers throughout the Middle East and elsewhere cynically and nervously maintain their own power by floating on the surface of an evil bargain: they allow fundamentalist Islamic extremists to flourish financially and organizationally in their countries as long as they spew their hatred onto America and Israel.

I feel a special responsibility as a Jew to speak out and assert that historical events are real, and that all sides in this conflict are not equal. Contemporary Jews have frequently found themselves at the wrong end of historical revisionism and postmodernist ideology. The most obvious examples of this pattern are found in the diverse claims of revisionists that the Holocaust never happened or that its events have been greatly exaggerated.

Even more insidious is the demand that only a pure and innocent government has the right to invoke historical events on its behalf. One Holocaust revisionist intellectual ploy, for example, is the argument that because the judgment and leadership of some Israeli leaders has at times been deeply flawed, the state of Israel has no right to remind the nations of the world that no country opened wide its doors to Jewish victims before Israel existed.

Some ideologues assert that the original capitalist "sins" of the United States have given the frustrated and desperate terrorists no choice but to strike out and get the world's attention. Many of them also believe that Hamas, Fatah, and other Middle Eastern terrorist groups have no choice but to get the world's attention through suicide bombings in Israel.

Although I have always been opposed to retaining the disputed West Bank territories for both ideological and practical reasons, I fail to understand the willful selective hearing loss of those who simply refuse to take at their word those Arab leaders who insist that taking back the territories is just a first step, a prologue to the "liberation" of all of "Palestine."

As someone who for years worked hard for Oz VeShalom, the religious Zionist peace movement in Israel, I have reluctantly come to accept the evidence that for many of our "partners in peace," the whole land of Israel is an unjustified colonial possession. This realization, like the destruction of the World Trade Centers and the mutilation of the Pentagon, is hard to swallow. But the very harshness of these facts serves as an important reminder that struggle is sometimes an unavoidable human condition. And in those situations in which a country has no choice but to struggle with entities that wish it ill, that country is duty-bound to do its best to win the conflict.

Critics of the American ethos often assert that the U.S. government ought to care equally about innocent people anywhere in the world. I believe that a democratic government—even an imperfect one—has a primary responsibility to defend the well-being of its own innocent citizens, and that these citizens have a right to demand this protection of their government. To me, these things are self-evident.

WAR

C. K. Williams

September–October 2001

1.

I keep rereading an article I found recently about how Mayan scribes,
who also were historians, polemicists, and probably poets as well,
when their side lost a war—not a rare occurrence, apparently,

there having been a number of belligerent kingdoms
constantly struggling for supremacy—would be disgraced
and tortured,
their fingers broken and the nails torn out, and then be sacrificed.

Poor things—the reproduction from a mural shows three:
one sprawls in slack despair, gingerly cradling his left hand with
his right,
another gazes at his injuries with furious incomprehension,

while the last lifts his mutilated fingers to the conquering warriors
as though to elicit compassion for what's been done to him. They,

elaborately armored, glowering at one another, don't bother
to look.

2.

Like bomber pilots in our day, one might think, with their radar
and their infallible infrared, who soar, unheard, unseen,
over generalized,
digital targets that mystically ignite, billowing out from vaporized
cores.

Or like the Greek and Trojan gods, when they'd tire of their
creatures,
"flesh ripped by the ruthless bronze," and wander off, or like
the god
we think of as ours, who found mouths to speak for him, then left.

*They fought until nothing remained but rock and dust and
shattered bone,
Troy's walls a waste, the stupendous Meso-American cities
abandoned
to devouring jungle, tumbling on themselves like children's
blocks.*

*And we, alone again under an oblivious sky, were quick to learn
how our best construals of divinity, our Do unto, Love, Don't kill,
could be easily garbled to canticles of vengeance and battle-
prayers.*

3.

Fall's first freshness, strange; the seasons' ceaseless wheel,
starlings starting south, the annealed leaves ready to release,
yet still those columns of nothingness rise from their own ruins,

their twisted carcasses of steel and ash still fume, and still,
one by one, tacked on walls by hopeful lovers, husbands, wives,
the absent faces wait, already tattering, fading, going out.

*These things that happen in the particle of time we have to be
alive,*

these violations which almost more than any altar, ark, or mosque
embody sanctity by enacting so precisely sanctity's desecration.

These voices of bereavement asking of us what isn't to be given.
These suddenly smudged images of consonance and peace.
These fearful burdens to be borne, complicity, contrition, grief.

E-MAILS FROM THE END
OF THE WORLD

Jonathan Mark

ANDREW ZUCKER WAS TWENTY-SEVEN YEARS OLD, with twenty-one nights left to live. He had just started work as an attorney on the eighty-fifth floor of the World Trade Center, where he had a spectacular view of the end of the world. On the hot night of August 21, at the end of America's endless summer, terrorists were already planning a twenty-first-century death camp in lower Manhattan. It was a night when most of us were less conversant about Talibans than about Chandra's vanishing. Andrew Zucker, who was soon to vanish, e-mailed an Internet petition among his friends: he could see the end of the world. The United Nations had to do more to contain the Taliban, he said. They were destroying Buddhas and making Hindus wear a yellow cloth. It reminded Zucker of Hitler. The e-mail added, "All it takes for evil to triumph is for good men to do nothing."

I did nothing. Even worse, I deleted it. Wait, did I say he sent that e-mail to friends? I flatter myself. We barely knew each other. I was never in his home, except in print. He never came to our office, except via e-mail. We met last autumn in the Riverdale Jewish Center, our neighborhood shul, after a concert of Jewish music. He was in the corridor, raising his voice as the music blared, encouraging people to sign up to monitor the media's coverage of Israel. It was biased, he said.

He was a severe critic, and I disagreed with him by half, but that soon gave way to tenderness. What was he really saying? It was less about any particular article than the fact that he couldn't bear Jewish death and vulnerability: "So two totally innocent [Jews in Israel] are shot in cold blood with machine guns," he e-mailed last December. "A fourth-grade teacher and a driver. Let's see what CNN and *The New York Times* have to say about this one."

Or he'd only ask that I say Tehillim. Someone was sick. Another died young and left children. As the world seemed more fragile, his e-mails became more personal: "It was good to see you the other day. . . . Thanks for the bracha."

He admitted to needing a blessing. His widow is expecting his baby and, back in the spring, his first baby, Abigail Bayla Rina, died. "[In] the short time that we knew her, in some way she touched all of us. Dayenu— that joy, the smiles she brought, the time we had. Somehow, even that was enough. It is excruciating for us to imagine that only having Abbe for the short time that we did is enough, but Hashem obviously had a special plan for her neshama."

Who can fathom a child's burial? He asked then, and so many ask it now. He e-mailed, "At our age, burial plots couldn't have been further from our minds. . . . May we celebrate many simchas together."

On September 16, another reader e-mailed a clip from OnlySimchas. com, a site requesting help in identifying the whereabouts of Jews who vanished on Black Tuesday. One item among many: "We are looking for information on Andrew Zucker. He is married to Erica (Konovitch). He is 6'1", about 300 lbs. He has brown hair and brown eyes and a 4" scar along his lower back from surgery. He works at Harris Beach, 85th floor in 2 WTC." Zucker was still written of in the present tense. Where was he?

How many times did Zucker e-mail about CNN? Now CNN had their say about Zucker: "Searching for a loved one—and hoping, praying." According to CNN online, "As her sister desperately wandered the streets of lower Manhattan, Erica Zucker spent Wednesday [September 12] making phone calls. Hoping. Praying. It's been nearly two days since she last spoke with her husband, a frantic call placed moments after the first jetliner careened into the north tower. . . . It was a short conversation. He reassured his wife. 'He said, "I'm OK. I'll call you back,"' Erica recalled. 'And he hung up.' Moments later a second jetliner crashed into the south tower—Andrew Zucker's tower."

Family and friends went from NYU Medical Center to Bellevue Hospital to Beekman Hospital, and then they looked to gather hair samples from his brown hair.

All these weeks later, souls hover in the night over lower Manhattan.

On 30th Street near the East River, three trucks from the Medical Examiner's office are loaded with body parts.

There is the sweetest of mitzvot known as shmira, in which a dead Jewish body is never left unattended before burial. There was difficulty finding shomrim over Shabbat. Stern College is near the trucks, so Jessica Russak, a Stern senior, put together a team of ten Stern women within an hour of hearing there was a problem. They took turns, sitting by the trucks, whispering Psalms through the midnight hours. "An immense number of Jewish souls were comforted by our prayers," Russak says. Is Zucker among those souls?

Perhaps Zucker is still at Ground Zero. I sat at Zucker's shomer on a milk crate on Maiden Lane and Broadway on a weeknight into the wee small hours. Ground Zero's death camp was flooded with brutally harsh light, creating its own perimeter in the blackness. Smoke was rising, made all the eerier by the illumination. Gnarled metal beams hung in midair like a frozen waterfall in the remains of the day. On Broadway, soldiers in camouflage rolled by on lorries. The smell of incineration and death wafted through the air when the winds blew east.

On one of the nights of watching, Jewish college students came by. They stood around a blue wax candle in a glass that shielded the flame from the wind. As the group's leader, Rav Binny Friedman, played Shlomo Carlebach and Breslov songs, young Barnard College freshmen rested their heads on each other's shoulders. Neshama Carlebach, Shlomo's daughter, listened to the old songs with her arms around a bride-to-be. They all came for Zucker, even if most didn't know him.

Rav Binny said, as he strummed his guitar, that Zucker was a friend of his. "He was an amazing person, Andrew Zucker. Chaim Zalman ben Zusha v'Sara." He told how Zucker, a former volunteer fireman, raced into the mailroom, grabbing two clerks by the arms, dragging them to safety, then racing back into the office to save another. "The incredible thing," says Rav Binny, "is that he was only working in that firm for six weeks. He didn't really know most of the people. And we can tell a story like that every day for the next five thousand days."

As the group dispersed, a woman from Borough Park who had come on her own said Sodom must have smoldered like this. Another said, no, there were righteous people in there, unlike Sodom. Rather, it was a havdalah candle, two flames, the end of an endless Sabbath. Neshama Carlebach said Jerusalem must have looked like this on the tenth of Av, with one small wall standing.

"Did you have any friends in there?" she asked.

"One. Well, we hardly knew each other," I said, before remembering that Zucker ran through fire for people he hardly knew at all. I sent a final e-mail to his mailbox; a prayer I'm sure he knew: "I am yours and my dreams are yours. I have dreamed a dream and I don't know what it means."

POSTTRAUMATIC LOVE
SYNDROME 9/11

Michael J. Bader

IN THE AFTERMATH OF THE WORLD TRADE CENTER ATTACK, we saw and experienced an outpouring of generosity, altruism, and heroism. And not only at Ground Zero. Many people found themselves talking to strangers on the street, on buses, sitting in a bar watching TV, or at a sports event. Many of us contacted friends we hadn't seen in years, reached out to family and acquaintances whom we hadn't had time for in the past.

Although more dramatic than most, this catastrophe wasn't unusual in the way it generated feelings of community. Catastrophes bring people together. They seem to bring out the best in people, breaking down barriers and walls that make us invisible to each other in daily life. Journalists have even described something that they call "terror sex," in which people lift their customary inhibitions and report intensified sexual experiences with spouses or even strangers. Since the goal of the Tikkun Community is to create exactly the type of society in which connections like this are the norm, we need to understand the essential psychological mechanisms at work at this moment and consider how we might promote them in everyday social and political life.

Why It's So Hard to Reach Out

The central mechanism at work, I believe, is safety. Catastrophes momentarily create the conditions of safety in which people can overcome their alienation from one another. In order to understand this paradoxical dynamic more fully, we have to look to its origins in childhood. From its beginnings, the human psyche is wired to seek psychological safety at any cost. This developmental fact has important implications, because it is under the sway of this need for a safe sense of relatedness that parents teach children about reality and morality. In the context of our dependence on our families, we all unconsciously learn how we're supposed to be and what we're supposed to want.

As children, safety depends entirely on the security and quality of our relationship with our caretakers. This is why we all grow up exquisitely sensitive to the nuances of our parents' moods and behavior. We will sacrifice any longing, need, desire, or pleasure, if we sense that it might endanger our connectedness to our parents.

For example, children will regularly inhibit the pleasures of independence if they believe that such autonomy will threaten their tie to a caretaker who cannot tolerate it. If a parent appears to be provoked by dependency, however, those same children will become stoic and overly self-reliant. Because our society privileges stoicism and self-reliance, experiences of loving tenderness and dependency seem to be especially threatening to developing children.

Let us consider our desires to lean on others and to nurture others who are leaning on us. These are perfectly normal and healthy needs, but their expression can often threaten our psychological safety. For example, we can be—and often are—rejected for such longings in our families. And when we feel rejected in this way, we feel ashamed because we automatically assume that the rejection is deserved. Self-blame of this sort is universal. Deep down, children take responsibility for their own rejection.

A patient of mine grew up in a family in which his alcoholic father was a cynical intellectual who repeatedly mocked displays of familial love as well as any displays of neediness. This patient grew up ashamed of wanting to be taken care of and identified with his father's disdain for emotional vulnerability. Whenever he felt dependent, he blamed himself for being weak. Whenever his children were too needy, he found himself becoming impatient and critical. My patient's perfectly normal and healthy longings for interdependence and love had been rejected in his childhood and, as an adult, he rejected them in himself and others.

At the same time, our normal and healthy need to be nurturing and altruistic often becomes co-opted and exploited, wittingly or unwittingly, by others, beginning with our parents; co-opted in the sense that we come to feel as if we're giving more than we're getting, that we're responsible for the welfare of others for whom we should not be responsible. In the language of popular psychology, we often become parentified, functioning as caretakers to our own parents. We then feel guilty about our need to be selfish, to separate, to have ambitions, and to experience successes and pleasures that our parents never did. Relationships often come to feel like obligations, burdens, rife with the possibility of self-sacrifice. Our underlying desire for relatedness has produced a paradigm of relatedness that is oppressive.

Connection becomes dangerous in this way as well.

A good example of this dynamic can be seen in a patient of mine who grew up in a household in which her mother was depressed, bitter about the burdens of taking care of four children, and disappointed in her weak and passive husband. My patient grew up trying to cheer her mother up. She tried to be "good" and was always exquisitely attuned to her mother's moods. She didn't date through high school because she didn't want her mother to feel inferior and left out. As an adult, she got involved in a series of bad relationships with depressed and self-preoccupied men whom she unsuccessfully tried to fix. In the course of her treatment with me, she realized that she was identifying with her mother because she felt so guilty about having a happier life than her. She experienced relationships as one-way streets, just like she had with her mother, and felt disloyal and uncomfortable when she became more independent and happy. Relationships, she unconsciously believed, were supposed to be self-sacrificial and disappointing.

These twin dangers of connectedness—rejection and compulsory responsibility—result in behavior and attitudes that are reinforced by our society. They become "adaptive" but are still ultimately pathological, as is the society that mirrors them. For example, people who are conflicted about their own dependency needs, and those of others, experience the American emphasis on meritocracy—the ideology that says that one's position in life is entirely one's own responsibility and reflects one's intrinsic value—as perfectly normal. According to this logic, people shouldn't go around asking for and getting help but should rise and fall on their own internal merits. People who are dependent are subtly scorned because of the unspoken rationale that "if I have to go it alone and on the basis of my own hard work, why should they get a handout?" We develop a hard shell of cynicism because we assume that to expose or express longings for caretaking or even love from others would be to invite either rejection or a one-way road to self-sacrifice and exploitation.

In this kind of world, too much social responsibility or relatedness is a dangerous thing. Instead, we cherish the values of rugged individualism, individual freedom, market competition, and self-interest. In this way, the personal meets the political in an unholy alliance that produces personal isolation and an aversion to social community.

Why WTC Changed Things

Enter: an external catastrophe. Suddenly, the psychological calculus changes. Suddenly, it becomes safe to connect with one another, to help one another, to acknowledge one's vulnerability and look upon that of others without disdain. What happened?

First, vulnerability and neediness are now socially sanctioned. After all, who can now say that their—our—need for help is illegitimate, weak, or shameful? The world is coming apart. People are supposed to be scared. Most important, negating the self-blame that flows from the edicts of our meritocracy, it is now nobody's fault that we're needy. Our consciences allow us to safely express our humanity without shame because external conditions seem to mandate it.

Second, not only is it permissible to be scared and dependent, but disasters dramatically provoke such feelings. Loss—or the potential for it— is all around us. Our innate longings for connectedness and attachment are stimulated to a tremendous degree. They overwhelm our normal inhibitions and we reach out to each other to beat back the darkness and danger that loss and helplessness create.

Third, massive external catastrophes such as the WTC attack and the anthrax scare affect all of us equally. The sense arises that "we're now all in this together." A natural disaster momentarily collapses racial and social distinctions. It's safe to recognize the other guy as similar to us because we've all been made into victims in a similar way. A common threat creates common interests.

Finally, following a disaster, we tend to ask, What do we have to lose? The world is crashing down around us. We're in the proverbial foxhole together. The perception arises that the rules no longer apply. We feel that normal social intercourse has come to a temporary halt as the social fabric lies in ruins around us. The lowering of external prohibitions promotes the lowering of internal ones, internal injunctions against being too vulnerable or about being too altruistic. When the external trappings of regulation, order, and control are lowered, one's forbidden longings and impulses can more safely flourish.

This model explains the surprising finding that people seem more sexual after a disaster. My own research suggests that so-called terror sex results, in part, from the sense that the old rules don't count any more. The characterological prohibitions based on shame and guilt that have inhibited sexual arousal are weakened in a postapocalyptic landscape because people feel that they have less to lose. Normally, we all inhibit our sexual desires because we fear that we'll be rejected or that we'll overwhelm or otherwise hurt the other person. In the aftermath of a huge disaster, however, we can sometimes momentarily shed the trappings of our old worries, our old identities, and safely connect with each other more directly, more lovingly, and more sexually. As Humphrey Bogart says at the end of *Casablanca*, "The problems of three little people don't amount to a hill of beans in this crazy world." Although Bogart and Ingrid Bergman couldn't shed their inhibitions enough to sexually reconnect in Casablanca, in other such crazy worlds, the outcome is more sexually satisfying.

Thus external ruin can be psychologically liberating precisely because it creates temporary conditions of safety in which people can experience and express the part of themselves that hungers for community but that is normally kept under wraps because of the potential dangers of rejection or guilty compliance.

What We Can Do

How can a social movement, then, committed to creating a new bottom line of caring and community, make use of these insights? First and foremost, we have to understand that even the language of our movement—"caring," "community," "love," "mutual recognition," and "spirituality"—will stir up resistance in people because such language puts into words longings that they have suppressed or cynically dismissed in themselves or in others because of the dangers of rejection and exploitation. By understanding how catastrophes bring people together, we can see how powerfully entrenched the fears of such connectedness must be. The world has to practically collapse around us before we can feel safe enough to come together. This understanding should help us feel compassion toward people who are dismissive or contemptuous of our ideas, as well as toward ourselves for not being able to sufficiently live them out.

This leads us to the centrality of addressing the issue of cynicism itself as part of our political work. In their heart of hearts, most people don't want to be cynical. They want to feel like they're part of something bigger than themselves while maintaining their freedom to realize their private ambitions. Their cynicism is a defense against the dangers of rejection and exploitation. Therefore, we should find ways to talk to people—in our literature, our conferences, our political proposals, and in the various social movements in which we participate—about the dynamics of cynicism. In particular, we should talk to people about how our political leaders continuously promote a cynical attitude toward idealism of any kind, how the mass media insidiously reflects the notion that everyone has dark and ulterior motives, and how our religions and communities often recreate the same sense of spiritual emptiness. We should find ways to remind people of movements like the civil rights and women's movements, which were genuinely idealistic and rejected the cynical belief that the way things are is the way they were destined to be.

All the while, it's crucial to call people to their true longings for connectedness and to systematically confront the psychological dangers that keep people from hearing that call. We need to try, in words and deeds, to make it safe for people to experience more of the interdependence that they secretly desire and to rebel against the institutions that tell them that such mutuality is shameful. We shouldn't need a catastrophe to open our hearts to each other and to feelings that are aching to be expressed.

SHOULD SCARED JEWS
BECOME TOUGH JEWS?

Michael Lerner

JEWS HAVE FACED THE SAME ISSUE as everyone else in the post-9/11 world: whether to retreat into fear or whether to use this moment to address how to heal the world. Both themes have deep resonance in Jewish experience, Jewish writing, and Jewish self-conceptions.

It is no surprise that the first response to the bombing of the World Trade Center and the Pentagon in the Jewish world mirrored that of the larger American society: anger and outrage. There is never any justification for acts of terror against innocent civilians—it is the quintessential act of dehumanization and not recognizing the sanctity of others, and a visible symbol of a world increasingly irrational and out of control.

It's *also* understandable why many of us in America, after grieving and consoling the mourners, felt anger. Unfortunately, demagogues in the White House and Congress moved quickly to manipulate our legitimate outrage and channeled it into a new militarism and a revival of the most deeply held belief of the conservative worldview: that the world is mostly a dangerous place and our lives must focus on protecting ourselves from the threat of others.

In this case, terrorism provides a perfect base for this worldview—it can come from anywhere and we don't really know who is the enemy, so everyone can be suspect and everyone can be a target of our fear-induced rage. With this as a foundation, the Bush team has been able to turn this terrible and outrageous attack into a justification for massive military spending, a new war against terror whose dimensions are open-ended, and the inevitable trappings: repression of civil liberties, denigration of "evil others," and a new climate of fear and intimidation against anyone who doesn't join this misuse of patriotism.

One did not need to see the videotape of Osama bin Laden gloat over the death of innocents to recognize the deep distortions and evil impulses in those who planned, encouraged, or participated in the murder of over 3,500 people on September 11, 2001. I rejoiced when the Taliban were overthrown in Afghanistan and the Al Qaeda network was crippled, not only because of the evil that they have done but because of the chance it opens for the women of Afghanistan to achieve some of the dignity that they were denied by these fanatic fundamentalists.

Yet a narrow focus on the perpetrators allows us to avoid dealing with the underlying issues. When violence becomes so prevalent across the planet, it's too easy to simply talk of "deranged minds." We need to ask ourselves, "What is it in the way that we are living, organizing our societies, and treating each other that makes violence seem plausible to so many people?" And why is it that our immediate response to violence is to use violence ourselves—thus reinforcing the cycle of violence in the world?

As a rabbi, I try to understand the world from the framework of Jewish spiritual wisdom. The increasing tendency to resort to violence to solve global political problems poses a real challenge for those of us who see the central problem of our times in a very different way; the growing global incapacity to recognize the spirit of God in each other—what we call the sanctity of each human being. But even if you reject religious language, you can see that the willingness of people to hurt each other to advance their own interests has become a global problem, and it's only the dramatic level of this particular attack that distinguishes it from the violence and insensitivity to each other that is part of our daily lives.

We may tell ourselves that the current violence has nothing to do with the fact that we've learned to close our ears when told that one out of every three people on this planet lives on less than $750 a year, and that one billion people are seriously malnourished. We tend to close our ears when the United Nations reports that approximately 32,000 children die of diseases related to malnutrition every single day (eight times the number of people killed at the World Trade Center). Yes, every single day.

We may reassure ourselves that the hoarding of the world's resources by the richest society in world history and our frantic attempts to accelerate globalization with its attendant inequalities of wealth have nothing to do with the resentment that others feel toward us. We may tell ourselves that the suffering of refugees and the oppressed has nothing to do with us—that that's a different story going on somewhere else. We reassure ourselves that the terrorists were themselves from well-to-do backgrounds, as though people who are economically well off could not possibly be moved to sacrifice for the interests of others who are not (ironically, the very argument used by some black nationalists to discount the role of Jews in making sacrifices for the civil rights movement). But we live in one world, we are increasingly interconnected with everyone, and the forces that lead people to feel outrage, anger, and desperation eventually impact our own daily lives.

I see this tendency in Israel, where some Israelis have taken to dismissing the entire Palestinian people as "terrorists" but never ask themselves, What have we done to make this seem to Palestinians to be a reasonable path of action today? Of course, there were always some hateful people and some religious fundamentalists who wanted to act in hurtful ways against Israel, no matter what the circumstances. Yes, there really are people who have come to hate so badly that nothing we can do would dissuade them.

Yet one need only compare the level of violence today with the level of violence that existed at moments when Palestinians thought that Israel was genuinely committed to withdrawal from the West Bank to see that violence is not just a steady phenomenon but one that varies with the levels of hope. When Israel failed to withdraw from the West Bank and instead expanded the number of its settlers, the fundamentalists and haters had a far easier time convincing many decent Palestinians that there might be no other alternative.

Similarly, if the United States turns its back on global agreements to preserve the environment, unilaterally cancels its treaties banning missile defense, accelerates the processes by which a global economy has made some people in the Third World richer but many poorer, shows that it cares nothing for the fate of refugees who have been homeless for decades, and otherwise turns its back on ethical norms, it becomes far easier for the haters and the fundamentalists to recruit people who are willing to kill themselves in strikes against what they perceive to be an evil American empire represented by the Pentagon and the World Trade Center. Most Americans will feel puzzled by any reference to this larger picture. It seems baffling to imagine that somehow we are part of a world system that is slowly destroying the life support system of the planet and quickly transferring the wealth of the world into our own pockets. Many people reassure themselves that they are just innocent victims of terror and don't feel personally responsible when an American corporation runs a sweatshop in the Philippines or crushes efforts of workers to organize in Singapore. Some of us don't see ourselves implicated when the United States refuses to consider the plight of Palestinian refugees or uses the excuse of fighting drugs to support repression in Colombia or Central America. Many of us didn't even see the symbolism when terrorists attack America's military center and our trade center—we talk of them as buildings, though others see them as centers of the forces that are causing the world so much pain.

We have narrowed our attention to getting through or doing well in our own personal lives, and who has time to focus on all the rest of this? Most of us are leading perfectly reasonable lives within the options that we have available to us—so why should others be angry at us, much less strike out against us? And the truth is, our anger is also understandable: the acts of terror against us are just as irrational as the world system that they seek to confront.

Yet our acts of counterterror will also be counterproductive in the long run—legitimizing the ethos of violence. We may at one moment be celebrating how easy it was to topple the Taliban, but we may also live to see the day when survivors of this battle come back at us with yet more sophisticated weapons. We should have learned that the current phase of the Israeli-Palestinian struggle—responding to terror with more violence, rather than asking ourselves what we can do to change the conditions that generated it in the first place—will only ensure more violence against us in the future.

And let's acknowledge that the world system of which we are part has already been at war with the peoples of the Third World for a very long time. Through military interventions and the support of coups d'etat in countries around the world, the Western powers have shaped a world to our liking, a world that is safe for our corporations and our media to penetrate, profit, and push toward our vision of the world.

We like to see ourselves as merely offering progress to the rest of the world—so we urge them to join us in modernizing. And, indeed, Western versions of modernity have some marvelous things to offer, the recognition of the importance of individual freedom and protection from state power, the insistence on a private realm free from public interference by the community, the freedom of individuals to choose their own level of religious belief and observance, the pursuit of science, and the rejection of sexist, racist, anti-Semitic, and homophobic worldviews.

Yet modernity has been tied to a capitalist system that has been militantly materialistic, insisting that institutions or social practices be considered rational, productive, and efficient only to the extent that they maximize money and power. It has created a culture in which consumption is the highest good and cannot be constrained for the sake of preserving the world's environment. It has produced individuals who know how to "look out for number one" but who are emotionally and spiritually illiterate, narcissistic, and have great difficulty in sustaining lasting relationships or building solid families. It has reduced human relationships to "what's in it for me?"

Most Americans don't see this as a price of corporate capitalist versions of modernity—they imagine that these developments are all just a product of human nature. How could it be the fault of "the system," when in other respects the system is economically successful in producing for them a good level of material well-being?

But that material cushion doesn't exist in many other places in the world. As we've become increasingly part of an integrated world system, the 5 percent of the world's population that lives in the United States has been living on 25 percent of the world's wealth. Globalized capital has been able to set conditions of trade that provide great advantage to the people in advanced industrial societies, but have simultaneously prevented Third World countries from benefiting. Instead, small elites of wealth and power in Third World countries commit their countries to policies that benefit the upper and upper-middle classes but hurt the majority, and in exchange for so doing they receive economic and military support from the advanced industrial world.

Along with economic domination comes a whole new religion: the religion of corporate capital, with its worship of individual freedom—which of course amounts to a whole lot more when you are living off the wealth of the planet than when you are on the verge of starvation—and its rejection of traditional values, spiritual understandings, or anything that places itself as more valuable than the accumulation of wealth and power.

There are a lot of reasons why people would resist this new world system and see it as a religion of its own that is trying to trample the local traditional religion. The problem is that the primary form this resistance to global capital has taken is often a religious fundamentalism that denigrates anyone outside the group of "the elect" or "saved." Women, gays, and Jews are just some of the groups that tend to be demeaned and repressed in these kinds of societies.

Few of us would survive in a world created in the image of the Taliban. Yet even now that the Taliban has been destroyed, the fundamentalist critique will continue to have abiding and even growing appeal as long as the only alternative is world domination by corporate capital and its religion of materialism and selfishness.

As the frenzy around anthrax by mail has demonstrated, no amount of bombings of other countries, rooting out particular networks of terrorists, or suspension of civil liberties can succeed in providing protection in a world in which our biological, chemical, and technological sophistication allows people to kill us if they hate us enough to be willing to lose their own lives. The only protection is to build a world where people won't have that desire.

Sure, there will always be a handful of deranged people. No one can guarantee a society free from terror. The United States saw its federal building in Oklahoma City blown up by terrorists, and criminal elements inside the United States continue to murder many more people per year than foreign terrorists. But the swamps of despair from which terrorists recruit their support and their "martyrs" can be dried up if the world begins to show generosity, open-heartedness, and genuine compassion toward those whom it has wounded.

The bin Ladens would be far less successful recruiting people to give up their lives in a world in which everyone knew America to be:

• The primary force seeking a worldwide redistribution of wealth to eliminate poverty and hunger (we could start by taking that $1.4 trillion tax cut, most of which goes to the rich, and using it to build the economic infrastructure of the world's poorest countries)

• The primary force for ecological sustainability (instead of the country that has been blocking the implementation of measures to prevent global warming)

• The country that embodies a spirit of generosity and open-heartedness in its dealings with the world, with a new bottom line so that it judged its own institutions to be productive, efficient, and rational to the extent that they maximized people's capacities to be loving and caring, ethically/spiritually/ecologically sensitive, and capable of responding to the world with awe and wonder (what I describe in my book *Spirit Matters* as an emancipatory spirituality)

Similarly, some Islamic fundamentalists may always be committed to eliminating a Jewish state in Palestine. But the number of Palestinians who identified with Hamas and that rejectionist position has always varied with the level of hope in the West Bank and Gaza about achieving Palestinian independence and economic well-being through negotiations. They would have far greater trouble recruiting people to martyr their lives were Israel to:

- End the occupation of the West Bank and Gaza
- Bring the settlers back to the pre-1967 borders
- Create and help make economically viable a Palestinian state in all of the West Bank and Gaza (with tiny border corrections to incorporate within Israel Gush Etzyion, the Jewish Quarter, French Hill, Mt. Scopus, and a few other minor changes)
- Acknowledge partial responsibility for the fate of Palestinian refugees and lead an international consortium of countries providing massive reparations for Palestinian resettlement within the new Palestinian state
- Take acts to punish settlers, police, and military who violate the civil liberties of Palestinians; take concrete acts of repentance for the pain imposed on the Palestinian people by the occupation
- Engage in a systematic campaign of internal reeducation to eliminate the dominant anti-Arab and anti-Palestinian discourse
- Act in a generous way, with a true commitment to reconciliation
- Eliminate all double standards in the daily treatment of Israeli Arabs and grant all citizens of Israel full equal treatment and legal equality

Would any of this really make a difference? Here we get to the nub of the issue both for Jewish society and for American society: Are we to believe that there are enough people inclined toward evil that our world must be built around protecting ourselves from them, or do we build a world on a more trusting vision of others and then deal with the exceptional cases when we must?

Or, to modify the question to fit the discourse of 2002, do we see the world through the framework of the terrorists or do we see it through the framework of outpouring of loving energy and generosity shown by so many police, firefighters, and ordinary people who risked (and in many cases, lost) their lives to care for others? If we see the world through this latter frame, we highlight the capacity and desire so many people have to care about each other. If we could legitimize people allowing that part of themselves to come out without having to wait for a disaster, we could empower a part of every human being that our social order marginalizes. Most people have a deep goodness—and that needs to be affirmed.

That same caring energy could be given a more positive outlet if we didn't live in a society that normally teaches us that our "natural" instinct is toward aggression and that the best we can hope for is a world that gives us protection. The central struggle going on in the world today vies between hope or fear, love or paranoia, generosity or trying to shore up one's own portion.

And this is really the central struggle going on inside the Jewish people as well. Many of the right-wing Jews who label as "self-hating" those Jews who offer criticisms of Israel's current policies are often very decent human beings themselves who are simply overcome with fear about the well-being of the Jewish people. They want what the peace forces want: a successful and safe Israel, but they believe the only way this can be achieved is through entering into the cycle of violence and showing that we can be tougher than our adversaries.

It's no surprise that a people nurtured on stories of pogroms and Holocaust would become fixated on how frightening the world is, how little one can count on or hope for support from a world that was capable of such levels of abuse, collaboration with the abusers, or indifference to the suffering of others. No wonder that such a people would use each act of fundamentalist terror as further confirmation of its "master narrative" that the whole world would always hate us, that we are always going to be unsafe, and that whoever is our current adversary will never be satisfied with anything less than our total annihilation. Given that worldview, Israel's actions become far more understandable. For the person who sees the world through the framework of fear, every situation can be reinterpreted from that standpoint. On the one hand, this has led many to insist that what we really need in the face of fear is to become "tough Jews" who can use the instruments of power and might to win whatever we think we need. On the other hand, our fear comes from a paranoia so deep that nothing in our contemporary experience is sufficient to dislodge it. Israel can be the strongest military power in the Middle East, and its army can occupy the towns and villages of a Palestinian people who have no tanks, no airplanes, no army, and yet the Israelis can see themselves as in mortal danger. And when they act from that supposition, smashing nonviolent demonstrations, humiliating on a daily basis the people they occupy, selecting some for torture and others for maiming or assassinations, they manage to create in the occupied the very hatred that they believed was there as an ontological reality.

In such a world, everything will be used as confirmation of our worst fears. Take, for example, the popular media trope that Ehud Barak offered "the most generous deal that Palestinians could ever hope for, and their rejection of it proved that they would settle for nothing less than the full destruction of the Jewish people."

When we look at the offers made by Israel at Camp David in 2000, it turns out that they were not so "generous" as the media and Ehud Barak portrayed. The West Bank and Gaza constitute 22 percent of the original land of Palestine—and the deal at Oslo was that the Palestinians would recognize Israel's right to the other 78 percent if the Palestinians could create a state in the remaining 22 percent of pre-Israel Palestine. Barak wanted to reduce this part that had already been agreed to at Oslo. Although supposedly offering 90 percent (of the 22 percent) of the land back to the Palestinians, that land was going to be crisscrossed by Israeli military roads and military garrisons, so that the Palestinian people would not be able to go from one place to another without traversing endless Israeli checkpoints. Imagine, if you will, someone who took over your house for thirty-four years, then offered to give you back 90 percent of it. Well, you might say that was generous, until you found out that the 10 percent they were still going to control was the hallways between the rooms! You wouldn't feel you had gotten back very much if you still needed their permission to go from any one room to any other!

And then imagine if the occupier demanded that you sign an agreement saying that this was "the final agreement" and that you publicly renounced all rights to raise modifications or other issues. Some people say, "sure, it wasn't a great deal, but Arafat should have taken it and then reopened other issues later." But Barak insisted that in the name of the Palestinian people Arafat agree to never reopen any further issues. Well, an agreement that left three million Palestinians as refugees with no reparations or any other compensation for what had been done to them would never be acceptable to the Palestinian people, and for legitimate reasons.

But few of us even knew about these complexities, because the dominant story in the Jewish media was so completely familiar: we were so good, "they" were so unreasonably hateful.

Every struggle needs two sides, and in this case, the Palestinians have their own distortions and self-fulfilling destructive perceptions. We at *Tikkun* magazine have long argued that the Jewish people could make huge progress against our own paranoid fantasies if the Palestinian people would adopt the strict guidelines of a nonviolent struggle developed by Mahatma Gandhi and Martin Luther King Jr. If the Palestinian leadership were to arrest Hamas activists, forbid all forms of rock-throwing, rein in all guns and mortars, and enforce a rigorous nonviolent discipline, and then engage in massive nonviolent civil disobedience, within five years they would have changed the hearts of sufficient Israelis to create a new political consensus for ending the occupation. That would require the Palestinians to acknowledge in their own minds that Jews are not fundamentally evil people, that the evil actions taken by the Israeli people in enforcing the occupation were not manifestations of an untransformable essence of hatred and desire to dominate, and that the hard crust of Israeli insensitivity could be melted by sustained love and generosity from the Palestinians.

Sure, I know it's "not fair" to ask that of the Palestinian people when it is they who are being occupied. It wasn't fair to ask that blacks fighting for their freedom in the United States engage in nonviolence either. But it was effective. Blacks could have been righteous losers—but instead they chose to win the battle by adopting a path of nonviolence. Martin Luther King Jr. made black demands seem credible and safe precisely because his language and his tactics affirmed the fundamental goodness of the majority white population. Palestinians should follow a similar path. They do not because they, too, are filled with resignation and despair, and so are more attached to "being right" than to winning their struggle.

The only way things will change is when both sides of this struggle are able to articulate the other side's story in a compassionate way. Building that kind of open-heartedness and generosity can't be done solely through traditional politics; it takes a new kind of spiritual awareness, a recognition of the sanctity of all humans, and a capacity for atonement and forgiveness. And this kind of spiritual consciousness is not only needed to deal with Israel; it's needed as well to address most of the fundamental political issues facing us in advanced industrial societies.

Within Jewish tradition there is a foundation for this other way of thinking about the world, detailed in my book *Jewish Renewal*. The fundamental reality of the universe is the potential for transformation from the status quo toward a world based on love, generosity, kindness, peace, economic justice, awe, and wonder. All forms of oppression can be overcome. We can build a world based on Torah principles like "thou shalt love the stranger," "justice, justice shalt thou pursue," and "thou shalt be holy." To see the world from this standpoint is not to claim that we are already in such a world, but it is to put on the agenda the question of how to develop strategies to build such a world. And strategy number one is this: don't talk as though the idea of a world based on love and justice is utopian nonsense that has no application in the "real world." If anything, understand that for Judaism the height of idolatry is realism—taking "that which is" as a criterion for "that which could be." Or at least for the strand of Judaism that I and my allies who are part of the Tikkun Community (Community@Tikkun.org) built around *TIKKUN* magazine have been seeking to reclaim and use as the cornerstone of the Jewish Renewal movement we are seeking to build. For us, September 11 does not translate to a new level of despair or proof that the world is irredeemably evil.

Rather, we *must try* to respond to September 11 as a potential wake-up call for the entire planet.

This is a moment in which all of us need to overcome our self-fulfilling pessimism, our certainty that we can't count on anyone else, our fears and our isolation, and instead begin to look at our situation with a new planetary consciousness. Instead of imagining that we can cleverly work out a private solution for the Jewish people by allying ourselves with the most powerful society in world history, we need instead to see our interdependence with the rest of humanity.

That planetary consciousness means that Jews will have to stop thinking of ourselves as separate from others, eternally persecuted, and instead begin to realize that the fate of the state of Israel, indeed, the fate of the entire Jewish people, is inextricably bound with the fate of everyone else on the planet. If they are doing well, we will do well. If they are in pain and oppression, we will not do well.

And this is the message that we Jews need to bring to America and other Western societies as well: the planet is one, indivisible, intrinsically interconnected. Don't imagine that you can dump your toxic wastes, your denials of human rights, your poverty, your ruling elites, on one part of the world to protect your interests, and that this will not eventually—and probably very soon—have dramatic impact on your own well-being. The world is one.

And humanity is one.

This does not mean that Jews should give up our separate identities, our history, our culture, or our religion. The unity we need in the human race is not a unity about these things. But it is a unity about sharing the world's resources rather than focusing on how to protect our own share, about modeling generosity and kindness toward others, about forgiveness and atonement for the ways that we have been insensitive to others, and about acknowledging that there are many equally valid spiritual paths. A Jewish people that can model this kind of consciousness has a chance of survival and deserves to survive. This is the only path to Jewish continuity.

It is this vision that I am inviting you to help make a reality by joining me to create the Tikkun Community: www.tikkun.org.

RED, WHITE, AND GOLD:
ON THE NUMBING OF A NATION

Danya Ruttenberg

WHAT ASTOUNDS ME THE MOST is how quickly it all happened. Within hours, it seemed—during all the sobbing, amidst the shock and disbelief and vulnerability and chaos and vigils and confusion and horror. Perhaps all the wireless cell phones and Internet communications we've been perfecting over the years paved the way for some sort of Coast-to-Coast Smoke Signal campaign, or maybe the semiotics of the national consciousness really are so well-established that we can effortlessly apply them to each new situation. Take one icon from column A, one from column B, and you've got yourself a campaign! Within minutes of people choosing to plunge to their deaths from the sixty-second and ninety-fifth floor, within minutes of people rushing up to help and not rushing back down, within minutes of a burning day that made everybody stop—within minutes, we had tricolor "cause ribbons," celebrity benefit concerts, and entire billboards rented out by Fortune 500 companies asking that G-d bless our dear America. Where did everybody get the four-by-nine flags for their cars?

More to the point, what lurks beneath the shiny "us-against-them" defense-line patriotism, replete with American machismo and, of all things, a mandate to shop? The speed and frenzy with which our nation jumped to its new, proud, post–September 11 existence clearly reveals some sort of coping mechanism. But of what sort?

The "justice, not vengeance" yelled from the Left claimed to be an antidote to the violin stirrings of "The Star-Spangled Banner." Sounds nice in theory, but what exactly does it mean? And what's the relationship between the pursuit of justice and this new rush of patriotism?

In the Torah, the classic statement "justice, justice, you shall pursue, that you may live and inherit the land" (Deut 16:20) is followed *immediately* by a series of prohibitions against idolatry. They start out fairly standard-issue: no Asherah trees next to G-d's altars, no erecting pillars, and so forth. The fourth line down, however, strikes me as particularly instructive: "If there is found among you a man or woman who transgresses the Covenant by going to serve other gods and worshipping them—whether the sun or the moon or any of the host of Heaven that I have forbidden—and it is reported to you . . ." then, well, here's how you evaluate the crime and issue possible punishment.

There's clearly a connection between the realization of justice and the problems posed by idolatry, and this particular line seems to be pointing us at one of the possible connections between the two. Interestingly, the line singles out the sun, moon, and stars as objects of idolatrous worship. There's a pretty natural human tendency to look skyward for signs of infinity, but what G-d's saying here is that settling for the stuff that's manifest, easy to pinpoint, just ain't gonna cut it.

The impulse to take the easy path also underlies the Golden Calf incident, Judaism's textbook case of idolatrous worship. As the story goes, G-d frees the Israelites from slavery in Egypt, enables them to cross the Red Sea, feeds them manna and water in the middle of the desert and *speaks to them on Sinai*—and the Israelites are *still* so insecure that while Moses is away talking to G-d, they put together a big, gleaming bull to worship. G-d is elusive, hard to perceive and even harder to see, and they have a hard time trusting that their needs will be cared for. It seems logical that they would be feeling uncomfortable and uncertain about their futures at this time, possibly even quite frightened after such a wild ride. But rather than sitting with their discomfort, they create something to focus on—that is, the calf—to distract themselves from the anxiety about their seemingly capricious fate in the desert.

Idolatry is about looking for distractions and easy answers. For a long time, now, in the face of grief, anger, fear, or hurt, individuals in our culture have thrown themselves at anything that might stave off the terror of ugly emotions: our work, the Internet, the TV set, a shopping binge, a new diet, the pursuit of cheap sexual gratification. We've built a nation of shallow entertainment, instant gratification, and consumerism, all of which seem to imply that just a little more—of what, we're not sure—will make it all better. And, not surprisingly, that same impulse has recently been grafted onto our feelings about war. We've begun staving off the guilt,

fear, insecurity, and feelings of vulnerability that broke through our consciousness like an airplane through a window; we've been staving them off
with flags and slogans and songs and yes, even fundraisers for the fireman's fund.

We seek distraction for the same reasons the Israelites did—to ignore
what is difficult, to drown out the fear and anger and hurt that seem overwhelming, overpowering, utterly and profoundly beyond our control. The
Israelites were scared stiff, and for good reason—their leader had vanished, and they were adrift in a barren wasteland, having left behind a
painful but at least more certain life of servitude back in Egypt. It's not
all that surprising that in the face of so much doubt and terror they'd
want to focus their attention on a big ol' shiny thing.

They did it for the same reasons we do—and we all do it.

I do. So do you.

In the world of contemporary spirituality, we often hear the story in
which "Kabbalah teaches that, with the creation of the world, the great
vessels of G-d's Light were shattered. As a result, the vessels' Most Sacred
contents rained outward in every direction, and each spark of the Divine
became a soul—a little piece of G-d embedded in each of us."

Yeah, well.

Personally, I think what we really got was a bunch of broken glass.

After all, each of us, in different ways, is deeply, profoundly, irrevoca-
bly broken. Those places of brokenness are, whether we're aware of it or
not, the lenses through which we see the world—the filters through which
we understand our own experience and the experience of the world. We
have a very human tendency to act out of broken places—out of the fear,
the hurt, the anger that in deep and fundamental ways mark us as exactly
who we are. Often from those places we behave badly to ourselves and
to other people—even or especially if we don't know it.

In the Torah, we're shown again and again a portrait of whiny, ungrateful Israelites—they get sick of manna and start begging for quail, they
lament for their lost safety in Egypt, and, of course, there's that calf thing
again. It's a portrait of people in the midst of what we might call posttraumatic stress disorder, really—they were so crushed by the brutalizing
experience of slavery that almost nothing G-d does can begin to help them
learn how to trust. After generations of oppression, the Israelites' victim
mentality is deeply embedded; they're utterly bereft of the tools that would
enable them to recognize sincere acts of love and respond in kind. Even
in the midst of signs and wonders, they're convinced that Moses and G-d
are out to get them.

We're broken, too—as individuals and as a nation. On a personal level, the nature of the shattered places vary as much as the whorl on a thumbprint; we all have stories to explain why we're angry, why we're scared, who hurt us beyond recognition and what debilitating losses we have suffered. What haunts us at night as we try to sleep and pretend that we don't feel the tightness in our chest. What we refuse to even remember. We all, in our own way, bear the indelible scars of living, and they shape who and how we are in the world in a myriad of ways.

And if the pain is often overwhelming on an individual level, how much more so when multiplied by an entire country? Something's been wrong for a long time—the evidence is in exploited Thai workers and bombed Iraqi children, in systems of oppression built to last—but the symptoms seem particularly acute now. Part of the reason, I think, that people became so patriotic so quickly, taking refuge in the ribbons and the billboards and the celebrity sing-alongs to benefit the fireman's fund, was a sense of shock and almost even chagrin that we should be the object of someone else's attacks. Whatever bombs we have dropped and whatever arms we have traded, we Americans have conceived of ourselves as a race of humans that were not, with a Manifest Destiny leap of logic, *meant* to suffer violence. It's a lot easier to design a "tribute to liberty" Website or to "adopt-a-victim" with a "memory plaque" than it is to acknowledge that, at core, our security and safety—our feelings of sheer invulnerability—are illusory. It's easier to shop the economy back to health than to stop assuming there's no moral ambiguity surrounding a "war on terrorism." We want to be the good guys who are happy because we deserve it, and we get frenetic at the prospect of any challenge to our preferred view of the cosmos.

The Rambam defines perfect tshuvah as returning to the same crossroads at which sin was originally committed and taking the other path. It's about revisiting the site of a wound in order to turn it on its head. In order to pass through pain, first we must feel it. It's natural to run in the opposite direction from our own suffering—but until we invite it to consume us, it will always be there, just throbbing beneath the surface. And we will constantly be acting from it—both reenacting destructive modes of thinking and making sudden, sharp turns in order to avoid feeling the emotions that are already there.

Our most broken place is our most open, most vulnerable—it's the place from which we can be closest to G-d. It is, in a way, who we really are. Where we are broken is the seat of our power, the place through which we are truly holiest.

In the *V'ahavta* we are told of the injunction to love G-d: *V'hayo hadvarim ha-eleh, asher anochi, mitzavchah al-livanecha* (and these words

which I command you this day shall be upon your heart). The Baal Shem
Tov asked, why are they upon your heart instead of in your heart? So that
when your heart breaks, the words fall in.

It's not even that we can't hear the words until we are broken—because
we are all broken—it's that hearing them—truly understanding how to
love ourselves and, by extension, G-d—must happen at precisely the point
of incision. It's not about "healing" from our wounds so that we can
move forward into the sacred—it's about using our wounds to encounter
the sacred.

What happens if we allow ourselves to feel them? The first impulse is that
the fear, the anger will threaten to consume us, drown us out until there's
nothing left but rage. Yet when we actually do stop and allow the burning
sensation to rise up, we discover that yes, it does flare hot for a while—
intensely hot—but eventually, once given permission to speak, the emotion
has its say and then departs, no longer a captive of the heart and mind.

Our broken bits and our divine spark are one and the same—what it
is about us that is our deepest hurt or shame or anger is our greatest power, when we open to it. Our greatest hurt or shame or sorrow is the raw
material of our greatest gift from G-d—and the raw material through
which we can offer what we have worth offering to the world. The trick,
of course, is to begin to understand that place, to see it, that we may go from
unconsciously acting out from it—idolatry—to using it to manifest profound goodness, to mirror the divine in ourselves and in the world.

America's anguish comes from the belief that our power makes us king.
And our power does make us king—we possess an overwhelming propor-
tion of the world's resources and we continue to dictate the terms of diplomacy, war, and trade for the rest of the world's inhabitants. We suffer when
we refuse to take responsibility for that. Our potential gift to the planet,
and ourselves, lies in the acknowledgment that we're not morally entitled
to any more than any other country or region, yet we do have more.

The implications of such an admission are innumerable; once we see
ourselves for what we are, without illusion, we'd necessarily have to take
a less militaristic and interventionist role in foreign policy; we'd have to
ensure that poorer countries, and their citizens, are protected in our trade
agreements. We'd have to reconsider how our national budget is allocated,
what role corporate interest has in shaping law, particularly environmental law. We'd have to understand our immigrant policies in an entirely new
way. We'd have to examine our diplomatic relationships with countries
that occupy, colonize, or violate human rights. In short, we'd have to understand each and every one of our actions as a nation in the bigger pic-

ture while acknowledging that the privilege we possess is not the privilege to which we are, in any special way, entitled.

This, then, is the true path to justice—to *tzedek*, the word the Torah uses: righteousness. Tricolored ribbons can't protect us from that, nor can slogans about standing united against—whatever we stand united against. Responsibility? Transformation?

I worry about us a lot. The Israelites were so overwhelmed by their brokenness that they had to wander in the desert for forty years—enough time for one generation to die out and another to take its place. The freed slaves were determined to protect themselves from the kind of suffering— the vulnerability, the fear—they had already endured, and they refused to let anyone into those places. Not even G-d. And as a result, they, in a way, died as slaves, forever beholden to the scars of servitude.

The path to justice, the Torah tells us, begins by letting go of the idols of easy answers and quick fixes. We're meant to look past the skyward glitter of the stars (and the stripes) to grapple with G-d directly, from our darkest recesses. On an individual level this process is profoundly difficult, and ripe with our greatest potential as human beings. And for us as a nation? How long we remain in the desert remains yet to be seen. Certainly, there's only one pathway to Zion.

"Justice, justice, you shall pursue," G-d tells us. "That you may live and inherit the land."

THE MANY
IDENTITIES
OF A JEW

PSALM

Joshua Weiner

When I sing to you I am alone these days
　　　　　and can't believe it, as if the stars

—while gazing up at them—just shut off.
　　　　　Astonished:

I search out the one light, brightest light
　　　　　in the night sky, but find

I cannot find it without weaker lights to guide me
　　　　　like red tail-lights on a car up ahead

after midnight when I'm sleepy, that illustrate
　　　　　how the highway curves,

curving to a hook, and maybe save my life
　　　　　and it means nothing to me

because nothing has happened, not the faintest
　　　　　glint of drama.

(Raining gently, the tarmac turns slick, moistened
　　　　　to life with renewed residues;

I can sense it with my hands on the wheel,
        the drops—not too heavy—

drumming off-time rhythms on the metal roof,
        the metal surface like a skin tense and sweating

and the road empty now, there are so many
        exits . . .)

Where is my family, both hearth and constellated trail of flicker
        I have always followed to your word?

There, but mastered by fear of dark compulsions
        and loathing atrocities committed in your name,

they hit the dimmer switch and extinguish themselves
        whenever I sing your praises . . .

Who can blame them?
        (I can't help but blame them.)

And anyway they are far from me
        (farthest when they come to visit)—

I should be self-reliant, in my armchair
        like Emerson reading by a single lamp;

I should not need them, finding in you
        myself, little firebug needing no outlet,

my soft light blinking as I oxidize my aimless flight
        to love, to the good,

even my glowing chemistry unnecessary now
        in the ultimate light of day.

But what good would that do me?
        With you, in you, perhaps others do not matter,

but this isn't heaven, and I cannot make a circle
        all on my own—

Photon, luciferin, meteor: as I burn myself
        to pieces, I only pray

let my sparking tail remain a moment longer
        than our physics might allow,

some indication, however brief, that there continues
        (amen) a path to follow.

PERMEABLE BOUNDARIES

Aryeh Cohen

A RABBI, ordained in the first decade of the twenty-first century, confronts an American Jewish community at an important crossroads. Fifty years after the end of the Shoah and fifty years after the creation of the state of Israel, some facts are brilliantly clear, even if, to some, unsettling.

The American Jewish community, in all its affiliations and forms, is far stronger and more vibrant than any European Jewish community in the more than one thousand years that Jews have lived and thrived on that continent. More Jews are involved in the study of Torah, whether in yeshivot, rabbinical seminaries, or universities, than ever in the history of Jewish life. While American Jews continue the centuries-old tradition of bemoaning the decline of Jewish existence—a tradition that can be traced back at least to tenth-century Persia in the Letter of Rav Sherira Gaon—Jewish existence is actually thriving.

At this moment in time, the paths of the state of Israel and the American Jewish community are consistently diverging. While the state of Israel was dependent on the Jews of North America for its creation and sustenance for most of the twentieth century (continuing the practice of the despised Old Yishuv), and while the political support and pressure of the Jewish community in the United States is important to the aims of the state of Israel (for better and for worse), the agenda of the Jewish community in the United States is no longer the agenda of the state of Israel—as the state of Israel is no longer merely a Jewish state (as it never really

46

was but for the films of the World Zionist Organization and the Jewish Agency) but a powerful nation-state whose democratic fragility is a direct result of its lack of egalitarian acceptance of its non-Jewish citizens.

This divergence is exacerbated by the stranglehold that the Chief Rabbinate has over the religious affairs of the state, leading to the dismissal of and contempt for every branch and expression of Judaism except Orthodoxy.

At the same time, the conservative movement maintains the structure of a Jewish community whose center is Israel. Every conservative seminary must have a year in Israel. Teaching modern Hebrew is an integral part of all Hebrew school curriculums (this being, of course, a symbolic act, since no one thinks that a child can learn to speak and understand a language in two one-hour sessions a week). Yet all the evidence points to the fact that the overwhelming majority of the American Jewish community has no intention of ever living in Israel. Moreover, this attention to the goings-on in Israel comes at a great price. The price is the lack of attention that is paid to the question of American Jewish identity. What does it mean to be a diasporic Jewish community? This is a question that our tradition has grappled with over and over again. In the following from Bavli Berachot, R. Yossi, who lived three generations after the Destruction of the Second Temple, is forced to come to terms with, and an understanding of, a Jewish life in exile. I will claim that this is the focal point of the conflict between an American diasporic Judaism and an Israeli Judaism. R. Yossi's education in this *beraitta* is the education that the rabbis needed (then and now), the radical transformation that was necessitated by the destruction of the temple and the ongoing sojourn in strange lands.

In Bavli Berachot (3a) the following *beraitta* is cited:

> It has been taught:
> R. Yossi says:
> One time I was travelling on the road and I entered into one of the ruins of Jerusalem in order to pray.
> Elijah, of blessed memory, came,
> and guarded the door for me,
> and waited for me,
> until I finished my prayer.
> After I finished my prayer, he said to me: "Peace be with you my master!"
> And I said to him: "Peace be with you my master and teacher!"

And he said to me: "My son, why did you go into this ruin?"
I said to him: "To pray."
And he said to me: "You ought to have prayed on the road."
And I said to him: "I feared lest passersby might interrupt me."
And he said to me: "You ought to have said an abbreviated prayer."
At that moment I learned from him three things:
—One must not go into a ruin,
—One must say the prayer on the road,
—And if one does say his prayer on the road, he says an abbreviated prayer.
And he said to me: "My son, what sound did you hear in this ruin?"
I said to him: "I heard a divine voice, cooing like a dove, and saying: Woe to the children!
For on account of their sins I destroyed my house
and burnt my Temple, and exiled them among the nations!"
And he said to me: "By your life and by your head!
Not in this moment alone does it exclaim thus,
But three times every day does it exclaim thus.
And not only this, but whenever Israel go into
the synagogues and study houses
and responds: May His great name be blessed!
The Holy One of Blessing, shakes his head, and says:
Happy is the king who is thus praised in his house!
What is there for the father
who had to banish his children?!
And woe to the children
who were banished from the table of their father."

R. Yossi's story is the story of the Exile.

R. Yossi was walking on the road and decided to go into "one of the ruins of Jerusalem." There is, of course, only one ruin in Jerusalem. All ruins point to the gaping hole in the center of the spiritual consciousness of the Jewish people—the destroyed temple. R. Yossi wanted to go back into the ruins of the temple to pray.

As soon as R. Yossi—the student of R. Akiva, who was the armsbearer for Bar Kochba, whom he considered the messiah—as soon as this scion of rabbinic messianism entered the ruin, Elijah, the harbinger of redemption, appears. R. Yossi prays and Elijah guards the door. Elijah waits patiently for R. Yossi to finish his prayer. Finally, R. Yossi finishes and Elijah greets him as one sage greets another.

At this moment, as we read the story, we are expecting Elijah to reveal news of the redemption. Instead, he interrogates R. Yossi's practice—and corrects it in the most radical way.

R. Yossi had wanted to pray at leisure, luxuriously, away from the madding crowd. Elijah tells him that he should not return to the ruins to pray but rather must pray on the road in an abbreviated form. Life has changed, Elijah is telling him. The temple has been destroyed, Israel is bereft, all there is, is the road. Now, an abbreviated prayer, a hastened prayer amongst and between the travails of the exile, is all the prayer we have.

This is not all. Elijah then proceeds to explain to R. Yossi the nature of exilic prayer.

"Did you not hear the cooing of the dove? That was the response to your prayer. That was the voice of God-in-Exile."

This is perhaps the most startling aspect of this aggadah. Elijah needed to point out to R. Yossi that he had heard a divine voice cooing like a dove mourning the destruction of the temple.

In the moment R. Yossi had not been able to hear it. R. Yossi was still looking for the temple in whose precincts dwelled the God who was "man of war," who would wreak vengeance on the enemies of Israel. When one prayed in the temple, the answer was thunderous.

Only after Elijah had taught R. Yossi that he could no longer go back into the temple to pray; that one prayed on the way; only then could R. Yossi understand that God's mourning and grieving *was* the reply of God-in-Exile to R. Yossi's prayer.

After the destruction of the temple, the balance of spiritual power has changed. It is God who draws strength from the prayers of the righteous. Prayer in exile is directed to a God in exile whose absence is an overwhelming presence.

These are the things that R. Yossi learned.

But there is more. What does it mean that we have to pray "on the way," "on the road"?

The *Kedushat Levi*, Reb Levi Yitzhak of Berditchev, explained God's charge to Abraham *lech lechah*, "go forth," in the following manner. God says to Abraham (and, of course, to all of us): "Go to yourself." "Every place that a person goes, he goes to the root of his soul." The "way" is the place that one needs to be. It is not some ultimate goal that is important. It is not, as Nachmanides writes, that in exile the commandments are merely signposts pointing back to the land of Israel.

It is, rather, that the challenge of being on the "way"—which is what diaspora is all about—is the challenge of attending to the moment and the place I occupy *now*. That moment and that place has something I need *and* something I need to take care of.

The destruction of the temple brings in its wake the possibility of serving God out of displacement. As the *Kedushat Levi* says elsewhere—pilgrimage on the festivals is commanded so that everyone worships God as a stranger, as a person not at home. This not-at-home-ness is perhaps the defining characteristic of exile—and, perhaps, its chief virtue. Displacement brings in its wake humility, according to Maimonides (*Laws of Tshuvah,* Chapter Two). Exile itself speaks against hubris.

The dangers of trying to replace the at-home-ness of the land with other forms of substitute mastery is addressed in several places in the Mishnah and the Talmud, with a skeptical eye cast on the virtues of complacency that are dressed up in the guise of ownership or mastery.

The first Mishnah in Shabbat, the Mishnah which maps Shabbat, which creates the Sabbatical geography of impermeable boundaries between public and private; this first Mishnah introduces the notion of public and private domain with a landlord and a poor person representing public and private. The transaction between them is one of life and death. Food passes from the hand of one to the other. When there is no way to pass food from private to public (or vice versa) someone dies.

The Talmud (b. Baba Bathra 6b) relates another tale of Elijah. There was a man to whom Elijah appeared regularly. The man was apparently righteous and worthy of these revelations. Once the man collaborated with his neighbors and built a fence at the entrance way to their courtyard—a fence and a partnership sanctioned by the Mishnah—once the fence was built, Elijah never returned.

The explanation in the Talmud (as understood by the medieval commentators) is that a fence that would prevent a poor person from entering the courtyard is forbidden. The boundaries between public and private must remain permeable.

This too is part of the "way." When walls of mortar and bricks or walls of dollars and cents or even walls of religion and ethnicity become impermeable boundaries between "our" private domain and the public "them" or "there," we are no longer on the way—we have lost our way.

There is another Torah that I draw from R. Yossi's encounter with Elijah. It is a Torah that is both very personal—in that it has been transformative in my own life—and, to my mind, of the highest importance for the American Jewish community in general and the conservative rabbinate in particular.

As Elijah guards the doorway and then escorts R. Yossi out of the ruins, back onto the road, he teaches R. Yossi the truth of the path chosen, yet not chosen by American Jews in the twentieth century. The Zionist enterprise, which, along with the Holocaust, has importantly defined and informed Judaism in North America in the past century, is based on the central claim that we can go back into the ruins; that we can return to the temple and pray. The most radical religious claim of Zionism was and is that the regeneration of Judaism is dependent on the reconnection with the land through which will flow a new Jewish person and a new Torah. Not only can we go back, but we must go back and pray in the temple.

While American Jews have never given more than a second's thought to moving to Israel, they still pay obeisance to this central tenet of Zionism—which is a large part of American Judaism. When I went to Israel in 1976 at the age of seventeen to study for a year at a Yeshivat Hesder, I was under the sway of this axiom of American Judaism—despite having been educated in right-wing orthodox yeshivahs in New York that deny the validity of Zionism.

Learning what was taught as *Torat Eretz Yisrael,* I could not reconcile living in *galut* with the existence of the state of Israel. I believed that there was no Jewish future outside of Israel. Therefore, I decided to stay in Israel and live the Jewish future. The Jewish future, I believed, was the path that led back into the temple—both metaphorically *and* literally. Living in this messianic future was, to a certain extent, dependent on certain cognitive blinders. I walked the streets of the Old City of Jerusalem, but I only saw the buildings that had been built and destroyed centuries ago. I was intimate with the occupants of the famous "burnt house"—which was destroyed in 70 A.D. with the temple—but did not speak Arabic nor did I really see the Palestinians who live in the Old City now.

It was a long and winding road that led me to see that truly we could not go back into the temple, since someone was living there. It was a road that went through Yamit and Lebanon, dead and missing friends and massacred Palestinians, places and faces that often I would rather forget but cannot.

It took me years to realize that Israel was not "a land without a people for a people without a land." The ruins had been covered with dust, and others had trod that dust for centuries, building cities and societies. I still felt a visceral attachment to the pathways, the walls, the hills of Jerusalem. I also felt its danger.

It was, however, only years later, after I had left Israel and was back on a short visit, that I was able to articulate the dangerous power aroused by the land. While standing at the top of Tel Bet Shean, I was able to see the whole sweep of the Jezreel Valley. The beauty of the land overwhelmed me. There was more to it than just its beauty. I felt a visceral connection to the mountains, the plateaus, the rocks, the dirt. I felt again the same feelings that I had felt every time I saw the approaching contours of the hills of Jerusalem. It was a feeling akin to love. The land was part of me. This must have been the pathos behind Maimonides' comment: "The greatest Sages would kiss the boundaries of the Land of Israel, and kiss her stones and roll around in her dust. As it says 'For Your servants take pleasure in its stones and love its dust' (Psalms 102:15)" (Laws of Kings 5:10).

This was, however, a dangerous attachment. The Deuteronomist's command to destroy the altars that were on every high mountain was followed in the breach as the power of the mountains and valleys were too hard to resist. It was exactly here that Israel was overcome with desire to worship a physical presence—the incarnation of the power that they felt as they looked out over the land. The land that God had given as an estate became itself a god, worshipped under the trees on the high mountains, with the sacrifice of the children (Isaiah 57:5).

It was only gradually that I was able to recognize the prophetic truth that the power of the land was a double-edged sword. Those who rolled around in the dirt of the land were those who declared "It is my strength and the power of my hand which has made all this for me" (Deut. 8:17).

This ever-growing cognizance of the dark side of the renaissance of the Jewish people in the land of Israel caused me to also question the centrality of Zionism and Israel to American Jewish identity. What is it that Israel gives to the American Jewish community? Are there truly paradigms of Jewishness, of community, of ethical polity that we would want to emulate? Is our focus on Israel not blinding us to the central questions of our own existence? Are we avoiding the questions that must be asked by this very affluent Jewish community with access to real political power? Should we not be putting questions of social and economic justice at the head of our list of priorities?

The existential situation of a Jewish community in the diaspora undermines the voice that says: "It is my strength and the power of my hand which has made all this for me." The challenge for the American Jewish community is to attend to the "diaspora-ness," the displacement, the margins that define our community and that our community occupies. The Jewish community is, by definition, countercultural in American society. The lens that this provides ought to be deployed as a critique to the comfort of being "inside" in many ways. The conservative rabbinate is uniquely positioned to lead along this path. We are a movement whose Torah bridges inside and out; we are a community which follows Maimonides' dictum of "learn truth from whomever speaks it." It is this very stance with which we begin to answer the pressing question of American Jewish identity. As a diasporic community, we are a community whose obligation it is to gather in the sparks of holiness in the visions of justice and truth that we encounter. We then add these as another layer in the immense structure of Torah on which we sit and which we continue to build. It is also our obligation to draw from that Torah in order to strike at the injustices that we see in this country, especially those directed at other marginal groups not as privileged or powerful as we. We also need to learn and understand and teach the Torah of permeable boundaries, of unlocked gates, of tents open to the four corners. We might bring that Torah back to our brothers and sisters in Israel, where it is so urgently needed.

This, then, can be our agenda. An agenda whose focus is substance and not numbers. We need not fear those who prophesize with statistics. There is a need for a rabbinic voice in North America (a rabbinic voice comprised of many voices) that demands a moratorium on programs that countenance "continuity" without context; a voice that loudly claims that the birthright of Jews is Torah, and that Torah is found in America and not only in Israel; a voice that says that those who lived marched also to Los Angeles and New York and Chicago and sowed the seeds for a vibrant Jewish community that can be the successor of Sura and Pumbeditha, Troyes and Dampierre, Provence and Barcelona, Baghdad and Livorno, and Warsaw and Berlin.

This is a way for which it is worth staking our careers and devoting our lives.

THE SECRET DIARY
OF A BAT MITZVA GIRL

Galina Vromen

THE TROUBLE BEGAN when my big brother married a shiksa. Not only was she Catholic. She was also pregnant—and religious, too. He was just twenty and brilliant. Well, at least he was considered brilliant until he married her. After that, everyone in our family thought he was dumb. Except me. I still think he's brilliant. He always has been. It's just that he's also horny. He always has been. At least as far back as I can remember. Is that such a crime? I guess even my parents would admit that it's not a crime. But they think getting a Catholic girl pregnant is a misdemeanor. Marrying her on account of her not believing in abortion is a felony.

But, like I said, I think Mort's brilliant. First of all, Cindy, the girl he married, is sweet in a naive sort of way. They eloped, which pissed off just about everybody. Me included. I mean I could have at least gotten an awesome new dress out of a real wedding. The baby, a girl, is called Ashley and she's really cute. And Cindy adores Mort. And Mort adores Cindy and is nuts about Ashley. They're kind of corny together. But if you ask me, adoring someone who adores you—the way Cindy and Mort do— that's got to be brilliant.

Not that I can speak from experience. I always seem to adore guys who don't even know I'm alive. And the guys who adore me are su-u-uch geeks. And ugly too. Except maybe for Charlie Ho. He's really smart but he's not a geek even though he's Chinese. Or at least his parents are. He's this amazing athlete at our school, really great at basketball and tennis. Tall and really funny. He knows I'm alive but he doesn't exactly adore me. We just kid around together sometimes. We both like Lenny Bruce and haiku poetry. Maybe that's not enough to base a relationship on, but at least it's *something*. I mean I don't adore him. But I could, if he adored me.

My Mom and Dad don't exactly adore each other. Half the time, they don't even talk to each other, especially since Mort married Cindy. They talk to each other through me. Like, "Ask your father when he wants to have dinner." Or like, "Ask your mother when she wants to leave for Aunt Amy's." Each one thinks it's the other one's fault that Mort married Cindy.

My mother thinks it's my father's fault for not sufficiently educating Mort about screwing around without using birth control. My father thinks that's a load of crap. He's right. I bet Mort knows a lot more about sex than Dad. (I walked in on Mort and Janet Schneider doing it in his bed one afternoon when Mort was fourteen. I didn't know what all that moaning and groaning was about at the time. I've grown up a lot since then. I should be so lucky—to lose my virginity at fourteen, I mean. At the rate I'm going, if I get kissed by the time I'm fourteen, it will be a miracle.)

My father thinks it's all my mother's fault that Mort married Cindy because Mom wouldn't let Mort go on a trip to Israel with United Synagogue Youth in his junior year of high school. "You were so afraid of terrorist attacks. Now we have a shiksa in the family instead. If he'd gone to Israel, maybe he would have understood what it means to be a Jew." My mother thinks that's a lot of crap. She's right. No one understands what it means to be a Jew.

This is something that I have been finding out recently because I'm preparing for my bat mitzva. I have been going to bat mitzva class since the beginning of the year. It is soooooo boring. We spend a lot of time talking about what being Jewish means. Rabbi Susan Fleishman says that being Jewish means knowing about Jewish tradition. Ha. The Orthodox rabbi in town won't talk to her because she's both a woman and a rabbi and that's not part of Jewish tradition. I happened to point this out in class. Which she admitted was an interesting point. So then she dropped the tradition bit and talked about Judaism as being flexible and changing with the times. But when I wanted to take pictures in synagogue after the bat mitzva of my best friend, Beth, Rabbi Fleishman stopped me because she said our synagogue is against taking pictures on the Sabbath. So much for flexible. I pointed that out, too. She said I'd made an interesting point. She said my observations helped to show up just how complex defining Judaism could be. That was her point, she insisted. Like, right.

There were some kids in class who said being Jewish meant being good to other people (like Maimonides said, the essence of the Torah is do unto others as you would have others do unto you; the rest is commentary).

But it seems at the soup kitchen where I go once a week, there are loads of Christians doing good, too. What I mean is Jews don't have a monopoly on the Golden Rule.

The soup kitchen is the one thing about this whole bat mitzva thing I really like (other than the presents and the money I'm going to get in the end). We have to do something of service to the community. It's supposed to make us good adults. Except the adults never do it. Just us kids. Down there in the soup kitchen, you get to see all these down-and-out types. You get to see what *real* life is like. It's so awesome. And it does make me feel lucky for our house, and the pool, for air-conditioning and heating. Most of the time, I wash dishes at the soup kitchen, and it makes me glad that we have a dishwasher at home.

Which may be the whole point of the exercise, really. To make us grateful for our comfortable Jewish homes. When I wash dishes at the soup kitchen with my friend Beth, we make up stories about anyone new who comes in for a meal. Then later, we try to get them to talk about themselves and see how far off our made-up stories are from reality. But some of the types that show up there are a little frightening to talk to—they seem totally flipped out. And a lot of people there don't like to talk about themselves. They yell at us or dismiss us with a wave of the hand. Which only makes us more curious. We have our own punishment for those who won't talk to us. We make up nicknames for them. Like Morty the Molester, Alan the Adulterer, Jimmy the One-Eyed Jailbird, Mark the Mother Killer.

Anyway, as I was saying, no one in our class, including the rabbi, knows how to explain what being Jewish means. One day, when we were talking about it (again) in our bat mitzva preparation class, someone said that being Jewish means sticking together with other Jews. I was considering mentioning my brother Mort. But I didn't want to get into it. As a matter of fact, it was one of the things a lot of the kids agreed about. Sticking with other Jews. What does that mean? Like when Jeff Finkelstein cheats on his algebra test, I'm not supposed to tell on him because he's Jewish? Well, I did. He got a 99 and I got a 98 and I wasn't going to let him get away with getting the best grade in class just because he cheated. So I squealed on him. He got into a shitload of trouble. So does that mean I'm not Jewish? Like, right. I pointed this out to Rabbi Fleishman. She wiggled out of it. Said it's sticking together on other things, as a family. By which she means not marrying shiksas, like my brother has.

Tell me about sticking together as a family. One of the things my parents have been talking about behind my back—like I don't know—is whether to invite Mort and Cindy to my bat mitzva. They don't know how they would explain Mort's absence to their friends. But they are afraid Cindy will not know how to behave, not stand up and sit down in the right places during the service. They're afraid she might do or say something that would show just how much of a shiksa she is. As my grandmother (she's dead) would have said, "Cindy doesn't know from Jews." I figure, if Cindy had, she probably wouldn't have gotten involved with Mort in the first place.

The problem with inviting Mort and Cindy is that my parents don't talk to Mort anymore. They are super pissed off at him, not only for marrying Cindy but also for everything he has done since then—quit college, let the baby be baptized. I think he baptized her out of spite. Then Mom and Dad threatened to cut him out of their will. He told them he wishes they live a long life and to go fuck themselves. I'm telling you, he's brilliant.

Well, my parents can discuss it behind my back all they want, but Mort is absolutely, definitely, coming to my bat mitzva. First of all, I had to be at his boring bar mitzva eight years ago. I even had to say something nice about him during the ceremony, which was hard at the time since he wasn't nice to me (or anyone else) during that particular period of his life.

Second, I want to get the present he'll have to buy me if I invite him. It will have to be a pretty big one. After all, I'm his only sister. Not that he's got a lot of money for presents these days. Since he quit college, he's been working as a floor manager at K-Mart. Not exactly big bucks. But he's brilliant, right? He'll get me something awesome. I'm sure of it. He's my brilliant big brother. Really.

Third, his being there will embarrass my parents. They've sort of downplayed his marriage. To put it mildly, I think they'd rather die than tell their friends what he's done.

Fourth, he'll look so bad for marrying a shiksa, it's sure to make me look good by contrast. I mean, until now I've never been considered the brilliant one. Bratty, yes. Energetic, definitely. Brilliant, no. So now maybe, finally, I'll look brilliant. (I am going to learn my damn Torah portion until I know it backward and forward and I'll think of something brilliant to say about it. Really.) So, anyway, my parents don't know it, but he's going to be there. Invited personally by yours truly.

About that Torah portion. I've been learning all that Hebrew stuff by heart for a couple of months. I even have the singsong down quite well. This week I got a brilliant idea. Really. Since I don't understand what I'm reading, I thought to look it up in English in a Bible so that I would actually know what it is I am going to be saying.

I couldn't quite figure it out, but it was something about Moses marrying a Cushite woman while he was leading the Jewish people through the desert for forty years and all about how Miriam, his sister, gets upset about it, and how God gets angry at Miriam for bad-mouthing Moses, and God wants to punish her with some horrible disease but Moses and Aaron beg God not to be so hard on her. In the end she is punished by being banished from the Jewish encampment for a week until she gets a grip. She got the opposite of grounded for bad-mouthing her brother. Now that's something I can relate to. I had no idea what a Cushite woman was. I thought maybe it meant low-class or something. There's one kid at school, Arieh, who comes from Israel and he actually knows Hebrew. So I asked him what "Cushite" means and he said black, as in black-skinned. Like Moses married an Afro-American. Or I mean the same thing as an Afro-American, although of course there weren't any Americans then. The equivalent then. At least I think that's what that portion means. Wow. I mean Moses was the flipping leader of the Jews and he goes and marries out of the faith! No wonder Rabbi Fleishman has us learn all this stuff only in Hebrew!

But I don't see why she should get out of 'fessing up to what the Bible says. So I decided to ask her about my Torah portion. I asked her if Moses marries an Afro-American in my portion. She looked at me funny. Then she sort of mumbled that although "Cushite" in modern Hebrew means black-skinned, in Moses' time it's not exactly clear what a "Cushite" was or who the "Cushites" were.

"But they weren't one of the twelve tribes of Israel, were they?" I asked.

"No, we know they were not one of the twelve tribes," she answered.

"So, like this portion is saying that Moses married someone that wasn't Jewish, right?" I pressed on.

"Yes, that's probably true," she answered.

"And Moses's sister criticized him for doing it, right?" I asked.

"Yes, she was very critical," Rabbi Fleishman answered.

"And God punishes her for bad-mouthing him for marrying a shiksa, right?"

"Well, that's not the way that passage is usually interpreted," the rabbi answered. "Traditionally, that passage has been viewed as dealing with leadership issues, establishing that Moses was God's favored. If you read the passage carefully, in context, it shows that God is letting Miriam and Aaron know their place as being subordinate to Moses. But we really don't have time to discuss this further right now. It's not fair to the rest of the class," she added quickly. "We can't just talk about your particular portion."

But I'm not willing to let it go. I go to the rabbi office later to talk to her.

"If Moses can marry a maybe Afro-American, why can't my brother marry a Catholic? Especially if God has nothing against it."

"That was then, this is now. I don't think you can take everything in the Torah literally. It has to be viewed in context," she says and then cuts our conversation short because she has a meeting with Nora Cohen, who is organizing the synagogue's annual tag sale.

So now I am wondering about all this. Then was then, now is now, she said. Can't take it all literally? Ha, tell that to the ultra-Orthodox. And who's to say what part to take and what not? Like *payot,* yes. But shiksas, no? Doesn't make sense to me. Know what I mean?

Anyway, I'm thinking of showing the passage to my parents. Like, get a grip, folks. But they'll probably only get angry at me for bothering them. They're really busy these days. They've been trying to hire a photographer and decide on a caterer. And then there's the fighting over the guest list.

I told them I want to invite Mort and Cindy and Ashley. My parents keep saying, "We'll see," which is usually their way of saying no. But I'll show them. I called Mort this week and made him promise to come if he got an invitation. He said he would if it was an official one. I get to invite some of my own friends to the bat mitzva and I get to address those envelopes myself. I'm inviting Beth and Charlie Ho and a bunch of others. (I think it's okay to invite Charlie Ho. He was at Beth's bat mitzva and I've seen him at a couple of other ones, so I don't think being at a Jewish service freaks him out or anything.) But I gave my mother the names of three friends I'm not inviting and sent the invitation to Mort, Cindy, and Ashley instead. I addressed the envelope in my mother's handwriting, which I'm very good at since I'm always practicing forging her signature so I can use her credit cards. (Don't worry, I only forge it with her permission— except when it comes to the sick notes I write to the school nurse after I've skipped out on a day of school.)

So anyway, happy bat mitzva to me. The day finally arrives. I missed Mort and Cindy's entrance. I don't know whether they came in when Aunt Amy took me aside to the vestibule of the synagogue to hand me an envelope, explaining to me in conspiratorial tones that she was giving me a bigger check than she gave my cousin Sarah a couple of years ago because I've been such a wonderful niece and Sarah never calls on her birthday. Or maybe it was when I was in the bathroom trying (again) to safety pin down my bra straps so they wouldn't show when I was up on the *bima.* (Though I wouldn't mind if Charlie Ho happened to notice that I'm wearing a bra these days, but still, it's embarrassing to have it show on the *bima.*) Anyway, by the time I came out of the bathroom, Mom had

on the sort of wobbly, distracted smile she puts on her face when something both unexpected and unpleasant happens. Next to her I saw Mrs.
Cohen who seemed about to head for me when I noticed my brother in a
corner, talking to the cantor and looking bored. I dove off in his direction,
almost toppling him over with a big hug.

"Hi brat," he smiled.

"Hi big brat," I retorted.

"Excuse us, cantor," he said, "I need to have a word with the birthday
girl." He grabbed my elbow and took me aside.

The moment we were out of the cantor's earshot, the smile disappeared.
"I can't believe you didn't tell Mom or Dad that we were coming," he said.

"But you promised me you would come."

"Yeah, but I assumed you'd tell them you were inviting us and they had
agreed."

I shrugged. "What does it matter? I wanted you here. You're here. That's
what matters."

He shook his head and rolled his eyes upwards. "I have half a mind to
leave."

"Don't," I said, grabbing his arm. "Please don't. I want you and Cindy
and Ashley to be here. And this is *my* party after all."

"Okay, okay. But you sure know how to create one hell of an uncomfortable situation," he hissed.

"That's rich. I'm the last one you should blame. You're the one who
eloped, and Mom and Dad are the ones who have decided not to have anything to do with you or Cindy. I'm the one who's trying to make everything
all right. Really."

"Sure, right." He smiled ruefully at me. "Brat," he said, tousling my hair.

"Stop it, you're ruining my hair."

"Like I said, brat," he said, tousling my hair again. I stuck out my tongue
and turned away.

"Hey, good luck up there," he called after me.

I beamed him back a smile. "Thanks, big brat."

People were beginning to take their seats in the hall and the rabbi came
to herd me and my parents up to the *bima*. Sitting up there during the service, I had plenty of time to get good and nervous. I once read that the
way to deal with stage fright is to imagine everyone in the audience is
naked. But with my grandfather and Aunt Amy sitting right up there in
the front row, I decided that I would rather suffer from stage fright than
throw up imagining how ugly they must look naked. I was trying to think
about Moses instead, and imagining how much he must have looked like

my grandfather—dressed or naked—when I heard Rabbi Fleishman call my name and invite me to read from the Torah.

If I say so myself, I read my portion flawlessly. My amen at the end was in gratitude for getting it all out of the way. Finally. Months of work. Gone, finished, done with. Then the rabbi asked me if I wanted to say a few words to the congregation. I nodded and went up to the podium again. I glanced at my parents, sitting behind me on the *bima* with self-satisfied smiles on their faces. The moment had arrived for the long-suffering folks to get their official gratitude from the bratty, ungrateful twerp—yours truly, of course. "Thanks to all of you for coming to my bat mitzva," I said. "And thanks to my parents for paying for all of the great food you're going to eat later . . . and for putting up with me for the past thirteen years," I added, getting a laugh from the audience.

"I want to talk to you a bit about the portion I just read," I continued. "Frankly, most of the time, the Bible seems to me to be full of stories I can't really relate to. But I must have lucked out, because the portion I got really speaks to me. I don't know how many of you really understood the text. I didn't understand it either until I decided to look it up one day. And I found out that it is about the reaction of Miriam and Aaron, Moses's sister and brother, when they find out that he has married a Cushite woman, in other words, a non-Jew. Miriam criticizes this marriage, so God strikes her with leprosy. Then, after Moses appeals to God, He lessens the punishment and orders that she be ostracized from the Is-raelites' camp for seven days. There are various interpretations of this story, as Rabbi Fleishman has pointed out to me," I paused and smiled at the rabbi. She smiled and nodded back.

"But I have my own interpretation. And it has to do with my brother, who I want you all to welcome here today. Mort, stand up."

Mort looked mortified, and keeping his head down, lifted himself half-way up off his chair before immediately sitting down again.

"That's my brother, for those of you who don't know him. If you are wondering why he is not sitting in the front row, where close family usu-ally sit, it is because he's my surprise guest here. You see, my parents never invited him to come."

My father suddenly looked uncomfortable.

"That's because, like Moses, Mort married someone who's not Jewish," I continued. Her name is Cindy. She's the woman sitting next to him with their baby, Ashley.

"Now the thing about my portion is, I don't see why Moses could marry a Cushite and have God punish Miriam because she didn't approve, but when my brother marries Cindy, my parents—and I guess a lot of you sitting here—think it's some big scandal.

"Everyone thinks kids of my generation are ignorant. That we don't know anything, that we are forgetting Jewish tradition. But if we bother to actually read the Torah, and to ask uncomfortable questions about certain parts, we are going to find parts of tradition that you don't really want us to talk about or to change the interpretation from the one you would like us to adopt. Who is to tell us what part to emphasize, what part is for our times, what part is not? The truth is—and I've been reading quite a bit of the Torah recently to get ready for this little lecture I'm giving you now—as far as I can figure out, marrying shiksas is part of Jewish tradition. Lots of Jews in the Torah did it. Sure, those were different times. But still. Who's to say that marrying a shiksa is less a part of Jewish tradition than keeping kosher? How do you judge? By how many rabbis tell you to keep kosher? Or by how many Jews over the course of Jewish history have married shiksas? I bet more Jews have married shiksas than have kept kosher. Do you see what I mean?" I glanced at Rabbi Fleishman, who had a don't-go-there look on her face. My parents looked dazed and seemed to be searchingly distractedly for familiar faces in the audience. I wondered if they were listening to me. It was time to get their attention.

"Mom, Dad, could you please come here and join hands with me?"

I could tell my parents were startled, but they obediently rose and stood by my side.

"I want you to repeat the following words after me: marrying a shiksa is okay. Moses did it. Mort did it. God punished Miriam for bad-mouthing Moses about it."

My mother bowed her head. Her bland smile vanished, and horror, then mortification, swept in to take its place. She looked as if she was about to cry. My father just glared at me. Then he decided to make it into a comic moment. He turned to the audience, "Didn't I always tell you I've got kids with guts?" And shaking his head, like he was just playing a good sport, he turned to me and said, "Whatever you want, dear."

"Good," I answered, ignoring his condescending tone and remaining dead earnest. "So, say the words."

"What were they again?"

"Marrying a shiksa is okay. Moses did it. Mort did it. It's okay. God punished Miriam for bad-mouthing Moses for it."

In a tone that left no one in the audience in doubt that he was merely indulging me, he repeated the words.

"Your turn, Mom." I said. She was crying softly, her head still down.

"Mort, come up here," I said. I couldn't believe I was doing what I was doing. But now I was on a roll. Hell, if I'd been born Christian, I might have considered becoming a television evangelist.

Mort remained glued to his chair. "Hey, Mort," I said. "Come up here. Come on, let's go. Get yourself up here."

He shook his head at me. Big brat was going to ruin this all, damn it.

But just then, Cindy touched his shoulder lightly, pushing him to go.

"Come on Mort, do this for you, for Cindy, for Ashley," I said. Cindy nodded at him. Hesitantly, he rose and then in a half-trot came up to the *bima*, almost tripping over the top step.

"Mort, hold Mom's hand." Mom was holding a handkerchief in one hand and crying into it quietly. He moved his hand over her other hand, which hung limply at her side, and she let him grasp it. "Okay, now say it, Mom."

She looked up at Mort, and her face was suddenly washed with love. I could tell she wasn't thinking of all the people in the audience any more. She could barely force her eyes from his face to glance back at me. "What was it I'm supposed to say?"

"Marrying a shiksa is okay. Moses did it. Mort did it. It's okay. God punished Miriam for bad-mouthing Moses for it."

In a daze, she turned back to look at Mort. "It's okay, Mort," she whispered. "It's okay, Mort." Mort put an arm around her in a hug. I could see he was trying not to cry. With his other arm, he motioned me to come over to him. He clasped my neck in a hug like a clumsy neck hold. We just stood there in a huddle. Dad hovered over us uncomfortably, trying to usher us off the *bima*. The embarrassed silence of the audience oozed around us.

Suddenly, someone in the audience began to clap. I looked out from under Mort's armpit. It was Charlie Ho, and he was beaming at me. "Mazel tov," Charlie yelled out. "Mazel tov to the bat mitzva girl." He clapped wildly and, putting his fingers to his mouth, whistled with all his might.

Didn't he know you're not supposed to clap and whistle at services? People around him tittered uncomfortably, then, slowly, as he kept clapping with abandon, an elated smile on his face, they began to join him, first hesitantly, but then with more conviction. Suddenly the hall was filled with their clapping, and we descended the *bima* to the din of their mazel tovs.

Over canapes afterward, no one said a word about my little ceremony. But believe me, Charlie Ho was one guy I definitely danced with at my disco party that night.

SHIK'SA GODDESS

Wendy Wasserstein

I CANNOT TELL A LIE. I feel compelled to bite the bullet and publicly reveal that I've just discovered my own denominational truth. I am Episcopalian.

I should have guessed a long time ago, because my parents never mentioned it. In fact, they hid it. They sent me to primary school at the Yeshiva Flatbush. It never crossed my mind that I was deliberately being isolated. On our classroom walls were portraits of Chaim Weizmann and Golda Meir in place of Dwight and Mamie Eisenhower. Our horror stories were not of being buried by Communists, but of being suffocated by nomad ham sandwiches.

We lived in a Jewish neighborhood in Flatbush. Our shopping strip included kosher butchers and Hymie's Highway Appetizers. For Sunday brunch, my mother produced bagels, belly lox, and cream cheese with scallions. Nobody told me that lox lived a double life as smoked salmon or that herring could ever be kippered.

Even the Christmas holidays were a setup. Every year on Christmas Eve, we were on a jet to Miami Beach. There wasn't even a chance for us to watch the WPIX Channel 11 Yule log burning as the Mormon Tabernacle Choir sang "Silent Night." We celebrated the holidays front-row center at the Versailles Room, with Myron Cohen warming up our crowd for Sammy Davis, Jr. Even our African Americans were Jewish!

Until now, I've had a happy life thinking of myself as a Jewish writer. I came to accept that when my work was described as being "too New

York" it was really a euphemism for something else. I belonged to a temple, and on my opening nights, my mother invariably told friends that she'd be much happier if it was my wedding. In other words, I had a solid sense of self. I knew exactly who I was.

Then the bottom fell out. I was speaking at the Lion of Judah luncheon in Palm Beach recently when I noticed a woman in a Lilly Pulitzer dress, one strand of pearls, and forty-year-old pink Papagallo shoes leaning against the door. She stood out from the crowd because, instead of the omnipresent Barry Kieselstein-Cord purse with lizard clasp, she was carrying a battered lacrosse stick.

At the conclusion of my talk, she approached the podium. "I hope you don't mind my speaking to you, but I believe we are related," she said.

I looked at her dead-straight blond hair and smiled politely. "I doubt it."

"Your name translates to Waterston," she continued. "Harry Waterston, your great-uncle twice removed, was my mother's fourth husband. They were married for one month." She looked at me as if only a simpleton wouldn't make the immediate connection.

I did have a distant relative, Dr. Harry Wasserstein, but I never heard of him marrying anyone but Aunt Rivkah. According to my mother, even though Harry was an educated man, he had never worked a day in his life, and Rivkah's live was miserable.

"I think you must be mistaken," I said, and tried to excuse myself.

"After he left my mother, Harry Waterston changed his name to Wasserstein because he wanted his son to go to an Ivy League college and to Mount Sinai Medical School. Harry Jr. became an educated man, but he never worked a day in his life."

I was *shvitzing*. I mean sweating. "Our name actually translates to Waterstone," I said.

"That's irrelevant!" She was almost haughty. "Look at that actor on *Law & Order*—what's his name, Sam? He's a Hasid if I ever saw one."

She handed me the lacrosse stick while I made a mental note to find out what Sam Waterston was doing for the High Holy Days. "This was Harry's lacrosse stick, which he used the year he was expelled from Hotchkiss," she said. "He made me promise to give it to the first Wasserstein relative I met in Palm Beach. He said it was inevitable that one of you people would show up here!" She winked and left the room.

Good or bad news had always made me hungry. But for the first time in my life, I needed a drink. Maybe she was onto something.

That week, I began eating chicken sandwiches with mayo on white bread, no crust, and getting full after two bites. For the first time in my life, I wrote in to the *Mount Holyoke Quarterly*: "Am looking to buy thirty-year-old Saab car and to apologize to all the Holyoke girls named Timothy and Kikky, whom I never spoke to. I now know you were very interesting people."

I began wearing faded cardigan sweaters and canceled all appointments for massages, pedicures, and exploratory liposuction. I gave up on my complicated relationship with a married Jewish Malaysian vibes player and learned to enjoy the company of a divorced asexual friend from Amherst who studies pharmaceutical stocks for J. P. Morgan. I began running ten miles every morning and sculling down the Hudson nightly. My approval ratings with my friends have gone up fifteen points.

But I was still, as I used to say in Yiddish, *"nit ahin nit aher,"* or, as I now say in the Queen's English, "neither here nor there."

That was when I decided to go on a listening tour of Fishers Island. I wanted to really hear the stories of my new Wasp ancestors, learn to make their cocktails, and wear their headbands. I want to live up to my true destiny and announce to the world how great it is to be *goyisheh* like me.

FROM PURE POETRY

Binnie Kirshenbaum

Chansons de geste: *the term by which the Old French epic poems
relating the deeds of Charlemagne and his barons were known.
"Geste" has additional senses of history and historical
document, and by further extension it comes
to mean "family, lineage."*

HENRY GIVES ME A GREEN PEPPER that is curvy and lascivious, and he says, "Here, chop this," which is both galling and sexy at once. I'm not sure whether to say, "Chop it yourself, asshole," or else drop to my knees and unzip his fly. The indecision results in a kind of freeze, where I'm stuck between two places. Also, if you invite me to dinner, I don't think I should have to do any of the cooking.

In a salad bowl on the countertop, Henry's goldfish dances in the water. Its hindquarters wiggle and its tail looks like something Esther Williams did in a pool. "Your fish dances," I remark, and Henry says, "Yes, that means he's hungry." Henry goes to the cabinet for fish-food flakes, which he sprinkles into the water. Then he says to me, "The knives are in that drawer there." With a cock of his head, Henry indicates the one to my left.

I am perfectly well aware that it is the wrong tool for the job, but still I take out a butter knife and squint at the fine print. Reed and Barton. Henry has sterling flatware from Reed and Barton. Fancy that. Fancy-schmancy that. Very fancy-schmancy that.

Nosy thing that I am, I rummage through the drawer to see what else he's got there. I come up with a stack of what appears to be six miniature gravy boats. Also sterling and monogrammed. "What is the purpose of these?" I ask.

"They're for almonds," Henry tells me. The little gravy boats are for almonds. Each place setting gets an individual serving of almonds so that there is no reaching into a bowl like pigs at the trough. An elegant concept, but the bowls are so small that you could fit no more than five or six nuts, tops, in each one, which is a chintzy portion. Especially if the almonds are salted.

If my mother were alive, she'd be peeing in her pants over Henry here and his Anglo-Saxon ways, that washed-out, oh-so-pale blue blood coursing through his veins, his Reed and Barton flatware. Her hope for me on this earth was that I'd stumble up the social ladder and into the land of lime green and pink. But the dead cannot pee in their pants, and I consider these almond boats an embarrassment.

Henry's bachelor pad is crammed with the effects of money minted generations ago. Silver candelabra and tea sets, lead crystal vases, Limoges battersea boxes, linen tablecloths. The stuff of a dowager. Old-lady tchotchkes. Generally speaking, recently divorced men have all of two bowls and a spoon they picked up at Pottery Barn. Henry has Wedgwood. Service for twenty-four, including the soup tureen.

As if that's not sufficiently peculiar, hanging on the wall in his foyer is a letter from then President Eisenhower. Matted in ecru and framed in a no-nonsense black. Eisenhower had written to Henry's parents congratulating them on the birth of their son. In reference to Henry, the president wrote, "It is with great joy that I welcome the littlest Republican into the world."

When I first saw that letter, I asked, "You're a Republican?" If my ghosts were to discover that I were boinking a Republican, they'd die all over again. Like me, Dora and Estella breathed left. Often, I hear the pair of them humming the "Internationale." I had to say, "I'll be square with you here, Henry. I'd blow a baboon before I'd suck a Republican dick. That's just how it is with me." Which is quirky of me. How I could do Nazi progeny, but I draw the line at Republican.

Henry swore up and down that he is a registered Democrat. "A liberal Democrat. Very liberal," he promised, but it could be that he was only trying to pass. "It's just that my mother was friendly with the Eisenhowers," he told me. "Mostly with Mamie. They were alumnae of the same finishing school or something. It was a social thing between them. My mother never talked politics. You would've liked my mother," he said.

I doubted that. A chum of Mamie Eisenhower's, and one that never talked politics, no less. I could just see Dora's face at hearing that. No, I would not have liked her. Only I didn't say so because it's bad form to insult a person's mother. Particularly when the mother in question is dead. Henry's mother has been dead for six years, and his father for seven. Yet they are with him, because Henry keeps their ashes in shoe boxes stacked in the hall closet. His mother's mortal remains are in a pink Pappagallos box, ladies' flats, size nine. His father is in a box from Johnston & Murphy, black cordovan, size ten and a half.

Henry has a reasonable explanation for this grotesque effrontery to the dead. Quite simply, he hasn't gotten around to burying his parents' ashes or sprinkling them as if they were fish food over a body of water, but he plans on it. "One of these days. Soon," he said, and he told me, "It was a very chaotic time in my life when they died."

That's his excuse, but I have ideas of my own as to why Henry's parents are in shoe boxes nestled between his ski boots and a gallon-sized jug of Spray 'n Wash. Ideas that rely on screws loose in his head as the result of the thinning of the blood line. You're always hearing about these kinds of kinks in royal families. Along with hemophilia A and the Hapsburg chin, they are prone to porphyria, which shows itself in behavior that is batty. It's the enrichment of homozygous genes that does it. In breeding, which produces dukes with six toes on each foot and poodles that do nothing but quiver and piddle on the carpet.

Each new apple on Henry's family tree put stress on the roots. Subsequent generations found themselves less well off, both in the pocketbook and in the head. Still, because there was a bundle to start out with, Henry might not be filthy rich but he is able to live quite comfortably off his inheritance. Which is a good thing because Henry has no job. "I haven't figured out what I want to be," he told me. "Mostly I like to putter."

Yet Henry refers to me as a princess. "Such a princess," he says. "You are such a princess. You don't even know how to chop a pepper." Apparently, I am not chopping to specifications. "We're making pasta sauce. We want small pieces for flavor." Henry takes hold of a ragged slice of pepper and waggles it as if it were a worm. "These are slices for a crudité." He tsk-tsks my inept handling of the pepper.

Pardon me for not employing proper chopping procedures. For not knowing there was a right way and a wrong way to chop a pepper. I don't know from chopping a pepper. I don't know from chopping peppers or making pasta sauce in jars from Waldbaum's supermarket.

On the boat to America, my paternal grandparents, Papa Moscowitz and Grandma Tessie, then newlyweds, shared their quarters with goats, which was step one to making a better life. My father and his sister Mitzie were born in a tenement in the Bronx, where Papa Moscowitz eked out a pathetic living washing windows. Schlepping a bucket and rags, he dragged his sorry ass from storefront to storefront asking, "Hey, Mister. You want I should wash your windows today?"

What with all those years of scrubbing pigeon shit off glass, it was enough to quiet any man's dreams. Whatever hope he had left, it was for his children.

While attending the City College of New York, my father took a class in industrial design. There, with the intent of easing his father's burden, he constructed a lightweight, lightning-fast industrial squeegee. Not the least bit taken with the newfangled gizmo, Papa Moscowitz preferred to stay with his rags and develop permanent elbow damage. My father, however, was frothy with first-generation enthusiasm. A man with a vision, pole-vaulting on his industrial squeegee, he launched a seriously profitable window-washing empire.

His sister Mitzie grew up to bleach her hair blond and become a real estate tycoon. She married some schmuck and together they spawned Howard, who was good with numbers.

With money in his pocket and looks like Tyrone Power the movie star, my father set out to win the affections of Isabelle DiConti, a Botticelli-like Venus whom he'd met at a party where City College men were introduced to Hunter College women. The DiContis were a once hoity-toity Italian-Jewish family who lost every nickel long before my mother was born. My mother and her parents lived on airs alone in an empty apartment on Riverside Drive. "We had no furniture," my mother told me, "but we had a good address." The DiContis didn't always have money for food, but my mother's winter coat was cashmere.

Like the young Jacqueline Bouvier, my mother was more than happy to trade her lineage for an infusion of hearty genes and a wad of cash. With the one small provision, as is so often the way in any fairy tale: a task to be performed. To prove his love, my mother requested that my father change his name because no way was she going to go through life as Bella Moscowitz, which was too too identifiably Jewish. It was okay to be Jewish, but it was not okay to be too too Jewish. As a result, I am Lila Moscowitz, née Morse.

Morse. Like the guy who came up with the code. Morse. As in Inspector Morse, the English detective whose eponymous show we get on our educational television stations.

"So, I Americanized it," my father said, justifying the rejection of his heritage.

"You did no such thing," I argued over the dinner table. "You anglicized it. Moscowitz is a perfectly good American name. Land of the wretched masses yearning to be free and all that crap. I am not ashamed of who I am." With the kind of moral indignation that only a teenager such as I was then can muster, I banged my fist on the table and sent a salad fork flying. "I will not live a lie," I proclaimed, while my brothers rolled their eyes at their loud-mouthed, obnoxious, too too Jewish sister.

If modern medicine could reattach the foreskin the way they are now able to stitch back an arm severed at the elbow or an amputated foot, my brothers would go for the procedure in a skinny minute. The two of them—Robert, the oral surgeon, and Michael, the professor of economics—wound up married to women cut from the same bolt of cloth, which was linen. Tall and thin and flat-chested, fair-haired, skinny-lipped things. In one of those delicious quirks of fate, Michael's wife is named Regan, leaving me no choice but to call Rob's wife Goneril, which irritates her. "My name is Kate," she reminds me, "Kate. Why is that so difficult for you to remember?"

"Because," I tell her, "you are such a Goneril."

Life mirrors art. She is such a Goneril. When my mother was alive, Goneril sucked up to her like milk through a straw. Kissy-poo to her face, but behind her back, my sister-in-law dished my mother for filth. The only time Goneril ever called me on the phone, it was to discuss a dilemma she was having in regard to my mother. "Do you think there is some way we can get her to give us money or gift certificates for Christmas this year?" she asked me.

"I doubt it. Why?"

"Because your mother has the worst taste. She gives us ugly things, and then I have to go to the trouble of exchanging everything."

I thought my mother had rather lovely taste. Not my taste, but not questionable. However, that was beside the point. "My mother," I said, "doesn't have to give you anything. You should be grateful. How good she is to you. I know how good she is to you because I know how jealous I am."

My brothers were determined to marry women who were not Jewish. Instead, they married a pair of Protestants who found their way around Bloomingdale's so fast it would make your head spin.

When I turned eighteen, I changed my name back to what it should have been all along. I forwent the brief and easily spelled Morse as a way to reclaim my heritage. To belong. I became Lila Moscowitz so I could say, "my people," and have it mean something. As with my ghosts, I sought an extended family, to be identifiably Jewish without all the hoopla, because I really could not keep up with the religious requirements. I embraced the European patriarchy, a legacy that amounted to three rubles and weekly pogroms, but mostly I did it because it irked my parents enormously.

My name reclamation remained the skeleton in the family closet until it was splashed over the pages of *People* magazine. No one reads poetry, but everyone reads *People*. Even if they deny it, they read it while standing on line at the supermarket or in the dentist's waiting room. "Moscowitz," Bella made excuses to her friends and neighbors. "Oh, that's her pen name. All the writers have pen names. Mark Twain, O. Henry, and Richard Whatever-It-Is is really Stephen King."

"Why do you lie about my name? Our name," I asked her, and she said, "Why do you want to embarrass us?"

They were so far gone, my parents, so in up to their eyeballs with Protestant envy, that when I owned up to the full truth about Max, about how he was a blood relative of Albert Speer, how he was practically Speer's nephew, all my mother said was, "Oh, well, now I know where Max got his good looks."

We were the sort of Jews who underwent baptism in the blue chlorinated waters of the swimming pool at Fox Hill Country Club. The way rich Romanians bought themselves titles to nobility, my parents bought the rights to an eraser. As if there were no history to contend with, as if nothing had ever happened, my parents considered themselves to be like Adam and Eve dwelling in the paradise of Westchester County. Adam and Eve, who were Jews, but not overtly Jewish. Nothing like Moses. That fanatic. Moses, he was the sort of Jew who disgraced my family, what with all the yelling and the miracles and that beard.

To be Jewish like Moses was un-American. Something for which Joe McCarthy could bring charges against you. Bella held that Jews should be unassuming and irreligious. She had it in big time for the Orthodox and especially for the Hasidim. As if they sullied her with guilt by association. She cursed them for wearing their faith—yarmulkes, beards, payas, tefillin, long black coats in summer yet, wigs and babushkas—for the world to see and to mock. "Filthy and ignorant. They give all Jews a bad name," my mother said.

Not that we newly rich American Jews didn't have our own ritualistic garb. Oh, but we did. Designer clothes with the labels showing. Oscar de la Renta emblazoned across the chest. Gloria Vanderbilt and her swan on the pocket of our jeans. Louis Vuitton pocketbooks, which—I'm sorry but it's true—look like diarrhea-colored vinyl totes that I wouldn't give five dollars for. We frosted our hair and we painted our fingernails with frosted polish. The way the baby Jesus was given gifts of gold, frankincense, and myrrh, I got goodies such as a birthstone ring, an add-a-pearl necklace, and a name necklace—*Lila* scripted in fourteen-karat gold, the *I* dotted with a diamond chip. I slept in a canopy bed, a pink princess telephone on the nightstand. I had cashmere sweaters by the yard and a junior fur, which was a jacket made from dead bunny rabbits and something like a training bra in that it was preparation for the mink coat of future womanhood.

If all had gone according to my parents' plan for me, instead of a small and haunted apartment on Morton Street, the ancestral digs, I'd be living in a big and new house in Connecticut, the gateway to New England. I'd be wearing tartan plaids in winter and pastels in the spring. My husband would have the pizzazz of a Ken doll and we would have a big dog, a setter or a retriever. Because we would not hunt—not even the most assimilated Jews play with guns—the dog would point toward Greenwich. Somehow, dominant and recessive genes notwithstanding, I'd have blue-eyed, blond-haired children, and my grandchildren would wind up like Henry, living off a dwindling trust amid the relics of better days.

Henry takes what is left of the pepper away from me and banishes me from the kitchen. "You're useless," he says. "Such a princess. Hopeless."

Henry may have his sterling flatware from Reed and Barton, but I've got hybrid vigor. While he's slaving over a hot stove, I'm in the living room with my feet up on the coffee table. I'm drinking chilled white wine from a crystal goblet. Like the princess I was raised to be.

They raised me to be a Jewish princess, but my parents wanted me to be an Episcopalian. Now Henry, an Episcopalian, wants me to be a Jewish princess, and let me never forget what Max wanted of me.

STOP ALL JEWISH COOKING NOW!

tova

1.

so many stories
from everyone, her sister, and me
of grandmothers' cooking.
truly, i weep for my long dead
gramma's prune strudel
but still,

i want it to stop

all jewish grandmothers
dead or alive,
stop cooking now!
no more kugel, blintzes, or tsimmis
no more minahs or bastilla
and while we're at it
let's stop eating what's called bagels
with or without shmears
(i won't even talk of cranberry and bacon bagels).

2.

it's all she knew to say
about being jewish.

my born again niece

my born again nieces and nephews
my catholic converted brother
my identityless sister
it's eating me up
jewishness that starts and stops
with grandma's cooking
and new age bagel stores.
i want to feed you midrash
jewish feminism, folk dancing
sephardic mizrahi ethiopian ashkenazi
tradition
i want you to relish the richnesses of judaism
savor the endless textures and tastes.
stop stuffing your face with romance and assimilation
spit out this betrayal to your people
build a sukkah
and maybe a bowl of shav
learn of the bund, zionism, or conversos
and maybe some borekas
listen to new women rabbis,
smear yourself with buttermilk as passover ends,
and dance from your soul to klezmer
     and maybe a knish.

3.

it will be decades
before anyone eats a bagel.
i will lament the loss
of this dense jewish circle
but now i need something better to bite into.
i cannot live with the holes any longer.

let me fill your pit with jewishness
let me teach you a labor of love
be born again to us
    to me
a circle of jews
hungering for their culture

and then i will truly weep again
while i cook you majestic jewish meals
          and tell you, finally,
eat, bubaleh, eat.

WAKING UP TO
MY FATHER'S WORLD

Jonathan Rosen

WHEN I WAS GROWING UP, my father would go to bed with a transistor radio set to an all-news station. Even without a radio, my father was attuned to the menace of history. A Jew born in Vienna in 1924, he fled his homeland in 1938; his parents were killed in the Holocaust. I sometimes imagined my father was listening for some repetition of past evils so that he could rectify old responses, but he may just have been expecting more bad news. In any event, the grumbling static from the bedroom depressed me, and I vowed to replace it with music more cheerfully in tune with America. These days, however, I find myself on my father's frequency. I have awakened to anti-Semitism.

I am not being chased down alleyways and called a Christ killer, I do not feel that prejudicial hiring practices will keep me out of a job, and I am not afraid that the police will come and take away my family. I am, in fact, more grateful than ever that my father found refuge in this country. But in recent weeks I have been reminded, in ways too plentiful to ignore, about the role Jews play in the fantasy life of the world. Jews were not the cause of World War II, but they were at the metaphysical center of that conflict nonetheless, since the Holocaust was part of Hitler's agenda and a key motivation of his campaign. Jews are not the cause of World War III, if that's what we are facing, but they have been placed at the center of it in mysterious and disturbing ways.

I was born in 1963, a generation removed and an ocean away from the destruction of European Jewry. My mother was born here, so there was always half the family that breathed in the easy air of postwar America. You don't have to read a lot of Freud to discover that the key to healthy life is the ability to fend off reality to a certain extent. Deny reality too much, of course, and you're crazy; too little and you're merely miserable. My own private balancing act has involved acknowledging the fate of my murdered grandparents and trying to live a modern American life. I studied English literature in college and in graduate school, where I toyed with a dissertation on Milton, a Christian concerned with justifying the ways of God to man. I dropped out of graduate school to become a writer, but I always felt about my life in America what Milton says of Adam and Eve entering exile—the world was all before me.

Living in New York, pursuing my writing life, I had the world forever all before me. I chose within it—I married and had a child. For ten years I worked at a Jewish newspaper. But my sense of endless American possibility never left me—even working at a Jewish newspaper seemed a paradoxical assertion of American comfort. My father's refugee sense of the world was something that both informed me and that I worked to define myself against. I felt it was an act of mental health to recognize that his world was not my world and that his fears were the product of an experience alien to me. I was critical of the Holocaust Museum in Washington. I didn't want ancient European anti-Semitism enshrined on federal land. But now everything has come to American soil.

Recently, I read an interview with Sheik Muhammad Gemeaha—who was not only the representative in the United States of the prominent Cairo center of Islamic learning, al-Azhar University, but also imam of the Islamic Cultural Center of New York City. The sheik, who until recently lived in Manhattan on the Upper West Side, explained that "only the Jews" were capable of destroying the World Trade Center and added that "if it became known to the American people, they would have done to Jews what Hitler did." This sentiment will be familiar to anyone who has been watching the news or reading the papers. In Kuwait, there were reports that New York rabbis told their followers to take their money out of the stock market before September 11; in Egypt, the Mossad was blamed for the attack. It is easy talk to dismiss as madness, I suppose, but because so many millions of Muslims seem to believe it, and because airplanes actually did crash into the World Trade Center, words have a different weight and menace than they had before.

So does history, or rather the forces that shape history—particularly the history of the Jews. It would be wrong to say that everything changed on the eleventh of September for me. Like the man in the Hemingway novel who went bankrupt two ways—gradually and then suddenly—my awareness of things had also been growing slowly. My father's sister escaped in the 1930s from Vienna to Palestine—now, of course, called Israel—and I have a lot of family there. I grew up knowing that Israel, for all its vitality, was ringed with enemies; I knew how perilous and bleak life had become after the collapse of the Oslo peace process a year ago and how perilous and bleak it could be before that.

I knew, too, that works like the *Protocols of the Elders of Zion*, the Russian forgery about demonic Jewish power, have been imported into Arab society, like obsolete but deadly Soviet weapons. By grafting ancient Christian calumnies onto modern political grievances, Arab governments have transformed Israel into an outpost of malevolent world Jewry, viewing Israelis and Jews as interchangeable emblems of cosmic evil. So when the Syrian defense minister recently told a delegation from the British Royal College of Defense Studies that the destruction of the World Trade Center was part of a Jewish conspiracy, I wasn't really surprised.

I'd gotten a whiff of this back in early September, while following the United Nations conference on racism and discrimination in Durban, South Africa, where the Arab Lawyers Union distributed booklets at the conference containing anti-Semitic caricatures of Jews with fangs dripping blood—a mere sideshow to the isolation of Israel and the equating of Zionism with racism that ultimately led to the United States' withdrawal. Singling out Israel made of a modern nation an archetypal villain—Jews were the problem, and the countries of the world were figuring out the solution. This was hardly new in the history of the United Nations, but there was something so naked about the resurrected Nazi propaganda and the anti-Semitism fueling the political denunciations that I felt kidnapped by history. The past had come calling.

I felt this in a different form reading coverage of Israel in European papers. Though public expressions of anti-Semitism are taboo in a post-Holocaust world, many Europeans in writing about Israel have felt free to conjure images of determined child killers and mass murderers. Earlier this year, the Spanish daily *La Vanguardia* published a cartoon depicting a large building labeled "Museum of the Jewish Holocaust" and behind it a building under construction labeled "Future Museum of the Palestinian Holocaust." The cartoon manages to demonize Jews and trivialize the Holocaust simultaneously. Tom Gross, an Israel-based journalist, recently pointed out to me that a BBC correspondent, Hilary Andersson, declared that to describe adequately the outrage of Israel's murder of Palestinian children one would have to reach back to Herod's slaughter of the innocents—alluding to Herod's attempt to kill Christ in the cradle by massacring Jewish babies. After leading an editor from the *Guardian* on a tour of the occupied territories, Gross was astonished at the resulting front-page editorial in that highly influential British paper declaring that the establishment of Israel has exacted such a high moral price that "the international community cannot support this cost indefinitely."

I understood that the editorial, speaking of the cost of the establishment of Israel—not of any particular policies—implied that Israel's very right to exist is somehow still at issue. (One cannot imagine something similar being formulated about, say, Russia, in response to its battle with Chechen rebels, however much the *Guardian* might have disagreed with that country's policies.) And this reminded me inevitably of the situation of the Jews in 1940s Europe, where simply to be was an unpardonable crime.

I had somehow believed that the Jewish Question, which so obsessed both Jews and anti-Semites in the nineteenth and twentieth centuries, had been solved—most horribly by Hitler's "final solution," most hopefully by Zionism. But more and more I feel Jews being turned into a question mark once again. How is it, the world still asks—about Israel, about Jews, about me—that you are still here? I have always known that much of the world wanted Jews simply to disappear, but there are degrees of knowledge, and after September 11 my imagination seems more terribly able to imagine a world of rhetoric fulfilled.

There are five million Jews in Israel and eight million more Jews in the rest of the world. There are one billion Muslims. How has it happened that Israel and "world Jewry," along with the United States, is the enemy of so many of them? To be singled out inside a singled-out country is doubly disconcerting. There are a lot of reasons why modernizing, secularizing, globalizing America, whose every decision has universal impact, would disturb large swaths of the world; we are, after all, a superpower. Surely it is stranger that Jews, by their mere presence in the world, would unleash such hysteria.

And yet what I kept hearing in those first days in the aftermath of the attack on the World Trade Center is that it was our support of Israel that had somehow brought this devastation down on us. It was a kind of respectable variant of the belief that the Mossad had literally blown up the World Trade Center. It could of course be parried—after all, the turning point in Osama bin Laden's hatred of the United States came during the Gulf War, when American troops were stationed in Saudi Arabia. But it had a lingering effect; it was hard to avoid a certain feeling that there was something almost magical about Israel that made it toxic for friends and foes alike.

This feeling will not go away, if only because our support of that nation makes it harder to maintain our coalition. Israel has somehow become an obstacle to war and an obstacle to peace simultaneously.

Lately, of course, bin Laden has added treatment of Palestinians to his list of grievances, and this may revive the sense that Israel bears some measure of responsibility. Large lies can be constructed out of smaller truths. The occupation of the West Bank by Israel, though it grew out of a war Israel did not want, has been a nightmare for the Palestinians and a disaster for Israel morally, politically, and spiritually. It is a peculiar misery to feel this way and to feel, at the same time, that the situation has become a weapon in the war against Israel. Bin Laden would not want a Palestinian state on the West Bank, because he could not abide a Jewish state alongside it.

Neither could many of our allies in the Muslim world, who keep euphemistically suggesting that if only the "Mideast crisis" were resolved, terrorism would diminish. It has a plausible veneer—and indeed, it would be an extraordinary achievement if the Palestinians got a homeland and Israel got safe borders. But since most of the players in the Middle East do not accept the existence of Israel, since "solving the Mideast crisis" would for them entail a modern version of Hitler's final solution, the phrase takes on weird and even sinister overtones when it is blandly employed by well-intentioned governments calling for a speedy solution. And this Orwellian transformation of language is one of the most exasperating and disorienting aspects of the campaign against Israel. It has turned the word "peace" into a euphemism for war.

I grew up in a post-Holocaust world. For all the grim weight of that burden, and for all its echoing emptiness, there was a weird sort of safety in it too. After all, the worst thing had already happened—everything else was aftermath. In the wake of the Holocaust, American anti-Semitism dissipated, the church expunged old calumnies. The horror had been sufficient to shock even countries like the Soviet Union into supporting a newly declared Jewish state. Israel after 1967 was a powerful nation—besieged, but secure. American Jews were safe as houses.

I am not writing this essay to predict some inevitable calamity but to identify a change of mood. To say aloud that European anti-Semitism, which made the Holocaust possible, is still shaping the way Jews are perceived; Arab anti-Israel propaganda has joined hands with it and found a home in the embattled Muslim world. Something terrible has been born. What happened on September 11 is proof, as if we needed it, that people who threaten evil intend evil. This comes with the dawning awareness that weapons of mass destruction did not vanish with the Soviet Union; the knowledge that in fact they may pose a greater threat of actually being used in this century, if only in a limited fashion, is sinking in only now.

That a solution to one century's Jewish problem has become another century's Jewish problem is a cruel paradox. This tragedy has intensified to such a degree that friends—supporters of Israel—have wondered aloud to me if the time has come to acknowledge that the Israeli experiment has failed, that there is something in the enterprise itself that doomed it. This is the thinking of despair. I suppose one could wonder as much about America in the aftermath of the September 11 attacks, since many American values will now be challenged and since, in fighting a war, you always become a little like your enemy, if only in accepting the need to kill. I grew up at a time when sex education was considered essential but what might be called war education, what a country must do to survive, was looked upon with a kind of prudish horror. I suppose that tendency will now change. In any event, Israel has been at war for fifty years. Without that context, clear judgment is impossible, especially by those accustomed to the Holocaust notion that Jews in war are nothing but helpless victims— a standard that can make images to the contrary seem aberrant.

I have a different way of looking at the Israeli experiment than my friends who wonder about its failure. It is connected to how I look at the fate of European Jewry. When the Jews of Europe were murdered in the Holocaust, one might have concluded that European Judaism failed—to defend itself, to anticipate evil, to make itself acceptable to the world around it, to pack up and leave. But one could also conclude in a deeper way that Christian Europe failed—to accept the existence of Jews in their midst, and it has been marked ever since, and will be for all time, with this blot on its culture. Israel is a test of its neighbors as much as its neighbors are a test for Israel. If the Israeli experiment fails, then Islam will have failed, and so will the Christian culture that plays a shaping role in that part of the region.

I am fearful of sounding as though I believe that the Holocaust is going to replay itself in some simplified fashion—that my childhood fantasy for my father is true for me, and it is I who am straining to hear Hitler's voice break over the radio. I do not. Israel has a potent modern army. But so does the United States, and it has proved vulnerable to attack, raising other fears. The United States spans a continent, and its survival is not in doubt. But experts who warn us about American vulnerability refer to areas the size of entire states that will become contaminated if a nuclear reactor is struck by a plane. Israel is smaller than New Jersey.

I am aware that an obsession with the Holocaust is seen as somehow unbecoming and, when speaking of modern politics, viewed almost as a matter of bad taste, if not bad history. I do not wish to elide Israel's political flaws by invoking the Holocaust. But that very reluctance has been exploited and perverted in a way that makes me disregard it. "Six million Jews died?" the mufti of Jerusalem, a Palestinian Authority appointee, remarked last year. "Let us desist from this fairy tale exploited by Israel to buy international solidarity." (The utterance is particularly egregious because the mufti's predecessor paid an admiring visit to Hitler in 1941.) The demonizing language that is used about Israel in some of the European press, and about Jews in the Arab press, is reminiscent of Europe in the 1930s. I grew up thinking I was living in the post-Holocaust world and find it sounds more and more like a pre-Holocaust world as well.

Ten years ago, I interviewed Saul Bellow in Chicago and in the course of the interview asked him if there was anything he regretted. He told me that he now felt, looking back on his career, that he had not been sufficiently mindful of the Holocaust. This surprised me, because one of his novels, *Mr. Sammler's Planet*, is actually about a Holocaust survivor. But Bellow recalled writing *The Adventures of Augie March*—the grand freewheeling novel that made his reputation—in Paris in the late 1940s. Holocaust survivors were everywhere, Bellow told me, and, as a Yiddish speaker, he had access to the terrible truths they harbored. But, as Bellow put it, he was not in the mood to listen. "I wanted my American seven-layer cake," he told me. He did not wish to burden his writing at that early moment in his career with the encumbering weight of Jewish history. *Augie March* begins, exuberantly, "I am an American."

I, too, want my American seven-layer cake, even if the cake has collapsed a little in recent weeks. There is no pleasure in feeling reclaimed by the awfulness of history and in feeling myself at odds with the large universalist temper of our society. Thinking about it makes me feel old, exhausted, and angry.

In World War II, American Jews muted their separate Jewish concerns for the good of the larger struggle to liberate Europe. I understand the psychological urge to feel in sync with American aims. But Israel sticks out in this crisis as European Jewry stuck out in World War II, forcing a secondary level of Jewish consciousness, particularly because the anti-Zionism of the Arab world has adopted the generalized anti-Semitism of the European world.

The danger to America, which has already befallen us, and the danger to Israel, which so far remains primarily rhetorical, are, of course, connected. And though it is false to imagine that if Israel did not exist America would not have its enemies, people making the link are intuiting something beyond the simple fact that both are Western democracies.

In *Cultures in Conflict: Christians, Muslims, and Jews in the Age of Discovery*, Bernard Lewis points out that after Christians reconquered Spain from the Muslims in the fifteenth century, they decided to expel the Jews before the Muslims. The reason for this, Lewis explains, is that although the Jews had no army and posed far less of a political threat than the Muslims, they posed a far greater theological challenge. This is because Jews believed that adherents of other faiths could find their own path to God. Christianity and Islam, which cast unbelievers as infidels, did not share this essential religious relativism. The rabbinic interpretation of monotheism, which in seeing all human beings as created in God's image recognized their inherent equality, may well contain the seeds of the very democratic principles that the terrorists of September 11 found so intolerable.

Is it any wonder that in the minds of the terrorists and their fundamentalist defenders, Americans and Jews have an unholy alliance? Expressing my separate Jewish concerns does not put me at odds with our pluralistic society—it puts me in tune with it, since it is here of all places that I am free to express all my identities—American, Jewish, Zionist. And if Jews kicked out of Spain clung, at peril of death, to a religion with such an ultimately inclusive faith in the redeemable nature of humanity, who am I to reject that view? Perhaps the optimistic American half of my inheritance isn't at odds with the darker Jewish component after all. In this regard, the double consciousness that has burdened my response to our new war need not feel like a division. On the contrary, it redoubles my patriotism and steels me for the struggle ahead.

FROM CLUB REVELATION

Allan Appel

The novel Club Revelation *follows a crisis in the lives of three Jewish/ Christian couples who unwittingly are drawn into the scheme of a young Christian evangelist who is attempting to convert Jews on New York's Upper West Side to Christianity by opening a Christian restaurant in the ground floor of the couples' brownstone. Although few customers are drawn to Loaves and Fishes, America's first Christian cafeteria, and the conversion-by-gastronomy scheme comically founders, one of the women, Marylee, is very taken by the plight of the young evangelist. She rediscovers her Christian roots and wants to bring her husband, Gerry, along on her religious journey. Gerry is quite willing to go along on the religious ride, not out of spiritual conviction but out of love for Marylee, his wife. When a date for Gerry's baptism is set, his friends Sam and Michael go on the offensive to save him for Judaism. In the section ex- cerpted below, Gerry brings his friends, one night after their weekly ten- nis match, to an undesignated location on the Upper West Side. It turns out to be the local mikveh, where Gerry tries to allay Michael and Sam's anxieties by illustrating the Jewish origins of his upcoming baptism. Like much in this satirical comedy of modern Jewish religious manners, the visit to the mikveh doesn't work out quite as planned.*

It is quite possible, Michael was thinking as he sprinted about on the base- line and covered for Sam—Sam was wearing an ancient, peeling pair of

Keds that were so tight, they made him flat-footed and slow—that if they did not have love of tennis in common, they might not be speaking with each other, period. To play effective doubles, however, required that you really communicate on the court. At minimum, you shouted "Switch" or "Cover the alley, you idiot" or "Forgive the decomposing frontal lobe neurons, what the hell is the score?" Michael and Sam, however, were not doing much of that minimal talk. Fortunately Sam's serve was nearly unreturnable tonight, and at least Michael could compliment him on that.

For Michael, this was also one of his Buddhist nights on the court. As Judy had told him many times when in his frustration he talked about giving up the game, he needed to adopt a Buddhist approach: no conscious thought should precede the hitting of the ball. The action and the thought should be one and instantaneous.

For most of the evening, Michael was conscious of being in this Buddhist zone. "You don't hit the ball," so Judy's tennis advice went. "Let the ball release itself from your racquet." Indeed, for a few games he had maintained an exceptional concentration. However, now the spell of good shots felt broken, and he expected to blow the one he was now engaged in: racing crosscourt, he caught up with Gerry's hard volley and returned it a millimeter over the net with so much angle and topspin that Gerry didn't even make a move for it. He just stared after it, declaring "Much too good," and then went back to serve the next one.

Michael and Sam, despite the communication breakdown, continued to do very well against Ganesh and Gerry, for whom the elusive chemistry was missing tonight. Perhaps Ganesh's game was just a little off because the amazing Iranian, still dressed in his cerulean blue hospital scrubs, had already performed two bypasses today, niftily finishing up the final suture just ten minutes before he was scheduled on the court.

If the crisp tennis were any measure, Michael, buoyed by self-satisfaction with his game, had at least forgiven Sam for his car trick of three weeks ago. Either that or the incident had altered their relationship in an indecipherable way (perhaps they took each other less for granted), with the result that their performance as a team against Gerry and Ganesh had rarely been better.

They had won two sets already and were screaming and jumping up and down as a third-set triumph, almost unheard of in the after–ten p.m. slot, seemed also to be materializing. But the games, especially the last three of the final set, continued to be hard fought, and the entire evening felt as if they had moved to a slightly new level—perhaps up to Ganesh's—with many points decided by all four combatants at the net, bam bam, very quick, like the professionals.

Of course, Gerry's imminent conversion to Christianity—a firm date had been set—and Michael and Sam's apparent failure to prevent this from occurring were never far from the tennis players' minds. After the first set, Sam had declared, "Jews one, Christian and Muslim nothing."

"And who might this Christian be?" Ganesh said as they all, having shaken hands, stood at the net and toweled off. "This is just an expression, your joke?"

"Nope," said Sam, "there is a Christian among us. Your teammate."

Gerry, with his back to this conversation, seemed to shrug.

Ganesh, who had sensed the presence of hard feelings, merely said with artful tact, "How fascinating."

He likely would have left it there had not Sam added, "The ceremony—the baptism—is coming up in a few weeks. Perhaps you want an invitation. Put it on your calendar. Sure to be a hot ticket."

"In the part of the world where I grew up, if you argue—or joke—about religion, you often end up regretting it, or dead."

"I'll be just fine," said Gerry.

"Well, you are launched on a new adventure, then," said Ganesh, extending his hand for Gerry to shake.

"That's the way I look at it too. An adventure."

"It is funny," Ganesh spoke, as he turned to leave. "If I had to pick out the fellow most likely to change his religion, I would not have picked Gerry. I would have picked you." He collegially snapped his towel toward Michael. "Of the three of you, you strike me as a man the most—what shall I say?—spiritually restless."

"You're lucky you didn't put money on it." Michael attempted a joke and wished he hadn't.

"I mean no disrespect to you," Ganesh turned to Gerry. "Only changing one's religion often has more consequences than changing one's wife."

"And how would you know?" Sam asked.

"Because I have done both. But I will tell you no details. We struggle in the dark toward the light, all of us. You see, that is an image from Zoroaster, the father of my current faith."

"You're not Muslim?"

"Of course not. I am a Zoroastrian."

"All these years," said Sam, "we had you wrong. Amazing."

"But it is truly nothing. You know it is my personal opinion that these baseball players"—he motioned toward the lounge and its set of elevated TVs with the baseball games visible from their court tonight—"who you see making the sign of the cross before the curveball comes at them, or the footballers thanking Jesus Christ for helping them throw a forward pass to victory in the Superbowl, this is very unseemly. You win because of your ability, not your faith. We will, I hope, continue to know each other as devotees of what we know is, however, the one true faith: worship of the little fuzzy eyeless green god Wilson. All hail the god Wilson. Gerry, I wish you only the best of luck."

At Gerry's unexpected urging, Michael and Sam left Caracas after the final set without even showering, having agreed to join him for late-night beer and burgers on Broadway near Seventy-Ninth Street. Ganesh's graciousness was on their minds, though his name was not invoked, as they drove back to the city through a persistent drizzle that taxed the Toyota's brittle wiper blades. They ate as they had driven, quickly, because Gerry had an additional destination for them a few blocks west of the restaurant: a low-slung building of worn stone, with two sets of steps descending to a common entryway guarded by an iron gate. At nearly midnight, as the trio stood beneath a ginkgo tree and observed it, the building appeared not only dark but also abandoned and foreboding, and a faint smell of bleach, ammonia, or the scent of a laundromat drifted up from the basement level.

"It's the mikveh, men," Gerry said. "It's the headquarters of the Jewish baptismal font and alcove. And I did a little research too: it predates Christianity. It is very Jewish, gentlemen. Why have I brought you here? So that you can relax about baptism. It's like washing your hands and saying the blessing. Only it's your whole body that's getting washed. Nifty, huh? And right in the neighborhood."

"Oy vey," said Michael.

"Now I understand why you are acting so screwed up," said Sam. "You're the only Jewish man on the West Side with a documented menstrual cycle. You come here often?"

"Gerry," Michael said—he aspired to Ganesh's patient tone and diplomatic style, but fell far short—"I don't want to shock you too much, but Jewish ablutions like washing your hands and saying the brocha before you sit down to a meal are not baptism. This is a place for traditional observant Jewish women, not for a businessman being driven out of his religion by his wife." Michael felt suddenly desperate to provoke a reaction. "How about finally grasping the gravity of what you're doing!" Gerry ignored the taunt. "It's not a joke."

"Gravity is in the eye of the beholder," Gerry said. "Come on down here and check this out." He led them, reluctantly, down the steps where they could peer in through the gated and mullioned windows. Not much was visible except a room with some kind of bench and closet area lit by what appeared to be a gloomy bulb.

"If you're so excited by this place," Sam said irritably—his white tennis shirt was hanging out, his hair was matted, and he was covered with sweat and beginning to feel itchy—"then why not cancel the ceremony at the kid's tub and get yourself baptized here? You can become a returning Jew, a what do you call it, Michael?"

"A *ba-al teshuva,* a repentant Jew."

"But gentlemen, I have already decided to allow myself to be baptized. Let this take the edge off for you. It's an ancient Jewish gesture, that's what it is."

"Gerry, Gerry," said Michael. "This is not a bubble bath. You know what Harp and Marylee are asking of you? By submerging, you relinquish all formal ties to Judaism. As you go under, you have to recite the catechism or whatever it is. The Nicene Creed. The articles of Christian faith."

"I know that."

"You have to say, 'I believe in the Holy Father and that Jesus Christ is the son of God . . .' the whole ball game."

"I will say it."

"But will you mean it?" said Sam as he leaned against the entry gate. "Even if you go swimming in it, you cannot possibly believe it!"

"Look," said Gerry, "we've been over this territory a dozen times. It's words, words, words. The Christians said for two thousand years that the Jews were responsible for Jesus' death, and one morning they woke up and changed their minds and got it right, and so they changed the words. That the Romans were now officially the bad guys. For thousands of years Catholics couldn't eat meat on Friday, and now you don't go to hell if you do. Why? They changed the words. Every deal, every contract can have an amendment."

"So you're faking it, Gerry. You're goddamn faking it for Marylee and Harp!" charged Sam.

"You're putting words into my mouth. What I'm doing is accommodating. That's all. I know I might not possess the greatest religious mind in the world, but at least I am keeping mine open. My mind can contain Jesus in it at the same time it can hold whatever you're supposed to hold if you're Jewish." He paused. "All that stuff."

"Try God," said Sam. "Try saying the word, the one God, damn it. As in 'Hear oh Israel the Lord our God the Lord is One.'"

"Let me ask you a question," Gerry said. "How do you know that the Trinity isn't a unity? Again, magic with numbers. Three in one. Frankly, I think Marylee is right that the Jewish God in Genesis mainly goes around checking up on people and dishing out the punishment; he's a little like you, Sam, or maybe Ellen when she's had a bad day with the freshmen. Things are not so simple."

"You can be both a Christian and a Jew?" Michael asked wearily. "That's news to me."

"And I'd appreciate your leaving my wife out of this," said Sam.

"And I'd appreciate it if you stop hounding Marylee. She should not feel persecuted in her own house."

"Calm down, boys," said Michael. "We're having a nice evening at the mikveh. Let's just keep it on a high intellectual level. The thing you have to understand, Gerry—I mean truly absorb—is that you, through the baptism, undergo a transformation. It is an official, external sign of what's supposed to be happening, or to have happened to you, internally. In a word, you are being reborn."

"Yeah," said Sam, "like that Swedish tennis player. He comes back from being down two sets, five-love to win the match. Björn Again Borg."

"Sam, please, for God's sake!"

"The man doesn't believe in what he is doing," said Sam, groping for the steps from the mikveh back up to the sidewalk. "And yet he does it. I'm reaching the point where I'm out of ideas. Let's just go home."

"Not yet," said Michael. For a change, he felt only bad, not sorrowful and dejected, and still possessed of some spiritual energy. He could see Gerry's effusiveness beginning to fade. He could see in Sam's irritation his own. Yet he decided to try once again. "Have I asked you to read Franz Rosenzweig's *Star of Redemption?*"

"You have, but I haven't."

"Why don't you read, Gerry? A Jew reads."

"Well, by that measure, maybe I'm not one. For me, a review or a digest takes the place of the book; sometimes it's even better. We're not all like you, Michael. And I know all about Franz Rosenzweig. I am not a philosopher, nor will I ever be one. I'm in floor tiles. I'm the great philosopher of linoleum."

"Please, Gerry. You will be a terrible loss to me," Michael said, "if you go through with this."

"I'm telling you I will pop up unchanged. It will be like a car's changing registration from New York to New Jersey."

"You're not a vehicle, Gerry. You're a human being. And the idea of baptism is—to stoop to the fine level we have attained tonight—that you get dunked as Jackie Mason and somehow emerge as Pat Robertson."

"Incidentally," Sam said, "there's a helluva difference between New York and New Jersey."

"To the car," Gerry said, "it makes a difference? Does the mileage change? Does the engine? The car just goes on running, with a new sticker in the window. It just goes on being itself, and that is my intention."

Michael sighed. "You talk to your mother?"

"Yes, thank you, my friend. I don't take offense. You did what you felt you had to do. I spoke to her. She understands."

"Like hell she does," said Sam. "If she understands, then I'm Golda Meir."

"I told my own father, Gerry. I was visiting him after I heard that the date of your ceremony had been set, and I just started to cry. I had to tell him. I couldn't stop myself. I told him how bad I felt that we couldn't change your mind about it."

"You were appealing to him to appeal to me?"

"Maybe," Michael said. "He always liked you, but, truth be told, when I mentioned it, I thought he was actually asleep and didn't hear me. Probably the way I wanted it: to get it off my chest without tormenting him. Why do I need to do this? Because you're making me feel like a lousy Jew myself. If I were any good, I could convince you that you're going down the wrong road. I could convince you, Gerry, that what you're doing isn't a name change, or a change of registration, or whatever you choose to dupe yourself with. I could convince you that you are washing away your memory—okay, not memory, but your formal connection—to all the Jews, and not only us, in the here and now, but also to those who were butchered, flayed, burned, garroted, had their tongues torn out, were shot, and gassed just because of their . . . registration. I'm sorry, Gerry."

Michael unshouldered his racquet case, and tried to give Gerry a hug; Gerry turned away slightly, and only half of him was embraced. Still, Michael was glad he had gotten this out. It had to be said, those words that had seemed like troops lined up at the back of his mouth, just waiting for the moment when they were ordered to march. Now they had come out. Would they do any good?

"You forgot drawing and quartering," said Sam despairingly. "You forgot drowning—"

"I will always be connected to all that," Gerry said.

"As a Christian, as a good Christian is connected to it," said Michael. "What a loss."

"Let's go, guys," said Sam. "We're getting nowhere."

"No, wait," Michael said. "Was it Marylee's vision? Is that what's gotten to you? Is that what she's holding over you?"

"What vision?" Gerry asked.

"You don't know? She saw Jesus in the bandages when she had her breast removed, man. She never told you this? That's when this all got started. That's what she told me. She said all this began with the operation. Oh, Gerry, back then, with the cancer, not with the preacher. She never told you?" Gerry did not answer. "What kind of marriage do you have?"

Gerry still did not answer, but his face grew vacant and disconsolate.

Michael was about to reach over and try that hug again when flashes filled their eyes, blue and red lights mingled alarmingly with the sounds of running feet and slamming doors. Large men brandishing sticks and now, Michael saw, guns were suddenly rushing down the steps toward them.

"Police officers! Put your hands high above your heads. Up, up. Now! Don't move!"

"Jesus Christ," said Michael. "Don't shoot."

"Keep your hands way up. Grown men pissing here again! What the hell is that? Holy shit, shotgun, shotgun!"

"No, no, no," Sam implored the cops. "Tennis racquets. We have only tennis racquets, cases . . . oh shit. . . ."

"Drop 'em, motherfuckers! Drop the weapons or we fire!"

"Racquets," cried Sam. "Wilson, Prince, Head."

"Move, move," another voice yelled. And then, "Whoa, sergeant, it is a shitload of tennis stuff."

"Move, move," they shouted.

Two officers hustled Gerry, Sam, and Michael up the steps and into the light of the street lamp, which poured down on their tennis-weary, disheveled forms. "Who the hell are you guys? What are you doing here?"

"Don't shoot. Please, for God's sake, don't shoot, officers," Michael begged. "We were only checking out the mikveh."

AGAINST CIRCUMCISION

Michael Kimmel

ALTHOUGH IT WAS A LITTLE LATE by traditional religious standards, the entire family and many friends gathered in our home three weeks after our son, Zachary, was born. We had gathered for his bris, the moment when a young Jewish boy is first brought into the family and the community, the moment of his formal entrance into the world of Judaism. At such symbolic moments, one feels keenly the sinews of connection to family and friends that sustain a life, animate it, give it context and meaning.

The mohel, of course, was running late. When he arrived, everyone gathered in the living room, where we had set up a table on which we had placed the various items we would use in the ceremony. A special chair had been reserved for the *sandek,* the honored family male elder, often the baby's grandfather or great-grandfather, who would hold the baby during much of the proceedings. (In our case, a godmother and godfather shared this role.)

As family and friends drew closer together, glasses of wine and champagne in their hands, the ritual began with prayers over the wine and bread. Our first toast to this new creature who had entered all our lives. Then the mohel began the naming ceremony, and some relatives and friends offered their wishes for this young life.

Amy, my wife, and I each offered a thought to the other and to Zachary as we entered this new phase of our lives as parents together. For my part, I quoted Adrienne Rich, who had written that "if I could have one wish for my own sons, it is that they should have the courage of women." I wished nothing more for Zachary than that he would have Amy's courage, her integrity, and her passion.

Then it was the moment for which we had all carefully prepared, about which we had endlessly talked, debated, argued, discussed. We took a pitcher of water and a bowl to the door of the house. Amy and I carried Zachary over to the threshold. With one hand I held his little body and with the other held his tiny legs over the bowl. Amy poured some water over his feet and rubbed it in. Then she held him and I did the same. Throughout, the mohel chanted in prayer. And in that way, we welcomed Zachary into our home and into our lives.

By now you are, of course, waiting for the "real" bris to begin, for the mohel to stuff a wine-soaked handkerchief into our son's mouth to muffle his cries and slightly anesthetize him, and then circumcise him, cutting off his foreskin in fulfillment of God's commandment to Abraham that he mark his son, Isaac, as a sign of obedience.

Sorry to disappoint, but that's the end of our story. Or at least the end of the story of Zachary's bris. There was no circumcision on that day. We had decided not to circumcise our son. Although he enters a world filled with violence, he would enter it without violence done to him. Although he will no doubt suffer many cuts and scrapes during his life, he would not bleed by our hand.

This was not an easy decision, but we had plenty of time to prepare—nine months to be exact. From the moment we saw the sonogram and read the results of the amniocentesis, the debate had been joined. Would we or wouldn't we? How would we decide? The remainder of this essay charts that process.

First, we talked. Constantly. Just when we thought the issue settled, we'd open it again. Each time one of us would read something, think something, pull something new off the Internet, we would reopen the discussion anew. We talked with friends, family members, religious authorities, doctors, and nurses. We asked our heterosexual women friends whether they had a preference for cut or uncut men. We each sought counsel from the e-mail discussion groups to which we belonged, and we consulted organizations like the American Academy of Pediatrics and the American Medical Association. We ordered and read more than a dozen books and pamphlets.

We contacted advocacy groups like National Organization of Circumcision Information Resource Centers (NOCIRC), National Organization to Halt the Abuse and Routine Mutilation of Males (NOHARMM), and Doctors Opposing Circumcision (DOC). But these organizations, while eager, were too one-sided and tended to minimize the difficulty of our decision.

And we didn't even bother calling organizations like Brothers United for Future Foreskins (BUFF), National Organization of Restoring Men (NORM), and RECover a Penis (RECAP) that encourage men who might "feel victimized by the unnecessary loss of their natural anatomical wholeness," as Joseph Zoske writes in *Journal of Men's Studies* (1998), to undergo penile reconstructive surgery to "correct" the circumcised penis. Such procedures (involving either attaching a new flap or pulling the remaining tissue down over the glans to create a pseudo-foreskin) seem as unnecessary as circumcision, and no doubt attend to psychological distress that has only the most tenuous connection to a small flap of penile tissue.

Pros and Cons

We heard a lot of arguments, for and against. To be sure, there is no shortage of arguments in favor of circumcision. Some are aesthetic and offer a psychological theory based on that aesthetic. Without circumcision, we heard, our son will look different from his father, and thus develop shame about his body. Our son will look different from other Jewish boys, especially in our heavily Jewish neighborhood, thus be subject to ridicule and teasing, and develop a sense that he does not belong. As one man on an e-mail list to which I posed the question wrote, "I don't want my kid to be an object of interest while taking public showers, such as in gym class or in athletic clubs" (David Garnier, personal communication).

Other arguments are medical. After all, male circumcision is the most common surgical procedure in the United States, and medical insurance carriers routinely cover hospital circumcision (which raises the incentives of medical practitioners to advocate the procedure). Our son's risks of penile infection, sexually transmitted diseases (STDs), and especially penile cancer would be significantly lower if he were to be circumcised. The likelihood of uterine cancer in his female sexual partners would be higher if he were not.

In addition, there were conflicting reports on the effects of circumcision on sexual functioning. There is some evidence from sex surveys that circumcised men are more sexually active and more sexually adventurous, especially as regards oral and anal sex. Circumcised men masturbate more often. And because circumcised men have less sexual sensitivity—after all, the foreskin contains about one thousand nerve endings, fully one-third of the organ's pleasure receptors—there is some evidence that circumcision delays ejaculation somewhat.

And, of course, the weight of family, history, and culture do not rest lightly on the shoulders of the new parent. As Jews, we knew full well the several-thousand-year-old tradition of following one of the most fundamental of God's commandments to Abraham—that "every male among you shall be circumcised . . . and that shall be a sign of the covenant between Me and you."

In the end, none of the arguments in favor of circumcision was fully persuasive. Taken together, however, they raised issues that spoke to the core of our identities as a man and a woman, as parents, as feminists, and as Jews. Each of the points of contention seems worth discussing in a bit more detail.

The Psychological Aesthetics of Difference

That our son would look different from his father was easily negotiated. We decided that we will simply tell him that Daddy had no choice about his own body and especially his penis, but that now, as parents, we loved him so much that we decided we didn't want to hurt him like that—turning something that could be a cause of embarrassment into a source of pride.

And he will look more and more like the other boys rather than different. Circumcision of newborns is decreasingly popular, performed routinely only in the United States (as a medical procedure in the hospital) and in Israel, where it remains a significant religious ceremony. (Adolescent circumcision remains the norm in most Islamic nations.) After these two countries, only Canada (25 percent) and Australia (10 percent) have rates of newborn circumcision in double digits; in European nations it is virtually nonexistent among non-Jews. Over four-fifths of all men in the world are uncircumcised.

Here in the United States, rates have fallen from well over 85 percent in 1960 to about 66 percent in 2000, so there was every reason to believe that more and more boys would look like Zachary and that he had little to fear by way of social ostracism. In our own neighborhood in heavily Jewish Brooklyn, about half the baby boys born in our local hospital are circumcised in the hospital (though there is no information about those who have it performed as a religious ceremony in their homes or elsewhere).

Medical Ambivalence

While it is true that the risk of penile cancer or infection is virtually nonexistent among circumcised men, rates among uncircumcised men, though higher, are still minuscule. In 1991, the American Academy of Pediatrics finally lifted its long-time advocacy of routine hospital circumcision for health reasons and now takes no position on the question, thus leaving the decision entirely up to the parents' aesthetic or religious beliefs. They concluded that there were no medical benefits to circumcision as long as the boy was instructed in proper cleanliness.

Even the redoubtable Benjamin Spock changed his mind over the years. Having always stood for the conventional wisdom that parents know best, Spock told *Redbook* in an interview in 1989 that his preference "if I had the good fortune to have another son, would be to leave his little penis alone." In a pamphlet, "Circumcision: A Medical or Human Rights Issue?" one doctor went so far as to suggest that removing the foreskin for strictly hygienic purposes was analogous to removing the eyelid for a cleaner eyeball.

Future sexual functioning didn't weigh particularly heavily in our minds either. For one thing, sexual functioning is so profoundly variable; we expect that if we teach Zachary to develop respect for his and others' bodies as well as their personal integrity, sexual pleasure will not be an issue for him or his partners. Second, the evidence is inconsistent. While circumcised men in the United States seem to have more sex, more varied sex, and masturbate more often, this may be more of a function of race, class, education, and religion than with whether or not the man is circumcised. It's middle-class white men—who tend to be the most secular and the most sexual—who still compose the majority of circumcised men. Among blacks and Hispanics, rates of oral sex and masturbation are significantly lower than among white men, and middle-class men are more sexually active and adventurous than working-class men. "People with graduate degrees are the most likely to masturbate," noted Ed Laumann, a sociologist and one of the principal researchers in the University of Chicago sex survey in the early 1990s.

Nor were we ultimately concerned about the eventual effect on potential women partners. An informal poll among heterosexual women friends yielded a mixed anecdotal response. Most said they preferred circumcised men, and one or two indicated significant aesthetic discomfort with intact men. But an article in the January 1999 *British Journal of Urology* reported that women who had slept with both circumcised and intact men preferred sex with men who were not circumcised. The article reported that the women achieved orgasm faster and were more likely to achieve multiple orgasms.

The Burden of History

Actually, the historical record of medical opinion consistently pushed us further into the anticircumcision camp. The more we learned about the medical history, the more we were convinced that concerns other than the health of the baby led doctors to make circumcision a routine practice. Before the 1870s, in the United States, routine medical circumcision was quite rare, hovering around 5 to 6 percent of all newborn baby boys. Subscribers to the new Victorian sexual morality sought to reduce what critics perceived to be rampant sexual promiscuity, and especially masturbation, which, they believed, resulted in all sorts of debilities and even death. Masturbation was said to cause all manner of emotional, psychological, and physiological problems, from bed-wetting to adolescent insolence, acne to mental retardation, insanity, psychological exhaustion, and neurasthenia.

Circumcision's well-established ability to curb sexual appetite and pleasure was prescribed as a potential cure for sexual profligacy. Lewis Sayre, a prominent New York physician hailed as "the Columbus of the prepuce" by his colleagues, experimented with circumcision as a cure for paralysis and other muscular ailments. Sayre's colleagues also noted that Jews had a lower rate of STDs than non-Jews, and hypothesized that this had to do with circumcision. (Actually this had to do with the fact that Jews had very little sexual contact with non-Jews.)

Another physician, Dr. Peter Remondino, advocated universal male circumcision since the foreskin, which he labeled "an unyielding tube," left the intact male "a victim to all manner of ills, sufferings . . . and other conditions calculated to weaken him physically, mentally, and morally; to land him, perchance, in jail, or even in a lunatic asylum." And Robert Tooke's popular *All About the Baby* (1896) recommended circumcision to prevent "the vile habit of masturbation."

J. H. Kellogg, pioneering health reformer, cereal inventor, and general medical quack also sounded the alarm; his best-selling health advice book, *Plain Facts for Old and Young* (1888), included nearly one hundred pages on the dangers of masturbation. Circumcision is almost always successful in curbing masturbation, he counseled, and he suggested that the operation be performed "by a surgeon without administering anesthetic, as the brief pain attending the operation will have a salutary effect upon the mind." (Though this may have begun the tradition of not using anesthesia to perform circumcision, Kellogg did not pretend that the baby feels no pain during the procedure. Anyone who has ever witnessed a routine medical circumcision performed without anesthesia knows only too well how much pain the infant does feel.)

Victorian morality was pervasive. And as waves of uncircumcised immigrants entered the United States, circumcision of newborns was a way to stake a claim for a truly "American" morality. Rates jumped to 25 percent by 1900. After World War II, when the *Journal of the American Med-*

ical Association reported that rates of STD were higher among blacks and uncircumcised white men, circumcision rates continued to climb, and by 1980, nearly nine of every ten American boys were circumcised.

But it now appears that the rapid spread of circumcision as a routine medical procedure had more to do with Victorian hysteria about sexuality than it did with hygiene. And given the American Academy of Pediatrics' recent backpedaling on the issue—from ritual endorsement to anxious agnosticism to its most recent resigned disapproval—there seems to be no medical argument—historical or hygienic—to compel the procedure.

The Weights of Tradition

The combined weights of family and religious culture were not so easily negotiated. As predicted, the future grandmothers were somewhat more sanguine about the prospect of noncircumcision than were the future grandfathers. It's ironic that it's always been women—even within Judaism—who have opposed circumcision as a violence done to their babies, and circumcised males who have supported it. Perhaps it is analogous to fraternity or military initiation ceremonies, where the salutary outcome of a sense of belonging to the larger homosocial group is deemed worth any price, including the removal of a third of one's potential sexual pleasure.

In our case, neither Amy nor I felt any strong compulsion towards circumcision, but I was more strongly opposed on moral grounds. Amy's opposition would come later, when she first held Zachary in her arms and she felt a visceral rage that anyone would do anything that would ever hurt this new creature. In very gender-stereotyped terms, Amy's opposition grew from her emotional, visceral connection to the baby; mine grew first from a principled opposition grounded in a sense of justice and ethics.

But equally gendered, I suppose, I felt that my Judaism had always given me the ability to stand up against injustice, that the imperative of the post-Holocaust generation of "Never Again!" impelled me to speak out against injustices wherever I saw them.

Ultimately, it came down to Judaism. Jewish law is unequivocal on the subject—it has been a time-honored tradition since the celebrated covenant with Abraham, the founding moment of monotheism. In Genesis 17, God appears before an aged Abraham—he's ninety-nine!—and commands that Abraham circumcise himself, his son, and all male members of his household (slaves and servants included).

Today circumcision is seen as a mitzvah, linking the family to a four-thousand-year history of a people. In his masterful compendium of Jewish law and lore, *Essential Judaism,* George Robinson writes that it is a mitzvah "one performs for its own sake as a subordination of oneself to a larger entity." What's a tiny foreskin compared to four thousand years of tradition? And so it appeared that Jewish tradition might yet extract its pound of flesh—well, more likely about a quarter of an ounce—from yet another innocent baby.

Yet Judaism today is hardly as monolithic as we once thought. Even in biblical times there seems to have been some dissent about the procedure. If one follows the ritual as prescribed by Jewish law, the baby is held during the circumcision on what is called the Chair of Elijah, named after the prophet "who railed against the Jews for forsaking the ritual of circumcision." What that says to me is that not long after circumcision was instituted, there were a lot of people who were already resisting it. Then, too, there is the law that the *brit milah* be performed on the eighth day after the birth of the son, a law so ironclad that it is perhaps the only Jewish ritual that may not be postponed for the Sabbath or even for Yom Kippur. Those who were interested in enforcing circumcision were determined that there be no excuses—no doubt because a lot of people were trying to wiggle their way out.

In her research, Amy found that even as recently as the mid-nineteenth century, in Eastern Europe and Russia there was a widespread move to stop the practice—ironically, just when it was becoming more widespread in the United States. Led by women—what a surprise!—who thought the practice barbaric and patriarchal, the movement eventually even convinced Theodore Herzl, the founder of modern Zionism, who refused to allow his own son to be circumcised.

It is, after all, quite perplexing: Why would God ask Abraham to do such a thing to himself and all the males of his household—especially his son? For years, I had a little cartoon in my study that depicted Abraham, standing alone on top of a mountain, looking up at the sky, forlorn and exasperated. The caption read, "Let me see if I have this right: You want us to cut the ends of our dicks off?!?!"

Sublimating Pleasure for Torah

The circumcision as ritual makes sense, however, in three ways—one sexual, one political, and one symbolic. Throughout history, commentators on circumcision have agreed that the goal was to transform men's (and women's) sexual experience, and thus make men more eager to study Torah. The only thing they disagreed on was how, exactly, circumcision would accomplish this feat of sublimation.

Most observers assumed it would make a man less sexually sensitive, reduce his sexual ardor, and constrain his sexual impulses. In his fascinating study, *Eros and the Jews,* David Biale finds two contradictory impulses leading toward the same conclusion. Ancient Jews, such as Philo, understood circumcision as "the symbol of the excision of excessive and superfluous pleasure." In *Guide to the Perplexed,* the great medieval philosopher Moses Maimonides prefigured J. H. Kellogg by nearly a millennium when he wrote that the commandment to circumcise was "not prescribed with a view to perfecting what is defective congenitally, but to perfecting what is defective morally." A chief reason for the ritual was "the wish to bring about a decrease in sexual intercourse and a weakening of the organ in question, so that this activity be diminished and the organ be in as quiet a state as possible." After all, he continued, "the fact that circumcision weakens the faculty of sexual excitement and sometimes perhaps diminishes the pleasure is indubitable."

While Maimonides argued that the physiological loss was "the real purpose" of the ritual, others believed that the psychological impact far outweighed the physical. Biale notes that an early medieval Midrash Tadshe suggests that the "covenant of circumcision was therefore placed on the genitals so that the fear of God would restrain them from sin." Later thinkers took the physical to new extremes. The early-nineteenth-century scholar Nahman of Bratslav, great grandson of the Baal Shem Tov, argued that circumcision symbolizes the complete excision of sexual pleasure so that the *true zaddik* (holy man) experiences pain, not pleasure, during intercourse.

On the one hand, writers were convinced that men would feel less— much less, and therefore their frustration would lead inevitably towards holier devotion to study. On the other hand, some writers were convinced that circumcised men would experience far more sexual excitement—so much more, in fact, that it would leave both him and his partner so frustrated that they wouldn't want to have sex again. In an astonishing passage, Isaac ben Yedaiah, a late thirteenth-century French follower of Maimonides, described the difference in such overheated prose that it borders on the salacious (which alone makes it worth quoting at length):

> [A beautiful woman] will court a man who is uncircumcised in the flesh and lie against his breast with great passion, for he thrusts inside her a long time because of the foreskin, which is a barrier against ejaculation in intercourse. Thus she feels pleasure and reaches an orgasm first. When an uncircumcised man sleeps with her and then resolves to return to his home, she brazenly grasps him, holding on to his genitals

and says to him, "Come back, make love to me." This is because of the pleasure that she finds in intercourse with him, from the sinews of his testicles—sinews of iron—and from his ejaculation—that of a horse—which he shoots like an arrow into her womb. They are united without separating and he makes love twice and three times in one night, yet the appetite is not filled. And so he acts with her night after night. The sexual activity emaciates him of his bodily fat and afflicts his flesh and he devotes his brain entirely to women, an evil thing.

But when a circumcised man desires the beauty of a woman . . . he will find himself performing his task quickly, emitting his seed as soon as he inserts the crown. . . . He has an orgasm first; he does not hold back his strength. As soon as he begins intercourse with her, he immediately comes to a climax. She has no pleasure from him when she lies down or when she arises and it would be better for her if he had not known her . . . for he arouses her passion to no avail and she remains in a state of desire [cited in Biale].

So more excitement means less pleasure—for both him and his female partner. Ancient rabbis, like Philo, had argued that not only did circumcision restrain male sexual ardor, but diminished women's pleasure. "It is hard for a woman to separate herself from an uncircumcised man with whom she has had intercourse." Everyone now seemed to agree that circumcision reduces the pleasure of the woman, which is precisely why it seems to have been prescribed. And precisely why Amy and I were growing increasingly suspicious.

There were political issues involved as well. It's interesting to observe the expansion of the ritual in terms of the relationship between Jews and their neighbors. Originally, apparently, the ritual consisted of only the *brit milah*—which is the excision of a small part of the foreskin. This enabled some Jewish men to continue to "pass" as gentiles in the ancient edition of those locker room showers that my friends continually discussed. Disgruntled rabbis then added the *brit periah,* which removed the entire foreskin, making it impossible to pass as gentile. (It's an ironic twist of history that it is the *brit periah* that was adopted by modern medicine when it still prescribed routine neonatal circumcision.)

But this expansion also raised, for us, the thorniest political and moral dilemma. A close friend, a child of Holocaust survivors, told me the story of his uncle, who was not so lucky. His was the now-classic story of the young man, sneaking his way onto a train leaving Germany, under the watchful eyes of the Nazis. When caught, he was forced to strip in the station, and when it was discovered that he was circumcised, he was shot on the spot.

Here was a political reason to circumcise, a slap in the face of anti-Semitism, a way to connect my son to a history of resistance against anti-Semitism, and to recognize the ways in which physical difference (whether congenitally or culturally derived) is grounds for discrimination. In fact, some historians claim that the *brit periah,* the more extensive circumcision, was first used by the Egyptians to mark their Hebrew slaves, so that they would be readily and permanently identifiable. Ironic then, that once free, these same Hebrews made the more dramatic statement a matter of their own inclusion.

Penile Patriarchy

But what was ultimately decisive for us was the larger symbolic meaning of circumcision, and particularly the gendered politics of the ritual. After all, it is not circumcision that makes a man Jewish; one can certainly be Jewish without it. Religious membership is passed on through the mother: if the mother is Jewish then the baby is Jewish, and nothing that the baby does—or that is done to him or her—can change that basic fact. A rabbi is trained to counsel parents of mixed religious backgrounds (in which the man is Jewish and the woman is not) that circumcision does not make their son Jewish, but that only the mother's conversion will make it so.

No, circumcision means something else: the reproduction of patriarchy. Abraham cements his relationship to God by a symbolic genital mutilation of his son. It is on the body of his son that Abraham writes his own beliefs. In a religion marked by the ritual exclusion of women, such a marking not only enables Isaac to be included within the community of men—he can be part of a minyan, can pray in the temple, can study Torah—but he can also lay claim to all the privileges to which being a Jewish male now entitles him. Monotheistic religions invariably worship male Gods and exhibit patriarchal political arrangements between the sexes. (Looked at this way, since both Judaism and Islam practice circumcision, it is really Christianity that is the deviant case, and it would be worth exploring how Christianity justified its evasion of the practice since it is certain that Jesus was circumcised.)

Circumcision, it became clear, is the single moment of the reproduction of patriarchy. It's when patriarchy happens, the single crystalline moment when the rule of the fathers is reproduced, the moment when male privilege and entitlement is passed from one generation to the next, when the power of the fathers is enacted upon the sons, a power which the sons will someday then enact on the bodies of their own sons. To circumcise our son, then, would be, unwittingly or not, to accept as legitimate four thousand years not of Jewish tradition, but of patriarchal domination of women.

Our choice was clear.

We welcomed Zachary into our family on that morning without a circumcision. We decided that we want him to live in a world without violence, so we welcomed him without violence. We decided that we want him to live in a world in which he is free to experience the fullness of the pleasures of his body, so we welcomed him with all his fleshy nerves intact. And we decided that we want him to live in a world in which male entitlement is a waning memory, and in which women and men are seen—in both ritual and in reality—as full equals and partners. So we welcomed him equally, his mother and I, in the time-honored way that desert cultures have always welcomed strangers to their tents: we washed his feet.

DEFENDING CIRCUMCISION

David Zaslow

IN 1984 OUR SON ARI had a beautiful, natural, home birth. Our daughter Rachel had been born in the same bed and into the same loving environment three years earlier. My wife, Devorah, and I were resolute about our decision not to circumcise our son. We felt like pioneers braving the obstacles of both family and Jewish tradition. We reasoned that if we made such an effort to create a loving welcome into the world, how could we inflict unnecessary pain upon this beautiful soul just because of an archaic tradition?

Oy, how we all change! In 1988 I had a spiritual awakening. I was forty years old when I "heard the call," and soon I was on the path to becoming a rabbi. At first my personal spiritual practices and study were not a contradiction to having an uncircumcised son. After all, my original reasoning against the ritual still seemed true.

But little by little something inside me was changing. Not a sense of returning to tradition. Not a sense of tribal loyalty. Not even a sense that our decision not to circumcise was a mistake. But a sense that there is a difference between a circumcision and a brit.

A brit is a covenant or partnership with the divine. I was experiencing this covenant myself. Firsthand. Connecting to the Holy One. Personally. Me. I no longer saw Jewish rituals as symbolic. They were, when administered properly, not symbols but parts of a spiritual technology for covenanting with G-d.

Shabbat candlelighting was no longer a quaint representation of an ancient fire ritual. The wine was not a symbol but an actuality. Candles and wine were signals to G-d that our family was ready for Sabbath. And when we sang "Shalom Alechem" to welcome in angels, it wasn't because it was symbolic. We sang it because we were actually welcoming real angels. We blessed our children because we were connecting the souls of our children to Shechinah.

Oh, how I had changed! I felt like Tevye about to tell Golde that their daughter's engagement was off! "Oy" I thought, "what am I going to tell Devorah about my new ideas about brit?" Could I conjure up a dream scene like in *Fiddler*? I opted for the truth—at least for "my" truth. Coincidentally, Devorah was coming to the same conclusion but for completely different reasons.

We arranged for Ari's belated circumcision when he was six years old. My change of mind was strictly spiritual. I believed that G-d's covenant was a real energy pact. I believed that Elijah was an animate energy force, and that his chair at a circumcision was not just symbolic. And if there was a psychological benefit for Ari to have his penis look like mine, then great.

For Devorah, the decision was strictly practical. She took the psychological path. Now that we were so fully immersed in daily Jewish life, what would it be like for our son to be at Jewish summer camp uncircumcised? Or on a summer trip to Israel?

We explained to Ari what was going to happen and told him that this was a special Jewish mitzvah. He picked an additional Hebrew name for himself. We bought him gifts and tried to make it special for him. In all honesty I cannot say how much of a choice this was for Ari, but in his six-year-old wisdom he completely consented.

In the operating room, while Ari was under anesthesia, Rabbi Aryeh Hirschfield conducted the sacred rite. The anesthesiologist placed a drop of wine on my son's lips. We welcomed Elijah. We prayed. The Jewish physician cut. We sang. I wept!

The next morning, while lying on the living room floor together, I told my son, my only son, that had I done this when he was eight days old there would have been hardly any pain. I told him that I didn't do it then because I didn't want to cause him any pain. I asked his forgiveness for causing him so much pain now.

His answer still gives me shivers, "Of course I forgive you, Daddy. But why didn't you do it then? I wanted you to do it then!" My mind went numb. I thought, "What did he mean by 'I wanted you to do it then?' Dare I ask?" I asked. He answered, "I wanted you to do it when I was eight days old." I asked, "You remember?" I was getting zapped by an angel. He repeated his cryptic words again, "I wanted you to do it then!" With tears streaming down both our cheeks we sat together in silence.

A Rabbi's Thoughts

Our rebbes teach us that there are three kinds of mitzvot. The first are called *mishpatim*, or judgments. These are the logical, universal, moral commandments discovered by all peoples in all spiritual traditions (don't kill, don't steal, honor your parents, and so forth).

The second category of mitzvot are *eidot*, or memorial rituals (make a seder on Passover to remember the exodus; read the story of Esther on Purim, and so on). They are not universal but strictly tribal reenactments to help those of us who are Jewish use the past for the benefit of the future.

The third category, under which brit milah falls, is the most mysterious. They are called *hukkim*, which we translate as statutes. These include kosher dietary laws and circumcision. What are they for? There is no clear answer. Why do we do them? There is no clear answer. The best we can do is rationalize. We do these mitzvot to show our love for G-d. We call it the practice of *bittul hanefesh*, to put the rational mind aside so that the heart and soul might open.

In Deuteronomy 30:6 the Torah says, "And YHVH, your God, will circumcise your heart, and the heart of your seed, to love YHVH, your God, with all your heart and with all your soul. . . ." It almost seems as if Torah Herself is trying to explain the profound impact of the ritual as a means of increasing compassion and empathy.

Okay, to abstain from shrimp I can give up reason, but must we cause needless pain to our sons? Torah says yes. When administered sensitively, the brit ceremony is the most incredible father-son bonding experience. It is not a means of "reproducing patriarchy, male privilege, and entitlement." On the contrary, it seems to be a means of reproducing male love and compassion. Our mothers, sisters, wives, and daughters experience the awesome spiritual bonding power of blood every month. Men have this opportunity only during circumcision.

The brit is the once-in-a-lifetime chance for the souls of father and son to bond in the deepest way imaginable. As a rabbi, this is the intention that I bring into the rite. I ask the dads to hold the hands of their sons and to whisper blessings of love to them. I tell them not to deny that there might be some pain, but to carry that pain for their sons. I encourage the dads to cry for their sons and for all the pain their sons will experience in their lives. I encourage the dads to weep and pray for all children. This is the essence, I believe, of making a covenant.

Reflection on Kimmel's Essay

My only serious criticism of Michael Kimmel's otherwise caring and moderate essay was in the fictitious imagining of his son's circumcision. He wrote that the "mohel, of course, was running late. " As the ceremony was about to begin he was waiting "for the mohel to stuff a wine-soaked handkerchief" into the baby's mouth to "muffle his cries." Mohels don't stuff handkerchiefs into babies' mouths! And I never met one who ran late. The whole image conjures up a weird, medieval caricature.

To ascribe the cause of male privilege and patriarchy to brit milah is incorrect. I can think of several aspects in Judaism that do contribute to patriarchy (required separation of men and women in prayer and not ordaining women as rabbis, for instance), but not the brit ceremony.

There is nothing moral or immoral about the choices we make about circumcision. This is not a moral mitzvah. It is a spiritual practice that is purposely not based on the issues that Kimmel and his wife struggled with: logic, aesthetics, good medicine, the weight of tradition, or the history of anti-Semitism.

It is a bonding ritual that I believe leads to higher levels of consciousness for both fathers and sons. I tell my non-Jewish friends that unless circumcision is done for spiritual or covenantal reasons, it is not necessary. To my Jewish friends who agonize about what to do I say, "I know exactly what you are going through. May the struggle be good!" I advise them to ask the Shechinah to help them make the decision.

THE RACIAL POLITICS
OF HEBREW

Loolwa Khazzoom

"I'VE LOST MY ÁYIN," I sadly confided to my Iranian friend on a recent trip to Israel. "Stay in Israel much longer, and you'll lose your 'het, too!" he laughed. Indeed, most of my Mizrahi friends speak the Ashkenaziized version of the Hebrew alphabet, as a result of the incessant ridicule and contempt their parents faced upon arriving in Israel. Scorn for the Mizrahi pronunciation of Hebrew was just another manifestation of the general disgust for anything Middle Eastern and North African. Leaving that accent behind was embraced as a method for escaping automatic classification as backward, primitive, dirty, uneducated, and violent—common stereotypes ascribed to Mizrahim.

Ironically enough, the Mizrahi pronunciation of Hebrew is the grammatically correct, original pronunciation. Hebrew originally had a different pronunciation for each letter of the Hebrew alphabet: alef and áyin; hey, 'het, and chet; gimmel with a dagesh (dot) in the middle and 'ghimmel without that dagesh. Originating in the Middle East, the sounds of the Hebrew alphabet were compatible with the sounds of other Semitic languages of the region. Accordingly, Jews who remained in the region over the millennia were able to preserve the original pronunciation of Hebrew through the modern day. Speaking Arabic or Farsi on a daily basis only served to reinforce the Semitic tongue.

Jews who migrated to Slavic and Germanic countries, however, lost the ability to make many of these distinct pronunciations. For example, there is no "w" sound in German, so the "waw" became a "vav." In total, about eighteen distinct sounds were mushed into nine, resulting in "duplicate" letters. Just as Ashkenazi culture came to dominate Jewish life globally, so did the Ashkenazi (mis)pronunciation of the Hebrew alphabet; and so these double letters are the commonly taught pronunciation today.

When I was five years old, I was the only child in my orthodox Hebrew school who got perfect scores on my Hebrew tests. "How are we supposed to know if it's a kouf or a kaf?" classmates would complain. I knew the distinctions because I learned them at home. When I prayed and sang, it was always with these distinctions. So at Hebrew school, I would go through a translation process in my head when learning new words, thinking of them as my family would pronounce them. Thus the secret to my success.

But as I grew up in the Jewish world, it seemed preferable to overlook this obvious advantage in favor of the more "enlightened" Ashkenazi pronunciation. I was regularly taunted for my pronunciation, to the point that I became afraid to open my mouth. In other words, sounding like me—like my family, like my ethnicity—was a shaming experience. And that was in America.

"It's amazing to me that I have to forfeit the correct pronunciation of Hebrew in order be considered educated enough to get a good job," one Mizrahi wrote in a letter to the editor of an Israeli newspaper about five years ago. In Israel, language politics are intertwined not only with identity politics but also with economics.

As I have taught Hebrew the past several years, I have been pointedly admonished from teaching the Mizrahi pronunciation to the children. "It will confuse them," I have been told by my supervisors. Meanwhile, my students have struggled with the elusiveness of figuring out how to spell with so many "double letters." Inevitably, I have sneaked in a lesson on the original pronunciations, praying the supervisor would not walk in during that moment. "For a number of political reasons I won't get into now," I said to one class last year, "modern Israeli Hebrew follows the European pronunciation of the Hebrew alphabet." "But wait," one red-haired, freckle-faced student asked me. "Why would they want to choose less sounds over more sounds? That's really dumb!" "Don't ask me," I said, hands surrendering in the air. "I'm with you!"

Indeed, why does the Jewish mainstream prefer to have nine Hebrew sounds for eighteen letters instead of eighteen sounds? On that note, why does it prefer to teach one traditional Hanukkah song instead of ten, one historical Jewish narrative instead of twenty, one menu for Shabbat dinner instead of thirty? Jewish (that is, Ashkenazi) leaders seem to be operating on an either-or model of perceived scarcity, threatened by the very mention of non-Ashkenazi heritage—as if our invitation to the dinner table would kick everyone else out of the room. In order to get rid of this perceived threat, Mizrahi, Sephardi, and Ethiopian Jewish heritage and communities have been devalued and degraded publicly.

Faced with the choice of preserving our heritage or being accepted and promoted in a Jewish society, the overwhelming majority of non-Ashkenazi Jews have assimilated and given up our traditions. Until Jewish leadership shifts to a model of abundance, we and our traditions will continue to be shut out. And the entire Jewish community will lose.

REVERSION

Adrienne Rich

This woman/ the heart of the matter.
This woman flung into solitary by the prayers of her tribe.
This woman waking/ reaching for scissors/ starting to cut her hair
Hair long shaven/ growing out.
To snip to snip to snip/ creak of sharpness meeting itself against
    the roughness of her hair.

This woman whose voices drive her into exile.
(Exile, exile.)
Drive her toward the other side.
By train and foot and ship, to the other side.
Other side. Of a narrow sea.

This woman/ the heart of the matter.
Heart of the law/ heart of the prophets.
Their voices buzzing like raspsaws in her brain.
Taking ship without a passport.
How does she do it. Even the ships have eyes.
Are painted like birds.
This woman has no address book.
This woman perhaps has a toothbrush.
Somewhere dealing for red/blue dyes to crest her rough-clipped
    hair.

On the other side: stranger to women and to children.
Setting her bare footsole in the print of the stranger's bare foot in
the sand.
Feeding the stranger's dog from the sack of her exhaustion.
Hearing the male prayers of the stranger's tribe/ rustle of the
stranger's river
Lying down asleep and dreamless in one of their doorways.

She has long shed the coverings.
On the other side she walks bare-armed, bare-legged, clothed
in voices.
Here or there picks up a scarf/ a remnant.
Day breaks cold on her legs and in her sexual hair.
Her punk hair/ her religious hair.

Passing the blue rectangles of the stranger's doors.
Not one opens to her.
Threading herself into declining alleys/ black on white plaster/
olive on violet.
To walk to walk to walk.
To lie on a warm stone listening to familiar insects.
(Exile, exile.)

This woman/ the heart of the matter.
Circling back to the city where her name crackles behind creviced
stones.
This woman who left alone and returns alone.
Whose hair again is covered/ whose arms and neck are covered/
according to the law.
Underneath her skin has darkened/ her footsoles roughened.
Sand from the stranger's doorway sifting from her plastic carry-all/
drifting into the sand whirling around in her old quarter.

RECLAIMING THE SPIRIT IN JUDAISM

SCIENCE AND RELIGION

A MARRIAGE MADE IN HEAVEN?

Rami Shapiro

SANTA FE, 2007—A spokeswoman for the Physics and Theology Institute (PTI) said today that recent breakthroughs in superstring theory have resulted in a startling discovery.

"Not only are we reading the mind of God," said Dr. Alice Weinstock, "we have found the essence of the Creator."

"In the past, religion and science were often in conflict," said Rev. Frank Macintosh, co-chair of a recent PTI symposium on the New Science of God, "but we are entering a new age of cooperation in which science as well as religion can reveal the God of creation."

Farfetched? Or just a matter of time? A growing number of scientists and theologians believe that the marriage of science and religion is inevitable and that science is revealing the very nature of God. But what kind of God does science reveal? If science is reading the mind of God, just what kind of thoughts is God thinking?

Almost four hundred years ago, Galileo Galilei invited the church fathers to look through his telescope and see for themselves that the earth orbits the sun. They refused, insisting instead that Galileo stop looking through the infernal device as well. Today the church has its own telescope, and theologians turn to science for the latest revelations of God.

If religion has found a use for science, science has finally discovered that the fundamental unity spoken of by religious mystics permeates every stratum of creation. However, the reductionist way scientists tend to view that unity shrinks God to the amoral building blocks of nature.

Just as religion will never discover superstrings, science will never imagine loving one's neighbor as oneself. Religion and science are different lenses through which we can catch glimpses of God, but to lay one atop the other is to distort them both. And yet we persist in blurring the boundaries between religion and science in hopes of having the latter prove the claims of the former so that faith can be bolstered by fact.

We lack a map of reality that would allow us to accept the truths of both science and religion without reducing either to a subset of the other. Such a map would unify but not reduce our sciences, both material and spiritual, and present an idea of God that incorporates and transcends them both. Such a map is not hard to find and has appeared in every culture throughout recorded history. It is called the Great Chain of Being.

Transpersonal philosopher and theorist Ken Wilber has done the most to bring the Great Chain into the twenty-first century, and I am indebted to him for much of my understanding of it. Wilber's map is far more complex than the one I will use here and speaks to issues beyond the narrow scope of this essay. Here, I draw upon the kabbalistic version of the Great Chain, the Five Worlds, to present a unified but not homogenized vision of science and religion within the greater unity of God.

Like a Russian doll concealing progressively smaller dolls within it, the Jewish mystics see all reality manifested as five distinct and nested dimensions or worlds. Just as the smaller doll is included in and transcended by the next larger doll, so are the less inclusive worlds included in and transcended by the next more inclusive world, and the whole nested reality is included in and transcended by God, the unconditioned and unconditional source and substance of all that was, is, and will be.

The first and least inclusive of the five worlds is called Assiyah. This is the realm of quantum mechanics, superstring theory, chaos, and complexity. The world of Assiyah is primarily the domain of physics. It is a world of constant wonder and, if Heisenberg is right, impenetrable mystery. It is the world to which both physicist and theologian turn to read the mind of God. Listen to Sheldon Glashow speak of superstring studies in Timothy Ferris' *Coming of Age in the Milky Way*: "[Exploring superstrings may be an enterprise] as remote from conventional particle physics as particle physics is from chemistry, to be conducted in schools of divinity by future equivalents of medieval theologians. . . . For the first time since the Dark Ages, we can see how our noble search may end, with faith replacing science once again."

Do we really want science to be replaced by faith? What advantage is gained by reducing the dialogue between science and religion to a monologue? And what kind of faith will this be? Glashow's vision is not the wonderful marriage of science and religion that some imagine. Spirit is replaced by superstrings, scientists are replaced by theologians, and faith in a moral universe calling us to justice, compassion, and humility (Micah 6:8) is reduced to faith in amoral multidimensional superstrings that speak to the origins of life, but not to its meaning or purpose.

The energies and forces studied by physicists in the Assiyah dimension of reality are called *nefesh,* which kabbalists take to be the most rudimentary manifestation of soul or consciousness. Without Assiyah and nefesh, no other worlds can exist, but to imagine that Assiyah reveals the final world (rather than the first) is to reduce the five dimensions to one, and the least inclusive one at that.

The second world or dimension of reality is called Yetzirah. In Yetzirah the quantum world of Assiyah reaches a new level of complexity, that dimension of life explored by biologists. Biology reveals a level of complexity that the world of quantum mechanics need not and cannot posit. Just as biology incorporates and yet transcends physics in its field of study, so the world of Yetzirah incorporates and goes beyond the world of Assiyah. The consciousness or soul manifest in Yetzirah is called *ruach.* Ruach, like nefesh, is not self-aware. It is the level of instinct and law, not yet reason and will.

Biology, no less than physics, has much to offer regarding the majesty of creation, and the universe it reveals is of such intricacy and wonder as to be a source of mystic amazement in and of itself. And herein lies the danger. To lose oneself in the wonder of Yetzirah is to fail to move beyond it. Ursula Goodenough, professor of biology at Washington University, gives a sample of this way of thinking: "Our story [of nature] tells us of the sacredness of life, of the astonishing complexity of cells and organisms. . . . Reverence is the religious emotion elicited when we perceive the sacred. . . . And so, I profess my Faith: For me, the existence of all this complexity and awareness and intent and beauty, and my ability to apprehend it, serves as the ultimate meaning and the ultimate value."

I cannot understand how the wondrous complexity of cells is the ultimate meaning and value of life. True, without cells, the world I revere could not exist, but to reduce that world to its cellular structure, or to point to cells as the carriers of meaning and value, seems extraordinarily reductionist.

A more reasoned approach comes from biologist Kenneth Miller of Brown University, who writes in *Finding Darwin's God* that "God uses physics, chemistry, biology to fashion and run the physical universe." Elsewhere Miller adds, "To a religious person, science can be a pathway towards God, not away from Him."

Science can move us closer to God manifested as the physical world. It cannot, however, reach those dimensions of God that transcend it. Or, when science does try to explain the spiritual yearnings of humankind with the biologic of Yetzirah, the results are inevitably similar to E. O. Wilson's sociobiology, which reduces the grandest capacities of human life and culture to the amoral transmission of genetic code. It is not that the science of biology is wrong; it is only that the world of Yetzirah is too small.

Beriah, the third dimension of the kabbalistic map, is the world of self-conscious beings: beings, human and otherwise, who are aware of creation, if not yet their place in it. It is in this world that life achieves the level of consciousness called *neshamah*, ego, the self that imagines itself to be separate from other selves. The dominant science of Beriah is psychology.

Where the sciences of physics and biology reveal an all-inclusive unity underlying their respective dimensions, the unity revealed by psychology is an egoic one, striving for an integration of forces present in the self to create a more harmonious self. Neshamah consciousness knows all about "I" but has yet to discover "Thou."

Just as a study of the physics of Assiyah does not require the biological complexity of Yetzirah, and the biological complexity of Yetzirah does not require the conscious ego of Beriah, so the psychology of Beriah does not mandate a more inclusive dimension of reality that incorporates and transcends it. On the contrary, speculation into an egoless spiritual unity and inclusivity is seen as an infantile wish to return to the supposed safety and security of the womb. Early forms of religion that do appear in this world are centered on the ego and its survival after death.

Higher, more inclusive expressions of religious consciousness—for example, the belief of ethical monotheism that one God necessitates one world (a united earth), one race (a united humanity), and one moral code (justice and compassion for all)—require a transpersonal perspective that cannot be found in the self-preoccupied dimension of Beriah.

For this perspective we have to move to the fourth world called Atzilut. It is at this level of reality that neshamah consciousness evolves into *chayya* consciousness, an appreciation of the transpersonal dimension of being. It is here that we find the creative energies of art, music, mathematics, religion, theology, and literature, and the quality of mind capable of using them.

The language of chayya is nuanced: dream, myth, and metaphor. When the nineteenth-century chemist Kekule discovered the atomic structure of the benzene molecule, he saw it first in a dream; that is, he leaped beyond the egoic world of Beriah to tap the transpersonal realm that is Atzilut. The science of Atzilut is transpersonal religion. It is here that the sacred traditions of the world begin to recognize that the egoic formulations of faith common to Beriah are too narrow, focusing as they do on division, chosenness, the saved, and the damned. They begin to look beyond these differences to discover a common ground from which to build a more compassionate and peaceful world. The "scientists" of Atzilut tend to be the prophets and visionaries who peer over traditional boundaries to embrace the whole of life—cultural, psychological, biological, and physical—as a network of mutually supportive and interactive systems all within the domain of God.

As integrative as Atzilut is, however, it is still not the final level of inclusiveness and transcendence. For this we turn to the fifth world, Adam Kadmon, Primordial Being. It is here that all selves dissolve into a selfless unity characterized best by the Hindu phrase *sat chit ananda:* being, consciousness, bliss. Not surprisingly, the level of consciousness that experiences this dimension of reality is called *yechida,* or unity consciousness. This consciousness belongs to no one in particular, for it does not see any separate beings at all, but only the One from whom all diversity flows.

The science of Adam Kadmon is mysticism, and her scientists are those rare beings—Abraham, Moses, Jesus, Mohammed, Lao Tzu, Buddha, Krishna, Eckhart, Hildegard of Bingen, to name a few—who master rigorous spiritual disciplines and momentarily drop body, mind, ego, and soul to experience God as the greater unity that is the singular source and substance of all worlds and levels of consciousness.

It is often difficult to distinguish between the fourth and fifth dimensions, as they seem to encompass similar, if not the same, things. The difference is the presence and absence of self. In the fourth dimension of Atzilut, chayya consciousness is still a form of self-consciousness. The person manifesting chayya consciousness is aware of both herself and her fundamental interdependence with all other selves. She is not without self, but sees that all selves are part of each other and a greater whole. It is this greater whole that is the realm of Adam Kadmon, the fifth world of the kabbalistic map. The yechida consciousness that manifests in this fifth dimension is aware of a seamless unity that leaves no room for variation or selves of any kind. Yechida consciousness is not aware of itself; it is awareness itself, consciousness without content.

Does yechida reveal the true nature of God? No more so than any of the other worlds. God is not limited to any one dimension. God is the parchment on which the map is drawn. God is present in every space, in every place. God permeates each and every dimension, for God is both the source and the substance of all reality. God is the superstring and the dark infinity of space. God is the cow in the stable and the neighbor next door. God is the immanent and the transcendent. There is nothing that is not God.

When we apply our Five Worlds map to our understanding of science and religion, we honor each discipline and its discoveries for what they are: various facets of an infinitely faceted God. When the physicist exploring Assiyah uncovers the primary forces of existence and thus the mind of God, she reveals the truth, just not the whole truth. It is not that the eye of the physicist sees poorly. It is that the lens of physics sees only what it can.

The same is true for the biologist exploring Yetzirah who discovers the vast interconnectedness of all life and thus the unity of God; for the psychologist exploring Beriah who lays bare the secrets of self and then suggests that God is only a projection of this self; for the ardent religious disciple exploring Atzilut who shows us the transpersonal ground from which all religions arise; and even for the mystic exploring Adam Kadmon who points toward the source from which all form and being arise and to which they return: if the mystic suggests that this realm is the only true realm, and that all other dimensions are illusory, she, like the religious disciple, psychologist, biologist, and physicist before her, reveals the truth, just not the whole truth. It is not that the eye of each sees poorly. It is that the lens of each world sees only what it can.

Whatever lens we use to view reality, we are reducing reality to what that lens reveals. All attempts to align God exclusively with any one aspect of reality are flawed. Physics is not theology, and while good theology must incorporate the truths of science and not deny or violate them, it must do so in the process of offering a more inclusive view of reality than science can reveal. There should be no conflict between good science and good religion, but neither should there be an equation of the two.

The quantum paradoxes of Assiyah, the biological wonder of Yetzirah, and the psychological genius of Beriah are all vital to the whole story of reality, but they do not contain the whole story. Physics may well be "nearing God," as Stephen Hawking said in the *Observer,* and the physicist may well desire with Albert Einstein "to know the thoughts of God," but they will know the thoughts of God only when God is thinking about the laws of physics.

What the kabbalistic map of the Five Worlds offers, indeed what all the expressions of the Great Chain of Being offer, is a means for integrating science and religion in a greater whole. Such a map allows us to honor and pursue the sciences appropriate to each dimension without forcing any one science to work in all dimensions. It provides us with a schema of reality that honors both science and religion, and reveals to us the truth that we are never apart from and always a part of that infinite reality we call God.

UNMASKING THE FAST
OF ESTHER

Bonna Devora Haberman

OFTEN WE THINK OF PURIM as a children's carnival. Yet the *Megilla,* the Scroll of Esther that we read on Purim, is a complex script for outrageous masquerade, tinged with macabre violence. The Talmud records the following story:

> Rava and Rabbi Zera made a Purim feast together and became drunk.
> Rava got up from the table and slaughtered Rabbi Zera.
> The next day when he understood what he had done, he prayed for mercy and brought him back to life.
> The next year, Rava said to Rabbi Zera:
> "Come let us make a Purim feast together!"
> Rabbi Zera replied:
> "No! A miracle doesn't happen at every single hour."
>
> (bTractate *Megilla* 7b)

This dark and dangerous Purim revelry derives from lethal themes present in the *Megilla*: the sexism of the beauty pageant for queen, the genocidal plot against the Jews, and the Jewish destruction of seventy-five thousand Persian lives in the ninth chapter of the *Megilla*. How do these elements fit with our Purim fun? The *Megilla* reveals how deadly orders issue from the sumptuous banquets of the heartless and powerful, with the swish and tilt of goblets, while we occasionally look up from our page, from our drink.

Feminist interpretation of the *Megilla* exposes the gendered root of racism, violence, and war. We unmask the *Megilla* as we unmask evil action in the world. Here I share the analysis that underpins a "textual activist" approach to Purim and invite you to participate in a grass-roots feminist social change process.

The dramatic excitement in the *Megilla* of Esther begins in the first chapter, when Persian Queen Vashti refuses to be taken to the King's drinking party wearing (only) her crown. King Achashverosh opts to banish the queen. Yet ridding himself of Vashti is insufficient; her insubordination generates fear of women's universal insurgence. Concerned that gender disorder in his court will ignite a women's liberation movement, the king decrees that every woman, young and old, must submit to her husband, the inviolable ruler of his house, and speak *his* language (Esther 1:2). The king's edict defends the patriarchy against Vashti. Paradoxically, Vashti accomplishes her revolt by means of her absence precisely when she is expected to be present. Refusing to be uncovered, she uncovers the king's dependency upon controlling her. The king's magnificent pomp conceals his weakness. Simone de Beauvoir wrote, "Woman is an object through whom the male subject fulfills himself; her beauty is a measure of him."[1] When he cannot expose her at his will, his vulnerability to her is exposed.

The king, hungry for beauty and sex to console himself, mobilizes the entire Persian Empire to satisfy his appetite. The beauty contest for the crown involves collecting virgin girls from throughout 127 states of Persia. Consider these parallel notices, one from the ancient Persian Empire, the other from the contemporary global empire of sex traffickers in Kiev last year:

> Let the King appoint officials in all the states of his empire. They will round up all beautiful young virgin girls and bring them to the capital city, Shushan, to the women's section [Esther 2:2–3].

> One typical ad used by traffickers read: "Girls: Must be single and very pretty. Young and tall. We invite you for work as models, secretaries, dancers, choreographers, gymnasts. Housing is supplied. Foreign posts available. Must apply in person" [Jan. 18, 1998, *Metro Final*, Sacramento, Calif.].

According to the *Megilla*, the girls are delivered into the custody of the eunuch Hegai, who oversees twelve months of primping and preening in myrrh and oil. This confinement under guard culminates in each taking her turn for a night with the king. On the morning after, she is passed along to Shaashgaz, who controls the harem of concubines. None is seen again by the king unless he summons her. This rule obtains for Esther even *after* she has been crowned queen (Esther 4:11). The enforced confinement of women to sexual service is practiced today throughout the global empire.

> The United Nations estimates that as many as four million people are trafficked around the world each year, resulting in profits to criminal syndicates of up to seven to twelve billion dollars annually. . . . The trafficked women often find themselves trapped in debt bondage contracts, or virtual slavery, working as prostitutes . . . where their invisibility makes them vulnerable to outrageous abuses.[2]

What about Mordecai, Esther's uncle and guardian, a hero of the scroll? Does he willingly tender Esther to the harem? There is no evidence that he hides her or resists. Unlike Yocheved, Moses' mother, who hides him from Pharaoh's edict against male babies, Mordecai does not critique the collection of the girls. Male sovereign entitlement to the women is presumed. Rashi comments that having been taken to lie with a heathen, there is no reason for Mordecai to fear for this righteous woman, for she will bring redemption to her people. By singling Esther out as an exception, this midrash implicitly accepts the sexual enslavement of the other women. Even if Mordecai values Esther's position as the potential savior of her people, he never expresses outrage about the sex role to which she and the other women in the harem must conform.

Just as the Passover Haggada inquires about the origins of enslavement, we ask about Jewish foundations of gender abuse. Where did all of this gender trouble begin? There is a biblical story about Avraham and Sara that addresses this question. When the famine was heavy in the land of Israel, Avraham sought refuge in Egypt. Fearful that Sara's beauty would bring harm to him, he asked her to pretend to be his sister. He also saw that he could *benefit* through her. Avraham obtained his wealth from Pharaoh when Sara was taken to the royal court.

> When Avraham arrived in Egypt, the Egyptians saw the exquisite beauty of the woman. Pharaoh's ministers saw her and praised her to Pharaoh. And the woman *was taken* to the king's palace. On her account, Avraham profited; he gained sheep and oxen, donkeys, servants and maids, asses and camels [my emphasis, Genesis 12:16].

The text uses the same verb that describes Esther being *taken*, on account of her beauty. Struck by God with great sickness, Pharaoh uncovers the deceit. He blames Avraham for not telling him the truth about Sara, that she is married to him (Gen. 12:17). Why was Pharaoh so clear about the impropriety of this ruse, while Avraham was not? And why was Avraham so willing to accept the "gifts" from Pharaoh, when earlier he refused to accept gifts from Malki Zedek, a priest who acknowledged the "Almighty God?"

This story is a microcosm of the exodus from Egypt; it is a liberation story on a family scale. Abraham and Sara went down to Egypt on account of famine in Canaan. Sara was taken into captivity in Pharaoh's court. On behalf of Sara, whose cries are not vocalized in the text, God sent a plague to deliver her from bondage. But did Avraham *sell* Sara to an imperial Pharaoh in exchange for sheep, cattle, donkeys, servants, maids, asses, and camels?!

While anguishing in my heart about the character of our forefather, I cannot close my eyes to the terrible scheme that Avraham, ancestor of the Jewish people, seems to have finessed. He willfully denied Sara's full humanity as his spouse and degraded her to the status of a beauty object in an economic exchange among men. Avraham appears to have "pimped" Sara to obtain his fortune. A few verses *after* this incident, God reveals for the first time the future destiny of the Israelites to be enslaved (Gen. 13:13–16). Avraham's core gender abuse is arguably the cause of the eventual enslavement of the entire Jewish people in Egypt for four hundred years.

While the rabbis did often stress that one of the greatnesses of our Torah is that the protagonists are fully *human,* surely they did not intend that we emulate their shortcomings. We refine our own humanity by revealing their assumptions, analyzing and engaging with their struggles. The goal of this interpretation is neither outrage nor alienation, but more embracing empathy and resolve to improve our own behavior, and that of our societies. There is evidence of this process in the text. Before Avraham merits conceiving a child with Sara, God commands Avraham to sanctify his sex organ through circumcision. I recommend adding the intention to prevent the violation of women as a vital part of the covenant of circumcision, *brit mila.* This powerful symbolic act will begin to redress the presumption of male entitlement to women's bodies that we find expressed in the *Megilla,* in the Torah, and in our global economy.

The sale of women and children into prostitution is one of the most egregious contemporary violations of human rights. The United Nations acknowledges the alarming increase in the scale of sexual "trafficking" from the South and East toward voracious and perverse appetites for abusive sex in the West and North. This burgeoning business embeds patriarchal and class structures based upon extreme exploitation of some of the most vulnerable members of humanity; it sustains a degraded conjunction of money with power.

In the Scroll of Esther, recruiting virgins for sexual service to the king intensifies the former royal edict that commands women's subordination. Each family that surrenders or "pimps" its daughter, each community that does not protect its daughters, spouses, and sisters, is complicit. Jewish communities have long been involved in trafficking women, throughout the period of what was known as the "white slave trade."

> Even before they had left their homes in Russia and other parts of Eastern Europe, Jewish girls had been frightened by stories of prostitution rings that preyed upon unaccompanied females on the ships and at the sea ports. Their fears are not unfounded. The Jewish underworld made a steady profit by supplying the brothels of Eastern Europe, Latin America and the Near East with "white slaves."[3]

> By 1909, of 199 licensed brothels in Buenos Aires, 102 (51 percent) were run by Jewish madams, often wives of the slavers. The agents would even pay their passage across the Atlantic to Buenos Aires. These unsuspecting women would make the trip only to be met by thugs who abducted them to houses of prostitution.[4]

Today in Israel, and throughout the world, as in the Persian Empire,

> Many of these women and girls become "commodities," literally bought and sold for thousands of dollars, literally held in debt bondage. They are locked up in apartments, and have their passports and travel documents confiscated. Many women are subjected to violence, including rape. Yet most of the people who commit such human rights abuses are never brought to justice by the Israeli government [Amnesty International, May 18, 2000].

Women are rendered a sexual commodity subject to exchange among men. In the *Megilla,* the king is the preeminent male. He achieves retribution for Vashti's disobedience through sexual dominance and enslavement.

Many cultures, including the rabbis' and our own, have sublimated aspects of this system of valuing women for sex. For example, in tractate *Pesachim,* the Talmud cites the description of the use of oils in Achashverosh's harem as authoritative about women's general use of cosmetics (43a). By this analogy, *every* woman is symbolically a potential member of a harem, preening herself for sex with men. Hypersexed images in our own media and fashion perform a similar function, psychologically enforcing standards of appearance and behavior, priming girls and women to perform their "proper" gender roles. Where we do not actively critique the beauty/sex value system, we are perpetuating it.

Haman's racism follows immediately upon the heels of the king's sexism. While Vashti's rebellion against her spouse appears domestic, and Mordecai's political and religious, the scroll bends the gender specificity of these domains and demonstrates their interconnectedness. A prominent aid to the king, Haman becomes obsessed against the Jewish piety of Mordecai, who refuses to prostrate himself. Haman's wrath against Mordecai and the Jews closely parallels the king's fury against Vashti and the women.[5] The cause is also similar: both Vashti and Mordecai refused to submit to a self-absorbed man. Disdain for and subordination of women are the underlying conditions for the progression toward more violent evils that threaten to prevail under the jester-king. As the text successively strips away masks of authority, macabre, vain, and fickle circumstance threatens moral order. Insurgent against this backdrop, Esther schemes to dissuade the king from allowing the slaughter of the Jews. The text indicates her gradual ascent to power. At the moment that Zeresh, Haman's spouse, is predicting that Haman will fall, the eunuchs arrive according to Esther's bidding and *take* Haman to her party. This scene is a complete inversion of the opening incident. Whereas Vashti defiantly resists a *king's* summons, Haman is subordinate to the *queen's* summons. This gender contrast foreshadows Esther's eclipse of Haman and highlights the feminist trend instigated by Vashti at the outset of the scroll.

At her own peril, in the presence of the evil protagonist Haman, Esther carefully formulates her appeal. In this climactic scene (in Chapter Seven), Esther performs a subversive transformation of identity and power. She compasses simultaneously contradictory positions. She both submits and presides. While she is part of the system and empowered by it as queen, she postures as a humble servant who seeks favor in the king's eyes. Esther deftly maneuvers past the dangers of alienating the irascible king. She begins with words that appear to plead, but conceal accusation. If it were *only* that she and her entire people had been sold into bondage, then she would not deem her cause worthy (Esther 7:4). It is only total death and annihilation that merit troubling the king(!). Do we detect sarcastic understatement here; or is it Esther's awakening? Indeed she and her people, women, have been sold into sexual slavery. Yet she did not, or could not, resist. Esther is becoming aware that her two subordinated roles converge: woman and Jew. She makes an eloquent plea against enslavement and violence:

Let my life be given me at my petition, and my people at my request; for we are sold, I and my people, to be destroyed, to be massacred and to be exterminated [Esther 7:3–4].

In this statement, Esther reveals her hidden *otherness*. She is a Jew marked for annihilation by the king's edict; *and* a woman, held captive in sexual slavery. She opposes oppression doubly, as both woman and Jew. Her call for liberation refers to her people, Jews, and to her people, *women*.

"Coming out" as a Jew is paradoxical in this context, for she "passed" so easily as a non-Jew. Does being Jewish affect her behavior, or is being Jewish easily hidden? Esther reveals that she is not what she seems. External identity is a mask for her internal being; she *is* what she did not seem, a Jew. At the same instant, Esther "comes out" as a woman. Similarly to the way she unmasks the truth of herself as Jew, she unmasks the truth of herself as woman. Having masqueraded as a submissive being, she manifests herself as a potent, commanding leader who imminently takes the king's authority in her hands, legislates, and makes a royal appointment. This unfathomable inversion of her status re-creates her identity as Jew and woman. Indeed the transformation of the Jews in Persia from oppressed people to empowered self-defenders hinges on the transformation of the identity of "woman." Esther transforms herself from oppressed object to strident commanding subject. Her rise to power, however, is not self-absorbed like the king's and Haman's. Esther's indomitable humane compassion drives her to risk her own life to oppose narrow and violent evil. "If I perish, I perish" (Esther 4:16).

In the next (ob)scene of the *Megilla*, the king goes off to his garden, stymied and infuriated by the unmasking of Esther's identity and her vulnerability to Haman's plan to kill the Jews. Meanwhile, in another gender inversion, Haman pleads desperately with Esther for his own life. Achashverosh returns to find Haman falling atop her couch and exclaims: "Have you come also to conquer the queen with me in the house?!" (7:8). The text is not clear about Haman's intention; was it physical or sexual aggression? The language of *conquering* underlines the commodification of woman as an object to be possessed or occupied by men. The sexual nuance of this bombastic scene is heightened by the previous phallic imagery of the golden sovereign scepter the king extends to Esther when she comes to see him (Esther 5:2). Haman's position *on the queen* signals his intention to usurp power. Esther's body becomes the contested territory for male conquest, the site where the king experiences an intolerable threat to his power. Defending his territory, Achashverosh immediately deposes Haman.

In contrast to the male violence, Esther's strategy expresses her commitment to life. She seeks to repeal the scrolls that mandate annihilation (Esther 8:5). Yet, having won the power and compliance of the king, Esther has a rude awakening. Even the *king* has no power to revoke his own seal. The only recourse is to issue new orders giving permission to the Jews to defend themselves against their assailants (Esther 8:11). The bloody denouement of Chapter Nine, the destruction of seventy-five thousand lives, seems to be an irrevocable outcome of the immutability of the King's ph/fallible decree. Whereas Esther's solution respects the integrity of the body by *de*constructing the text, the monarch's solution destroys the body, while maintaining the text intact. The outcome in the story enacts the horrific consequences of the displacement of integrity from human life to text. Yet the celebration of Purim promulgated by Esther's scroll affirms her humane kindness. The obligations of Purim are giving gifts to the poor, exchanging food with friends, feasting and rejoicing, and listening to the scroll. These commandments reflect Esther's desire to nurture caring and mutual sustenance. By contrast, the violent outcome is a perverse inversion, a mockery of divine immutability, and a displacement of the sacred from our texts and table.

In the *Megilla,* racism is brought down, but sexism is not explicitly uprooted. This "activist" reading demonstrates one of the claims of feminist theory: human dignity is embedded in the relations between women and men, in families, in daily respect for the full humanity of girls and women. Violation of the female gender is one of the most prevalent sources of oppression. The messages of sexual oppression are broadcast in subliminal ways, internalized, and fulfilled in subtle and extreme abuses.

During the three days preceding her meeting with King Achashverosh, Esther, a prostituted woman, declares a communal fast in solidarity with herself as she incubates her strategy and steels her resolve to foil Haman's evil plan to destroy her people. Esther's fast creates a unique opportunity to inspect and strategize against the gendered roots of evil. As in Persia, while many of us feast on our material blessings and human freedoms, treacherous acts of inhumanity are plotted and implemented.

Esther was an activist whose potent insurgence foiled a plot of global proportions. Ultimately, Esther's liberation struggle is affirmed by her control over the text; Esther wrote the final authorized version of the scroll (Esther 9:29). According to some commentaries, the acceptance of the oral law by the Jewish people is undertaken at this time (Esther 9:27). Following Esther's lead, let us make a ritual innovation: sanctifying Ta'anit Esther, the Fast of Esther that precedes Purim. By the order of Esther, we fast in solidarity with all girls and women who are dehumanized on account of gender. The Fast of Esther is a day to begin to incubate *our* strategy and steel *our* resolve to foil the gendered roots of evil. The oppression of women is latent in the *Megilla* as it is latent in the structure of our families, communities, and nations, in our global economy and politics.

According to the legendary kabbalist Rabbi Isaac Luria, the concealment of the divine presence during the Babylonian exile is a reenactment of the drowse God imposed upon Adam during the creation of Eve. This feminist reading interprets the *Megilla* as a wake-up call to the Jewish people. It is time to unmask and dismantle the tacit sexist global consensus. It is time to deconstruct the perverse desire that makes trafficking profitable.

NOTES

1. Simone de Beauvoir, *The Second Sex,* trans. H. M. Parshley (New York: Vintage, 1989), 248.

2. Donna Hughs, "The Natasha Trade: The Trans-national Shadow-Market of Trafficking in Women," special issue of the *Journal of International Affairs,* 53(2), spring 2000; Global Survival Network, Jan. 1998.

3. Susan A. Glenn, *Daughters of the Shtetl* (Ithaca, N.Y.: Cornell University Press, 1990), 52.

4. Robert Weisbrot, *The Jews of Argentina* (Philadelphia: Jewish Publication Society, 1979), 60.

5. Athalya Brenner mentions this parallel in "Looking at Esther through the Looking Glass," in her collection *A Feminist Companion to Esther, Judith, and Susanna* (Sheffield, England: Sheffield Academic Press, 1995), 74.

VEGETARIANISM: A GLOBAL AND SPIRITUAL IMPERATIVE?

Richard H. Schwartz

WHILE RARELY DISCUSSED IN THE JEWISH COMMUNITY, a widely accepted aspect of modern life—the mass production and widespread consumption of meat—contradicts many fundamental Jewish teachings and badly harms people, communities, and the planet.

1. Judaism mandates that we should be very careful about preserving our health and our lives. The Talmud teaches that Jews should be more particular about matters of well-being than about ritual matters. If it is necessary to possibly save a life, Jews generally *must* (not may) violate the Sabbath, eat nonkosher foods, and even eat on Yom Kippur. The only laws that cannot be violated to preserve a life are those prohibiting murder, idolatry, and sexual immorality.

While the preservation of human health and life is arguably Judaism's most important *mitzvah,* animal-based diets have been strongly linked to heart attacks, strokes, various types of cancer, and other degenerative diseases. Migration studies show that when people from areas where disease rates are low migrate to the United States or another country with a high consumption of animal products, disease rates rise sharply. Dr. Dean Ornish has demonstrated that a very low-fat, almost vegan (no animal products at all) diet, along with other positive lifestyle changes can significantly reduce coronary blockages. The China/Oxford/Cornell study, called the Grand Prix of epidemiology by the *New York Times,* investigated sixty-five villages throughout China and found that disease rates correlated strongly with the consumption of animal products. The American Dietetic Association has stated that a well-balanced vegetarian diet is not only nutritionally adequate, but can reduce the risk of many diseases.

Unfortunately, few doctors are strongly promoting plant-centered diets, since medical training stresses medicinal and surgical treatments, rather than disease prevention. Also, animal-based industries have been spending vast amounts of money misleading people about the alleged health benefits of their products. This has led to many misperceptions, perhaps the most serious being what can be called the protein myth and the calcium myth. Believing that large amounts of dietary protein are necessary, most people consume far too much, and this is harmful to the kidneys and contributes to osteoporosis. The reason for this myth is that early research results on protein were obtained from experiments on rats. However, rats need far more protein than humans, as is shown from the facts that a rat mother's milk has almost half of its calories in protein, while a human mother's milk has only about 5 percent of its calories in protein. The excess protein acidifies the blood, and calcium is drawn from the bones to neutralize this excess acidity. This calcium is later excreted, along with the excess protein (since the human body cannot absorb extra protein), contributing to a negative calcium balance. This is why the countries that consume the most calcium, including the United States, Israel, and Scandinavian countries, have the highest rates of osteoporosis. Diets that have a variety of fruits, vegetables, whole grains, and legumes (such as soy products) provide adequate protein and calcium, without the hormones, antibiotics, and high cholesterol and fats of animal-based diets.

2. Another reason that Jews should seriously consider vegetarianism is Judaism's powerful teachings on compassion for animals. Judaism forbids *tsa'ar ba'alei chayim,* inflicting unnecessary pain on animals. Proverbs 12:10 teaches that "The righteous person considers the life of his or her animal." The psalmist states that "The Lord is good to all, and His tender mercies are over all His creatures" (Psalms 145:9). Concern for animals is even expressed in the Ten Commandments, which indicate that animals, as well as people, are to be permitted to rest on the Sabbath day. Moses and King David were chosen for leadership and Rebecca was deemed suitable to be a wife for the patriarch Isaac because they were kind to animals. Many Biblical laws command proper treatment of animals. For example, one may not yoke a strong animal to a weak animal and one may not muzzle an ox while he is working in a field of grain. The Talmud teaches that one must feed his or her animals before sitting down for a meal.

Contrary to Judaism's strong teachings on compassion to animals, most farm animals today—including most raised for kosher consumers—are raised on "factory farms," where they live in cramped, confined spaces, and are often drugged, mutilated, and denied fresh air, sunlight, exercise, and any enjoyment of life, before they are slaughtered and eaten. Since Jews are to be *rachmanim b'nei rachmanim* (compassionate children of compassionate ancestors), can we justify the force-feeding of ducks and geese to create pâté de foie gras? Can we justify taking day-old calves from their mothers so that they can be raised for veal in very cramped conditions? Can we ignore the killing of over 250 million male chicks immediately after birth at egg-laying hatcheries because they cannot produce eggs and have not been genetically programmed to have much flesh? Can we fail to protest when hens are kept in spaces so small that they cannot raise even one wing? Can we justify artificially impregnating female cows every year so that they will be able to produce more milk? Can we ignore the many other ways that modern intensive livestock agriculture violates Jewish teachings on compassion for animals?

3. Judaism teaches that "the earth is the Lord's" (Psalm 24:1) and that we are to be God's partners and co-workers in preserving the world. The Talmudic sages indicated great concern about reducing pollution. While God was able to say, "It is very good," when the world was created, today the world faces many environmental threats.

In 1993, more than 1,700 of the world's top scientists, including 104 Nobel laureates, signed a World Scientists' Warning to Humanity in which they indicated that "Human activities inflict harsh and often irreversible damage on the environment and critical resources. If not checked, many of the current practices put at serious risk the future that we wish for human society and the plant and animal kingdoms, and may so alter the living world that it will be unable to sustain life in the manner that we know." Perhaps the greatest threat facing humanity today is that of global climate change. There is overwhelming scientific agreement that the earth's average temperature may rise from 2.5 to 10.4 degrees Fahrenheit in the next century. Since the one-degree-Fahrenheit increase experienced in the last century has resulted in the melting of glaciers, the bleaching of coral reefs, an increase in the number and severity of storms, droughts, and wildfires, and other negative impacts, it can be seen that the projected temperature increase for the next century would have devastating consequences.

While recent increased public concern about global warming is very welcome, the many connections between typical American and other Western diets and global warming have generally been overlooked. Current modern intensive livestock agriculture and the consumption of meat contribute greatly to the four major gases associated with the greenhouse effect: carbon dioxide, methane, nitrous oxides, and chlorofluorocarbons.

The burning of tropical forests releases tons of carbon dioxide into the atmosphere and eliminates the ability of these trees to absorb carbon dioxide. The highly mechanized agricultural sector uses an enormous amount of fossil fuel to produce pesticides, chemical fertilizer, and other agricultural resources, and this also contributes to carbon dioxide emissions. Cattle emit methane as part of their digestive process, as do termites who feast on the charred remains of trees that were burned to create grazing land and land to grow feed crops for farmed animals. The large amounts of petrochemical fertilizers used to produce feed crops create significant quantities of nitrous oxides. Likewise, the increased refrigeration necessary to prevent animal products from spoiling adds chlorofluorocarbons to the atmosphere.

Modern intensive livestock agriculture contributes substantially to soil erosion and depletion, air and water pollution, overuse of chemical fertilizers and pesticides, the destruction of tropical rain forests and other habitats, global climate change, and other environmental damage.

Nearly six billion of the seven billion tons of eroded soil in the United States has been lost because of cattle feedlot production. Grazing animals have destroyed large areas of land throughout the world, with overgrazing having long been a prime cause of erosion. Over 60 percent of all U.S. rangelands are overgrazed, with billions of tons of soil lost each year. Cattle production is a prime contributor to every one of the causes of desertification: overgrazing of livestock, overcultivation of land, improper irrigation techniques, deforestation, and prevention of reforestation. In the United States, more plant species have been eliminated due to overgrazing by livestock than by any other cause.

Mountains of manure produced by cattle raised in feedlots wash into and pollute streams, rivers, and underground water sources. U.S. livestock produce an astounding 1.4 billion tons of manure per year (this amount works out to almost 90,000 pounds per second!), or about 130 times the amount excreted by the U.S. human population.

The tremendous amount of grain grown to feed animals requires extensive use of chemical fertilizer and pesticides, which cause air and water pollution. Various constituents of fertilizer, particularly nitrogen, are washed into surface waters. High levels of nitrates in drinking water cause illnesses to people, as well as animals.

Demand for meat in wealthy countries leads to environmental damage in poor countries. Largely to turn beef into fast-food hamburgers for export to the U.S., the earth's tropical rain forests are being bulldozed at a rate of a football field per second. Each imported quarter-pound fast-food hamburger patty requires the destruction of fifty-five square feet of tropical forest for grazing. Half of the rainforests are already gone forever, and at current rates of destruction the rest will be gone by the middle of this century. What makes this especially ominous is that half of the world's fast disappearing species of plants and animals reside in tropical rain forests. We are risking the loss of plant species that might hold secrets for cures of deadly diseases or might be good sources of nutrition. Also, the destruction of rain forests is altering the climate and reducing rainfall, with potentially devastating effects on the world's agriculture and habitability.

4. Based on Deuteronomy 20:19, 20, which prohibits the destruction of fruit-bearing trees in time of warfare, the Talmudic sages prohibited the waste or unnecessary destruction of all objects of potential benefit to people. Rabbi Samson Raphael Hirsch stated that this prohibition (*bal tashchit*) is the first and most general call of God: we are to "regard things as God's property and use them with a sense of responsibility for wise human purposes. Destroy nothing! Waste nothing!" He also stated that destruction includes using more things (or things of greater value) than is necessary to obtain one's aim.

Animal-centered diets require far more land, fuel, grain, water, pesticides, fertilizer, and other agricultural resources than vegetarian diets. The standard diet of a meat-eater in the United States requires 4,200 gallons of water per day (for animals' drinking water, irrigation of crops, meat processing, washing, cooking, etc.). A person on a vegan diet requires only 300 gallons per day. The production of only one pound of beef for human consumption in a semi-arid area such as California requires as much as 5,200 gallons of water, as contrasted with only 25 gallons or less to produce a pound of tomatoes, lettuce, potatoes, or wheat. *Newsweek* reported in 1988 that "the water that goes into a 1,000-pound steer would float a (naval) destroyer."

An animal-based diet also wastes energy. While an average of 10 calories of fuel energy is required for every calorie of food energy produced in the United States, many other countries obtain 20 or more calories of food energy per calorie of fuel energy. To produce one pound of steak (500 calories of food energy) requires 20,000 calories of fossil fuels, most of which is expended in producing and providing feed crops. It requires 78 calories of fossil fuel for each calorie of protein obtained from feedlot-produced beef, but only 2 calories of fossil fuel to produce a calorie of protein from soybeans. Grains and beans require only 2 to 5 percent as much fossil fuel as beef. The energy needed to produce a pound of grain-fed beef is equivalent to one gallon of gasoline.

5. Judaism stresses that we are to assist the poor and share our bread with hungry people. The Talmud states, "Providing charity weighs as heavily as all the other commandments of the Torah combined" (Baba Batra 9a). Farmers are to leave the gleanings of the harvest and the corners of the fields for the poor. On Yom Kippur, the holiest day of the Jewish year, while fasting and praying for a good year, Jews are told through the words of the Prophet Isaiah that fasting and prayers are not enough; they must work to end oppression and "share thy bread with the hungry" (Isaiah 58:6–7).

Over 70 percent of the grain grown in the United States is fed to animals destined for slaughter, while an estimated twenty million people worldwide die because of hunger and its effects each year. It takes up to sixteen pounds of grain to produce one pound of beef for human consumption in a feedlot. While the average Asian consumes between three hundred and four hundred pounds of grain a year, the average middle-class American consumes over two thousand pounds of grain, 80 percent of which comes in the form of meat from grain-fed animals. If Americans reduced their beef consumption by 10 percent, it would free up enough grain to feed all of the world's people who annually die of hunger and related diseases.

This evidence indicates that the food being fed to animals in the affluent nations could, if properly distributed, potentially end both hunger and malnutrition throughout the world. A switch from animal-centered diets would free up land and other resources, which could then be used to grow nutritious crops for people. This new approach would also promote policies that would enable people in underdeveloped countries to use their resources and skills to raise their own food.

Many people feel that there is plenty of grain being stored and that it is the actions of repressive Third World regimes that is causing hunger. While there has been some truth to this claim, there are signs that animal-centered diets are increasingly threatening world food security. Increasingly, affluent people are shifting toward diets involving meat and other animal products. One result is that China, with about 21 percent of the world's people, shifted in 1995 from being a grain-exporting country to a major grain importer. If this trend, promoted by agribusiness and global financial groups, continues, it will have severe consequences for future food security.

6. Judaism stresses that we must seek and pursue peace and that violence results from unjust conditions. While not a pacifist religion, Judaism mandates a special obligation to work for peace. While many commandments require a certain time and/or place for their performance, Jews are

to constantly "seek peace and pursue it" (Psalms 34:15). According to the Talmudic sages, God's name is peace, peace encompasses all blessings, and the first words of the Messiah will be a message of peace. While the Israelites did go forth to battle, they always yearned for the time when "nations shall beat their swords into plowshares . . . and not learn war any more" (Micah 4:3,4).

The Jewish sages taught that one of the roots of war is a lack of bread and other resources. Hence, although not commonly discussed, another argument for vegetarianism is that animal-centered diets, by their wasteful use of land, water, energy, and other agricultural resources, help to perpetuate the widespread hunger and poverty that frequently lead to instability, violence, and war.

In view of these important Jewish mandates to preserve human health, attend to the welfare of animals, protect the environment, conserve resources, help feed hungry people, and pursue peace and nonviolence—and since animal-centered diets violate and contradict each of these responsibilities—Jewish vegetarians argue that committed Jews, and others, should sharply reduce or eliminate their consumption of animal products.

One could say *dayenu* (meaning "it would be enough") after any of the arguments above, because each one constitutes by itself a serious conflict between Jewish values and current practice that should impel Jews to seriously consider a plant-based diet. Combined, they make an urgently compelling case for the Jewish community to address these issues. Making the situation even more urgent is the efforts of livestock agriculture and transnational financial groups to sharply increase the production of meat and other animal products.

Hence it is urgent that vegetarianism be put squarely on the Jewish agenda, and on other agendas, and that the many moral issues related to our diets be discussed. The revitalization of Judaism and the sustainability of the global environment depend on a shift to plant-based diets. A commission of rabbis, other Jewish scholars, health experts, nutritionists, environmentalists, and other objective experts should be formed to investigate the realities of the production and consumption of animal products and how they impinge on basic Jewish values.

The Biblical Case for Vegetarianism

God's first dietary regimen was strictly vegetarian: "And God said: 'Behold I have given you every herb yielding seed which is upon the face of the earth, and every tree, in which is the fruit of a tree yielding seed—to you it shall be for food'" (Genesis 1:29). That God's first intention was that people should be vegetarians was restated by Jewish classical Biblical commentators, such as Rashi, Abraham Ibn Ezra, Maimonides, and Nachmanides. It is significant that after giving this dietary law, God saw everything that He had made and "behold, it was very good" (Genesis 1:31). Everything in the universe was as God wanted it, in complete harmony, with nothing superfluous or lacking. The vegetarian diet was a central part of God's initial plan.

What about God's permission, given to Noah and his descendants, to eat meat? According to Rabbi Abraham Isaac Hakohen Kook, first Chief Rabbi of prestate Israel and one of the outstanding Jewish thinkers of the twentieth century, this permission was a temporary concession to human weakness. He felt that God, who is merciful to all of His creatures, would not institute an everlasting law that permits the killing of animals for food.

According to Isaac Arama, author of *Akedat Yitzchak,* God established another nonmeat diet, manna, when the Israelites left Egypt. Manna is clearly described in the Torah as a vegetarian food, "like coriander seed" (Numbers 11:7). This diet furthermore kept the Israelites in good health for forty years in the desert. When the Israelites cried for flesh, God only reluctantly provided it (in the form of quails). A great plague subsequently broke out, and many people died. The place where this occurred was named the Graves of Lust, perhaps an early warning of the negative health effects of the consumption of meat.

This argument is further supported by the belief of Rabbi Joseph Albo and Rav Kook that in the days of the Messiah, people will again be vegetarians. They base this belief on the prophecy of Isaiah: And the wolf shall dwell with the lamb. . . . And the lion shall eat straw like the ox. . . . And none shall hurt nor destroy in all My holy mountain (Isaiah 11:6–9). In the future ideal time (the Messianic age), people and animals will again not eat each other's flesh.

Although most Jews eat meat today, God's high ideal—the initial vegetarian dietary law—stands supreme in the Torah for Jews and the whole world to see. It is the ultimate goal toward which all people should strive.

Responses to Counterarguments

The above arguments strongly indicate to me that vegetarianism is the diet most consistent with Jewish values and God's preferences. I invite the reader to further investigate these arguments and sources, including other explanations and understandings that would defend meat consumption as acceptable within the ideal diet for Jews. I believe that my position would still remain strong. I feel, however, that to complete my arguments, I should address some of the challenges to my assertion that the ideal diet for Jews is vegetarianism.

> COUNTERARGUMENT 1. The Torah teaching that humans are granted dominion over animals (Genesis 1:26) gives us a warrant to treat animals in any way we wish.

Response: Jewish tradition interprets "dominion" as guardianship or stewardship: we are called upon to be co-workers with God in improving the world. Dominion does not mean that people have the right to wantonly exploit animals, and it certainly does not permit us to breed animals and then treat them as machines designed solely to meet human needs. In *A Vision of Vegetarianism and Peace,* Rav Kook states: "There can be no doubt in the mind of any intelligent person that [the Divine empowerment of humanity to derive benefit from nature] does not mean the domination of a harsh ruler, who afflicts his people and servants merely to satisfy his whim and desire, according to the crookedness of his heart. It is unthinkable that the Divine Law would impose such a decree of servitude, sealed for all eternity, upon the world of God, Who is 'good to all, and His mercy is upon all his works' (Psalms 145:9), and Who declared, 'The world shall be built with kindness'"(Psalms 89:33). This view is reinforced by the fact that immediately after God gave humankind dominion over animals (Genesis 1:26), He prescribed vegetarian foods as the diet best suited to humans (Genesis 1:29).

> COUNTERARGUMENT 2. The Torah teaching that only people are created in the divine image means that God places far less value on animals.

Response: While the Torah states that only human beings are created "in the Divine Image" (Genesis 5:1), animals are also God's creatures, possessing sensitivity and the capacity for feeling pain. God is concerned that they be protected and treated with compassion and justice. In fact, the Jewish sages state that to be "created in the divine image" means that people have the capacity to emulate the divine compassion for all creatures. "As God is compassionate," they teach, "so you should be compassionate."

> COUNTERARGUMENT 3. Inconsistent with Judaism, vegetarians elevate animals to a level equal to or greater than that of people.

Response: Concern for animals and the refusal to treat them cruelly and slaughter them for food that is not necessary for proper nutrition and, indeed, is harmful to human health, does not mean that vegetarians regard animals as being equal to people. Also, as indicated, there are many reasons for being vegetarian other than animal rights, including concern for human health, ecological threats, and the plight of hungry people.

Because humans are capable of imagination, rationality, empathy, compassion, and moral choice, we should strive to end the unbelievably cruel conditions under which farm animals are currently raised. This is an issue of sensitivity, not an assertion of egalitarianism with the animal kingdom.

COUNTERARGUMENT 4. Vegetarianism places greater priority on animal rights than on the many problems related to human welfare.

Response: As indicated, vegetarian diets are beneficial not just to animals. They also improve human health, help hungry people through better distribution of food and other resources, put less stress on endangered ecosystems, conserve valuable resources, and reduce the potential for war and violence. In view of the many global threats related to today's livestock agriculture, working to promote vegetarianism may be the most important action that one can take for global survival.

COUNTERARGUMENT 5. By putting vegetarian values ahead of Jewish teachings, vegetarians are in effect creating a new religion with values contrary to Jewish teachings.

Response: Jewish vegetarians are not placing so-called vegetarian values above Torah principles. They are saying that basic Jewish teachings that mandate that we treat animals with compassion, guard our health, share with hungry people, protect the environment, conserve resources, and seek peace, point to vegetarianism as the ideal God-directed diet for Jews today. Rather than rejecting Torah values, Jewish vegetarians are challenging the Jewish community to apply Judaism's glorious teachings.

COUNTERARGUMENT 6. Jews must eat meat on Shabbat and Yom Tov (Jewish holidays).

Response: According to the Talmud (T. B. Pesachim 109a), since the destruction of the temple, Jews are not required to eat meat in order to rejoice on sacred occasions. This view is reinforced in the works *Reshit Chochmah* and *Kerem Shlomo* and Rabbi Chizkiah Medini's encyclopedic work *Sdei Chemed,* which brings many classical sources on the subject. Recent scholarly articles by Rabbi Alfred Cohen and Rabbi J. David Bleich also conclude that Jews do not have to eat meat in order to celebrate the Sabbath and Jewish festivals. The fact that several chief rabbis, including Shlomo Goren, late Ashkenazic Chief Rabbi of Israel, and Sha'ar Yashuv Cohen, Ashkenazic Chief Rabbi of Haifa, have been or are strict vegetarians also strengthens this argument.

COUNTERARGUMENT 7. The Torah mandates that we eat korban Pesach and other korbanot (sacrifices).

Response: The great Jewish philosopher Maimonides believed that God permitted sacrifices as a concession to the common mode of worship in Biblical times. It was felt that had Moses not instituted the sacrifices, his mission would have failed and perhaps Judaism would have disappeared. The Jewish philosopher Abarbanel reinforced Maimonides' position by citing a *midrash* (rabbinic teaching) that indicated that the Israelites had become accustomed to sacrifices in Egypt, and thus God tolerated the sacrifices but commanded that they be offered only in one central sanctuary in order to wean the Jews from idolatrous practices.

Without the temple, sacrifices are not required today. And Rav Kook felt that there will only be sacrifices involving vegetarian foods during the Messianic Period. He based this on a *midrash* that states, "in the Messianic era, all sacrifices will cease, except thanksgiving offerings (which could be non-animal) which will continue forever."

COUNTERARGUMENT 8. Jews have historically had many problems with some animal rights groups, which have often opposed *shechita* (kosher slaughter) and advocated its abolishment.

Response: Jews should consider switching to vegetarianism not because of the views of animal rights groups, whether they are hostile to Judaism or not, but because it is the diet most consistent with Jewish teachings. It is the Torah, not animal rights groups, that indicates how far the treatment of animals is from fundamental Jewish values. The powerful Jewish teachings on proper treatment of animals was eloquently summarized by Samson Raphael Hirsch: "Here you are faced with God's teaching, which obliges you not only to refrain from inflicting unnecessary pain on any animal, but to help and, when you can, to lessen the pain whenever you see an animal suffering, even through no fault of yours."

COUNTERARGUMENT 9. The restrictions of *shechita* minimize the pain to animals in the slaughtering process, and thus fulfill Jewish laws on proper treatment of animals.

Response: This ignores the cruel treatment of animals discussed above in the many months prior to slaughter.

COUNTERARGUMENT 10. If Jews do not eat meat, they will be deprived of the opportunity to do many *mitzvot* (commandments).

Response: By not eating meat, Jews are fulfilling many *mitzvot,* such as showing compassion to animals, preserving health, not wasting, feeding the hungry, and preserving the earth. In addition, by abstaining from meat, a Jew reduces the chance of accidentally violating several prohibitions of the Torah, such as mixing meat and milk, eating nonkosher animals, and eating forbidden fats or blood.

There are other cases where Torah laws regulate things that God would prefer that people not do at all. For example, God wishes people to live at peace, but he provides commandments related to war, knowing that human beings quarrel and seek victories over others. Similarly, the Torah laws that restrict taking beautiful female captives in wartime are a concession to human weakness. Indeed, the sages go to great lengths to deter people from taking advantage of such dispensations.

COUNTERARGUMENT 11. Judaism teaches that it is wrong not to take advantage of the pleasurable things that God has put on the earth. Since He put animals on the earth and it is pleasurable to eat them, is it not wrong to refrain from eating meat?

Response: Can eating meat be pleasurable to religious persons when they know that as a result their health is endangered, grain is wasted, the environment is damaged, and animals are being cruelly treated? One can have pleasure without doing harm to living creatures. There are many other cases in Judaism where actions that people may consider pleasurable are forbidden or discouraged, such as the use of tobacco, drinking liquor to excess, sexual relations out of wedlock, and hunting.

COUNTERARGUMENT 12. A movement by Jews toward vegetarianism would lead to less emphasis on *kashrut* (dietary laws) and eventually a disregard of these laws.

Response: Quite the contrary. In many ways, becoming a vegetarian makes it easier and less expensive to observe the laws of *kashrut*. This might attract many new adherents to keeping kosher and eventually to other important Jewish values. As a vegetarian, one need not be concerned with mixing *milchigs* (dairy products) with *fleichigs* (meat products), waiting three to six hours after eating meat before being allowed to eat dairy products, storing four complete sets of dishes (two for regular use and two for Passover use), extra silverware, pots, and pans, and many other considerations incumbent upon the nonvegetarian who wishes to observe *kashrut* strictly.

COUNTERARGUMENT 13. I enjoy eating meat.
Why should I give it up?

Response: If one is solely motivated by what will bring pleasure, perhaps no answer to this question would be acceptable. But Judaism wishes us to be motivated by far more: doing *mitzvot,* performing good deeds and acts of charity, sanctifying ourselves in the realm of the permissible, helping to feed the hungry, pursuing justice and peace, and so on. Anyone who takes such Jewish values seriously should, I believe, be a vegetarian. And in view of the current agricultural, health, and environmental realities discussed above, there has never been a better time to switch to vegetarianism.

Even if one is primarily motivated by considerations of pleasure and convenience, the negative health effects of animal-centered diets should be taken into account. One cannot enjoy life when one is not in good health.

Additional information may be obtained at jewishveg.com, from my book *Judaism and Vegetarianism,* and from books by Roberta Kalechofsky, especially *Vegetarian Judaism.*

MY FATHERS, THE BALTIC

Philip Levine

Along the strand stones,
Busted shells, wood scraps,
Bottle tops, dimpled
and stainless beer cans.
Something began here
A century ago,
A nameless disaster,
Perhaps a voyage
To the lost continent
Where I was born.
Now the cold winds
Of March dimple
The gray, incoming
Waves. I kneel
On the wet earth
Looking for a sign,
Maybe an old coin,
An amulet
Against storms,
And find my face
Blackened in a pool
Of oil and water.

My grandfather crossed
This sea in '04
And never returned,
So I've come alone
To thank creation
As he would never
For bringing him home
To work, defeat,
And death, those three
Blood brothers
Faithful to the end.
Yusel Prishkulnick,
I bless your laughter
Thrown in the wind's face,
Your gall, your rages,
Your abiding love
For women and money
And all that money
Never bought,
For what the sea taught
You and you taught me:
That the waves go out
And nothing comes back.

BRINGING MESSIANIC CONSCIOUSNESS

David A. Cooper

AS THE CONVENTIONAL WORLD CELEBRATES the arrival of the third millennium in the Gregorian calendar, the Hebrew calendar marks the coming of the seventh millennium—in about 240 years. While the dating of the "Common Era" is based on the birth of Christianity, the dating of the Hebrew calendar is built upon a different concept. On the literal level, it is said that 5,761 years ago was the birth of Adam and Eve. On an esoteric level, the kabbalist would say that adamic consciousness came into its fullness 5,761 years ago—that the world witnessed a new realization of the relationship between each individual and the Source of Being. That is, human consciousness (as opposed to animal consciousness) was born as we became aware of our own awareness. This is what distinguishes human consciousness from other forms of consciousness. While animal life has extraordinary awareness, humans have the ability to be aware of and to contemplate our own awareness.

This ability to be aware of our own awareness has opened up vast possibilities. For, while most life is fully dependent upon divine providence, we humans, because of our consciousness, have the potential to participate in the unfolding of each moment. This potential, from a kabbalistic point of view, puts humanity in the position of being a continuing co-partner in creation with the Source of Being. Or, said another way, we have the potential of fully realizing the role we play as the Divine expresses Itself through us.

As our intrinsic awareness of this process becomes more developed, we become more wise, more compassionate, more enlightened. We gain more understanding of the way things work and an ever greater appreciation of the continuing dance of Creator and Creation, which are not two separate things but a single process we call Life. The Jewish perspective is that the full ripening of this understanding is a key purpose of human existence.

The kabbalists tell a story to express the progress of our understanding. They remind us that Adam/Eve was born during the "last hour" of the sixth day, just before Shabbat. Adamic consciousness could not come to fruition until almost all of the six days of creation had passed; similarly, the ripening of adamic consciousness—our enlightenment—will take time too. How much time? One thousand years for each day, or a total of six thousand years. Thus, the Jewish mystic believes that within the next 240 years human potential will reach a new plateau and we will enter a thousand-year era of Shabbat, a time when a new consciousness will transcend the way we view reality today. This, some would call "messianic consciousness."

What will things look like when the world is imbued with messianic consciousness? And more important, what is our individual and collective role in helping to bring about this new level of understanding of life? Some assume that we need only survive until the messiah arrives and fixes everything. Judaism suggests, however, that each and every one of us, and each and every act that is done, is a significant element in the birthing of messianic consciousness. In mystical terms, while a new consciousness for humanity will ultimately take the form of a profound paradigm shift, the real focus of our attention must be on the moment-to-moment awareness that leads up to that shift. The way each and every one of us works with our own awareness right now, again and again, is the crucial element in the unfolding of messianic consciousness.

As we reflect upon our lives, we face many important questions: who are we, how are we living our lives, how do we handle relationships, how do we earn a living, how do we serve the community, what are our goals and our ideals, and so forth. One fundamental arena that has enormous potential for deeply informing people in many of these vital areas I would like to generally call "spiritual development." In particular, as there is a mandate in the Torah for Jews to be a light unto the nations, I would like to look more closely at the potential role Judaism could play in daily life in a way that would more profoundly engage the process of raising awareness, thereby smoothing the way for the paradigm shift for all humanity.

There are at least ten key areas that invite exploration. Others are likely to arise. But the following ten subjects are so rich in possibilities that they are likely to keep us busy for some time to come.

1. Defining God in Absolute Versus Relative Terms

The primary issue in Judaism is how Jews present "God" to the world. The emphasis on the dualistic God, the God out there, the God with a temperament, is probably the most confusing aspect of the Jewish tradition for Jews and non-Jews alike. Kabbalah has always been clear that Ein Sof, the boundless Source, is nondual, has no attributes, is a simple, all-inclusive Oneness. This is the essential truth of Jewish teaching. The faces of God to which we relate in dualistic terms meet many needs, but we must also explore and clearly articulate the true nature of Ein Sof and the interplay of this Oneness with god-names like Yod-Hey-Vov-Hey, Adonoy, El, Elohim, Shaddai, Tzevaot, Makom, Shalom, and so forth.

2. Inclusivity and Impartiality versus Exclusivity and Chosenness

The understanding of the Oneness of Ein Sof must be brought to bear on clarifying the interconnectedness of everything. Nothing can be separated from the Source, and thus exclusivity is a self-contradiction. This means that the issue of chosenness must be illuminated in a way that does not alienate Jews and non-Jews alike. Clearly chosenness is not a reference to a hierarchical structure which implies some kind of superiority; rather it has to do with the role individual parts play in a wholeness which could not exist without the sum of its parts. Every individual and every organic structure is chosen, so to speak, for the role it plays in this universe. In this context, the mystical role Judaism plays in the unfolding of the universe has profound consequences, particularly from a kabbalistic perspective, for it has been "chosen" to reveal the interconnectedness of all creation with Ein Sof, the boundless Source.

3. Full Integration of the Feminine

Although major advances have been made in this generation for the full integration of the feminine, there are vast areas that continue to need attending in Jewish "law," in the wording of the Talmud, in the Midrash, and in virtually all parts of the Jewish world. The most offensive example that continues full-blown is the insistence on referring to "God" as He or Him, when everyone "agrees" that God has no gender. An enormous healing awaits and is dependent upon the full integration of the feminine in action and deeds, not in words alone.

4. Deep Psycho-Spiritual Exploration of the Wounded Jew

There is a widespread, almost epidemic dis-ease among Jews today that has not been clearly investigated. It expresses itself in a kind of self-hatred, a feeling of embarrassment for anything done by a fellow Jew or the state of Israel, by self-criticism, fear, frustration, anger, bitterness, and a sense of alienation. It is often expressed in a sense of entitlement for exceptional treatment in Jewish environments, in unwarranted expectations for what Judaism is supposed to deliver, in highly charged reactions to evocative language, in strong opinions, in ethnocentrism, and in xenophobia. This alienated feeling—what I would call woundedness—can be found in a large percentage of the Jewish population; it is one of the key elements of the phenomenon, especially present in the latter half of the twentieth century, of extraordinary numbers of Jews seeking spiritual engagement in other traditions, in anything but Judaism.

5. New Emphasis on What It Means to Be a Jew

The definition of what it means to be a Jew continues to confuse and lead to contention. Not even the state of Israel has been able to find a resolution to this problem. Up to now, the emphasis tends toward legalisms, bloodlines, maternity, and talmudic debate. It may well be that this question of Jewishness is one that ultimately leads toward what is called a "teku" in the Talmud, an argument that will not be resolved until the messiah comes. Meanwhile, the essential heartfulness, compassion, openness, love, and caring that are fundamental teachings of Judaism seem to be given short shrift to the extent that "lovingkindness" is generally viewed as a Buddhist teaching, "charity" as something that Christians believe in, "devotion" as something Hindus are good at, and "ecstasy" as something owned by the Sufis. The time has come to ask ourselves what Judaism might look like when messianic consciousness has fully come into its own, and then ask ourselves why we need to wait for the messiah to live this kind of Judaism in its fullness right now? What an amazing light that questioning would cast on the real treasures that are easily accessible in Judaism today.

6. Exploration of Alternative Practices

The rapid proliferation of communication and networking is one of the most prominent signs of the increasing integration of the world. There is a cross-fertilization of a wide variety of ideas and technologies, and the ghetto mentality of walling oneself or one's community behind barriers to keep the world out is becoming less and less feasible as a strategy to maintain group coherence. Religion faced a similar tidal wave when science challenged it in the eighteenth and nineteenth centuries. Judaism can learn much and be nurtured by a wide variety of alternative practices, as well as learning from other traditions. This does not mean it will be necessary to merge into one world tradition; rather to respect the plurality of individual teachings while understanding places where there are common touchpoints and universal goals. By opening our arms and hearts to each other, everyone gains.

7. The Community at Large: Social Action

Secular Jews have traditionally played an active role in social action. A large number of Jewish institutions and synagogues have programs for helping others. To a great extent, however, many of these programs are defined in a Jewish context, channeling financial and other support to Jewish organizations, Israel, and so forth. Such intracommunal support is, of course, important. On the other hand, even though many Jews are involved in a wide spectrum of social issues, Judaism itself is not known for its international concerns with environmental issues, ecology, hunger, poverty, and the like. The Jewish renewal movement is clearly making inroads in these arenas, and activists like Arthur Waskow stand out for bringing a Jewish presence to many of these areas of concern. Jewish renewal rabbi and leader Reb Zalman Schacter-Shalomi has even called for a rethinking of what is kosher to include these social action issues.

His initiative offers precisely the attitude of inclusivity and interconnectedness that will mark the times of messianic consciousness. Meanwhile, however, a great deal more awareness and activism is needed in the mainstream Jewish community to bring home the younger generations of Jews who are highly motivated to become involved in social action.

8. The Relationship of a Congregation with Its Rabbi

One of the most important points often missed in discussions of Jewish life is the relationship between a congregation and its rabbi. This is a sensitive subject and rabbis don't like to bring it into the open, even though it is often a major topic of conversation when rabbis are privately discussing their pulpit with each other. Many congregations are respectful and generous in their treatment of the rabbi. However, there are also many situations in which the rabbi is not treated as a spiritual guide, but as a performer who is rated on how he or she fills seats, how much money is raised, how many new members join the congregation, how wonderful and innovative—particularly at High Holiday time—is each sermon, and so forth.

Some of this is simply the name of the game, and clergy in other traditions suffer the same problems as rabbis. But it is known that rabbis generally have a higher burnout and dropout ratio than other denominations, and it is known as well—joked about in many circles—that presidents and officers of synagogues often play power games with the rabbi, making for a dysfunctional situation. This phenomenon has not been adequately studied, and many rabbis, as well as their congregations, suffer the consequences.

Part of such a study should address such questions as, What do Shabbat and Holy Days mean for a rabbi who is always working at these times? What would be the potential of balancing the load with a co-rabbi, particularly with a gender balance as well? What financial arrangements should be made to protect the rabbi from those holding the purse strings? How much time is acceptable to take off? and How much do rabbis themselves invite abuse through codependency and insecurity? These are important issues for the health of a congregation.

9. Greater Exposure to Mystical Judaism

People continue to be afraid and uninformed or misinformed about the mystical side of Judaism, both in terms of Kabbalah and Hasidism. Most mainstream rabbis have had only modest training in this aspect of the tradition. Many yeshivas continue to focus on the *halachah,* the law, without much balance in study of the *agadata,* which provides profound teachings that illuminate a vast amount of hidden wisdom in the Talmud. Very little has been done to look at Torah, halachah, prayer, Shabbat, and the Holy Days through the eyes of Kabbalah. Yet this is clearly a thirst expressed again by Jews and non-Jews alike. The entire scope of Yiddishkeit will benefit by looking more closely into mystical understanding.

10. Rediscovering Contemplative Judaism

In many ways the opening of the mystical side of Judaism goes hand-in-hand with rediscovering contemplative Judaism. Much of Judaism was built on contemplative practices, but they were not as clearly defined as in Buddhism, for example. In Judaism, prayer, study, devotion, celebration, fasting, chanting, visualization, repetition, memorization, and silence are all natural parts of the daily life of normative Jewish practice. All of these have elements of meditative techniques. Many of the Jewish sages would today be called great meditators; we can see this clearly in their writings.

Many Orthodox Jewish practitioners today have great concentration skills, which is the foundation of most meditation techniques. Traditional Jewish lifestyle is imbued with meditative techniques like these. The question is how Jews who choose not to be Orthodox will be able to develop the contemplative skills and understanding which are in many ways a prerequisite for gaining a view of the layers of wisdom hidden under the surface of Jewish teaching. Moreover, how do we make a breakthrough with Orthodox practitioners to appreciate the contemplative tools already in their hands? I don't think it is an overstatement to say that the contemplative approach, specifically meditation, has been the single most attractive aspect of the practices that have accompanied the growth of Buddhism in the West over the past forty years. Yet although such practices are a natural part of Judaism, many rabbis do not understand them—indeed they often fear them—and thus they are unable to bring these simple meditative practices to their own congregations. What is needed is a much broader program, not simply "mindfulness" training, but a program that deals with the many meditative techniques that can be easily adapted to a Jewish lifestyle.

All of the points noted above are part of a holistic approach to bring Judaism to the fullness of its potential in our times. None of the points individually is the solution; all of them collectively need to be addressed and attended. The riches of Judaism are extraordinary. Many of these gems remain buried under confusion, antipathy, and outright alienation. But the direction is for greater understanding of each other and the world at large. Judaism could play a major role in this process of bringing messianic consciousness, or it could stay on the sidelines. Yet Jewish input will be sorely missed if it is not heard. It is up to us.

PRAYER AS REBELLION

Leonard Felder

FROM INTERVIEWING OVER 250 MEN AND WOMEN about why they pray or why they don't pray, I have found that the reasons are almost never theoretical or theological. Rather, they are highly personal. If you want to understand what draws someone into a deep relationship with spirituality or what sends an individual far away from belief, ask that person to tell you his or her personal story.

Thirty years ago, when I entered Kenyon College in Ohio as a freshman psychology major, I was just about ready to stop believing in God and to start taking a break from Judaism. For two summers in high school I had volunteered with my temple youth group to teach in the inner city of Detroit, only to find out that the slum landlord who was gouging the families of the students at my summer school was actually the president of my temple. In addition, my mother had died at the age of forty-six after a four-year battle with cancer that kept getting worse despite my frequent prayers for her recovery.

So when my brilliant and charismatic Kenyon English professor insisted during a well-composed lecture that "religious faith is for cowardly sheep," I was more than ready to sign up for his brand of elitist atheism. For the first time in my life I imagined breaking free of the shackles of being a Jew, the son of a Holocaust survivor—where at each family meal if I didn't finish my vegetables my father told me it was a "victory for Hitler."

My atheism felt good for a while, until I began to read some fascinating books that made me skeptical about my skepticism. The turning point came when I began to devour the writings of Dr. Viktor Frankl, which explored the possibility of finding daily meaning, purpose, and dignity, even in Auschwitz. Despite losing his father, mother, brother, and wife to the Nazis, Frankl continued to help people in the camps focus on the powerful inner voice deep inside us that looks for holiness, creativity, and meaning even in the most awful and oppressive conditions.

Essentially, Frankl's message was that even if you can't control many of the externals of life, you can still find strength and a profound humanity by looking deep within for a connection to your own soul and to the soul of the universe, which many call God. He demonstrated, both in his own life as a camp survivor and as a rebel against the atheism of Freud, that if you search for a spiritual connection to a loving Source that co-partners with human beings to repair this broken world, you may be able to create a life of dignity and purpose.

For over twenty years I have been working as a psychotherapist with a specialty in spiritual and religious issues, in many cases helping men and women regain their connection to Jewish spiritual teachings that can help keep them on track toward co-creating a better world. Like Viktor Frankl, whom I later studied with personally, I have been amazed at how much a person's spiritual search for meaning and ways of being of service can improve his or her sense of health and fulfillment. I've seen repeatedly that intelligent men and women, especially those who have lost faith in God or religion, are still very hungry for a connection to a sense of spiritual meaning and daily purpose.

I had thought as a freshman at Kenyon that atheism was the most rebellious thing I could do. From working with hundreds of courageous and passionate counseling clients, I now believe that finding progressive ways to use prayer and daily spiritual practice for connecting with holy energies of compassion and creativity is an even more rebellious act. Following are a few brief examples of what I mean by "prayer as rebellion."

1. Rebelling Against the Mortal Kings and Queens

When I was a teenager reading the prayer books at temple, I never warmed up to the Hebrew phrase found in many prayers, "Melech ha-olam," which often gets translated as "King of the world." It seemed patriarchal, anthropomorphic, and old-fashioned to my child-of-the-1960s sensibilities to be praying to a "King" or a "Sovereign." It reminded me of servants in ancient and medieval times bowing down to corrupt kings and queens, or to modern sheep following lock-step behind a political party or a flawed politician who was telling them what to do.

But during more than twenty years of courses, readings, and study with some outstanding rabbis from all branches of Judaism, I have come to see the prayers that seek to connect with "Melech ha-olam" in a very different light. I think of Jews in ancient times and the Middle Ages who were able to stand strong against corrupt kings and queens because we Jews believed there was a higher morality, a more universal guiding force, a Source of justice and compassion that was far more profound than some mortal king or queen. To pray each day for guidance and strength from an energy source that is the quintessence of mercy and caring, even while a mortal king or queen is threatening to kill us for not being loyal to the local despot, is quite a radical concept. It has made Jews continue to be a dangerous thorn in so many corrupt leaders' power grabs over the centuries.

During these twenty years of study with numerous Jewish scholars and teachers, I've also learned to see "Melech ha-olam" not as a ruler, but rather as a Ruling Force, a Guiding Principle, or a Preeminent Source that is perpetually expressing and co-creating the world. In Jewish spirituality, we are not cowardly sheep but rather important partners and repairers in the ongoing process of creation. To pray each day and to ask for guidance on how to help create justice, fairness, compassion, and healing is a bold act of strength and dignity.

But what if you don't believe in a God who co-creates the world or expresses the whole of the world in daily life? For example, I recently counseled a very intelligent woman named Sheila who teaches biochemistry at a nearby university. During her third session, when we happened to be discussing her estrangement from Judaism, Sheila told me, "My husband and my daughter want me to come with them more often when they go to synagogue, but I simply do not feel comfortable in a cavernous sanctuary saying, 'Help me! Help me!' to a nonexistent father figure or heavenly king."

I didn't try to change Sheila's mind, but several weeks later I was struck by the way she explained why she loves biochemistry: "There's this indescribable sense of mystery and wonder I feel when I'm trying to understand the nature of how cells communicate with each other and turn into such remarkable life forms. It is beyond words to contemplate the beauty of how life unfolds." Sheila's passionate description of the miracle of life sounded to me a lot like Rabbi Abraham Joshua Heschel's theology of "radical amazement," in which humans are essentially connecting with the Preeminent Source of life during those moments when we feel deeply moved by the wonder and mystery of it all.

I suggested to Sheila, "The next time you are in a synagogue with your family, or if you are out in nature taking a walk, or if you're at home about to connect with your loved ones before a meal, try an experiment for a moment. Offer up a prayer to the same mysterious force that animates the cells and creates such amazing life forms. Whether you call that mysterious ruling force God, or higher wisdom, or the guiding principle of the universe, imagine yourself connecting with it directly and expressing what a blessing it is to live in such a world. Instead of translating the words 'Melech ha-olam' in your blessing as King of the Universe, see how it feels if you translate these words as Ruling Force or Pulsing Source of all that is. Try and connect with that same radical wonder and mystery that you feel for the miracle of cells, biochemistry, and amazing life forms."

Sheila told me a few weeks later, "At first I was hesitant. Could I really think of God as the ruling force or hidden pulse that underlies all of biology and chemistry? I felt skeptical until one Saturday at synagogue during a silent prayer when I was holding my daughter's hand and I imagined connecting with the ever-present pulse of the universe that I sometimes can feel between her and me. At times like that, I feel as though she and I are connected on a soul level far beyond just biology. In those moments, I tend to be somewhat open to the possibility that we might be connected through the Preeminent Source of all that is, through some sort of higher wisdom, or maybe even God."

2. Prayer as a Rebellion against the Tyranny of the Anxious Human Mind

In 1927, at the University of Berlin, a Jewish woman named Bluma Zeigarnik, who was researching brain psychology mechanisms, came upon an important finding that says a lot about how human beings respond to prayer and spirituality. She showed a large number of human subjects a circle that was seven-eighths complete and found that the vast majority focused their eyes and their attention on the one-eighth of the circle that wasn't complete. This phenomenon, which was later named "the Zeigarnik effect," explains why our anxious, problem-seeking brains can't seem to notice what's going right in our lives but seem to be pulled toward the next unsolved problem. Is it any wonder your spouse, your boss, your parents, or your own self-critical brain tends to focus only on what's incomplete and takes for granted or ignores what is healthy or going well?

Jewish spirituality recommends saying a prayer or reciting a blessing whenever you notice, even for a moment, that something is going right. It's as though the ancient rabbis knew that our brains were good at problems but lousy at appreciating life or moments of peace. It is a radical liberation step to rise above anxiety for at least a few moments each day to appreciate that some things are going well, even in tough times.

If you want to outsmart the anxious, never-satisfied brain, Jewish spirituality offers you the chance to get in the habit of starting each day with Modeh Ani (if you are a man) or Modah Ani (if you are a woman), a profound twelve-word Hebrew prayer that can be translated in English this way: "I am so grateful in front of You, ruling force of time and existence, for renewing my soul with compassion and purpose. You are dependable beyond measure."

Instead of starting the day with immediate worries, discomforts, or a sense of falling behind already on your schedule, Jewish teachings recommend saying essentially to God or the universe, "I have a beautiful soul and it's being renewed for another day so that I can be of service and experience the wonders of being alive. Modah/Modeh Ani, I am very grateful for this." You may find that if you start some or all of your days with this spiritual practice, your mind becomes more adept at noticing not just what's a problem but also what's a source of joy.

For some of my counseling clients, saying thank you to God for renewing our souls each morning has made these individuals significantly less anxious and more productive. But for many of my counseling clients who are skeptical or not interested in talking to a mysterious and indescribable Divine Presence, the prayer can be just as effective if you use it to offer heartfelt thanks each morning to the universe or to nature.

As one counseling client told me recently, "If I imagine myself feeling grateful to God, that starts a whole argument in my head about what God is or isn't. But if I say the Modeh prayer and express my gratitude to life or the universe, I feel immediately more energized and I just might be including God or the Divine Presence in this thank-you message."

3. Prayer as a Rebellion Against Passivity or Withdrawal

I think back again to the Kenyon College professor and to the dualistic view of human beings he offered. He said there were those who fought for justice and there were those who did nothing more than pray and ask God to do it all for them. Only by studying Jewish history and theology for many years did I begin to realize just how wrong this professor was with regard to the way prayer is viewed in Judaism. Rather than being a passive act or a withdrawal from the world, Jewish prayer is a way of waking up the soul, clarifying the mind, and summoning up strength for doing good in the world. I have found a few specific Jewish blessings (which I've detailed in my book *Seven Prayers That Can Change Your Life*) that I have seen numerous counseling clients use on a daily or weekly basis in order to make sure they follow through on their goals and visions for repairing the world.

One of the most remarkable prayers I have been prescribing to men and women for many years is the Netilat Yadayim ("raising up the hands") prayer that includes washing your hands and asking God or the Creative Source to help you raise up your actions to make an impact on your corner of the world. In English this prayer can be translated this way: "Blessed are You, Eternal One, Source of all that is, Who guides us on ways to become holy, and Who inspires us to lift our hands, to raise up our actions, and be of service."

I have seen many men and women use this prayer midmorning when they're procrastinating or having trouble staying on track. Simply by running water over your hands and connecting with a Creative Source, it has been effective for over 70 percent of my counseling clients who have used it. Far from being passive, this ancient prayer has helped many men and women bounce back from disappointments and get back on track with their progressive goals. Rather than being held back by feelings of sluggishness or discouragement, this prayer can clarify the mind and lift up your spirits by renewing your efforts at making each day meaningful and productive.

For example, Joyce is an extremely brilliant woman and talented social worker who grew up with leftist parents who had given up on Jewish theology but had stayed involved in secular Jewish activism. Like many atheists, Joyce had always assumed prayer was a passive activity and that repairing the world demanded that people stop waiting for God's help.

But one afternoon we were discussing Joyce's tendencies toward procrastination and distractibility. Like many innovative people, Joyce has several good ideas and projects she hasn't been able to focus on or complete. I asked her if she'd be willing to try an experiment—to wash her hands and offer up a prayer. In Joyce's case, this prayer was being offered up to the infinite Source of justice and compassion, asking for help in following through on a project Joyce had thought up for assisting unwed mothers who were falling through the cracks of the social services system. Joyce's innovative ideas regarding how to help these moms and their children were excellent, but she'd been too busy and distracted by other demands on her time to focus sufficiently on this important project.

A few days after our discussion, Joyce noticed she was procrastinating again and so she went to the sink, washed her hands, and asked silently for help with focusing and following through. As she later reported, "There was a part of my brain that was still skeptical and hesitant. I'd say maybe 90 percent of my mind was still not sure if it was OK for a nice Jewish atheist like me to be saying a prayer. But there was also 10 percent of my mind that was curious about the possibility that maybe there truly is a higher source of justice and compassion. And that if I asked this

Source to give me strength and focus, it might help me stay on track and get a very important project done."

In fact, that is what happened. Like many others, Joyce found the radical act of connecting with a higher wisdom did help her stick to her goal of putting together a program that has been very useful for assisting numerous unwed mothers. As Joyce admits, "I still don't know for sure if there is a God or if my parents were right and it's all an illusion. But I do know that letting myself open up to the possibility of making a commitment 'to be of service' and declaring that commitment to an infinite Source of justice and compassion has helped me get the job done. I've learned that true prayer is not about being passive—true prayer is a way to make sure you boost your energy and push for positive changes to happen."

The attacks on the World Trade Center and the Pentagon, along with the bioterrorism that followed a few weeks later, caused a marked increase in anxiety for many of us. Even if you tried not to be fearful or upset, you may have noticed yourself feeling just a little bit more impatient, short-tempered, or easily agitated by people and events in your daily life. You may have found yourself getting worked up by what you saw on the television news and then later inadvertently taking out your frustrations on co-workers, loved ones, or even on a slower-than-molasses clerk who was making you wait for a painfully long amount of time.

One of the purposes of Jewish prayer is to help us creatively rise above fear, edginess, and impatience. For example, there is a spiritual practice in Judaism that if your child, parent, spouse, friend, or a nearby stranger is starting to get on your nerves, you need to stop yourself from lashing out with hurtful remarks and instead take a moment to say a blessing for this individual. You will need to catch yourself right before you lash out with a shaming comment or a dirty look, so you can take a moment to say silently the familiar ancient blessing that comes from the Book of Numbers, "May God bless you and keep you. May God illuminate your way and be gracious unto you. May God raise up in your direction and guide you and give you peace and wholeness."

For instance, I was counseling a man named Brian who had lost a beloved family member in the World Trade Center and who was telling me how fearful he'd become and how impatient and short-tempered his reaction had been recently with his wife. Brian admitted, "The last thing I want to do now is to take out my pain on my wife, but I'll tell you my fuse is very short these days." When I asked Brian if he would be willing say a silent blessing for his wife right at the moment when he was about to lash out at her with a barbed comeback, he wasn't sure at first. Brian commented, "Are you saying I need to let her walk all over me because I'm a little too edgy right now?"

I replied, "No, you don't need to let her 'walk all over you,' but you might want to say a silent blessing and see if that helps you stand up for yourself in a less abrasive way. Over the next few weeks, Brian tried using these ancient words to calm himself during stressful moments. He reported back, "I was surprised at how quickly I could snap out of my impatience and remember that I really do love my wife. Asking God to bless her made it very hard to trash her with my words. And it gave me a few extra seconds to calm down and talk to her like a human being."

As I've discovered with many of the people I've counseled, each of us has a different story and a different set of issues to overcome if we are to live up to our potential as spiritual human beings, guided by a tradition that asks us to be instruments for healing and repair. I hope that if you, too, have been held back—by personal frustrations with parts of Judaism, or by bad experiences with people who were not living up to their spiritual values, or by a professor or other role model who told you that atheism was more courageous than prayer—that you will consider reexamining the power and the intelligence found in prayers that are meant to stir up our rebelliousness and our strengths. Even though most people go through their entire lives without knowing the deeper meanings of the prayers that are recited each day by millions of Jews, I hope you will take the time to find out what these prayers have to say about courage, renewal, and commitment to doing good. You may find that even some of the prayers you never took seriously are in fact an important source of strength and clarity for making each day count.

THE WORSHIP REVOLUTION

Eric H. Yoffie

*I propose that we proclaim a new Reform revolution which will
make synagogue worship our foremost concern.*

REFORM JEWS ARE REDISCOVERING the power and the purpose of prayer.
We sense that our Judaism has been a bit too cold and a bit too domesticated; we yearn to sing to God, to let our souls fly free. And we feel that
through prayer we can rediscover our inner selves, and tie ourselves to the
collective body of Israel.

There is nothing surprising about this. Prayer is an irrepressible expression of the human spirit, and we Jews appeared on the historical scene
as a praying people. Yes, we know how hard prayer is. We know that moments of true inspiration are rare; we do not expect that every Shabbat
we will leave the synagogue personally transformed. But we do expect to
be gently moved each time we come to temple. And we do expect, from
time to time, that our prayers will make us feel closer to God.

Does this mean that Reform Judaism is abandoning the rationalism and
intellectual rigor which are the foundations of Jewish belief? Heaven forbid. When Reform Jews enter the synagogue, we refuse to check our brains
at the door.

Reform Judaism welcomes exuberance and song as well as ideas, celebrates the cerebral but pulsates with emotion. Judaism has always prescribed two paths to tradition: the path of the mind and the path of the heart. Torah study is the way of thinking, prayer the way of feeling. And even though these paths are parallel, the Jew has always been required to walk them both. Therefore, the Reform Jew must be both a studying Jew and a praying Jew.

We must ask ourselves: What is happening with worship in our synagogue? I have found that the prayers in many congregations are heartfelt, the music uplifting, and the participation enthusiastic. But far too often, services are tedious, predictable, and dull. Far too often, congregants pray without fervor or concentration. Far too often, the music is dirgelike and the Torah readings lifeless, incapable of triggering true emotion and ascent. Forty percent of Americans attend congregational worship every week; for Jews, the figure drops to 10 percent. We joke about two-day-a-year Jews, but we know in our hearts that the fault is not entirely theirs. We need to ask ourselves why so many of these Jews feel religiously unsatisfied in our synagogues.

There is a certain irony in these numbers. The Jews gave prayer to the world and authored the Psalms—the most passionate, poetic, and beautiful prayers ever composed. How is it that we are today the least worshipful of peoples in North America?

It is also ironic that we Reform Jews find ourselves in this situation, because our Movement came into being as a liturgical revolution. Reform Judaism did not begin with ethics, social justice, or personal autonomy; it was a reaction to the chaos, incomprehensibility, and mechanical mumbling of the then-dominant forms of Jewish prayer. Worship reform was the very heart of early Reform Judaism; classical Reform Jews, then as now, brought a deep earnestness to issues of prayer.

So what happened? Nineteenth-century innovations no longer suffice, but we are uncertain of what should come instead. And we Reform Jews are, on the whole, quite conservative in our worship patterns. We say we want prayer that is authentically Reform, but this usually means "what I remember from *my* temple when I was growing up." And no two of us ever seem to remember the same thing. Generational differences are particularly pronounced. Our congregations, therefore, often confront a multiplicity of conflicting worship demands. Older members threaten to vote with their checkbooks if worship is changed, while younger members threaten to vote with their feet if it is not.

The pressures of the worship wars have created a turf consciousness unusual for our Movement. Caught in the crossfire, rabbis and cantors sometimes insist they alone have authority over worship. Lay leaders seem to alternate between indifference and the expectation that their rabbi will do their worshiping for them. And finger-pointing is all too common. Lay leaders complain to me that their rabbi has introduced too much Hebrew, or too little Hebrew, too many changes, or too few changes; and that their cantor does not let them sing, or sings music they do not like. Rabbis and cantors tell me how frequently their members greet every new idea with that well-worn refrain: "But we've never done it that way before!" In such an atmosphere, even some of our most dynamic congregations have grown fearful of innovation.

But there is no reason for despair. A collective resolve is emerging in our Movement to overcome this paralyzing fear of change. We have leaders and congregations whose creativity and commitment to renewal will light our way.

I propose, therefore, that we proclaim a new Reform revolution. Like the original Reform revolution, it will be rooted in the conviction that Judaism is a tradition of revival, redefinition, and rebellion; and like the original, this new initiative will make synagogue worship our foremost concern.

I further propose that this worship revolution be built upon the premise of partnership: rabbis will be its architects, cantors its artists, and lay people its builders. This has always been our way. No other religious movement in Jewish life has been as democratic, as open, and as rooted in the collective partnership of rabbi, cantor, and lay person. And prayer is not a noun but a verb; it is not something that is done to us or for us, but by us; it is not something that you create and give to the congregation; it is something that the congregation creates with you. So it is critical that vested interests be put aside and that the laity be admitted into the dialogue, even as we acknowledge that Jewish wisdom is ultimately the rabbis' expertise.

The revolution that I propose will require an accurate understanding of what we mean by "tradition." The heart of the worship tradition is the order of prayers that has become standardized over the last two millennia. And while Reform has revised this liturgy so that it is fully inclusive, the Shema, the Amidah, and the Torah service are not very different from what they were in the synagogue of the third century.

However, everything else—the chanting styles, the music, the aesthetics—has been ever-changing. In fact, much of what we now refer to as "tradition" is not tradition at all, but a reflection of eighteenth- and nineteenth-century European culture.

Yes, communal prayer requires recognizable constants that bind worshiper to worshiper and congregation to congregation, but we need not be bound by cultural precedents that no longer resonate. Eighteenth-century Minsk is not our worship ideal. Neither is Berlin of the 1850s nor suburban America of the 1950s.

And just as we reject nostalgia disguised as tradition, so too do we reject "contemporary" worship that is faddish or trendy. There is no Jewish worship without age-old prayers and time-honored chants. In short, we need not choose between "traditional" worship and "contemporary" worship. As Reform Jews, we insist on the best of both worlds: continuity with our tradition *and* constant reformation.

Finding the right balance requires both innovators and conservators—those who push the envelope and those who hold back. At this moment, it is the innovators we need most. We must give our leaders the freedom to experiment and to develop forms of communal prayer that are both Jewishly authentic and fully indigenous to North America.

What will be the single most important key to the success or failure of our revolution? Music. Every congregation that has revived its worship has begun with music that is participatory, warm, and accessible. Our wisest synagogues invite their members to join in song because they know that Jews feel welcomed, accepted, and empowered when they sing. Ritual music touches people in a way that words cannot. Music converts the ordinary into the miraculous, and individuals into a community of prayer. Music enables overly intellectual Jews to rest their minds and open their hearts.

There is nothing new in this. At the very moment of Israel's liberation, Miriam led her people in song on the far shore of the Red Sea. But somehow, for some reason, many of us have lost our voices. The music of prayer has become what it was never meant to be: a spectator sport.

That is why our cantors, soloists, and choirs are working so hard to sing with us, and not for us.

In many instances this work is just beginning. It is not easy for a congregation that has never sung to begin to sing. And when the congregation finds its voice, the prayer leader—whether cantor or soloist, rabbi or layperson—may find it difficult not to be completely in control. Also, because East European melodies—soaring and rich—are often difficult to sing, a simpler American *nusach* is only now being developed.

Still, despite these challenges, I am convinced that music will be the foundation of our worship revolution. And this means that Jews in large numbers will return to our sanctuaries only when we offer them music that is vibrant, spiritual, community-building, and that speaks directly to the soul.

The other great challenge of our worship revolution is to bring young families and young children back into our sanctuaries. A 27-year-old rabbi, newly ordained from the Hebrew Union College-Jewish Institute of Religion, will often look out at her congregation on Erev Shabbat and find that she is the youngest person there by several decades. Why has this happened?

Many of our leaders have suggested that we may have unwittingly driven young people away. Convinced that exuberant children could not be accommodated at regular Shabbat worship, and that their baby-boomer parents would not be drawn to the somber melodies of the older generation, we created the shorter, more energetic, and more spontaneous monthly Shabbat family service. And it has succeeded. The average family service, while a bit disorderly, is filled with wonder and dissonance and natural enthusiasm, and our sanctuaries are often filled to overflowing.

But by creating the family service, we may have signaled that young parents and children are not welcome at other times—that for them, in effect, Shabbat falls but once per month. How do we change this perception and put Shabbat back on their weekly schedule?

Some suggest that Shabbat morning is the best time for family prayer. But this means confronting a myriad of conflicts, including the choice between soccer and synagogue. As Rabbi Jeffrey Salkin has put it: "The God of soccer is a vengeful God." An even greater obstacle is the Shabbat morning bar or bat mitzvah, which in most cases has alienated the uninvited, young and old, and appropriated the worship service as a private affair of the bar mitzvah family. This is far from a simple matter. For many Reform Jews, the rite of bar mitzvah is the single most significant religious event in their lives, and we should be respectful of its impact. Still, Judaism is a collective enterprise, not a private pursuit, and we must be troubled by the prospect that a family celebration is displacing Shabbat morning communal prayer.

But Reform Judaism is ever-evolving. And so some of our congregations have proclaimed that the regular Erev Shabbat service will no longer be the domain of adults and a Shabbat morning service the domain of b'nai mitzvah families. Instead, every worship service will be intergenerational, welcoming all. Others have undertaken to provide family-oriented worship, in addition to regular services, not once a month but every week. Whatever the solution, young children and young families in our community must be part of our revolution. The children in turn, through their simple faith and playful eagerness, will help us to breathe new life into our prayer.

To realize the worship revolution, I urge each UAHC congregation to devote a major segment of two upcoming board meetings to define a worship agenda. The starting place for worship reform is a forward-looking lay leadership, invested as partners by rabbi and cantor, assuming responsibility for congregational prayer which they see as their own. The UAHC has prepared a suggested plan for these board deliberations.

Second, I propose that we call upon all our congregations to do what many have already done: enlist the best and brightest to serve on the temple ritual committee, transforming it from one that too often has focused on ushering and High Holiday tickets to one that works with rabbis and cantors on worship renewal. The ritual committee must now become the primary venue for rethinking the congregation's worship agenda. The first step is studying, with the rabbi or cantor, the history and theology of Jewish prayer. Just as one cannot pray without appropriate preparation, one cannot engage in the transformation of worship without preparation and knowledge. The Union has created a detailed curriculum for course leaders.

Ritual committees also need to undertake an in-depth self-evaluation of current worship practices. Does Shabbat prayer capture the heart and soul and kishkes of the congregation? Is the music uplifting? Are congregants creative worshipers or captives to sameness? As part of this self-assessment, I recommend that each synagogue evaluation team commit itself to visiting at least four other congregations. We are sometimes terribly parochial, unaware of what our sister congregations have done to bring dignity, reverence, and beauty to their worship. It is important that rabbis and cantors be included in these visits; we ask our clergy to be experts in matters of prayer, and yet it is difficult to lead if one lacks exposure to other models of *tefillah*. The UAHC has assembled a comprehensive self-study document that congregations may use both to evaluate their own worship practices and to assess the practices of others.

Third, I propose that we initiate an on-line, Movement-wide dialogue on prayer. My hope is that hundreds of temple presidents, ritual chairs, laypersons, rabbis, and cantors will join this on-line discussion, and that the number of participants will eventually reach into the thousands.

Fourth, I propose that the Union, the College-Institute, the Central Conference of American Rabbis, and the American Conference of Cantors cooperate in sponsoring retreats for rabbis and cantors, where our worship leaders can consider the scholarly and professional dimensions of worship reform and generate many of the creative ideas that will power our revolution and assure its success.

Fifth, I propose that we enrich our worship by undertaking a program of adult Hebrew literacy. Some see the increased use of Hebrew in prayer as contrary to Reform principles, but I disagree. Every Reform service contains an ample number of English prayers so that all worshipers can pray with comprehension. And the Hebrew language is more than a vehicle of expression; it is part of the fabric and texture of Judaism, vibrating with the ideas and values of our people.

The division that exists in our Movement is not between those congregations that use more Hebrew and those that use less; these differences are not very significant. The important division is between those congregations where many worshipers know some Hebrew and those where they do not. Why? Because absence of Hebrew knowledge is an obstacle to heartfelt prayer; because inability to pray with the congregation at peak moments becomes a source of frustration; and because the full participation for which our members yearn is that much more difficult without some access to the sacred language of the Jewish people.

Let me put it plainly: we value Hebrew for many reasons, but it is most of all the great democratic tool of Jewish worship, the vehicle which "opens the gates of prayer" to the average Jew. If we fail to learn at least the basics of Hebrew, then we are treating our rabbis and cantors as priests—as an ecclesiastical elite which enjoys sole access to the secret code of Jewish worship. But they do not want to be cast in this role, and we should not force it upon them. We want to be empowered to pray on our own, and this is so much easier when we turn those little black dots and boxes on the page of the *siddur* into a conversation with God.

The UAHC is developing two Hebrew primers exclusively for adults. They focus not only on phonetic reading but on comprehension of basic prayers and texts. I propose that following the High Holidays next year, our congregations make use of these texts, offering ten-session adult Hebrew courses in both the fall and spring.

I do not wish to mislead you. The revolution that I am calling for is as daunting a challenge as any that we have faced. We Reform Jews are never more recalcitrant than when we deal with issues of prayer. But I am convinced that our Movement possesses the spiritual courage for just such a revolution. Indeed, it is already underway.

Let us then join together in creating a synagogue that is a center of Jewish life in all its sweep and scope, but that is first and foremost a center of *avodah*—of worship, reverence, and awe. And we will do this because we are the most creative movement in Jewish life; because, in the absence of prayer, all our crowded congregational calendars are for naught; and because to live without prayer is to live without God.

PSALM 37 AT AUSCHWITZ

Jacqueline Osherow

Nourish yourself with faith
Psalm 37.3

*Just a little longer and there will be no wicked one; you'll
contemplate his place and he'll be gone*
Psalm 37:10

*I was young; I've also grown old and I've never seen a righteous
man forsaken or his children begging bread*
Grace after meals, Psalm 37:25 and *Birkat Hamazon*

All those boys who'd started *heder* at three,
After licking a page of letters smeared with honey,
Who, legend has it, by the age of ten,
Could track the route of an imaginary pin

Stuck through the *Gemarah,* word for word—
Surely it was nothing to the likes of them,
Who clung to every holy thing they heard,
To learn by heart the words of every psalm,

And surely, even given the odds, one,
Despite his scholar's pallor and his puniness,
Made it, by some miracle, to the workers' line
And didn't go directly to the gas.

What I want to know is: could he have tried,
Before his slow death from starvation,
To bring himself a little consolation
By reciting all those psalms inside his head?

Just a little longer and there will be no wicked one,
He'd murmur to a shovel full of ash,
You'll contemplate his place and he'll be gone.
Unless he was too busy saying *kaddish*

For his father—lost a few days before
Along with his own reservoir of psalms,
Still stunned by the crudeness of the cattle car,
A man known to go hungry giving alms,

Who'd walk to *shul* the long way on a muddy road
So as not to crush a blade of grass on *shabbos*—
Was he to say his father wasn't righteous
That his only son should go in search of bread?

Though the psalm does say *begging* bread:
And begging was of little use at Auschwitz:
There, you had to have something to trade—
A sock, a shoe, a blanket, cigarettes—

For what someone who did favors for a dishwasher
Had managed to scrape off dirty SS plates.
Our scholar wouldn't eat—it wasn't kosher—
Though the rules didn't *really* apply at Auschwitz;

The Torah, after all, says, *to live by them*;
You can even eat vermin in the face of death
But our young man kept singing that one psalm
Over and over: *nourish yourself with faith.*

(Is that why David says he's never seen
The children of the righteous begging bread?

They're meant to be sustained by faith alone?)
And was our scholar, singing that line, comforted?

And his fellow prisoners? Could they have heard?
Did he sing the other psalms or just that one?
Maybe all the psalms had left his head.
He'd contemplate their place and they'd be gone.

I could try asking my father-in-law
If, in all his years at Auschwitz-Birkenau,
He ever once overheard a psalm.
But I know the answer just imagining him

Giving me the slightly baffled stare
He keeps in reserve for these conversations
That says: where do you find these foolish questions?
And then: how could you know? You weren't there;

If I hadn't been, I wouldn't believe it either. . . .
Aloud, he'd tell me: *Psalms, I didn't hear,*
You were lucky to put two words together
Without some SS screaming in your ear

But this was nothing. This was nothing.
Most of his descriptions end like this.
He almost never says what *something* was.
Whatever it may have been, he'll always sing

That bit about the children begging bread
When it's quoted in the *Birkat Hamazon*.
I refused to sing it as a kid—
Though, unless you're counting television

I could honestly have said I'd never seen
Or known I'd seen, a single person starving—
My poor rabbi found me so unnerving
When I'd balk at this effort to explain

That the line wasn't meant to be historical
But something to hold onto as a dream.
I love to sing it now. Only a fool
Would try to be literal about a psalm

But then I'd argue: but it says *seen.*
The past tense. A single person's life-span.
Read it. *I've been young and I've grown old.*
Even now, singing it, I'm still compelled

To wonder what the line's supposed to mean.
Maybe the key word really is *seen*
And David's trying to make us a confession:
That, for all his affect of compassion,

He never, even once, bothered to look.
Or maybe it was just that he couldn't see.
A man who, with a slingshot and a rock,
Could conquer a nation's greatest enemy . . .

A slingshot at Auschwitz? Can you imagine?
Though once, in a film, I heard a Vilna partisan
Describe his girlfriend crippling a Nazi train
Loaded with guns and bombs and ammunition

With a single handmade ball of yarn and nails . . .
But that was only one Nazi train.
She did, for a week or so, tie up those rails,
But, before she knew it, trains were running again,

Taking whoever hadn't died of gunshots
In graves they'd dug themselves in nearby woods
To slower, but less messy, deaths at Auschwitz—
Some, with entire books inside their heads—

And what I'm saying is, there were so many of them—
Let's forget about my scholar with the shovel—
I'd admit it; he had no thought of a psalm—
But think of the others, many religious people,

Standing there, waiting in the other line,
First, for the barber, to have their hair cut,
Then, for whoever did the tooth extraction,
All these things took time, they had to wait.

I know it sounds crazy, but couldn't one of them—
Not that it matters, they all died anyway—

But still, so many people, and enough time
For reciting what the dying are supposed to say

(*Hear O Israel,* etc.) and a psalm.
Or not even a whole psalm. Just one line.
All those people waiting. Couldn't one of them
Have mumbled to a brother, a father, a son

(The women, of course, were on another line
And this was not a psalm they would have known)
Just a little longer and there will be no wicked one;
Just a little longer . . . he'll be gone.

THE CURSE OF BEING RIGHT

David Suissa

IT'S A DRUG. It's intoxicating. It tastes better than wine. It's so seductive it makes people go nuts, desperate for another fix. It's today's drug of choice.

It's the drug of being right.

Such simple words, "I'm right and you're wrong," and we're off to the races. Hide the children. "I'm right and you're wrong," and bang just like that, I'll break my own rules. I'll hit you where it hurts most; I'll break your heart.

Religious versus secular, left versus right, businessman versus poet, politician versus politician, spouse versus spouse, parent versus kid, driver versus driver, it doesn't matter who, it doesn't matter where: being right seems to give people a severe case of amnesia. Suddenly, when they're right, Torah scholars forget basic Torah teachings. Noble people make ignoble statements. Sweet people say bitter words. Humility? Dignity? Ahavat Israel (love of your fellow Jew)? Gone. All in the name of being right.

When one is wrong, humility comes cheap. It's no big deal to be humble or contrite when caught with your hand in the cookie jar. But how about when your spouse or friend is an hour late without a good excuse? Or when we feel so terribly right about an issue because we believe we have the law, the facts, the Torah, history, science, or whatever squarely on our side?

Can we then resist the irresistible? Can we resist the urge to throw stones, the rush to emotion, the instinct to dominate?

Those who are obsessed with being right often find that their cause gets ambushed by their methods. A Midrash on our forefather, Abraham, gives us a vivid example of this idea. An old stranger once came to Abraham's tent. Abraham was known as the most hospitable of men, and the only thing he asked from this ninety-five-year-old man after he ate was to bless God. "Which god?" said the old man. "The God of everything," said Abraham. "I worship the god of fire," said the old man. "And I don't know the god of everything, so I'd rather pay for my meal than bless your god." Abraham tried to convince the old man that there is only one God who makes fire, water, and everything else, and he used the most beautiful arguments to sway him. But the old man wouldn't have it. "Set your price and let me go," he said. "I will not change." Abraham tried everything he could, to no avail. "Wicked old man!" he exclaimed. "Are you not ashamed to refuse to bless the Most High who made you as well as the Fire that you worship?" And with that Abraham chased the old idolater from his tent. Whereupon God appeared to Abraham, asking him, "Abraham, why did you chase the old man from your tent?" "He refused to bless you for the meal he ate at your servant's house," said Abraham, "so I chased him to teach him a lesson."

"Think, Abraham," said God. "You could not suffer this idolater for one hour and one meal in your tent while I fed him meals every day for ninety-five years and never asked anything from him in return? Had you treated him more respectfully, your words could have made him love me." I've always loved that story. It shows how even the greatest among us are vulnerable to the curse of righteousness.

But the cure doesn't come easy: there's no twelve-step program for Self-Righteous Anonymous. It's more a matter of reprogramming our mindsets to calmly and clearly see the other side. I like to tell my ultra-Orthodox friends that if they were raised Reform, they too would be Reform! And vice versa, of course. Somehow we find it so difficult to put ourselves in the shoes of others. And it is those among us with the most "truth," who feel the most "right," that are often the most vulnerable.

It's as if we've all forgotten the sanctity of dignified debate in the Jewish tradition. Debate allows us to handle the multiplicity of views in this world and treat it as a blessing. It is through dignified debate that our sages have kept Judaism alive. In Pirkey Avot we learn that "a debate for the sake of Heaven shall remain for later generations, but a disrespectful debate shall vanish." For our sages, being engaged in a destructive debate is using the Divine crown for one's own purposes, and even being right doesn't help at that stage. The crown of the righteous is worn by those who don't brag that it sits on their head and, in fact, by those who don't even *notice* the crown is there.

The Talmud, which is the core expression of the wisdom of Israel, is a book of constant debate, questioning, and redefinitions. As exemplified in the Hillel versus Shammai debate—when the Heavenly voice declared that both of their opinions were a "reflection of the living God"—no one in the Talmud is absolutely right. Absolutely right would smack, for us, of non-Jewishness, and God knows the Jews have suffered enough at the hands of those who believed themselves to be "absolutely right." At its heart, absolutely right is also a distortion of life, which is nothing if not a tapestry of nuances and complex connections. It is these which enrich our quest for a greater divine truth, a quest that has always been at the center of the Jewish ethos.

I long for the day when respect, dignity, and intellect become the new tools of choice in this never-ending quest for divine truth: when we will, like the sages of the Talmud, learn to disagree without being disagreeable, and when we will teach the world by acting right, even when we are right.

ZOHAR

Alicia Ostriker

Not until the lower world
was made perfect was the other world also made
perfect. . . . and it is thus the yearning from below
which brings about the completion above.
The Zohar

and so I am reading the zohar
and they are so splendid these old rabbis in their splendor
and their words are blazing light sparks gushing springs
and their hopes are palaces pomegranate trees perfumes
     ascending

glorious
but as for me
their gates stand closed
fastened against me

what must I do outside here
shake the latches and wail, they are deaf

mount a lawsuit against them, they are expert lawyers
scratch my scabs go on hunger strike

forget it they own the cameras, oh my beloved
how long before you tell them who I am

CAIN AND ABEL

THE TERRIBLE POWER OF A MINOR GUILT

Abraham B. Yehoshua

What Was the Real Punishment Inflicted on History's First Murderer?

The Biblical Story of Cain and Abel, Genesis 4

And the man knew Eve, his wife; and she conceived and bore Cain saying, I have acquired a manchild from the Lord. And she bore again, his brother Abel. And Abel was a keeper of sheep, but Cain was a tiller of the ground. And in the process of time it came to pass, that Cain brought of the fruit of the ground an offering to the Lord. And Abel, he also brought of the firstlings of his flock and of the fat parts thereof; but to Cain and to his offering he had not respect. And Cain was very angry and his face fell. And the Lord said to Cain, Why art thou angry? And why art thou crestfallen? If thou doest well, shalt thou not be accepted? And if thou doest not well, sin crouches at the door, and to thee shall be his desire. Yet thou mayest rule over him. And Cain talked with Abel his brother and it came to pass, when they were in the field, that Cain rose up against his brother Abel and slew him. And the Lord said to Cain, Where is Abel thy brother? And he said, I know not, am I my brother's keeper? And he said, What hast thou done? The voice of thy brother's blood cries to me from the ground. And now cursed art thou from the earth, which has opened her mouth to receive thy brother's blood from thy hand; when thou tillest the ground, it shall not henceforth yield to thee her strength, a fugitive and a vagabond shalt thou be on the earth. And Cain said to the Lord, My punishment is greater than I can bear. Behold, thou hast driven me out this day from the face of the earth; and it shall come to pass, that anyone that finds me shall slay me. And the Lord said to him, Therefore whoever slays Cain, vengeance shall be taken on him sevenfold. And the Lord set a mark upon Cain, lest any finding him should smite him. And Cain went out from the presence of the Lord and dwelt in the land of Nod, to the east of Eden. And Cain knew his wife, and she conceived and bore Hanokh and he built a city, and called the name of the city after the name of his son, Hanokh.

We are told at the end of this story what happened to history's first murderer, according to the Bible. Following an exchange of harsh words with God, who places a curse on the murderer and forces a nomadic existence on him, Cain has the audacity to ask to be protected against any adversary who might want to kill him—whether in retribution for the murder of Abel or as a result of the increased vulnerability of the nomadic lifestyle God imposes on him (the text is unclear on this point). Indeed, God accedes to the murderer by stamping him with a sign that will warn off any potential attacker, and in order to make this sign effective and clear to all, the Maker issues a warning of the serious consequence to be suffered by anyone who dares lay a finger on history's first murderer.

Fully armed against any eventual harm or revenge, Cain leaves the presence of God, but not to take up a harsh nomadic existence detached from human society, as decreed by God. What he does is make his way to a new settlement in a place that is not far from the Garden of Eden and is known as the Land of Nod. Is the Land of Nod the right place for implementing the punishment of nomadism? Not necessarily. The Land of Nod is connected to nomadism only in that the Hebrew word for nomad is *navad* or "noded." Actually, according to the biblical text, Cain successfully undertakes the life of a settler. Not only does Cain's wife (did she exist before the murder?) give birth to a son, but from then on, he has no desire to eke out a livelihood by working the land, and quite rightly so, for after God curses the land for being partner to the murder of his brother, it becomes hard and rebellious, and makes life difficult for anyone trying to grow his daily bread out of it. Cain undergoes a "modern" transition from a rural to an urban lifestyle (the exact opposite of what is considered the life of a nomad), and the new town he builds and inaugurates is indeed his new home in all senses, if the name he gives it is the same as that of his son, Hanokh. When we go back to make a close and perfectly lucid study of the closing chapter of the story of Cain and Abel, as it is presented in the Bible, we are thus surprised to learn that not only does the murderer avoid severe punishment for his crime, but the less severe punishment decreed for him by God is not even carried out in the end. Thus, the murderer does not even return to the situation he was in prior to the murder, and a close study of the text shows us that his situation has even *improved.* But the second surprise is that the story's author has actually managed to deceive us. Not because he does not present all the facts—on the contrary, there is something cruelly honest in the biblical report of Cain's happy end—but in the way in which he anesthetizes and dims our natural sense of justice. Indeed, the story of Cain and Abel is not saved forever in our awareness as a terrible miscarriage of justice on the part of God, who is a hero and partner in the story. The story does not cause us to come out in protest and to say, "If this is the way that Genesis begins, with the story of a cruel murder and such a happy ending for the murderer, not only is it no wonder that our world has been so full of murder stories ever since, but the question is, If this is the level of God's justice, should we be willing to accept his moral control of the world?

On the other hand, if we were to ask people who read about Cain and Abel in their youth what they remember of the story and what happened to Cain, many might remember that Cain did not pay with his life for the murder he committed. Most of them would describe him as a wild animal, alone and neglected in some remote cave, rejected by human society, suffering and persecuted, with the sign of God stamped like an ugly horn on his forehead, signaling more than a warning to potential assailants, but the disgrace of the murder.

In order to live in peace with this story, we have been obliged to balance the biblical picture in our moral imagination. But the question that has to be asked is: If the author of the story did indeed put to sleep our moral senses, what was his purpose in doing so? In other words, what is the *true* moral objective of this story?

We shall follow the story, paragraph by paragraph.

"And the man knew Eve his wife." This is the first time in the Bible that the act of copulation between a man and a woman is described with a nice word, *knew,* a word that has in it something spiritual and noble— knowledge as a challenge of love, for the purpose of giving birth. The wife is the mysterious text that needs to be deciphered, and the man deciphers her through the act of love. Although according to this description the active initiative is the man's, the woman's material passivity is explained in the wealth and the mystery imbedded in her.

"And she conceived and bore Cain, saying, I have acquired a manchild from the Lord." Indeed, Cain was born as a result of this act of knowing love, and the author attaches great significance to the name given to the child by his mother—from the Hebrew word *kin* or "acquire." His birth took place with the help of God, and through it the mother has a renewed connection to God, acquisition being tantamount to ownership. In any case, the entire story of Cain's birth and naming bears witness to a great sense of respect on the part of the author for Cain and his status.

This status is reinforced when it comes to describing the birth of Abel, which is almost the exact opposite of that of Cain. "And she again bore, his brother Abel." Abel seems to have been born of Eve alone, without the need for Adam's *knowledge* of her. Not only does his name have no significance, but it has an almost cruel antisignificance—*hevel,* the Hebrew word for "nonsense," that which is meaningless. From the beginning, the only significance for Abel's existence lies in his being Cain's brother. Right from the start, the author singles out the main hero of this story, the one whose task it is to shoulder the drama—Cain.

From here on, Adam and Eve disappear from the story, and their disappearance is extremely significant from the point of view of the author's moral interests. Their presence or any mention of them would have certainly made it difficult for the author to lead the story in the way in which he intends.

"And Abel was a keeper of sheep, but Cain was a tiller of the ground. And in the process of time, it came to pass, that Cain brought of the fruit of the ground an offering to the Lord. And Abel, he also brought of the firstlings of his flock and of the fat parts thereof." These new neutral facts with regard to the significance of the text give no indication as to a moral preference for one occupation over the other. Is there any special meaning to the fact that Abel is mentioned first? I think there is, if we expect that the firstborn son should be mentioned before his younger brother. The change in order creates in us a certain sensitivity with regard to the sequence in which things related to the brothers are presented. Thus, when one line down, it says that Cain was the first to bring his offering to the Lord, we do not conceive of this statement as merely a routine technicality that presents the seniority of the firstborn over his younger brother. If the order was changed in the first sentence, then this is not a case of mechanical but of palpable order. Cain is the first to bring an offering to the Lord. In other words, the initiative for proffering the offering is Cain's; Abel merely follows on.

Here stands the anchor that many readers grasp in order to give a moral rationale to the story and especially to justify the question of why God had respect for Abel's offering and no respect for Cain's. Abel "brought of the firstlings of his flock and of the fat parts thereof," whereas Cain brought *only* of "the fruit of the ground"—as if Abel had brought choicer examples of his efforts and Cain's offerings were more mundane. As far as I am concerned, there is no foundation for this hypothesis. Abel did indeed bring the firstlings as an offering, but is the cause of Cain's downfall that he did not bring his firstlings, of which no mention is made? True, although there is a symbolic value to the offering of firstlings, this significance is not acute. Is it possible that for so trivial a fact the Lord would make so harsh a discrimination between the two brothers that would ultimately result in murder?

I reject this notion for the simple reason that the Lord does not explain his nonacceptance of Cain's offering as being because Cain did not bring firstlings, but for a much more substantial and serious reason. If that had been the reason for the Lord's preference of Abel's offering, Cain could have easily remedied the matter and achieved the Lord's approval. I believe that as soon as the reader reaches the moment in which Abel's offering is accepted and Cain's is rejected, and it says in the Bible, "And Cain was very angry and his face fell," it is quite easy to understand the pain and insult he is suffering from the rejection of his offering.

God is very important to Cain, who is the first to make his offering and who is deeply angered and insulted by God's rejection of the offering. Thus, God's questions—"Why art thou angry? And why art thou crestfallen?"—appear to be rhetorical, superficial, and superfluous. But it seems that they are not from God's point of view, who believes that Cain should have understood the reason for the rejection of his offering. The Lord respects the way in which Cain's self-awareness cannot only understand the reason for the rejection, but also justify it.

And here comes the key sentence in the text, which is complex and difficult, but also full of profound meaning: "If thou doest well, shalt thou not be accepted? And if thou doest not well, sin crouches at the door, and to thee shall be his desire." A possible explanation is: if you do well, you will enjoy an advantage; if you do not do well, you will be stricken by sin, and although sin is drawn to you, you are still able to control it.

In essence, Cain is substantially inferior from a moral point of view not because of any sinful acts he has committed, but because his thoughts and his drives are drawn to sin. He is a man who is *destined to sin,* although he has the ability and the strength to overcome the evil within him. A gift from a person who implicitly has bad and criminal thoughts in his heart is seen by the Lord as an act of falsehood and is rejected. When the heart is impure, it is not possible to legitimize an external ritual of gift giving. What could Cain have done, then? In actual fact, nothing. No allegation is made of a specific sin that Cain committed (in which case the Lord could have admonished him), rather only of thoughts and ugly intentions. Abel symbolizes here a person who is pure of mind and has no sinful tendencies, perhaps through lack of imagination or perhaps because of a simple and uncomplicated mental structure. In any case, God's statement can be summed up thus: "Although you are two brothers, in fact you are not equal in my eyes, not because of anything you have done but because of what is inside of you."

The arena here is an internal one. The debate is on something internal—on a moral feeling about potential thoughts and eventualities—and not on concrete situations. Although the world is not yet demanding moral decisions in clear human situations, the moral context exists in the fact of the internal moral attitude to it. Good and bad stand beyond action. Cain is disqualified (not punished!) not for what he did, but for what is happening within him.

This concept is serious and harsh. It is easier to avoid committing a sin than it is to refrain from sinful thoughts. Cain feels a stinging pain because the blessing that is withheld from him is given so freely to his brother, so it is quite natural that after his conversation with God, he turns first and foremost to his brother, Abel, whether to be helped by him or to do away with him.

"And Cain talked with Abel his brother." Something seems to be lacking in this part of the text. I say *seems* because in this debate we are relating to the biblical text not as some ancient archaeological text, but as a purely literary text. The fact that the author does not go into detail over the words spoken by Cain to Abel might indicate a weak and unclear attempt at dialogue, an attempt that by its mere content is destined to fail because how can Abel explain to his brother his own pure and natural quality?

"Cain rose up against his brother Abel and slew him." Abel does not respond to Cain, and, gripped with the power of jealousy, Cain kills Abel, his brother. Because Cain is unable to be what the Lord asks of him, he wants to destroy the criterion according to which he is being judged. Is the fact that the word *brother* is constantly repeated beneficial to the murderer or not? I venture to believe that in the end it is to the murderer's benefit. In murdering his brother, he is also murdering something of himself. I admit that this issue is debatable and that opinions differ as to crimes committed within a family framework. There are those who would tend to be very severe in judging such crimes in the belief that a crime committed against family members who had faith in their relative is worthy of the worst kind of punishment. On the other hand, there are also those who would try to find a mitigating side to such crimes. It might be assumed that anyone who has reached a state where he can harm a person dear to him—his parents, children, spouse, or another family member—and thereby also harms himself must have had good reason for doing so (extenuating, sometimes), such as troubled personal interaction with them. An attack on a total stranger, on the other hand, always gives the impression of being more severe and more cruel because it is apparently more thoughtless and mercenary.

Attention should be paid to the fact that the Bible gives no description of the murder itself. There is no description of the murderer's feelings or of his parents' reaction to the act. The only words that echo from the description of this murder are *rose up, brother, slew.*

"And the Lord said to Cain, Where is Abel thy brother? And he said, I know not: am I my brother's keeper?" It is at this moment that our revulsion for Cain is at its peak, more even than at the moment of the murder itself, which we conceive as being more tragic than vile because we are still under the hold of the desperation that brought Cain to committing the murder, the criterion that determines his inferiority. But the moment he tries to *deny* the murder is the moment we feel the full measure of revulsion toward the murderer. It is clear that God knows where the murdered man's body is laid, but he wants to prove to Cain the depth of the lie that he is living, and through his rhetorical question, God reveals the weight of the lie.

Using his literary means, the author creates not simply a story about a disagreement between two brothers, but a dramatic dialogue between a man called Cain and the Lord his God. Abel is no more than a completely sufferable tool in this dialogue, so that in himself he is not important; he is *hevel* (in Hebrew, "air, mist"). His death is less central than Cain's lie to God, to the extent that right from the beginning God is indifferent to the murder, and his only intention is to prove to Cain his criminal tendencies, which are completely unworthy of the grace of God—to prove the justice of his first assessment of Cain's corrupt nature and by doing so to justify his refusal of Cain's offering.

Even the words "What hast thou done? The voice of thy brother's blood cries to me from the ground" refer to more than the actual murder. They aim at proving that nothing is lost to the eye of the Lord or that the attempt at lying has failed because God can hear the call of blood from within the earth.

Thus, it is clear that the right punishment in this particular context is not the execution of the murderer, because revenge for the murder is not what is necessary in the dialogue that this story spreads before us, but rather the absolute and total discontinuation of contact with the Lord and the loss of his grace. "And from thy fact I shall be hid," says Cain in shame.

The punishment of nomadism is seen therefore as a constant escape from the Lord, as a lack of inner equilibrium, rather than true wandering. Thus, the happy ending as it appears at first sight is misleading. As soon as Cain's equilibrium is shaken, from the moment a feeling of unrest is planted within him, he is in a state of constant flight from the Lord: building the town and producing a son are only the outer peelings of the Lord's presence from which Cain shall hide.

I am trying to lead my commentary in this direction because otherwise it is impossible for us to reconcile ourselves to Cain's "happy ending," which should have aroused in us a powerful feeling of disgust, both toward the biblical storyteller, who finds it fitting to tell us so immoral a tale, and toward the Lord, who finds himself partner to a story that is so problematic.

But let's imagine to ourselves that the story of Cain and Abel was written differently, without making any factual change in the original text:

> And the man knew Eve his wife, and she conceived and bore Cain, saying, I have acquired a manchild from the Lord. And the man knew his wife Eve and she conceived and bore Abel and said, Even the air from his mouth is dear to my heart. Abel was a tender of sheep and Cain a tiller of the land. And it came to pass that Cain brought of the fruit of the earth an offering to God, and Abel brought also of the firstlings of his flock and of their milk. And the Lord had respected Abel and his offering, and he rejected Cain's offering. And Cain was very angry. And the Lord said to Cain, Why are you angry and why are you crestfallen? If you do well, shall you not be accepted? And if you do not well, sin crouches at the door and to thee shall be his desire. And Cain talked to Abel, his brother. Let us go for a walk in the breeze of the day. And while they were in the field, Cain rose up against Abel his brother. And Abel begged for his life, and Cain did not listen to his brother's pleading, but thrust the knife into his throat.
>
> And Adam and Eve heard of the murder and hurried to the field and saw Abel their son lying in a pool of blood, and they rent their clothes and cried bitter tears and laid a terrible curse on Cain. And the Lord said to Cain: Where is Abel, your brother? And he said I know not, am I my brother's keeper?

This "new" text contains no fact that contradicts the original text, and all the additions are perfectly feasible with regard to what was written in the original text. Only an elaboration on the point of view—the description of the murder, the parents' reaction, the previous value that was given to Abel's name—and this elaboration makes it difficult for the reader to reconcile himself to the story's other ending, the so-called "happy ending." Employing new literary means, moving aside the focal point, elaborating on the story—all these techniques cause a shake-up in the moral map, yet they are based on the very same facts.

The question is, What went to work on our moral feelers, which were supposed to have reacted differently to the injustice of Cain's light sentence? In that same book of Genesis, five chapters after the story of Cain and Abel, and after the Noah's Ark affair, there comes a moral rule that is completely different with regard to punishment due to any murderer: "Who so sheds a man's blood by man shall his blood be shed: for in the image of God made he man." This is a social law of the first order, according to which human society protects itself against the acts of injustices and evil that take place within it. But in the story of Cain and Abel, this firm moral code is not implemented; rather, another set of moral sensitivities is presented, one that is more complex and therefore also more profound and richer, but also more problematic. In this set of sensitivities, God is given a more important active role than the "in the image of" that serves as a uniform standard after the flood. God is a partner in the profound discourse with man on his inner self, on the truth and the lie that is within him, on his thoughts and on his potential for evil and his ability to overcome it. Thus, Abel, who is murdered in the course of this story, does not turn into a victim that demands immediate vengeance worthy of murder; rather, he is only one component of this complicated discourse.

According to the story of Cain and Abel, from the very beginning, human beings are not equal to each other in the sight of God because their inner selves—whether as a result of congenital traits, their destiny, their education, or consequences—are individual, differing from one person to the next. People are not judged merely on their actions, but also on what is inside their souls, their thoughts, and their personalities because all these elements are important in motivating their actions. God takes the responsibility for the significant difference between one person and the other. He does not content himself with the uniform "image" of God with which he stamps every person; he also deals with the various qualities ingrained in people. Thus, just as God will refuse to accept an offering from a man whose inner self is bad, so too he cannot judge this man too harshly for having committed a murder that resulted from this very rejection. God is responsible for his rejection, which makes him circumspectly responsible for the murder committed as a result of the rejection, giving us the reason for the light punishment.

The line that differentiates substantially between two people in accordance with the moral weight of their inner selves is developed and preserved throughout the Bible (alongside and in contradiction to other lines). Moreover, its strength will be stressed specifically because it is tested—as in the story of Cain and Abel—in the midst of biological families, between siblings and other relationships (Cain and Abel, Abraham and Lot, Isaac and Ishmael, Jacob and Esau, Joseph and his brothers, Israel and the other nations, and so on). I believe, in the end, that this line is tragic and problematic, constantly arousing contention. Against this line comes another one, a more open and democratic one, by which a person's moral rights and obligations are being examined in accordance with the simple and all-powerful criterion of the "image"—"Whoso sheds a man's blood by man shall his blood be shed: for in the image of God made he man." There is but *one* image, and the personality behind it is of no importance. The thoughts, the dilemmas, the inner selves—all these are not placed under any moral scrutiny, only the acts.

According to the "in the image" principle, I daresay that it would have been contingent upon God to accept Cain's offering; he would not have discriminated against him on the basis of his inner self. But then, if Cain had committed murder, for any reason, he would have been executed immediately. God, who is cruelly selective before the murder and lenient with the punishment he metes out to the murderer, is a different God from the one about whom it is asked, "Shall not the Judge of all the earth do right?"

The thing that interests us in the story of Cain and Abel is the private moral correction made by many readers in their imagination in order to atone for God's miscarriage of justice in not inflicting any real punishment on Cain. Thus, a moral analysis such as the one made here not only exposes the true substance of the story but also explains why we were wrong about it.

AUTHORITY, RESISTANCE, AND TRANSFORMATION

JEWISH FEMINIST REFLECTIONS ON GOOD SEX[1]

Judith Plaskow

IT IS STRIKING THAT, when issues of sexuality are discussed in religious contexts, a handful of texts are often cited and argued about over and over, as if they were the only sources relevant to shaping norms around sexual behavior. In the Jewish community, debates around homosexuality have often revolved around two verses in Leviticus and rabbinic commentary on them, while Christians add to the scanty resources in the Hebrew Bible a third verse in Romans. This approach ignores the host of other injunctions in the Bible and rabbinic tradition about forming ethical relationships, creating community, and ensuring social justice. It fails to view sexuality as just one dimension of human relationship, embedded in a constellation of familial, interpersonal, and communal connections that shape, support, or deform it. Instead, sexuality is seen as a peculiar problem for ethics, a discrete and troublesome domain requiring unique regulation. In addition to confronting problems around grounding sexual values, therefore, feminist accounts of sexuality also need to locate the issue in a larger social context. Building on the early feminist insight that the personal is the political, feminists need to insist that good sex on the interpersonal level is possible only in the context of just social, political, and economic relations.[2]

Thinking about Compulsory Heterosexuality

I choose to begin thinking about good sex by reflecting on a central oppressive element in my tradition, because I believe that it is the negative aspects of tradition that most profoundly shape women's current sexual situation, and that most require attention and transformation. In my view, the starting point for feminists in thinking about good sex must be resistance. Feminists must begin by examining and dismantling the institutions that stand in the way of women even imagining fully our needs and desires.

The concept of "compulsory heterosexuality," which Adrienne Rich placed on the U.S. feminist agenda through her well-known essay on the topic, refers to the complex social and political processes through which people learn how and are made to be heterosexual.[3] The first and simplest way in which heterosexuality is made compulsory is that other modes of sexual expression are forbidden on pain of punishment or death. Such a prohibition on male/male anal intercourse appears in Leviticus 18:22 and 20:13 and forms the starting point for all Jewish discussion of homosexuality—as well as Jewish gay and lesbian resistance to traditional attitudes toward homosexuality. Although lesbianism is not mentioned explicitly in the Bible, the rabbis find a reference to it in Leviticus 18:3, "You shall not copy the practices of the land of Egypt . . . or the land of Canaan." They interpret the practices in question as a man marrying a man and a woman marrying a woman. Both the Palestinian and Babylonian Talmuds also contain brief discussions of whether women who "rub with each other" are considered to have committed an illicit sexual act and are therefore forbidden to marry a priest. The rabbis' consensus that such acts are "mere licentiousness," that is, not real sex, and therefore not disqualifying, reveals another weapon in the arsenal of compulsory heterosexuality; rendering sex between women invisible by defining it as impossible.[4]

While contemporary Jewish debates about homosexuality generally revolve rather narrowly around these verses in Leviticus and the few rabbinic sources interpreting them, I find this material less useful for understanding heterosexuality as an institution than the pervasive assumption in biblical and rabbinic texts that heterosexual marriage is the norm for adult life. In getting at this larger context of Jewish attitudes toward marriage and family relations, Genesis 3:16—"Your desire shall be for your husband and he shall rule over you"—is far more revealing than Leviticus 18 and 20, because it names the connection between gender complementarity, compulsory heterosexuality, and the subordination of women. Gayle Rubin, in her classic essay "The Traffic in Women," argues that, in traditional societies, the social organization of sex is built on the links between "gender roles, obligatory heterosexuality and the constraint of female sexuality."[5] Gender roles guarantee that the smallest viable social unit will consist of one man and one woman whose desire must be directed toward each other, at the same time that men have rights to exchange their female kin and control their wives in marriage that women do not have either in themselves or in men.

Genesis 3:16–19, which describes God's punishments of Adam and Eve for eating the fruit of the tree of knowledge, offers a remarkable condensed and powerful statement of the connections laid out by Rubin. In increasing Eve's pain in childbearing and punishing Adam with having to sweat and toil to gain his bread, God assumes or ordains differentiated gender roles and, at the same time, defines them asymmetrically. Eve's (heterosexual) desire for her husband will keep her tied to childbearing, despite its painfulness, and will allow him to "rule over" her. My point is not that compulsory heterosexuality as a Jewish institution is rooted in this story, but rather that this myth of origins provides a lens for examining interrelationships that are spelled out at length in Jewish narrative and law. In the Jewish case, as in the traditional societies Rubin discusses, rigid gender roles support the channeling of sex in marriage. A man who is not married (the texts speak from a male perspective) is seen as less than whole, for only a man and woman together constitute the image of God. The extensive laws regulating women's sexuality and placing it under the control of fathers or husbands ensure that women will be available for marriage to men who can be fairly certain that their wife's sexuality belongs only to them.

In a context in which good sex is defined as sex that is under male control, the question of what constitutes good sex from women's perspectives simply cannot be asked within the framework of the system. For the Bible and for the rabbis, good sex is sex that supports and serves a patriarchal social order. The so-called divinely ordained laws concerning marriage and divorce, adultery, rape, and so on, allow for the regular and orderly transfer of women from the homes of fathers to the homes of husbands, or, if need be, from one husband to another. Women's fears, desires, and preferences, their efforts to find meaning in or to resist this legislation, are nonissues and "nondata" that are also nonsense in the context of the rabbinic world view.[6] As Rachel Adler points out in a powerful article about women's role in the Jewish covenant community, the categories of a system of thought determine the questions it can ask, allowing it to pile up huge amounts of information on certain questions while rendering others invisible. The problems that receive extensive attention in Jewish law are the "status problems of marriage, desertion, divorce and *chalitzah* (leverite marriage) which the tradition itself created and from whose consequences it now seeks to 'protect' women, since by its own rules they can never protect themselves."[7] Insofar as the rabbis do attempt to "protect" women—for example—they indicate some awareness of the limits and injustices of the system they have created and, in this sense, offer some resources for criticism. But insofar as they are willing to address these injustices only within the framework of the system that gives rise to them, they close off any possibility of women entering as subjects and reframing the issues in genuinely new terms.

As Rubin's analysis suggests, however, control of women's sexuality is just one dimension of the institution of compulsory heterosexuality, which is also spelled out in *halakha* (Jewish law) in terms of property rights, work roles, and religious obligations and exemptions. In her book on the construction of gender in Roman-period Judaism, Miriam Peskowitz examines a Mishoaic passage that shows the rabbis in the act of extending a husband's power over the property his wife acquired before marriage, so that, while the wife may continue to own property, the husband controls it and is entitled to the profits that flow from it. In their ensuing debate about the validity of this legal innovation, the rabbis involved presuppose that a man has authority over his wife. What they need to determine is the extent of that authority in the sphere of property ownership, much as in other contexts they will discuss a husband's power over this wife's sexuality. The conversation, Peskowitz argues, reveals that there are many nodes "in the construction of sexual difference," sexual control constituting only one area in which marriage allows a man to "rule over" his wife.[8]

The Jewish division of religious labor also presupposes and helps construct a social structure in which heterosexual marriage is the norm. The exemption of women from positive time-bound commandments—in particular, set times for daily prayer—assumes that they are involved in household obligations that are their first responsibility and priority. In caring for small children, observing the rules of *kashrut* (dietary laws), and preparing for holy days by cooking special foods and making their homes ready, women free men for their own prayer and Torah study and enable them to observe the dietary laws and the Sabbath and holidays fully. For their part, women need men to take the ritual roles in the home that they themselves are neither obligated nor educated to assume. In other words, the whole series of laws that exclude women from public religious life, laws that Jewish feminists have analyzed and criticized from the perspective of women's spiritual disempowerment, are also part of the system of compulsory heterosexuality. That system is not just about sex, but also about the organization of daily life around gender role differentiation and the power of men over women.

Because compulsory heterosexuality is interstructured with a whole network of sexual, social, economic, and religious relations in Jewish law, creating the preconditions for good sex cannot end with questioning the few biblical and rabbinic passages on same-sex relationships. The material on such relationships is scanty and specific, so that those advocating expanded rights for gays and lesbians have been able to challenge it from a number of directions. Are other forms of male sexual interaction, other than anal intercourse forbidden by Leviticus?[9] Did the Torah or the rabbis have any concept of homosexuality as an orientation, or were they condemning homosexual acts performed by heterosexuals?[10] While such critical questions are important and useful in trying to gain acceptance for gays and lesbians within the framework of Jewish law, they never step outside that framework to confront the broader system of compulsory heterosexuality. That system controls and marginalizes all women, whether or not they are heterosexual, and whether or not they are married. It also makes illegitimate any sexual or life choice outside of heterosexual marriage, so that self-pleasuring, celibacy, singleness, cohabitation without marriage, and so forth, all constitute forms of resistance to compulsory heterosexuality.[11]

Starting Points

I would argue that the feminist critic must begin not by allying herself with dissenting voices within her tradition, but by questioning the authority of tradition, resisting any framework that leaves no room for women's agency, and then proceeding to transform tradition by placing women at the center.[12] Feminism begins in resistance and vision, a resistance and vision that are not simply personal but are rooted in "communities of resistance and solidarity" that are challenging specific forms of oppression out of concrete experiences of alternative ways of being in the world.[13] Thus, the feminist and the lesbian, gay, and bisexual movements have allowed women to feel the power and potential of bonds between women; to experience an intimacy, sexual and otherwise, that often has been trivialized or undermined; and to claim our power as agents to participate fully in society and religious communities on terms that we define. This experience of the power of being, as Mary Daly described it early on, over the institutions that have consigned women to nonbeing, does not of itself threaten these institutions or render them harmless, but it does provide starting points for imagining a different future and criticizing the forces that stand in its way.[14] To my mind, this experience, rather than any dissident strands within patriarchal religion, is the authoritative foundation of resistance and transformation. Given the conflicting voices within any normative text, the decision to claim such strands must come out of some experience of their greater power to support fullness of life for a larger group of people. Out of participation in a community of resistance and transformation, one then looks for and consciously claims the resistive elements in a particular tradition, in order to mobilize them toward a different future.[15]

What does this mean and not mean in relation to compulsory hetero-sexuality? Beyond the dimension of critique, which I see as central to a feminist appropriation of tradition, there are several ways in which feminists can find resources for resistance and transformation within our religious traditions. One is by deliberately allying ourselves with the self-critical strands in texts that have been understood as normative. In her early and influential reinterpretation of Genesis 2–3, Phyllis Trible pointed out that the explicit statement in Genesis 3:16 that a woman's "desire shall be for her husband, and he shall rule over (her)," occurs in the context of divine punishment for disobedience. Remarkably for a pa-triarchal society, the story does not depict women's subordination as nat-ural and divinely ordained, but as a perversion of the created order that is a result of sin. Trible thus reads this story not as prescribing male su-premacy but as describing it—not as legitimating but as condemning it.[16] For her, the insight that male supremacy is a distortion of creation con-stitutes the true meaning of the biblical text, which thus stands over against patriarchy.

Given that the description of compulsory heterosexuality is part of the same passage, one could make a similar move, arguing that this aspect of social life too appears under the sign and judgment to sinfulness. But aside from the fact that such an approach would ignore Genesis 1, in which male and female together constitute the image of God, there are deeper problems with claiming to have found the true meaning of any biblical text. Just as every text was written in a specific historical, social, and re-ligious context, so texts are interpreted in particular contexts that give rise to particular exegetical needs.

The current desire to find an underlying nonsexist or nonheterosexist vision in scripture comes out of a political and religious situation in which various forms of fundamentalism are on the rise all over the globe and are attempting to tighten control over every area of women's lives. In the United States, the Christian Right has claimed the mantle of Christian au-thenticity, equating authenticity with control of sexuality and women, and the same dynamic is taking place within Judaism. As contemporary Judaism has become increasingly diverse and fragmented, issues of sexuality and women's roles have become the battleground for arguments about Jewish legitimacy. In a religious context in which the reactionary side of an increasingly heated debate claims divine authority for its position, it is tempting to argue that the essence or fundamental core of the tradition supports a progressive stance. But this is finally to get into an irresolvable shouting match in which each party claims God on its side. It also means that feminists accept in principle the authority of texts that are at many points antithetical to women's power and agency, and that can be used against the feminist cause as easily as for it.

Although the difference may be subtle, I see the claim to have discovered the authentic meaning of a tradition as different from self-consciously drawing on the dissident voices within it, while grounding oneself in a community that is actively working to create a Jewish future in which women are full Jews and full persons. For the purposes of resistance, it can be strategically useful to point to the contradictions or mementos of self-criticism within normative texts, showing how opposing positions can be justified on the basis of the same sources. Yet it is not useful to debate about which position is finally more authentic. From the perspective of the texts, the question of authenticity has no meaning; the texts encompass genuine disagreements. The argument over texts is in reality an argument over competing social visions. Whose version of the future will hold sway? Who will have the right to determine the distribution of society's goods and resources, to say whether a given social or religious system meets basic human needs? Precisely because this is the real issue in question, however, it is important to highlight the dissident strands within a sacred text in order to crack open or challenge dominant religious and social perspectives and thus enlarge the space for change. From this point of view, it is useful to notice that women's subordination is conjoined with heterosexuality in the context of punishment for sin, not because this renders invalid two thousand years of sexist and heterosexist readings, but because it helps us to imagine an alternative future.

A second way to mobilize resources for resistance and change is to look at Jewish sources with an eye to the historical possibilities that they simultaneously conceal and reveal, so that one can make visible the existence of "forbidden" sexual practices of transgressive gender relations. Thus, for example, the same rabbinic passages that can be read as denying the possibility of sexual activity between women can also be seen as acknowledging the existence of such activity, but regarding it as inconsequential. When the rabbis discussed the question of whether a woman who "rubs" with another woman is permitted to marry a priest, they may have been aware of the female homoeroticism amply attested to in Roman sources but seen it as not worth punishing.[17] From this perspective, the relative silence of Jewish tradition regarding both female and male homoerotic behavior may be construed as a form of permission. To take this view is not to deny the importance of heterosexuality as an ideology and an institution, but it is to suggest that behavior that did not threaten heterosexual marriage may not have been regarded with much seriousness. Reading Jewish texts in light of what we know of cultural attitudes and practices at the time they were written begins to uncover the complex historical reality masked by an exclusive focus on official prohibitions. It also broadens the sense of historical possibilities on which feminists can draw in seeking to transform the tradition in the present.

Still a third strategy of resistance and transformation that is especially important in dealing with issues of sexuality involves broadening the context of teachings on sexuality by looking at them through the lens of attitudes toward social justice. Rabbi Lisa Edwards, in a sermon on the Torah portions that contain Leviticus 18 and 20, argues as follows:

> We are your gay and lesbian children: 'You must not seek vengeance, nor bear a grudge against the children of your people' (Lev. 19: 18); we are your lesbian mothers and gay fathers: 'Revere your mother and your father, each of you' (19:13) . . . we are the stranger: 'You must not oppress the stranger. You shall love the stranger as yourself for you were strangers in the land of Egypt' (19:34).'[18]

In reading the prohibitions against male/male sex in the context of surrounding injunctions about just social relations, Edwards risks getting drawn into arguments about which is the more fundamental or essential dimension of the tradition. But by focusing on broader social justice themes, she also makes the critical point that any choice of sources in a debate about the meaning and intent of tradition always involves selecting from conflicting perspectives. Moreover, she places the biblical passages on homosexuality in the context of the gay and lesbian community of resistance, focusing on the interconnections between sexual ideologies and social injustice, rather than on private sexual behavior. Her sermon thus supports the crucial point that the authority for singling out the self-critical and dissident elements in our textual traditions comes not from the traditions themselves, but rather from the new possibilities envisioned and created by particular communities of solidarity.

NOTES

1. An expanded version of this essay was initially written in the context of a series of feminist conversations on the meaning of good sex in the world's religions. The results of these conversations are published in *Good Sex: Feminist Perspectives from the World's Religions*. eds. Patricia Beattie Jung, Mary E. Hunt, Radhika Balakrishnan (New Brunswick: Rutgers University Press, 2001).

2. This was a central and recurrent theme in all our Good Sex conversations, as many chapters in this volume bear witness.

3. Adrienne Rich, "Compulsory Heterosexuality and Lesbian Existence," *Signs: Journal of Women in Culture and Society* 5/4 (1980), 631–660.

4. For some introductory material on these issues, see Rachel Biale, *Women and Jewish Law* (New York: Schocken, 1984), 192–197; and Rebecca Alpert, *Like Bread on the Seder Plate: Jewish Lesbians and the Transformation of Tradition* (New York: Columbia University Press, 1997), 25–34.

5. Gayle Rubin, "The Traffic in Women: Notes on the 'Political Economy' of Sex," in *Toward an Anthology of Women,* ed. Rayna R. Reiter (New York: Monthly Review, 1975), 179–180.

6. Mary Daly, *Beyond God the Father* (Boston: Beacon, 1973), 12.

7. Rachel Adler, "I've Had Nothing Yet So I Can't Take More," *Moment* 8/8 (Sept. 1983), 24.

8. Miriam B. Peskowitz, *Spinning Fantasies: Rabbis, Gender, and History* (Berkeley and Los Angeles: University of California Press, 1997), 35.

9. Saul Olyan, "And with Male You Shall Not Lie the Lying Down of a Woman: On the Meaning and Significance of Leviticus 18:22 and 20:13," *Journal of the History of Sexuality* 5/2 (1994), 185.

10. Bradley Artson, "Gay and Lesbian Jews: An Innovative Jewish Legal Position," *Jewish Spectator* (winter 1990–1991), 11.

11. It is remarkable how little has been written criticizing the Jewish insistence on marriage from other gay and lesbian perspectives. See Laura Geller and Elizabeth Koltun, "Single and Jewish: Toward a New Definition of Completeness" in the first anthology of Jewish feminist work, *The Jewish Woman: New Perspectives,* ed. Elizabeth Koltun (New York: Schocken, 1976), 43–49. Also see the section "Being Single" in *Lifecycles: Women on Life Passages and Personal Milestones,* ed. Debra Orenstein (Woodstock, Vt: Jewish Lights, 1994), 99–116.

12. I am very grateful to the group conversation at the Good Sex meeting in Amsterdam for pushing me to be clearer about the ways in which Jewish feminists have moved beyond simply resisting women's traditional roles to creating new forms of practice, identity, and community.

13. Sharon D. Welch, *Communities of Resistance and Solidarity* (Maryknoll, N.Y.: Orbis, 1985).

14. Daly, *Beyond,* chapter 1.

15. See Daniel Boyarin, "Justify My Love," in *Judaism Since Gender,* eds. Miriam Peskowitz and Laura Levitt (New York: Routledge, 1997), 131–137.

16. Phyllis Trible, "Eve and Adam: Genesis 2–3 Reread," in Womanspirit Rising, eds. Carol P. Christ and Judith Plaskow (San Francisco: HarperCollins, 1979), 80.

17. Rebecca Alpert, "Like Bread on the Seder Plate," 29–34; Bernadette Brooten, *Love Between Women: Early Christian Responses to Female Homoeroticism* (Chicago: University of Chicago Press, 1996).

18. Lisa A. Edwards, "A Simple Matter of Justice" (Sermon, April 29, 1993).

FROM OUR IMMORAL SOUL

A MANIFESTO OF SPIRITUAL DISOBEDIENCE

Nilton Bonder

Betrayals of Culture: Adam and Abraham

Let us research our primitive understanding of the human being by relying on the oldest story in the Bible: the Creation. The Book of Genesis speaks of three stages in the creation of humanity: Adam, Abraham, and Jacob. Each of these three archetypes is associated with an important moment in the evolution of the story recorded in Genesis. Adam represents a break with nature; Abraham, a break with society; and Jacob, a break with the family.

Adam transgresses when he discovers that, unlike the other animals in the garden, he is faced with not only the absolute purpose of reproduction but also a prohibition that must be obeyed or disobeyed.

Abraham—to whom God promises progeny as numerous as the stars of heaven and as the sands of the seashore—is the man who inaugurates history. This focus on him and on the "multitude" that will descend from him is a clear option to tell history through a story. But what is so special about this man that he was chosen to found a nation? Like Adam, Abraham was a transgressor. His personal story begins when he hears an order: "Get out of your country, and your birthplace, and your father's house, to the land that I will show you. I will make you into a great nation" (Genesis 12:1–2). The verb "get out," which is in an emphatic form in the original, implies "break with"—in other words, betray.

Jacob is one who commits a transgression against someone else. He represents the betrayal of personal relationships within the family. He steals his brother Esau's birthright as firstborn son, committing grave treason against his father and his brother. He takes advantage of his father's blindness—not unusual in situations of betrayal—to appropriate the blessing that was meant for Esau, and with the help of his mother (symbol of good), he breaks with his father (symbol of right). His flight and the suffering provoked by this betrayal initiate an exemplary process: the establishment of the first family. It is this family that will be "potent" enough to found the twelve tribes of Israel and represent the true "multitude" promised to Abraham, the social transgressor.

Earlier, we looked at the first example of betrayal: the evolutionary traitor who discovers that not only rules may be transgressed but the game itself. Now let us look at the second case—the social traitor—to help us gain a better grasp of the act of betrayal and the immorality of the soul.

Abraham's story begins with a rupture. The Bible tells us nothing about his childhood, probably because it is not of great interest. This becomes important to our focus on Abraham's initial act and how it relates to what is so special about Abraham. Leaving behind his culture and his past for the sake of the future means knowing how to reconstitute the tension between body and soul, learning to make this break in light of the demands of the future and not just the demands of the past.

This is the "chosen" status that is proposed to Abraham and his multitude in the form of a pact, or covenant. Traitors usually like the idea of being a "chosen one," because it seems to compensate for the fact that society sees them as deviants. From the perspective of the body, someone who "gets out" of his father's house is not a model to be emulated. Yet from the perspective of the soul, he is. The notion of a "chosen one" is the soul's interpretation, while the body sees it as something dangerous, requiring immediate corrective action.

Michael Lerner, in his book *Jewish Renewal*, offers an enlightening interpretation of Abraham's act of breaking with his "house" in order to begin the search for a "new house." According to Rabbi Lerner, the question raised by Abraham's saga is whether or not we can break with the violence of the past. All of us have constructed the notion of "body" through conditioning imposed from our past. Our parents (particularly when considered from the analyst's couch); our experiences, from which we glean "certainties" and a fear of the unknown; and our culture, which indicates what is "right" and sees this right as "good" by definition—all imprint our destiny on us. It is this destiny that Lerner sees as the violence of the past. The proposition that we ought to remain the same and never leave our "father's house" is more than indecent: it does violence to a person. To remain the same means that we keep on doing what was done in the past. If we were unfortunate enough to be abused by our parents, we will be much more likely to repeat this with our own children. How many times did we have to suffer hearing our parents say, "*I* had to put up with such and such—why can't *you*?" Here is an educational concept where the past is surely the determinant of what is right and good. The son who makes the break, who does not take up his father's profession or his culture, is not the doctor his parents dreamed of but a musician, a deformed mutant, because he listens to the demands of the future and is detached from the past.

Abraham was not what his parents dreamed of. Knapsack on his back, off he went in search of his own land. Prototype of the "bad child," Abraham questioned the violence inherent to the inevitability of his destiny.

But what lends special import to Abraham's decision to transgress, to leave home, is the test to which life puts him later on. The real question is not whether Abraham will manage to break with the violence of his father's past but whether he will manage to accept this as a behavioral attitude toward life and therefore refrain from imposing violence on his own child. In other words, did Abraham take up his search for good, in detriment of right, solely for his own purposes, or did he inaugurate a transforming process between generations? If the answer to the latter question is yes, then Abraham ushered in a history that is not merely cyclical and repetitive from generation to generation but which, when each one of these generations breaks with its past, opens the way to a future grounded on the needs of the soul and not of the body—a future that belongs to the mutant and not to a body preserved as is. It would not be the land of our grandparents but a strange land, a land that is in strong tension with the land of our memory, which constitutes our "house."

Was Abraham to social reality what Adam was to evolutionary reality? Was Abraham to the option for evolution within the social realm what Adam and his transgression were to the option for evolution within the realm of nature? If so, then the future would be different from the past. The violence of the past would be filtered out of the future, and a new social being would be possible. The concept of reaching a messianic future depends upon the human possibility of transgressing against what is right, of transcending the house and territory of our past.

The test came. In an atmosphere reminiscent of the betrayal committed in his youth—when he was told, "Get out of your country, and your birthplace, and your father's house"—Abraham hears a new order, similar in structure: "Take your son, the only one you love—Isaac—and go away to the land of Moriah [the Temple Mount in Jerusalem]; and offer him there as a burned offering on one of the mountains that I will designate to you" (Genesis 22:2).

It was evidently the practice in that region that a father should offer his firstborn son in sacrifice. As a good citizen of Canaan, Abraham obeyed the design of his culture. It is interesting that the same God of transgression is now the God who speaks for culture. Abraham's experience when he receives this order is identical to the first occasion, and the question is whether Abraham will be able to perceive the hidden hook. The God of the soul now speaks in the same tone and in similar fashion, hiding his true identity—as the God of the body.

Abraham walks with his son. His inner doubt is terrible: Should he do what is right as if it were good, without questioning it? The denouement of Abraham's moment alone is awesome. He does not obey the original order. Neither does he disobey it. Abraham hears God say something different from what he had originally said. Instead of "Sacrifice your son," he hears, "Do not harm the boy. Do not do anything to him" (Genesis 22:12). Abraham does not disagree with God but learns to hear a different order from the same God. Here the divine figure is symbolic of the deepest understanding of what life, of what reality, expects of Abraham, who betrays neither God nor himself; instead, he legitimates his transgression as being God's true will. Abraham's secret lies in this nonrebellion, where good is practiced to the detriment of right, ushering in a new morality—the morality of the body, whose mutation was a product of the soul. Abraham proclaims his faith in the demands of the future and, therefore, of the soul. He is immoral, for he legitimates a different morality, which springs from the same source as the morality of the past.

It is only at this moment in his life that Abraham closes the cycle, not passing on to his son the violence of his morality and culture. In Abraham's relationship to his father's generation, we only know that Abraham has perceived his path—to leave home—but it is when he is faced with the possibility of having to offer up his own son that Abraham is choosing to see his son live in another "house" and another "land." As his legacy, he leaves Isaac a new world, where the nonsacrifice of his firstborn son represents the search for a land that does not belong to his contemporaries or compatriots. Abraham is disobedient. Within the social realm, he stands not only as fulfiller of the positive commandment to become "father of a multitude" but also of the negative commandment to transgress the expectations, or violence, of his generation.

Abraham learns not only to opt for the "good" but also to decree it as the new "right," the one that will replace the old and "betrayed" right.

There is no treason in this action, and the tension between past and future, between body and soul, is restored. Were it not for Abraham's ability to hear God express a divine will that differed from what had originally been ordered, he would have failed to recapture the perspective of the body, and a loss of tension would have occurred. Abraham would have been betraying by choosing the soul without achieving reconciliation with the body. His mistake would have been no different than if he had obeyed the initial commandment and enforced the violence of his generation. In this hypothesis, in addition to opting for the body to the detriment of the soul, Abraham would not have truly left his home.

This point is very important. Leaving home does not just mean abandoning a body that belongs to others—it is the act of abandoning one's own body. Transgressing our own convictions is essential. It is like the case of a law whose legitimacy depends upon the hypothesis that under certain circumstances disobedience is the best form of compliance. For Abraham, being absolutely human—fulfilling what is expected of us—means accepting the hypothesis that the best way of preserving his integrity may lie in relinquishing this same integrity.

Abraham establishes the possibility of a new law, a new understanding of orders—he opts for the immorality of the soul. From the perspective of the body, this immorality is what allows the evolutionary process to take place, where the new order is always legitimate. The fact that Abraham waited to hear this new order means he recovered the lost tension and eliminated any risk of committing a real act of betrayal.

We can see that Abraham could also have decided to make a new "good" fit the old "right," sacrificing his son and coming to peace with himself by finding a convincing justification that he had done a "good" thing. But Abraham couldn't do that; his solution had to be finding a new "right" for this "good."

Abraham is consistent and allows his son to find another "house" or another "land," just as he had—the promised land of which Abraham had dreamed, a land whose tradition includes ruptures. With the founding of a new religion, one that recognizes the soul's transgressive nature, a better future became possible. Abraham enjoys a cathartic moment, for he understands how wonderful the future can be if we legitimate our transgressions.

Betrayals of Family: The Story of Jacob

The third archetype is Jacob, the one who transgresses within the realm of the family. He does not betray his nature or the violence of his society; his specialty is betraying "the Other."

Jacob represents the transgressions that all his children and descendants will repeat. Let us not forget that it was Jacob who received the name Israel and that the twelve tribes of the Jewish people were descended from his twelve children. Jacob's betrayal and transgressions were to have a profound effect on the historical destiny of the Hebrews, inaugurating a process that transcends the individual.

The Bible uses the question of firstborn rights for symbolic purposes. Being the firstborn child meant inheriting the family name and history. The firstborn was the chosen one who would ensure continuity and carry on the future. Jacob breaks with the law of the firstborn, as does his son Joseph—an action that has become the stereotype of the Jew. Down through the ages, powerful and domineering peoples who came to view themselves as the legitimate heirs of civilization's history in a certain generation have labeled the Jews usurpers of the rights of the firstborn.

What, however, is Jacob's model? Abraham had made a break in his past and did so again at the end of his life. He legitimized betrayal by hearing in a new way, one that was more compatible with what he perceived as good. Jacob's experience was similar. He stole his brother's birthright and fled. His theft is only legitimized decades later, when he and his brother are reunited.

This reunion is preceded by a struggle with God. In a mysterious account at the end of Genesis 32, Jacob finds himself alone, facing the night, before his reunion with his brother. He's afraid of his brother and anxious because he stole his inheritance. A being then appears and wrestles with Jacob throughout night. Struggle—a word that denotes tension—is the process of instability in quest of a renewed balance. The being proves to be God. In prevailing in this struggle, Jacob receives the name Israel, the meaning of which is recorded in the text: "you have struggled with God and with men, and have prevailed" (Genesis 32:28).

Jacob represents the act of opting for a new "right" in his relationship with his peer, with the Other. But it is not simply a matter of his stipulating the new "right" for the identified "good." Jacob cannot do the same as Abraham, who heard God retract His order. God is not going to ratify the new "right" with new words. The alternative is to struggle with God and with men so that the new "right" will prevail. This hand-to-hand struggle, which begins as a fight between men, in the end proves to be a dispute with God. Doubt is not eliminated through deep self-examination and self-betrayal, as was the case with Abraham. Doubt is eliminated by showing the courage to assert a new "right," to betray the Other, and legitimize oneself in the process.

Abraham is like the father who accepts his musician son and dances with him, recognizing that his dream of a medical career for his son is not the right that best fits what is good. Abraham does not merely tolerate; he dances with his son, who goes off in quest of his own land. Jacob is the brother who follows the life of the artist and intellectual, leaving the presidency of his father's companies to his entrepreneurial, administrative brother. Jacob is the one who will have to legitimize his choice, resolving his own doubts and gaining the maturity to realize that he is the true heir. This heir is, of course, not the heir of the body, of companies and assets, but the heir of the soul, of the deep-seated desire to venture forth in life instead of following well-traveled roads.

The complications that ensue when we break with a peer or a brother are what cause the Other to see this as a betrayal. The traitor threatens the person who preserves his body. Legitimizing the Other's right to be an artist, recognizing that this is a valid option, means questioning yourself about your own ignored potentials. For someone who preserves and protects the body, this doubt causes a pain that can often result in violence and accusations of betrayal.

Jews carry this stigma. As questioners, they have been looked upon with suspicion by the Christian world—a world that inherited this civilization but that feared its brother, the "usurper of inheritances," because his mere presence stimulated profound doubts.

The Jewish people occupy a dangerous position in the Western world. In a sense, the Jews are examples to the world, for in deeming themselves chosen and seeking a new land lost long ago, they are exploring questions of the soul. This is why the Jews provoke a strong reaction from the world of the body.

Later I will explore how Christian tradition set itself the task of making Judas the prototypical Jew. A traitor from the cradle, the Jew is the most vivid example—and one never replicated in the history of civilization—of treason and betrayal.

From the perspective of the Jew, of Israel (Jacob)—the one who fights with God and with men—it is not easy to legitimate the position of "chosen one" without resorting to violence. The challenge is to wholly legitimate the new "right," not with arguments or justifications but through a deep belief in the soul and its transgressions.

Salvation through Betrayal: The Messianic Lineage

One of the most intriguing questions in biblical genealogy concerns the Messiah's family roots. Traditionally identified as a descendant of the House of David, the Messiah is heir to a fascinating lineage marked by profound transgressions, as observed by the anthropologist Claude Lévi-Strauss.[1] Let us take a brief look at this genealogy.

The Book of Genesis tells the story of the destruction of two wicked cities, Sodom and Gomorrah. Wracked by major convulsions in the realm of "right" and "good" in the eyes of the Eternal One, these societies met with catastrophic destruction. The only nuclear family to escape with their lives was Lot, his wife, and two daughters. But when Lot's wife turned around to see what was happening and watch how the cities were being destroyed, she was turned into a pillar of salt. In terror, Lot and his two daughters hid in a cave. Believing the whole world had been destroyed, the older daughter says to the younger one: "Our father is growing old, and there is no other man left in the world to marry us in a normal manner. Come, let's get our father drunk with wine, and sleep with him, and we will survive through children of our father." The text goes on to say: "That night, they got their father drunk with wine, and the older girl went and slept with her father. He was not aware that she had lain down or gotten up. The next day, the older girl said to the younger, 'Last night it was I who slept with my father. Tonight, let's get him drunk with wine again. You go sleep with him, and we will survive through children of our father. . . .' Lot's two daughters became pregnant from their father. The older girl had a son, and she named him Moab. He is the ancestor of [the nation] Moab that exists today. The younger girl also had a son, and she named him Ben-Ami. He is the ancestor of the people of Ammon who exist today" (Genesis 19:31–38, Aryeh Kaplan translation).

Believing that the entire world had been destroyed, Lot's daughters felt responsible for the continuity of the species. In biblical terms, they were guaranteeing that their father's endangered seed would live on. The sons begotten of these relations carry this distinction in their names: Moab (whose name means "from the father") is a son of his father, and Ben-Ami, ("from my people") a son of the people. Lot's daughters ensured the survival not only of their father's seed but of the entire people's seed. Yet the solution they found—incest—transgresses biblical law. "Good"—in this case, survival of the species—is saved by a new "right," and this entails a betrayal of the law that is neither condemned nor judged by the biblical text. Thus began one of the lines of the House of David and, consequently, of the Messiah.

Later on, in Chapter 38 of Genesis, we find a second lineage. This is the episode where Judah, son of Jacob, fails to obey the law of the levirate. According to this law, if a married man died without leaving children, his brother (or closest relative) had to take the widow as his wife and impregnate her to ensure continuity of the deceased's lineage. These "redeemers of the seed" played an important, respected role in biblical times.

Judah had three sons—Er, Onan, and Shelah—and he found a woman named Tamar to be his firstborn's wife. When Er died without leaving any descendants, Judah obliged Onan to fulfill his obligation as brother-in-law. But, the Bible tells us, since Onan knew that the offspring would not be his, he spilled his semen on the ground whenever he went to his brother's wife, so that he would not have children in his brother's name (Genesis 38:9). This is the origin of the term "onanism" (masturbation), derived from Onan's decision to deny his sperm to Tamar, wasting it instead.

Judah told his daughter-in-law Tamar to live as a widow in her father's house until Judah's son Shelah was grown, because he feared that Shelah would die too, like his brothers. A long time passed without any redeemer propagating the seed of Judah's sons through Tamar. Meanwhile, Judah's wife died, and Tamar heard that he was going to Timnah to shear his sheep. Tamar dressed as a prostitute and sat waiting for her father-in-law on the road, to seduce him. Since Judah had no way of paying Tamar on the spot, he left "pledges" with her (his signet, cord, and staff) as proof of his debt. Since the "prostitute" disappeared, Judah never got his belongings back.

Some months later, Judah was told his daughter-in-law was pregnant, and he demanded she be put to death for committing adultery. So Tamar showed him his belongings and Judah shamefully recognized she had acted correctly when she ransomed the seed that had been denied her. Tamar bore twins: Perez and Zerah.

Once again, the redemption, or preservation, of the seed transpired in irregular fashion. Tamar is not only dissimulating when she passes herself off as a prostitute (as when Lot's daughters got him drunk); the story likewise involves signs of incest, since Tamar redeems her husband's seed through her father-in-law rather than her brother-in-law. Transgression—once again committed by a woman—recaptures the possibility of propagation. The law is fulfilled through disobedience and betrayal.

Traced back to transgressions committed to preserve continuity, these two genealogical lines cross in the story of Ruth. Set in the countryside during harvest time, the story uses the word *seed* in two senses.

A member of the tribe of Judah called Elimelech migrated with his wife, Naomi, and their two sons to the land of Moab, fleeing a severe drought. There his sons married Moabite women, and Elimelech passed away. Not long afterward, his two sons died as well. Naomi released her two daughters-in-law of any responsibility toward her, insisting they rebuild their own lives, since they were still young. But one of them, Ruth, refused to abandon her mother-in-law because she knew that without Ruth, Naomi would never be able to redeem her husband's seed. With no living sons, it was as if Naomi made use of the law of the levirate to redeem her husband's lineage.

Full of details rich in symbolism, this story tells how Ruth managed to recover the potential for propagating the family. Like a beggar, Ruth went to glean "seeds" remaining in the field of Boaz, a rich relative of Elimelech. Boaz took an interest in Ruth, even though he was of an older generation—the same as Elimelech, Ruth's father-in-law—and he offered her "seeds" so she would not die of hunger.

Naomi and Ruth grew excited over the possibility of redeeming their husbands' seeds. With Naomi's help, Ruth made plans to seduce Boaz. In the middle of the festivities to celebrate the end of harvesting, surrounded on all sides by seeds, Ruth got Boaz drunk. The Bible is unclear about whether or not Ruth got the desired "seed" from the rich farmer in order to continue her husband's lineage.

Boaz in any case ends up coming to Ruth's aid, taking her as his wife, and in the final chapter of Ruth, the reader discovers that Boaz was a descendant of Perez, Judah's son by his daughter-in-law Tamar. The Moabite Ruth was a descendant of Moab, the incestuous son of Lot by his eldest daughter. From the union of these two transgressive lines—through Boaz and Ruth—King David will be born. And from the House of David will come the Messiah—in truth, a descendant of "saviors and redeemers" of seeds through transgressive acts.

What we inarguably have here is a pattern initiated by Eve, who gets Adam involved; the eldest daughter, who gets Lot drunk; the daughter-in-law, who fools Judah; and Ruth, who seduces Boaz. In all of these cases, it is the woman who, through disobedience, constructs humanity's road and redeems not only its seed but its very future.

Lévi-Strauss points out this gradual cloaking of the incestuous act, which began quite explicitly with Lot and his daughters but almost disappears in the case of Boaz and Ruth. Transgression is disguised but it in fact guides the body's destiny.

The fundamental issue here appears to be the fact that natural processes, the law, and that which is deemed "right" fail to achieve the desired "good." It becomes necessary to create a new order, one that can be extremely immoral at a given moment but which will ensure continuity and preservation. If you are able to follow this road, you endow the soul with its due value while bringing about the demise of the body and its animal morality.

We find the same transgression within the family of Moses. Although he is not of messianic lineage, Moses will play the historical role of Israel's redeemer in the episode where the Hebrews flee Egypt. In a comment apparently of little importance to the accounting of events, Exodus 6:20 makes a point of telling us that Moses' father was Amran, who married his own aunt, Jochebed. The Bible prohibits such a marriage (Leviticus

18:12), deeming it incestuous. Moses' history reveals this same theme of the endangered seed. Pharaoh decrees the annihilation of the seed, yet it is preserved—not simply through the prohibited marriage of Moses' parents but, once again, through a woman's initiative in the act of redemption.

As in the stories of the Messiah's ancestors (Lot's daughters, Tamar, and Ruth), it will be up to women to decide the paths of this redemptive transgression. In this particular case, the women act together: midwives (who disobey the order to kill newborns), Moses' mother and sister (who redeem the seed, placing the baby Moses in a basket in the Nile), and Pharaoh's daughter as well (who completes the redemption by adopting the baby). It falls to the woman to redeem the seed, albeit using strategies that transgress the reigning morality in order to reach the final goal.

The Messiah's ancestors were traitors of the reigning morality and customs, and in the eyes of the establishment there is nothing more devilish or threatening than the interests of those who break with the status quo in order to assure the best possible chances for individual and collective survival. Seen from the perspective of preservation, the Messiah is represented within the collective human imagination as a subversive, a nihilist, and a heretic.

NOTE

1. Claude Lévi-Strauss, "The Structural Study of Myth," in *Structural Anthropology* (New York: Anchor Books, 1967).

THE TENTH PLAGUE

Jill Hammer

Aaron took to wife Elisheva, daughter of Aminadav and sister of Nachshon, and she bore him Nadav and Avihu, Elazar and Itamar. . . . And Elazar, Aaron's son, married one of the daughters of Putiel, and she bore him Pinchas.

Ex. 6:23, 25

Shifrah and Puah the Hebrew midwives were Yocheved and Miriam, and some say Yocheved and Elisheva.

Adapted from Sotah 11b

Elisheva had five joys more than all the daughters of Israel . . .

Zevachim 102a

EVEN DURING THE HAIL, Yocheved had gone to deliver babies. Life does not stop even for acts of God. Egyptian women had special need for midwives who would not be waylaid by hailstones or hungry locusts. The plagues, Yocheved had said, were no excuse for failure to do one's job. But tonight Yocheved's biting voice was absent. She had run to the communal ovens to bake for the journey. Miriam had gone to dispense her wisdom in the huts of the slave-chieftains. Neither would attend a birth tonight. Tonight the Angel of Death had descended. Tonight Elisheva was alone, a midwife sitting quietly by the hearth.

Elisheva dried her hands on her apron. She hummed a small song to her youngest. Family was her comfort in this time of wonders and dangers. Elisheva's father and mother had died years before of overwork and disease. Her younger brother had a friend, Aaron, whom she had loved. So it had been her fate to marry Yocheved's son, older brother to the mysterious Moses. Aaron was kind. She had needed kindness. Her pain at losing her own family prompted her to learn from Yocheved and Miriam their family trade. With that trade had come skill, patience, and enough courage to disobey Pharaoh's decrees. But now that blood had filled the Nile, she was as frightened as everyone else. That morning, she had seen how the firstborn of Egypt were shunned in the streets and even in their homes. Moses said the plagues came from God, but Elisheva found herself questioning why a merciful God would allow such suffering.

There was a knock at the door.

The girl was spotted with the remnants of boils and insect bites. Her dress was Egyptian, her face a wrinkled dot of fear. Elisheva drew away sharply from the child's outstretched hand.

"Please," the child said, "it's my sister's time."

Elisheva turned slightly away, toward the fire. The boys were asleep in the house's inner reaches. "You'll have to wait," she said. "The midwives have gone out."

Having told the lie, she wished to comfort the child. "Shall I bring you some herb tea?" she said.

The girl did not move. "Please," she said, "I've seen you at birthings before. My sister's bleeding. The baby's wedged inside her somehow. Please come."

Elisheva had never been afraid of death before. Tonight she thought of the plague feeling its way along Egypt's rough-edged alleyways. She could not bear the thought of leaving her four sons alone without their mother.

"Why haven't you gone to an Egyptian midwife?" Elisheva asked.

"My sister's a firstborn, and so is the baby," the girl admitted softly. "I've been all over. Everyone else is afraid."

Elisheva was silent for a long moment. Anger welled up within her that because of an Egyptian child, she should be in fear of her life the night before freedom.

"I won't come," she said harshly. She turned away and roughly poked the embers with a stick.

The girl was silent then. She slunk toward the low door, brushing against the dead reeds poking from the shabby wall. Elisheva made a small noise, watching her go.

The girl turned back suddenly, her face like ash with a single cinder left.

"My sister is in pain," she said with a clenched face. "She can't even speak. She can barely sit up. She has no strength left. She could die, and you're going to sit here by your warm fire and stir your ashes because she's an Egyptian and because you're scared. What kind of midwife are you? Aren't you supposed to care about all babies?"

The girl's voice was like Yocheved's, toothed and copper-plated. The bruised face of the Egyptian girl seemed to mirror every desperate pregnant woman Elisheva had ever attended. The risk seemed great, the reward small.

"I will come," Elisheva conceded, and reached for her warm robe.

The alleys of the Hebrews soon led to Egyptian streets. There was no sound, except the weeping of the bereaved, which was quickly silenced by fearful households. There were no cattle or insects to fill the streets with noise. The firstborns who were still alive huddled in the byres and ruins where others had driven them. Elisheva became grateful that the night was completely dark. There were no moving shadows to remind her of the angel who walked over Egypt. Her gratitude ceased when her foot landed on a corpse. Then she merely walked forward and thought of nothing.

When they arrived at the house, hunch-walled and topped with reed bundles, it smelled of blood. Elisheva felt herself begin to retch from fear. She swallowed and straightened her back. Then she stooped to enter the low opening into the house. The girl scurried ahead of her, breathing hard.

The scene before her—disarranged bedclothes and pots of hot water steaming—was like any other lying-in. Yet a pall hung over the room. There were no anxious voices. An Egyptian god lay useless on a table. The husband had long since run from the house.

The woman in the bed looked up at her with bloodshot eyes. Elisheva was afraid to touch her, for fear she might be slain herself. Like the woman in labor, Elisheva was a firstborn. Yet the white cloths lent some sense of normalcy, and she could not believe an angel of death lurked outside. The smoky brown walls of the hut seemed sturdy and safe. Elisheva went briskly to work.

Hours began to pass, punctuated by cries from other houses. The mother had lost much blood, but had enough energy to squeeze out a small body with Elisheva's help. The wet man-child was born backward. An omen of the times, Elisheva thought. She pulled him from the depths of his mother in one clean, practiced motion. His wisp of hair was the color of grated ginger, his skin a shade of horseradish. He was beautiful.

The midwife wrapped up the child and spoke words of comfort to the mother. The mother nursed and smiled at her son. Elisheva thanked God for the instant bond between mother and child. She had seen it so often, but it was always a miracle. The new mother's young sister, eyes fastened on her nephew, finally fell asleep on a reed mat. Elisheva packed her things and got ready to leave. She put on her robe and belted it, but she lingered and kept lingering. She wanted to get home to her own children, but somehow she couldn't seem to set her foot on the doorsill. Four hours passed, then five. A lightening of the sky came, and then it was almost dawn. Elisheva began to hope that, although there was no blood on the lintel, death had passed over the house.

When the gray shadow entered the room, Elisheva saw it first. She felt her old anger return, toward Egyptians, toward this mother and her child. She turned her back to the shadow and held her breath. She thought of Aaron, of his kind mouth pressed against hers.

A minute later, Elisheva could feel the mother's pulse slipping away. The child's lips were turning blue. She herself felt healthy. She breathed a sigh of relief that the plague had not touched her. She began to think of returning home.

Home made her think of all that this home was about to lose. Elisheva whipped around and faced the angel, her anger suddenly focused on the unfair decree that took away innocent life.

"Why are you here?" she screamed into the mist. "Being firstborn isn't a crime! What have this mother and child done worthy of death? They don't deserve to perish for being born!"

Then Elisheva became aware of something within the grayness, something small and shining and still, like a beacon in a storm. From the shining came a voice.

"Why are *you* here, Elisheva?" it asked.

"I belong here," she said, weeping. She hugged the mother and child to her with a strength she had known in herself only when she was near her own family.

The soft voice was audible only to her. Mother and infant had slipped into unconsciousness. The Egyptian girl stood open-mouthed near her bed, staring at the smoky light.

"Your vigil this night has not been in vain," the voice told her. "This mother and child will live because of you, and there will be an end to the plague on the firstborn: no one else will die on this night. Because you were not afraid to follow a stranger into her suffering, I will bless you and build you a great posterity. I will give to your hands the power of saving life. I will give to your house the priesthood. Your children will offer sacrifices for the nation. They shall be holy to me. And because you loved this family as your own, your grandchildren will descend from it. With them I will make my covenant of peace."

Through a daze of wonder, Elisheva imagined her sons growing into men. The light faded suddenly, like the end of a dream. On the doorpost was a smear of red like the ones on Israelite doorposts. She felt the new mother pull at her hand.

"We're still alive." The woman spoke with great awe.

"Yes, and you have a beautiful healthy baby," Elisheva told her. She began packing up herbs and cloths. Her family was no doubt waiting for her.

"Wait," the mother said, and held her gaze. "I want you to take us with you. I know you are going to a place where the stranger will be protected. Please give us a chance to live in such a place."

Elisheva was startled. She wanted to refuse. Surely the Israelites would not accept these Egyptians as comrades. Then she considered the vision she had seen.

"We need to leave right away," she said.

"I understand," the mother answered. "We have nothing to pack."

"What is your name?" Elisheva asked her.

"Putiel," the woman said. She squeezed the hand of her young sister, who for the first time shyly smiled.

A generation later in the Sinai wilderness, on a golden dawn, Putiel's second daughter gave birth to Elisheva's grandson. Elisheva and her apprentices, Putiel's sister and daughters, delivered the child. They gave him the name Pinchas, meaning "dark one." His name was in memory of the night of the tenth plague, and in honor of the night sky above Sinai, which Putiel had lived to see.

ISRAEL IN CONFLICT

HOW COULD A JEW DO THAT?

Letty Cottin Pogrebin

THIS IS A COLUMN ABOUT SHAME, an emotion I don't usually feel in relation to Jews. Lately, however, a sense of personal and communal shame has overwhelmed me, triggered by news stories from Israel or eyewitness reports from friends who live there. What I've reacted to in each case is an act of cruelty that strikes me as unthinkable not just because of its inherent heartlessness or severity, but because it was committed by a Jew.

Perhaps the problem is the deeply held—read, smug—beliefs I was taught as a child: that Jewish behavior is guided by strong moral and ethical imperatives; Jews don't oppress other peoples; Jews empathize with the underdog, having ourselves been oppressed in Mitzrayim and everywhere else; the Jewish people tries to be a light unto the nations and the Jewish state a model state; and, finally, Israel has the toughest, smartest army in the world, but also the most humane.

Sadly, in last twelve months these beliefs have been shaken to the core. Reading about documented Israeli human rights abuses, instances of Israeli Defense Force (IDF) brutality, and provocations by right-wing settlers, I ask myself, Can this be happening? Can Jewish people actually be behaving this way?

Which is not to say that any Jew should be passive or defenseless in the face of attack, or that Israel's enemies who bomb, shoot, ambush, terrorize, kidnap, and torture Jews should not be prosecuted to the fullest extent of the law. Such behavior, moreover, should arouse Arab shame. But when we Jews do such things nondefensively, when some of us treat all of "them" as if every single Palestinian is a terrorist and every Arab fundamentally subhuman, then the shame becomes ours—or, at least, mine.

Though Israel's occupation of the West Bank and Gaza has long been problematic (and illegal), I first felt this new kind of shame a year ago, at the start of the second intifada, when thirteen unarmed Israeli Arabs were killed by Israeli police who shot at them with rubber bullets from a distance of fifteen meters, though the projectiles are known to be fatal if fired closer than thirty meters. (The victims, citizens of Israel who were exercising their democratically protected right to political expression, reminded me of the thirteen students gunned down—four fatally—by the U.S. National Guard in the Kent State massacre of 1970.) When Physicians for Human Rights confirmed that the IDF had been using live ammunition and rubber bullets "excessively and inappropriately" against unarmed demonstrators, I thought, how could Jews do that?

Since then, there have been many reasons for shame and despair:

• Human Rights Watch observers spent five weeks last winter evaluating conditions in the conflict-ridden Hebron area and found that, among other things, thirty thousand Palestinians were being confined to their homes by "a near-permanent round-the-clock curfew" for the convenience of Jewish settlers who were allowed to move freely at all times. Innocent or guilty, old or young, sick or well, Palestinians experienced severe food shortages, twenty-one thousand pupils were unable to attend classes, workers lost their jobs, and ambulances were delayed. Knowing what Jews know about being penned up in ghettos, I asked myself, How could a Jew do that to others?

• B'Tselem, an independent Israeli human rights monitoring group, reported last March that Jewish settlers throughout the West Bank had been provoking Palestinian violence or acting as vigilantes while the IDF and Israeli police stood on the sidelines like a virtual shield doing nothing to prevent the violence or protect its victims. When wounded Palestinians appealed to them for help, "the soldiers refused to assist or responded with contempt." As the months went by, I continued to read accounts of Jewish settlers freely marauding through Palestinian villages, firing at vehicles and homes, breaking windows while people were trapped inside under curfew, burning a mosque, keeping farmers from tending their fields, preventing the entrance of firefighters who were responding to fires lit by settlers, and attacking journalists and medical teams. I remembered what the Cossacks had done to us and I wondered, How could a Jew do that to others?

• In early spring, I read of a pregnant Palestinian detained at an Israeli checkpoint who gave birth attended by IDF rifles; with the newborn on the ground still attached by its umbilical cord, the woman was still being interrogated. On June 8, Israeli soldiers refused passage to a forty-year-old woman in advanced labor who was forced to give birth in a car. When finally allowed to proceed to Jericho Hospital, she was hemorrhaging and the baby was in serious condition. On July 10, a baby died by the time its mother could receive medical care. What happened to the humanity of those young soldiers? How could a Jew do that?

• According to Adi Kuntsman, cofounder of the new group Machsom (Checkpoint) Watch, "We see examples of humiliation [of Palestinians] on an almost daily basis. People have their IDs taken from them, . . . sometimes waiting an hour or two to get them back." Kuntsman has "witnessed people forced to stand with their hands up in the air and their faces to the wall, or sit in the baking sun or pouring rain. And when we asked the soldier, 'Why can't they stand where it is isn't raining?' the soldier says, 'Because this is how I want it—I want them to do that." What bizarre distortion of power could make a young Jew that cruel?

• Last July 3, the IDF bulldozed a large number Palestinian homes in retaliation for the murder of a Jewish settler from Susiya, though the man's killer had not been identified or arrested. Nonetheless, in what can only be termed an act of free-ranging Israeli vengefulness, five hundred Palestinians were left without shelter, their wells destroyed, farms ravaged, and olive trees uprooted. Given our people's long history of victimization by collective punishment, how could a Jew do that to another people? (The strategy of demolishing Palestinian homes and property has proven an ineffective deterrent against terrorism, though it has made the possibility of future cordial coexistence increasingly remote.)

Israel's heartless or sadistic treatment of the "Other" seems to be proliferating. In response, right-wing apologists would probably say, "these people" deserve it, all of them, because every Arab would destroy us if he could. But at this point in history—given Israel's unquestionable military superiority—I believe we should be less worried about external enemies than about the internal existential threat to the very essence and meaning of Judaism and the Jewish State. In short, If we stop acting Jewish, are we still Jews?

EVIL UNLEASHED

Tanya Reinhart

IN MAINSTREAM POLITICAL DISCOURSE, Israel's recent atrocities are described as "retaliatory acts"—answering the last wave of terror attacks on Israeli civilians. But in fact this "retaliation" had been carefully prepared long before. Already in October 2000, at the outset of the Palestinian uprising, military circles were ready with detailed operative plans to topple Arafat and the Palestinian Authority. This was before the Palestinian terror attacks started. (The first attack on Israeli civilians was on November 3, 2000, in a market in Jerusalem.) A document prepared by the security services at the request of then-Prime Minister Barak, stated on October 15, 2000, that "Arafat, the person, is a severe threat to the security of the state [of Israel] and the damage which will result from his disappearance is less than the damage caused by his existence." (Details of the document were published in *Ma'ariv,* July 6, 2001.) The operative plan, known as Fields of Thorns, had been prepared back in 1996 and was then updated during the Intifada (Amir Oren, *Ha'aretz,* Nov. 23, 2001). The plan includes everything that Israel has been executing lately, and more.[1]

The political echelon for its part (Barak's circles) worked on preparing public opinion for the toppling of Arafat. On November 20, 2000, Nahman Shai, then public-affairs coordinator of the Barak government, released in a meeting with the press a sixty-page document titled Palestinian Authority Noncompliance: A Record of Bad Faith and Misconduct.

The document, informally referred to as the White Book, was prepared by Barak's aid, Danny Yatom.[2] According to the White Book, Arafat's present crime—"orchestrating the Intifada," is just the last in a long chain of proofs that he has never deserted the "option of violence and 'struggle.'" "As early as Arafat's own speech on the White House lawn on September 13, 1993, there were indications that for him, the D.O.P. [declaration of principles] did not necessarily signify an end to the conflict. He did not, at any point, relinquish his uniform, symbolic of his status as a revolutionary commander" (Section 2). This uniform, incidentally, is the only "indication" that the report cites of Arafat's hidden intentions on that occasion.

A large section of the document is devoted to establishing Arafat's "ambivalence and compliance" regarding terror. "In March 1997 there was once again more than a hint of a 'Green Light' from Arafat to the Hamas, prior to the bombing in Tel Aviv . . . This is implicit in the statement made by a Hamas-affiliated member of Arafat's Cabinet, Imad Faluji, to an American paper" (*Miami Herald,* April 5, 1997). No further hints are provided regarding how this links Arafat to that bombing, but this is the "green light to terror" theme that Military Intelligence (Ama'n) has been promoting since 1997, when its anti-Oslo line was consolidated. This theme has since been repeated again and again by military circles and eventually became the mantra of Israeli propaganda—Arafat is still a terrorist and is personally responsible for the acts of all groups, from Hamas and the Islamic Jihad to Hizbollah.

The Foreign Report of July 12, 2001, disclosed that the Israeli army (under Sharon's government) has updated its plans for an "all-out assault to smash the Palestinian authority, force out leader Yasser Arafat and kill or detain its army." The blueprint, titled The Destruction of the Palestinian Authority and Disarmament of All Armed Forces, was presented to the Israeli government by chief of staff Shaul Mofaz on July 8. The assault would be launched at the government's discretion after a big suicide bomb attack in Israel, causing widespread deaths and injuries, and the bloodshed would be cited as justification.

Many in Israel suspect that the assassination of the Hamas terrorist Mahmoud Abu Hanoud—just when the Hamas had respected for two months its agreement with Arafat not to attack inside Israel—was designed to create the appropriate "bloodshed justification" on the eve of Sharon's visit to the United States. (Alex Fishman, senior security correspondent of *Yediot,* noted that "whoever decided upon the liquidation of Abu Hanoud knew in advance that would be the price. The subject was extensively discussed both by Israel's military echelon and its political one, before it was decided to carry out the liquidation" [*Yediot Aharonot*, Nov. 25, 2001].)

Israel's moves to destroy the PA thus cannot be viewed as a spontaneous "act of retaliation." It is a calculated plan, long in the making. The execution requires first weakening the resistance of the Palestinians, which Israel has been doing systematically since October 2000, through killing, bombarding of infrastructure, imprisoning people in their hometowns, and bringing them close to starvation. All this while waiting for the international conditions to "ripen" for the more advanced steps of the plan. Now the conditions seem to have ripened. In the power-drunk political atmosphere in the United States, anything goes. If at first it seemed that the United States would try to keep the Arab world on its side by some token of persuasion, as it did during the Gulf War, it is now clear that they couldn't care less. U.S. policy is no longer based on building coalitions or investing in persuasion, but on sheer force. The smashing "victory" in Afghanistan has sent a clear message to the Third World that nothing can stop the United States from targeting any nation for annihilation. They seem to believe that the most sophisticated weapons of the twenty-first century, combined with total absence of any considerations of moral principles, international law, or public opinion, can sustain them as the sole rulers of the world forever. From now on, fear should be the sufficient condition for obedience.

The U.S. hawks, who push to expand the war to Iraq and further, view Israel as an asset: there are few regimes in the world like it, so eager to risk the lives of their citizens for a new regional war. As Professor Alain Joxe, head of the French CIRPES (peace and strategic studies) put it in *Le Monde,* "American leadership is presently shaped by dangerous right-wing Southern extremists who seek to use Israel as an offensive tool to destabilize the whole Middle East area" (December 17, 2001). The same hawks are also talking about expanding the future war zone to targets on Israel's agenda, like Hizbollah and Syria.

Under these circumstances, Sharon got his green light in Washington. As the Israeli media keeps raving, "Bush is fed up with this character" (Arafat), and "Powell said that Arafat must stop his lies" (Barnea and Schiffer, *Yediot,* December 7, 2001). As Arafat hides in his bunker, Israeli F-16 bombers plow the sky and Israel's brutality generates new desperate human bombs every day, the United States, accompanied for awhile by the European Union, keeps urging Arafat to "act."

But what is the rationale behind Israel's systematic drive to eliminate the Palestinian Authority and undo the Oslo arrangements? It certainly cannot be based on disappointment with Arafat's performance, as is commonly claimed. The fact of the matter is that from the perspective of Israel's interests in maintaining the occupation, Arafat did fulfill Israel's expectations all these last years.

As far as Israeli security goes, there is nothing further from the truth than the fake accusations in the White Book or in subsequent Israeli propaganda. To take just one example, in 1997—the year mentioned in the White Book as an instance of Arafat's "green light to terror"—a security agreement was signed between Israel and the Palestinian Authority, under the auspices of the head of the Tel Aviv station of the CIA, Stan Muskovitz. The agreement commits the PA to take active care of the security of Israel—to fight "the terrorists, the terrorist base, and the environmental conditions leading to support of terror" in cooperation with Israel, including "mutual exchange of information, ideas, and military cooperation" (clause 1 [translated from the Hebrew text, *Ha'aretz,* December 12, 1997]). Arafat's security services carried out this job faithfully, with assassinations of Hamas terrorists (disguised as accidents) and arrests of Hamas political leaders.[3]

Ample information was published in the Israeli media regarding these activities, and "security sources" were full of praise for Arafat's achievements. For example, Ami Ayalon, then head of the Israeli secret service (Shab'ak), announced in a government meeting on April 5, 1998, that "Arafat is doing his job—he is fighting terror and puts all his weight against the Hamas" (*Ha'aretz,* April 6, 1998). The rate of success of the Israeli security services in containing terror was never higher than that of Arafat; in fact, much lower.

In left and critical circles, one can hardly find compassion for Arafat's personal fate, as opposed to the tragedy of the Palestinian people. As David Hirst writes in the *Guardian,* when Arafat returned to the occupied territories in 1994:

> He came as collaborator as much as liberator. For the Israelis, security—theirs, not the Palestinians'—was the be-all and end-all of Oslo. His job was to supply it on their behalf. But he could only sustain the collaborator's role if he won the political quid pro quo which through a series of "interim agreements" leading to "final status" was supposedly to come his way. He never could. . . . [Along the road], he acquiesced in accumulating concessions that only widened the gulf between what he was actually achieving and what he assured his people he would achieve, by this method, in the end. He was Mr. Palestine still, with a charisma and historical legitimacy all his own. But he was proving to be grievously wanting in that other great and complementary task,

building his state-in-the-making. Economic misery, corruption, abuse of human rights, the creation of a vast apparatus of repression—all these flowed, wholly or in part, from the Authority over which he presided ["Arafat's Last Stand?" *Guardian*, Dec. 14, 2001].

But from the perspective of the Israeli occupation, all this means that the Oslo plan was essentially successful. Arafat did manage, through harsh means of oppression, to contain the frustration of his people and guarantee the safety of the settlers, as Israel continued undisturbed to build new settlements and appropriate more Palestinian land. The oppressive machinery—the various security forces of Arafat—were formed and trained in collaboration with Israel. Much energy and resources were put into building this complex Oslo apparatus. It is often admitted that the Israeli security forces cannot manage to prevent terror any better than Arafat can. Why then was the military and political echelon so determined to destroy all this already in October 2000, even before the terror waves started? Answering this question requires a look at the history.

Right from the start of the "Oslo process" in September 1993, two conceptions were competing in the Israeli political and military system. The one, led by Yosi Beilin, was striving to implement some version of the Alon plan, which the Labor Party has been advocating for years. The original plan consisted of annexation of about 35 percent of the territories to Israel and either Jordanian rule or some form of self-rule for the rest, the land on which the Palestinians actually live. In the eyes of its proponents, this plan represented a necessary compromise, compared to the alternatives of either giving up the territories altogether or eternal bloodshed, as we witness today.

It appeared that Rabin was willing to follow this line, at least at the start, and that in return for Arafat's commitment to control the frustration of his people and guarantee the security of Israel, he would allow the PA to run the enclaves in which the Palestinians still reside in some form of self-rule, which may even be called a Palestinian state.

But the other pole objected to even that much. This was mostly visible in military circles, whose most vocal spokesman in the early years of Oslo was then Chief of Staff Ehud Barak. Another center of opposition was of course Sharon and the extreme right wing, who were against the Oslo process from the start. This affinity between the military circles and Sharon is hardly surprising. Sharon, the last of the leaders of the "1948 generation," was a legendary figure in the army, and many of the generals were his disciples, like Barak. As Amir Oren wrote, "Barak's deep and abiding admiration for Ariel Sharon's military insights is another indication of his views; Barak and Sharon both belong to a line of political generals that started with Moshe Dayan" (*Ha'aretz*, January 8, 1999).

This breed of generals was raised on the myth of redemption of the land. A glimpse into this worldview is offered in Sharon's interview with Ari Shavit (*Ha'aretz*, weekend supplement, April 13, 2001). Everything is entangled into one romantic framework: the fields, the blossom of the orchards, the plow, and the wars. The heart of this ideology is the sanctity of the land. In a 1976 interview, Moshe Dayan, who was the defense minister in 1967, explained what led to the decision to attack Syria. In the collective Israeli consciousness of the period, Syria was conceived as a serious threat to the security of Israel, and a constant initiator of aggression towards the residents of northern Israel. But according to Dayan, this is "bullshit"—Syria was not a threat to Israel before 1967—"Just drop it . . . I know how at least 80 percent of all the incidents with Syria started. We were sending a tractor to the demilitarized zone and we knew that the Syrians would shoot." According to Dayan (who at the time of the interview confessed some regrets), what led Israel to provoke Syria this way was the greediness for the land—the idea that it is possible "to grab a piece of land and keep it until the enemy gets tired and gives it to us" (*Yediot Aharonot*, Apr. 27, 1997).

On the eve of Oslo, the majority of Israeli society was tired of wars. In their eyes, the fights over land and resources were over. Most Israelis believe that the 1948 Independence War, with its horrible consequences for the Palestinians, was necessary to establish a state for the Jews, haunted by the memory of the Holocaust. But now that they have a state, they long to live normally with whatever they have. However, the ideology of the redemption of land has never died out in the army or the circles of the "political generals," who switched from the army to the government. In their eyes, Sharon's alternative of fighting the Palestinians to the bitter end and imposing new regional orders—as he tried in Lebanon in 1982—may have failed because of the weakness of a spoiled Israeli society. But given the new war philosophy established in Iraq, Kosovo, and Afghanistan, they believe that with the massive superiority of the Israeli air force it may still be possible to win this battle in the future.

While Sharon's party was in the opposition at the time of Oslo, Barak, as Chief of Staff, participated in the negotiations and played a crucial role in shaping the agreements and Israel's attitude toward the Palestinian Authority.

I quote from an article I wrote in February 1994, because it reflects what anybody who carefully read the Israeli media could see at the time:

From the start, it has been possible to identify two conceptions that underlie the Oslo process. One is that this will help reduce the cost of the occupation, using a Palestinian patronage regime, with Arafat as the senior cop responsible for the security of Israel.

The other is that the process should lead to the collapse of Arafat and the PLO. The humiliation of Arafat and the amplification of his surrender will gradually lead to loss of popular support. Consequently, the PLO will collapse or will enter power conflicts. Thus, Palestinian society will lose its secular leadership and institutions. In the power-driven mind of those eager to maintain the Israeli occupation, the collapse of secular leadership will be misinterpreted as an achievement, because it would take a long while for the Palestinian people to get organized again and, in any case, it is easier to justify even the worst acts of oppression when the enemy is a fanatic Muslim organization. Most likely, the conflict between the two competing conceptions is not settled yet, but at the moment the second seems more dominant. In order to carry out the first, Arafat's status should have been strengthened with at least some achievements that could generate support of the Palestinians, rather then Israel's policy of constant humiliation and breach of promises."[4]

Nevertheless, the scenario of the collapse of the PA did not materialize. Palestinian society resorted once more to their marvelous strategy of *zumud*—sticking to the land and sustaining the pressure. Right from the start, the Hamas political leadership and others were warning that Israel was trying to push the Palestinians into a civil war in which the nation slaughters itself. All fragments of the society cooperated to prevent this danger and calm conflicts as soon as they were resorting to violence. They also managed, despite the tyranny of Arafat's rule, to build an impressive amount of institutions and infrastructure. The PA does not consist only of corrupt rulers and various security forces. The elected Palestinian council, which operates under endless restrictions, is still a representative political framework and a basis for democratic institutions in the future. For those whose goal is the destruction of the Palestinian identity and the eventual redemption of their land, Oslo was a failure.

In 1999 the army regained power through the "political generals"—first Barak and then Sharon. (They collaborated in the last elections to guarantee that no other civil candidate would be allowed to run.) The road opened to correct what they view as the grave mistake of Oslo. In order to get there, it was first necessary to convince the spoiled Israeli society that the Palestinians are not willing to live in peace and are threatening our very existence. Sharon alone could not possibly have achieved that, but Barak did succeed, with his "generous offer" fraud. After a year of horrible terror attacks combined with massive propaganda and lies, Sharon and the army feel that nothing can stop them from turning to full execution.

Why is it so urgent for them to topple Arafat? Shabtai Shavit, former head of the Security Service (Mossad), who is not bound by restraints posed on official sources, explains this openly: "In the thirty-some years that he [Arafat] has led, he managed to reach real achievements in the political and international sphere. . . . He got the Nobel Peace Prize, and in a single phone call he can obtain a meeting with every leader in the world. There is nobody in the Palestinian gallery that can fill his shoes in this context of international status. If they [the Palestinians] lose this gain, for us it is a huge achievement. The Palestinian issue will be off the international agenda" (interview in *Yediot* weekend supplement, December 7, 2001).

Their immediate goal is to get the Palestinians off the international agenda, so slaughter, starvation, forced evacuation, and "migration" can continue undisturbed, leading possibly to the final realization of Sharon's long-standing vision embodied in the military plans. The immediate goal of anybody concerned with the future of the world should be to halt this process of evil unleashed. As Alain Joxe concluded his article in *Le Monde*, "It is time for Western public opinion to take over and to compel the governments to take a moral and political stand facing the foreseen disaster; namely a situation of permanent war against the Arab and Muslim people and states—the realization of the double fantasy of Bin Laden and Sharon" (December 17, 2001).

NOTES

1. For the details of this operative plan, see Anthony Cordesman, "Peace and War: Israel versus the Palestinians—A Second Intifada?" Center for Strategic and International Studies (CSIS), December 2000, and its summary in Shraga Eilam, "Peace with Violence or Transfer," *Between the Lines*, December 2000.

2. The document can be found in www.gamla.org.il/english/feature/intro.htm

3. For a survey of some of the PA's assassinations of Hamas terrorists, see my article "The A-Sherif Affair," *Yediot Aharonot*, April 14, 1998, www.tau.ac.il/~reinhart/political/A_sharif.html

4. The article can be found (in Hebrew only) at www.tau.ac.il/~reinhart/political/01GovmntObstacleToPeace.doc

EIGHTY THESES

Uri Avnery

1. The peace process has collapsed—and taken down with it a large part of the Israeli peace camp.

2. Transient circumstances, such as personal or party political matters, failures of leadership, political self-interest, domestic and global political developments—all these are like foam over the waves. Important as they may be, they cannot adequately explain the peace process's total collapse.

3. The true explanation of this collapse can only be found beneath the surface, at the roots of the historical conflict between the two nations.

4. The Madrid-Oslo process failed because the two sides were seeking to achieve conflicting goals.

5. The goals of each of the two sides emanated from their basic national interests. They were shaped by their historical narratives, by their disparate views of the conflict over the last 120 years. The Israeli national historical version and the Palestinian national historical version are entirely contradictory, both in general and in every single detail.

6. The negotiators and the decision-makers on the Israeli side were completely oblivious to the Palestinian national narrative. Even when they sincerely wished to reach a solution, their efforts were doomed to fail because they could not understand the national desires, traumas, fears, and hopes of the Palestinian people. While there is no symmetry between the two sides, the Palestinian attitude was similar.

7. Resolution of such a long historical conflict is possible only if each side is capable of understanding the other's spiritual-national world and

willing to approach it as an equal. An insensitive, condescending, and overbearing attitude precludes any possibility of a mutually agreed-upon solution.

8. The Barak government, which had inspired so much hope, was afflicted with all these attitudes; hence the enormous gap between its initial promise and its disastrous results.

9. A significant part of the old peace camp (also called the Zionist Left or the Sane Constituency) is similarly afflicted by these attitudes and therefore collapsed along with the government it supported, paving the way for the ultra-Zionist, Sharon-led National Unity Government.

10. The primary role of a new Israeli peace camp is to get rid of the false myths and the one-sided view of the conflict. This does not mean that the Israeli narrative should automatically be rejected and the Palestinian narrative unquestionably accepted. But it does require open-minded listening and understanding of the other side's position in the historical conflict, in order to bridge the two national narratives.

11. Any other way will lead to a perpetuation of the conflict, with periods of ostensible tranquility and conciliation frequently interrupted by violent hostile actions between the two nations and between Israel and the Arab world. Considering the pace of development of weapons of mass destruction, further rounds of hostility could lead to the destruction of all sides of the conflict.

The Root of the Conflict

12. The Israeli-Palestinian conflict is the continuation of the historical clash between the Zionist movement and the Palestinian Arab people, a clash that began at the end of the nineteenth century and has yet to end.

13. The Zionist movement was essentially a Jewish reaction to the emergence of the national movements in Europe, all of which were hostile to Jews. Having been rejected by the European nations, some of the Jews decided to establish themselves as a separate nation and, following the new European model, to set up their own national state where they could be masters of their own fate. The basic Zionist tenet, drawn from the European model, that a minority cannot exist within a nationally homogeneous state, subsequently led to the practical exclusion of the Palestinian national minority in the Zionist state that came into being about fifty years later.

14. Traditional and religious motives drew the Zionist movement to Palestine (*Eretz Israel* in Hebrew) and led to the decision to establish the Jewish state in this land. The maxim was "a land without a people for a

people without a land." This maxim was not only created out of ignorance but also reflected the general arrogance towards non-European peoples that prevailed in Europe at that time.

15. Palestine was not empty—not at the end of the nineteenth century
nor at any other period. At that time, there were half a million people living in Palestine, 90 percent of them Arabs. This population objected, of
course, to the incursion of another nation into their land.

16. The Arab national movement emerged almost simultaneously with
the Zionist movement, initially to fight the Ottoman Empire and later to
fight the colonial regimes created upon its destruction at the end of World
War I. A separate Arab-Palestinian national movement developed in the
country after the British created a separate state called Palestine, and in
the course of the struggle against the Zionist infiltration.

17. Since the end of World War I, there has been an ongoing struggle between two nationalist movements, the Jewish-Zionist and the Palestinian-
Arab, both of which aspired to accomplish their goals—which entirely
negate each other—within the same territory. This situation remains unchanged to this day.

18. As Jewish persecution in Europe intensified, and as the countries
of the world closed their gates to the Jews attempting to flee the inferno,
so the Zionist movement gained strength. The Holocaust, which took the
lives of six million Jews, gave moral and political force to the Zionist claim
that led to the establishment of the state of Israel.

19. The Palestinian people, witnessing the growth of the Jewish population in their land, could not comprehend why they were required to
pay the price for crimes committed against the Jews by Europeans. They
violently objected to further Jewish immigration and to the acquisition of
lands by the Jews.

20. The complete blindness of each of the two peoples to the national
existence of the other inevitably led to false and distorted perceptions that
took root deep in the collective consciousness of both. These perceptions
affect their attitude towards each other to this day.

21. The Arabs believed that the Jews had been implanted in the country by Western imperialism, in order to subjugate the Arab world and take
control of its treasures. This conviction was strengthened by the fact that
the Zionist movement, from the outset, strove for an alliance with at least
one Western power (Germany, Great Britain, France, the United States)
to overcome the Arab resistance. The results were a practical cooperation
and a community of interests between the Zionist enterprise and imperialist and colonialist forces, directed against the Arab national movement.

22. The Jews, on the other hand, were convinced that the Arab resistance to the Zionist enterprise—intended to save the Jews from the flames

of Europe—was the consequence of the murderous nature of the Arabs and of Islam. In their eyes, Arab fighters were "gangs," and the uprisings of the time were called "riots."

(Actually, in the 1920s, the most extreme Zionist leader, Ze'ev Jabotinsky, was almost alone in recognizing that the Arab resistance to the Zionist settlement was an inevitable, natural, and, from this point of view, just reaction of a "native" people defending their country against foreign invaders. Jabotinsky also recognized the fact that the Arabs in the country were a separate national entity and derided attempts made to bribe the leaders of other Arab countries to put an end to the Palestinian Arab resistance. However, Jabotinsky's conclusion was to erect an "iron wall" against the Arabs and to crush their resistance by force.)

23. This total contradiction in Arab and Jewish perceptions of the facts affects every aspect of the conflict. For example, the Jews interpreted their struggle for "Jewish Labor" as a progressive social effort to transform a nation of merchants and speculators into one of workers and farmers. The Arabs, on the other hand, saw it as a criminal attempt by the Zionists to dispossess them, to evict them from the labor market, and to create, on their land, an Arab-free, separatist Jewish economy.

24. The Zionists were proud of their "Redemption of the Land." They had purchased it for full value with money collected from Jews around the world. *Olim* (new immigrants, literally pilgrims), who had been intellectuals and merchants in their former life, now earned their living by the sweat of their brow. They believed that they had achieved all this by peaceful means and without dispossessing a single Arab. For the Arabs this was a cruel narrative of dispossession and expulsion: the Jews acquired lands from rich absentee Arab landowners and then forcibly evicted the *fellahin* who had for generations been living on and earning their living from these lands. To help them with these evictions, the Zionists engaged the Turkish and later the British police. The Arabs looked on despairingly as their land was taken from them.

25. Against the Zionist claim of having successfully "turned the desert into a garden," the Arabs cited the testimonies of European travelers who spoke of a Palestine that, for several centuries, had been described as a populated and flourishing land, the equal of any of its regional neighbors.

Independence and Disaster

26. The contrast between the two national versions peaked in the war of 1948, a war called the "War of Independence," or even the "War of Liberation," by the Jews, and El Naqba, the disaster, by the Arabs.

27. As the conflict intensified in the region, and with the resounding impact of the Holocaust, the United Nations decided to divide the country into two states, Jewish and Arab. Jerusalem and its environs were supposed to remain a separate unit, under international jurisdiction. The Jews were allotted 55 percent of the land, including the unpopulated Negev.

28. The Zionist movement accepted the partition plan, convinced that the crucial issue was to establish a firm foundation for Jewish sovereignty. In closed meetings, David Ben-Gurion never concealed his intention to expand at the first opportunity the territory given to the Jews. That is why Israel's Declaration of Independence did not define the state's borders and Israel has remained without definite borders to this day.

29. The Arab world did not accept the partition plan and regarded it as a vile attempt by the United Nations, which essentially was at the time a club of Western and Communist nations, to divide a country that did not belong to it. Handing over most of the country to the Jewish minority, which represented a mere third of the population, made it all the more unforgivable in their eyes.

30. The war initiated by the Arabs after the partition plan was inescapably an "ethnic" war; a kind of war in which each side seeks to conquer as much land as possible and evict the population of the other side. Such a campaign (which later came to be called "ethnic cleansing") always involves expulsion and atrocities.

31. The war of 1948 was a direct extension of the Zionist-Arab conflict in which each side sought to fulfill its aims. The Jews wanted to establish a homogeneous national state that would be as large as possible. The Arabs wanted to eradicate the Zionist Jewish entity that had been established in Palestine.

32. Both sides practiced ethnic cleansing as an integral part of the fighting. Not many Arabs remained in territories captured by the Jews, and no Jews remained in territories captured by the Arabs. However, as the territories captured by the Jews were by far larger than those captured by the Arabs, the result was unbalanced. (The ideas of "population exchange" and "transfer" were raised in Zionist organizations as early as the 1930s. Effectively this meant the expulsion of the Arab population from the country. On the other side, many among the Arabs believed that the Zionists should go back to wherever they came from.)

33. The myth of "the few against the many" was cultivated by the Jews to describe the stand of the Jewish community of 650,000 against the entire Arab world of over a hundred million. (The Jewish community lost 1 percent of its people in the war.) The Arabs painted a completely different picture: a fragmented Arab population with no national leader-

ship to speak of, with no unified command over its meager forces, with poor, few, and mostly obsolete weapons, confronted an extremely well-organized Jewish community that was highly trained in the use of its weapons. The neighboring Arab countries betrayed the Palestinians and, when they finally did send their armies, they primarily operated in competition with each other, with no coordination and no common plan. From the social and military point of view, the fighting capabilities of the Israeli side were far superior to those of the Arab states, which had hardly emerged from the colonial era.

34. According to the United Nations plan, the Jewish state was supposed to include an Arab population amounting to about 40 percent. During the war the Jewish state expanded its borders and ended up with 78 percent of the area of the land. This area was nearly devoid of Arabs. The Arab populations of Nazareth and a few villages in the Galilee remained almost incidentally; the villages in the Triangle had been given to Israel as part of a deal by King Abdullah and therefore could not be evacuated.

35. In the war a total of 750,000 Palestinians were uprooted. Some of them fled out of fear of the battle, as civilian populations do in every war. Some were driven away by acts of terror such as the Dir-Yassin Massacre. Others were systematically evicted in the course of the ethnic cleansing.

36. No less important than the expulsion is the fact that the refugees were not allowed to return to their homes when the fighting was over, as is the practice after a conventional war. Quite to the contrary, the new Israel saw the removal of the Arabs very much as a blessing and proceeded to demolish totally some 450 Arab villages. New Jewish villages were built on the ruins, and new Hebrew names were given to them. The abandoned houses in the cities were repopulated with new immigrants.

A Jewish State

37. The signing of the cease-fire agreements at the end of the war of 1948 did not bring an end to the historical conflict, which was in fact raised to new and more intensive levels.

38. The new state of Israel dedicated its early years to the consolidation of its homogeneous national character as a "Jewish state." Large sections of land were expropriated from the "absentees" (the Arab refugees), from those officially designated as "present absentees" (Arabs who physically remained in Israel but were not allowed to become citizens), and even from the Arab citizens of Israel, most of whose lands were taken over. On these lands a dense network of Jewish communities was created. Jewish

"immigrants" were invited and even coaxed to come en masse. This great effort fortified the state's power several times over in but a few years.

39. At the same time the state vigorously conducted a policy of obliterating the Palestinians as a national entity. With Israeli help, the Trans-Jordan monarch, Abdullah, took control over the West Bank and since then there has been, in effect, an Israeli military guarantee for the existence of the kingdom of Jordan.

40. The main rationale of the deal between Israel and the Hashemite Kingdom, which has been in effect for three generations, was to prevent the establishment of an independent Arab-Palestinian State, which was considered—then and now—an obstacle to the realization of the Zionist objective.

41. A historical change occurred at the end of the 1950s on the Palestinian side when Yasser Arafat and his associates founded the Fatah movement designed to free the Palestinian liberation movement from the custody of the Arab governments. It was no accident that this movement emerged after the failure of the great pan-Arab concept whose most renowned representative was Gamal Abdel Nasser. Up to this point many Palestinians had hoped to be absorbed into a united all-Arab nation. When this hope faded, the separate national Palestinian identity reemerged.

42. The Palestinian Liberation Organization (PLO) was created by Gamal Abdel Nasser to prevent autonomous Palestinian action that might involve him in an undesired war with Israel. The organization was intended to impose Egyptian authority over the Palestinians. However, after the Arab defeat in the June 1967 war, Fatah, led by Yasser Arafat, took control over the PLO and the PLO has been the sole representative of the Palestinian people ever since.

The Six-Day War

43. The June 1967 war is seen in a very different light by the two sides, as is every incident over the last 120 years. According to the Israeli myth, the Six-Day War was a desperate war of defense that miraculously placed a lot of land in Israel's hands. According to the Palestinian myth, the leaders of Egypt, Syria, and Jordan fell into a trap set by Israel in order to capture whatever was left of Palestine.

44. Many Israelis believe that the Six-Day War was the root of all evil and it was only then that the peace-loving and progressive Israel turned into a conqueror and an occupier. This conviction allows them to maintain the absolute purity of Zionism and the state of Israel up to that point in history and preserve their old myths. There is no truth to this legend.

45. The war of 1967 was yet another phase of the old struggle between the two national movements. It did not change the essence; it only changed the circumstances. The essential objectives of the Zionist movement—a Jewish state, expansion, and settlement—were making great strides. The particular circumstances made extensive ethnic cleansing impossible in this war, but several hundreds of thousands of Palestinians were nevertheless expelled.

46. Israel was allotted 55 percent of the land (Palestine) by the 1947 partition plan, an additional 23 percent was captured in the 1948 war, and now the remaining 22 percent across the Green Line (the pre-1967 armistice line) was also captured. In 1967 Israel inadvertently united the Palestinian people (including some of the refugees) under its rule.

47. As soon as the war ended, the settlement movement began. Almost every political faction in the state participated in this movement—from the messianic nationalistic Gush Emunim to the "leftist" United Kibbutz movement. The first settlers received broad support from most politicians, left and right, from Yigal Alon (the Jewish settlement in Hebron) to Shimon Peres (the Kedumim settlement).

48. The fact that all governments of Israel cultivated and advanced the settlements, albeit to different extents, proves that the settlement aspiration was restricted to no specific ideological camp and extended to the entire Zionist movement. The impression that has been created of a small minority driving the settlement movement is illusory. Only a consolidated effort on the part of all government agencies since 1967 could have produced the legislative, strategic, and budgetary infrastructure required for such a long-lasting and expensive endeavor.

49. The legislative infrastructure incorporates the misleading assumption that the Occupation Authority is the owner of "government-owned lands," although these are the essential land reserves of the Palestinian population. It is self-evident that the settlement movement contravenes international law.

50. The dispute between the proponents of "greater Israel" and those of "territorial compromise" is essentially a dispute about the way to achieve the basic Zionist aspiration: a homogeneous Jewish state in as large a territory as possible. The proponents of "compromise" emphasize the demographic issue and want to prevent the inclusion of the Palestinian population in the state. The greater Israel adherents place the emphasis on the geographic issue and believe (privately or publicly) that it is possible to expel the non-Jewish population from the country (code name: transfer).

51. The general staff of the Israeli army (under Ariel Sharon in particular) played an important role in the planning and building of the settlements. It

created the map of the settlements—including blocs of settlements and by-pass roads, lateral and longitudinal—so that the West Bank and the Gaza Strip are chopped up into pieces and the Palestinians are imprisoned in isolated enclaves, each of which is surrounded by settlements and the occupation forces.

52. The Palestinians employed several methods of resistance, mainly raids across the Jordanian and Lebanese borders and attacks inside Israel and everywhere in the world. These acts are called "terrorist" by the Israelis, while the Palestinians see them as the legitimate resistance of an occupied nation. The PLO leadership, headed by Yasser Arafat, had long been considered a terrorist leadership by the Israelis but has gradually come to be internationally recognized as the sole legitimate representative of the Palestinian people.

53. At the end of 1987, when the Palestinians realized that these actions were not putting an end to settlement momentum, they launched the Intifada—a grassroots uprising of all sectors of the population. In this Intifada, fifteen hundred Palestinians were killed, among them hundreds of children, several times the number of Israeli losses.

The Peace Process

54. The October 1973 war, which commenced with the surprise victory of the Egyptian and Syrian forces and culminated with their defeat, convinced Yasser Arafat and his close associates that there is no military way to achieve the national Palestinian objectives. He decided to embark upon a political path to reach agreement with Israel and to pursue at least a partial achievement of the national goals through negotiation.

55. To prepare the ground for this goal, Arafat created contact for the first time with Israeli personalities who could make an impact on public opinion and on government policy in Israel. His emissaries, Said Hamami and Issam Sartawi, met with Israeli public figures, the peace pioneers who in 1975 established the Israeli Council for Israeli-Palestinian Peace.

56. These contacts, as well as the growing fatigue felt by the Israelis during the Intifada, the Jordanian withdrawal from the West Bank, changing international conditions (the collapse of the Communist bloc, the Gulf War), led to the Madrid Conference and, later, to the Oslo Agreement.

The Oslo Agreement

57. The Oslo Agreement had positive and negative features.

58. On the positive side, this agreement brought Israel to its first official recognition of the Palestinian people and its national leadership and

brought the national Palestinian movement to its recognition of the existence of Israel. In this respect the agreement (and the exchange of letters that preceded it) were of paramount historical significance.

59. In effect, the agreement gave the national Palestinian movement a territorial base on Palestinian land, the structure of a "state in the making," and armed forces—facts that would play an important role in the ongoing Palestinian struggle. For the Israelis, the agreement opened the gates to the Arab world and put an end to Palestinian attacks—as long as the agreement was effective.

60. The most substantive flaw in the agreement was that both sides hoped to achieve entirely different objectives. The Palestinians saw it as a temporary agreement paving the way to the end of the occupation and the establishment of a Palestinian state in all the occupied territories. The respective Israeli governments regarded it as a way to maintain the occupation in large sections of the West Bank and the Gaza Strip, with the Palestinian self-government filling the role of an auxiliary security agency protecting Israel and the settlements.

61. Therefore, Oslo did not represent the beginning of the process to end the conflict but rather a new phase of the conflict.

62. Because the expectations of both sides were so divergent and each remained entirely bound to its own national narrative, every section of the agreement was interpreted differently. Ultimately, many parts of the agreement were not carried out, mainly by Israel (for example, the third withdrawal and the four safe passages).

63. Throughout the period of the Oslo Process, Israel continued its vigorous expansion of the settlements, primarily by creating new ones under various guises, expanding existing ones, building an elaborate network of "bypass" roads, expropriating land, demolishing houses, and uprooting plantations. The Palestinians, for their part, used the time to build their strength, both within the framework of the agreement and outside it. In fact, the historical confrontation continued unabated under the guise of negotiations and the "peace process," which became a proxy for actual peace.

64. In contradiction to his image as an unequivocal supporter of reconciliation with the Palestinians, Yitzhak Rabin continued many of the practices of the occupation while simultaneously managing the political process to achieve peace on Israeli terms. As he was a disciple of the Zionist narrative and accepted its mythology, he suffered from cognitive dissonance when his hopes for peace clashed with his conceptual world. It appears that he began to internalize some parts of the Palestinian historical narrative only at the very end of his life.

65. The case of Shimon Peres is much more severe. He created for himself an international image of peacemaker and even designed his language

to reflect this image—"the New Middle East"—while remaining essentially a traditional Zionist hawk. This became clear in the short and violent period when he served as prime minister after the assassination of Rabin and again in his current acceptance of the role of spokesman and apologist for Sharon.

66. The clearest expression of the Israeli dilemma was provided by Ehud Barak, who came to power completely convinced of his ability to cut the Gordian knot of the historical conflict in one dramatic stroke, in the fashion of Alexander the Great. Barak approached the issue in total ignorance of the Palestinian narrative, showing utter contempt for its importance. He presented his proposals as ultimatums and was appalled and enraged by their rejection.

67. In his own eyes and in the eyes of Israel as a whole, Barak "turned every stone" and made the Palestinians "more generous offers than any previous prime minister." In exchange, he wanted the Palestinians to lend their signatures to an end to the conflict. The Palestinians considered this offer preposterous, since Barak was effectively asking them to relinquish their basic national aspirations, such as the right of return and sovereignty in East Jerusalem and the Temple Mount. Moreover, while Barak presented the claims for the annexation of territories as a matter of negligible percentages ("Settlement Blocs"), according to Palestinian calculations Barak's offer amounted to an actual annexation of 20 percent of the land beyond the Green Line.

68. In the Palestinian view, they had already made the decisive compromise by agreeing to establish their state beyond the Green Line, in merely 22 percent of their historical homeland. Therefore, they could only accept minor border changes in the context of territorial swaps. The traditional Israeli position is that the achievements of the war of 1948 are established facts that cannot be disputed and the compromise required must focus on the remaining 22 percent.

69. As with most terms and concepts, the word *concession* has different meanings for both sides. The Palestinians believe that they already conceded 78 percent of their land when they agreed to accept 22 percent of it. The Israelis believe that they are conceding when they agree to "give" the Palestinians parts of that same 22 percent (the West Bank and the Gaza Strip).

70. The Camp David Summit in the summer of 2000, which was imposed on Arafat against his will, was premature and brought things to a climax. Barak's demands, presented at the summit as Clinton's, were that the Palestinians agree to end the conflict by relinquishing the right of return and the return itself; accept complicated arrangements for East

Jerusalem and the Temple Mount without achieving sovereignty over them; agree to large territorial annexations in the West Bank and the Gaza Strip; agree to an Israeli military presence in other large areas; and agree to Israeli control over the borders separating the Palestinian state from the rest of the world. No Palestinian leader would ever sign such an agreement and thus the summit ended in deadlock.

The Al-Aqsa Intifada

71. The breakdown of the summit, the elimination of any hope for an agreement between the two sides, and the unconditional pro-Israeli stance of the Americans inevitably led to another round of violent confrontations, which earned the title of the al-Aqsa Intifada. For the Palestinians, this Intifada is a justified national uprising against the protracted occupation, which has no end in sight and allows continual, daily pulling of their land out from under their feet. For the Israelis, it is an outburst of murderous terrorism. The perpetrators of these acts appear to the Palestinians as national heroes and to the Israelis as merciless criminals who must be liquidated.

72. The official media in Israel no longer mention settlers but speak of "residents" upon whom any attack is a crime against civilians. The Palestinians consider the settlers the forefront of a dangerous enemy force whose intention is to dispossess them of their land and who must be defeated.

Another feeble effort was made in December 2000 at Taba, when both delegations moderated their positions and got closer to each other. The Israeli map of "settlement blocs" shrunk, new proposals for Jerusalem were considered, and it was reported that even on the refugee question the parties had come closer to one another (both sides proposed actual numbers of refugees who would be allowed back into Israel). However, nothing was put on paper and eventually Barak called off the talks and repudiated all the proposals made. The whole Taba episode is questionable, because it occurred in the middle of the election campaign in Israel, when an unparalleled defeat of Barak had already become a virtual certainty, making Palestinian "concessions" even more difficult. Also, it could be asked why the Israeli delegation made such concessions at Taba but not five months earlier at Camp David, when they could have made a difference. In the meantime, of course, the armed confrontation had broken out.

73. A great part of the Israeli "Peace Camp" collapsed during the al-Aqsa Intifada. Especially after Barak had "turned every stone" and made "more generous offers than any previous prime minister," Palestinian behavior was incomprehensible to this part of the "Peace Camp," since it

had never performed a thorough revision of the Zionist narrative and did not internalize the fact that there is a Palestinian narrative too. The only remaining explanation for these peaceniks was that the Palestinians had deceived them, that the Palestinians had never intended to make peace, and that their true purpose was to throw the Jews into the sea, as the Zionist right had always claimed.

74. The collapse of the "left Zionists" and the contention of Barak, Ben-Ami, and their followers that "Arafat has rejected the offers which gave him everything he wanted" and that therefore "there is no partner for peace" led inevitably to the landslide victory of Ariel Sharon in February 2001. As a result, the dividing line between the Zionist right and left disappeared. The leaders of the Labor Party joined the Sharon government and became his most effective apologists (Shimon Peres) and military executives (Binyamin Ben-Eliezer). This again proves that the Zionist narrative is the decisive factor unifying all factions of the political system in Israel, making the distinctions between Avigdor Lieberman and Avraham Burg, Ehud Olmert and Yossi Sarid insignificant. This is also proven by the uniform backing given by all Israeli media without exception to extremist government policies.

While concealing his real intention with the help of Peres, Sharon set out to destroy the Oslo agreement and its actual manifestations on the ground, shatter the Palestinian authority and its armed forces, and kill or expel Yasser Arafat—the very same aims he had tried to achieve by his 1982 invasion of Lebanon. Cautiously but consistently, mindful of the need to gain and preserve the support of the U.S. administration, he tried to do this by making life in the Palestinian territories intolerable, destroying the people's means of subsistence, employing harsh military measures (including the assassination of political leaders), destabilizing the Palestinian authority, strengthening the extreme fundamentalist organizations, and trying to isolate Arafat.

At the beginning, the Bush administration paid lip service to peace and conciliation in the Middle East, while supporting Sharon in practice. After the September 11 outrages in New York and Washington, D.C., it seemed for a while that this policy was being changed in the interest of building the great coalition deemed necessary for the pursuit of the War against Terrorism. Bush spoke about a Palestinian state and Colin Powell set forth a reasonable plan for peace. However, after the easy victory in Afghanistan, Bush reverted to his earlier stance, supporting Sharon to the hilt.

75. There is a notable decline in the Palestinian willingness to reopen a dialogue with the Israeli peace forces. This is a consequence of their utter disappointment with the "leftist government" that had inspired so much

hope after the Netanyahu years, as well as a consequence of the fact that, apart from the voice of small radical peace groups, no Israeli outrage at the brutal reactions of the occupation forces has been heard. The tendency to tighten ranks, typical of any nation in a war of liberation, makes it possible for the extreme nationalistic and religious forces on the Palestinian side to veto any attempt at Israeli-Palestinian cooperation.

A New Peace Camp

76. The breakdown of the old peace camp necessitates the creation of a new Israeli peace camp that will be real, up-to-date, effective, and strong, that can influence the Israeli public and bring about a complete reevaluation of the old axioms in order to effect a change in the Israeli political system.

77. To do so, the new peace camp must lead public opinion toward a brave reassessment of the national narrative and rid it of false myths. It must strive to unite the historical versions of both peoples into a single narrative, free from historical deceptions, that will be acceptable to both sides.

78. While creating this new narrative the peace camp must also make the Israeli public aware that along with all the beautiful and positive aspects of the Zionist enterprise, a terrible injustice was done to the Palestinian people. This injustice, which peaked during the Naqba, obliges us to assume responsibility and correct as much of it as is possible.

79. With a new understanding of the past and the present, the new peace camp must formulate a peace plan based on the following principles:

A. An independent and free Palestinian state will be established alongside Israel.

B. The Green Line will be the border between the two States. If agreed upon by the two sides, limited territorial exchanges may be possible.

C. The Israeli settlements will be evacuated from the territory of the Palestinian state.

D. The border between the two states will be open to the movement of people and goods, subject to arrangements made by mutual agreement.

E. Jerusalem will be the capital of both states—with West Jerusalem the capital of Israel and East Jerusalem the capital of Palestine. The state of Palestine will have complete sovereignty in East Jerusalem, including the Haram al-Sharif, the Temple Mount. The state of Israel will have complete sovereignty in West Jerusalem, including the Western Wall and the Jewish Quarter. Both states will reach agreement on the unity of the city at the physical, municipal level.

F. Israel will recognize in principle the Palestinian right of return as an inalienable human right. The practical solution to the problem will come about by agreement based on just, fair, and practical considerations and will include return to the territory of the state of Palestine, return to the state of Israel, and compensation.

G. The water resources will be controlled jointly and allocated by agreement, equally and fairly.

H. A security agreement between the two states will ensure the security of both and take into consideration the specific security needs of Israel as well as of Palestine.

I. Israel and Palestine will cooperate with other states in the region to establish a Middle Eastern community modeled on the European Union.

80. The signing of a peace agreement and its honest implementation in good faith will lead to a historical reconciliation between the two nations based on equality, cooperation, and mutual respect.

THE ASYMMETRY OF PITY

Yossi Klein Halevi

MY MOST INSTRUCTIVE CONVERSATION on the Middle East conflict was not with a politician or a journalist but with a soft-spoken Palestinian Anglican minister named Naim Ateek, whose group, Sabeel, promotes a Palestinian version of liberation theology. During a long and friendly talk about two years ago, we agreed on the need for a "dialogue of the heart," as opposed to a strictly functional approach to peace between our peoples. In that spirit, I acknowledged that we Israelis should formally concede the wrongs we had committed against the Palestinians. Then I asked him whether he was prepared to offer a reciprocal gesture, a confession of Palestinian moral flaws. Both sides, after all, had amply wronged each other during our hundred-year war. The Palestinian leadership had collaborated with the Nazis and rejected the 1947 UN partition plan and then led the international campaign to delegitimize Israel that threatened our post-Holocaust reconstruction. What was Reverend Ateek prepared to do to reassure my people that it was safe to withdraw back to the narrow borders of pre-1967 Israel and voluntarily make ourselves vulnerable in one of the least stable and tolerant regions of the world?

"We don't have to do anything at all to reassure you," he said. He offered this historical analogy: when David Ben-Gurion and Konrad Adenauer negotiated the German-Israeli reparations agreement in the early 1950s, the Israeli prime minister was hardly expected to offer the German chancellor concessions or psychological reassurances. The Germans had

been the murderers, the Jews the victims, and all that remained to be negotiated was the extent of indemnity.

"So we are your Nazis?" I asked.

"Now you've understood," he replied, and smiled.

I have thought often of that conversation since the collapse last fall of
any pretense of a mutual process of reconciliation between Palestinians
and Israelis. With disarming sincerity, Reverend Ateek offered the most
cogent explanation I had encountered for why the Oslo peace process never
had a chance to succeed.

From the start, Palestinian-Israeli peacemaking was burdened by asymmetry. The gap between Israeli power and Palestinian powerlessness was
translated into a political process that required tangible Israeli concessions—
reversible only through war—in exchange for Palestinian promises of peace:
in essence, land for words. But the deepest and most intractable asymmetry has been psychological: it has been an asymmetry of pity or, more precisely, of self-pity. The Palestinians, as losers of the conflict, continue to see
themselves solely as victims, without guilt for helping maintain the conflict
or responsibility for helping to end it; indeed, for many Palestinians, the
war is not over borders but absolute justice, a battle between good and evil.
Because history has been kinder to them, Israelis can afford to concede complexity and, indeed, the Israeli mainstream now perceives the conflict as a
competition between two legitimate national movements over the same tortured strip of land. Aside from the hard-right minority, most Israelis acknowledge that both sides share rights and wrongs.

Zionism's Victory over Jewish Self-Pity

The first generation of Israelis after statehood resembled Palestinians
today in their simplistic view of the struggle over the land as an absolutist
moral conflict. In every generation, as the Passover Haggadah puts it, a
new enemy rises to destroy the Jews and, for most Israelis, this was the
Arabs' turn. A popular Yiddish pun emphasized the point: Hitler fell into
the water, it went, and emerged *nasser*—Yiddish for "wet" and a reference to Egypt's president, Gamal Abdul Nasser, Israel's great antagonist
during its formative years.

Only gradually did Israelis begin to see the conflict with the Palestinians and the Arab world generally as a fundamental break from the pattern of Jewish history—that Zionism's hard gift to the Jews was to restore
to us our collective free will, transform us from passive victims of fate to
active shapers of our own destiny, responsible for the consequences of our
decisions. A key turning point was the November 1977 visit of Anwar

Sadat to Israel. Remarkably, a mere four years after Egypt's surprise attack against Israel on Yom Kippur, the holiest day of the Jewish year, Sadat was welcomed as a hero in the streets of Jerusalem. The Israeli notion of the Arab world as an impenetrable wall of hostility began to change. So, too, Israeli certainty about the justness of its cause was subtly challenged: many Israelis, including Ehud Barak, began to suspect that Israel could have prevented the 1973 Yom Kippur War had it agreed to withdraw from the Sinai in the early 1970s. The subsequent invasion of Lebanon in 1982, followed in late 1987 by the first intifada, reinforced for Israelis the moral ambiguity of the Middle East conflict.

At the same time, Israel's sense of siege began to ease. The collapse of the Soviet Union, the repeal of the UN "Zionism is racism" resolution, the post–Gulf War optimism in the Middle East, the mass Russian immigration and resulting Israeli prosperity—all reinforced the same message that Israel had entered a new era and was about to fulfill the long-deferred Zionist promise of Jewish normalization. Finally, a new generation of native-born Israelis that could take Jewish sovereignty for granted no longer saw itself as living in the pathology of Jewish history but in a new Israeli reality.

Indeed, young Israelis became so distanced from the traumas of exile that the Israeli Ministry of Education felt impelled in the 1990s to introduce pilgrimages to Nazi death camps in Poland for high school students, as an emotional crash course in Jewish history. In politics, too, the Holocaust lost its centrality: only the hard Right and the ultra-Orthodox continued to cite the genocide of European Jewry as a potentially recurring threat. Whereas former Israeli Prime Minister Menachem Begin once routinely invoked the Nazi era—and even publicly compared himself, during the invasion of Lebanon, to an Allied commander closing in on Hitler's bunker—his equally right-wing politician son, Benny, confined his traumas to the Middle East. Thanks largely to the effects of Israeli sovereignty on the Jewish psyche, a wound that should have taken generations to heal began to recede into history. By the time of the Oslo agreement in September 1993, a majority of Israelis had been weaned from the self-defensiveness of the victim and educated in the moral dilemmas of the conqueror.

The Weight of Palestinian Self-Pity

It would be unrealistic to expect a similar evolution among Palestinians who, after all, lack fifty years of sovereignty to compensate for their historical trauma. The Palestinians are at a different stage of their national development, resembling Israel in its early years, celebrating nationalism and self-sacrifice and mistrusting moral complexity as weakness. Yet that psychological gap between Israelis and Palestinians was precisely Oslo's great structural flaw. The problem with the Oslo process, as Ariel Sharon has noted, was not its goals but its timetable, its lack of ample "process." Oslo's implicit expectation was that Israel would return to approximately the June 1967 borders after a mere seven years of tenuous relations with the Palestinian entity, well before the Palestinians could be emotionally prepared to offer Israelis even the most minimal sense of safety and acceptance in the region.

On the Israeli side, a vigorous and successful effort was made by Labor Party leaders to wean the public from its emotional attachment to the biblical borders of "greater Israel." Yitzhak Rabin and Shimon Peres repeatedly told the Israeli people that the dream of greater Israel was unrealistic and self-destructive. That message was reinforced by the Israeli media, often by what we journalists chose to omit as much as to publish. I recall, for example, reading an account in the *Jerusalem Post*'s media column, written by right-wing commentator David Bar-Ilan, just after the White House handshake of September 1993. The column reported on a speech delivered by Yasser Arafat in Amman in which the Palestinian chairman noted that by signing the Oslo Accords he was merely implementing the "stages" policy—that is, the 1974 PLO decision to accept whatever territory Israel evacuated and continue struggling until the demise of the Jewish state. My instinctive reaction was that the account must be exaggerated: Bar-Ilan, after all, was a right-wing ideologue. Despite the devastating implications of that speech, I did not bother checking whether Bar-Ilan's report was accurate, precisely because I feared that it might be. Nor did I want to be tainted by association with the right-wing opposition. That combination of wishful thinking and cowardice characterized most Israeli journalists, at least in the early years of the Oslo process.

In contrast with Israel's contortionist efforts to adapt to Oslo's false promise, no attempt was made by Palestinian leaders to accommodate the Jewish state in their people's mental map of the Middle East. Indeed, the self-justifying myths of the Palestinians have only become more entrenched since Oslo. The Palestinian people are routinely told by their controlled media that the temple never existed on the Temple Mount, that the biblical stories did not occur in Israel/Palestine, and even that the Holocaust is a lie. The consistent message is that the Palestinians are victims of a false Jewish narrative.

Rather than challenging the Palestinians' wholesale expropriation of justice and truth, the international community has encouraged their self-perception as innocent victims of the Middle East conflict. Every year on May 15, as Palestinians violently mark the *nakba,* or tragedy, of 1948, much of the world's media dutifully replays the Palestinian version of that event. Few journalists challenge Palestinian spokesmen with the fact that Arab rejectionism was at least partly responsible for their people's uprooting and occupation. Indulging that sense of blameless victimization has only reinforced the Palestinian inability to assume the role of equal partner in negotiations and take responsibility for helping to end the conflict. As Naim Ateek put it, the Palestinians' only obligation to peacemaking is to show up and receive concessions. The Palestinian leadership has felt no moral obligation to fulfill its stated commitments under Oslo—such as curbing terrorism and ending incitement or even the straightforward matter of revoking the Palestinian Covenant that calls for the destruction of Israel. (To this day it is uncertain whether the Palestinians have legally revoked the covenant, and their deliberately created ambiguity has negated any positive impact its revocation may have had on the Palestinian psyche.)

The apologetics offered by much of the international community—and by part of the Israeli Left—for Arafat's violent rejection of Barak's peace offer have reinforced the pathological tendencies of Palestinian self-pity. Especially absurd has been the claim that Barak's settlement-building was a sign of bad faith that undermined Arafat's trust in the process. Nearly all the housing starts begun under Barak were concentrated in areas intended to become settlement blocs—whose permanence the Palestinians accepted during negotiations at Camp David. According to Barak's chief negotiator with the Palestinians, Gilad Sher, settlements—whose total built areas cover a mere 1.5 percent of the West Bank—were not even among the five major issues of disagreement during the Camp David negotiations. Instead, the major issues were the Palestinian insistence that Israel assume full moral blame for the flight of the refugees in 1948 (ignoring the Arab world's invasion of Israel that preceded the refugee crisis) and the Palestinian refusal to acknowledge any Jewish connection to the Temple Mount, Judaism's holiest site.

When confronted with the continued ideological intransigence of the Palestinians, the Israeli left-wing retort was invariably a sarcastic dismissal: "We don't expect them to become Zionists." Even as it successfully compelled a reluctant Israeli public to confront at least some truths of the Palestinian narrative, the Left refused to demand any reciprocity from its Palestinian partner. In so doing, the Left ignored its own argument: that without accommodating the other's narrative, peace would be impossible.

The Israeli Left committed one more fatal tactical mistake: it divorced itself emotionally from Judea and Samaria, even as the Palestinians reinforced their emotional claim to pre-1967 Israel. The moral basis for partition of Israel/Palestine is that two peoples, profoundly rooted in the entirety of the land, must each sacrifice part of its legitimate claim to accommodate the legitimate claim of its rival. But by tacitly rejecting even a theoretical Israeli right to Judea and Samaria, the Left created a moral imbalance: the Palestinians were offering a traumatic concession by ceding parts of historic Palestine, whereas Israel was merely restoring occupied— that is, stolen—land. That imbalance reinforced the Palestinians' refusal to compromise on the 1967 borders, even though no independent Palestinian state had ever existed on any part of the land.

The success of Oslo was predicated on the Palestinians' ability to convince Israelis to trust them enough to empower them. But soon after the White House signing, increasing numbers of Israelis began to suspect they had been deliberately deceived. That process accelerated with Arafat's 1995 speech in a Johannesburg mosque, in which he compared Oslo to a cease-fire the Prophet Muhammad signed with an Arabian tribe he later destroyed. By dismissing that speech as mere rhetoric intended to appease domestic opposition, the Israeli Left made a fatal miscalculation of its devastating effect on the Israeli public. Then came the wave of suicide bombings in early 1996, which further eroded Oslo's credibility among even centrist Israelis and provided a link between Arafat's incitement and intensified terrorism.

The inevitable result was a revolt by the Israeli majority that had initially welcomed the Oslo accords and that had been willing to make far-reaching concessions for genuine peace. The first revolt occurred in 1996, with the election of Benyamin Netanyahu. Apologists for the Palestinians insist that Israel under Netanyahu helped destroy the Oslo process by resuming massive settlement-building, largely frozen under Rabin, thereby eroding Palestinian trust in Israeli intentions. That argument ignores the fact that the election of Netanyahu was a self-inflicted Palestinian wound— a direct result of Arafat's refusal to fulfill his most minimal obligations under the Oslo accords. The erratic voting pattern of the Israeli public throughout the Oslo process—repeatedly veering between Left and Right, from Yitzhak Rabin to Benyamin Netanyahu to Ehud Barak to Ariel Sharon—reflected both the growing skepticism of Israelis and their reluctance to repudiate the hopes raised by Oslo. Only with the landslide election of Sharon, who had warned for decades against empowering the PLO, did the Israeli people deliver its definitive judgment on the Oslo process as one of the gravest mistakes in the history of Israel.

Unchanged Palestinian Goals

By refusing to "partition" justice and insisting that historical right belongs exclusively to them, the Palestinians have preempted the need, in their minds, to revise their long-term goal of undoing the "injustice" of Israel's existence. Indeed, when Palestinian leaders speak of a "just and lasting peace," it is now clear that they mean, in the long term, peace without a Jewish state. Mainstream Palestinian leaders no longer invoke the old crude slogan of throwing the Jews into the sea. Instead, the scenario has become more complex, a gradual eroding of Israel that includes undermining its will to fight and to believe in itself; loss of territorial intactness; a compromising of its sovereignty via international commissions, observers, and "peacekeepers"; increased radicalization of Arab Israelis, leading to demands for "autonomy" and even the secession of those parts of the Galilee and the Negev where Arabs could soon form a majority.

Indeed, the key element in the "stages" plan is the massive return—both through Israeli consent and illegal infiltration—of embittered and unassimilable Palestinian refugees to pre-1967 Israel. By refusing to concede the "right of return," the Palestinian leadership belies its claim that it has recognized Israel in its pre-1967 borders. For Palestinians, the great crime of Zionism was artificially transforming the Jews into a majority in any part of Israel/Palestine—through Jewish immigration ("colonization") and Arab expulsion and flight. In a stunning speech to Arab diplomats in Stockholm in 1996, Arafat laid out his vision of undoing the Jewish majority even within pre-1967 Israel. By overwhelming the land with refugees and expropriating water and other resources, as well as turning a blind eye to ongoing Palestinian terrorism, Arafat would ensure that a large part of the Israeli middle class would emigrate in despair to the west. The remaining Jews would be so disoriented and demoralized by the departure of Israel's most talented citizens that the state would eventually collapse from within.

That this was no mad fantasy on Arafat's part but an accurate reflection of mainstream Palestinian strategy was confirmed by the late Faisal Husseini, long considered by the Israeli peace camp to be among the most pragmatic Palestinian leaders. In an interview with the Egyptian newspaper *Al-Arabi*, Husseini made the remarkable admission that the Oslo process was a "Trojan horse." He explained: "When we are asking all the Palestinian forces and factions to look at the Oslo Agreement and at other agreements as 'temporary' procedures, or phased goals, this means that we are ambushing the Israelis and cheating them." The goal, he concluded, was "the liberation of Palestine from the river to the sea"—that is, from the Jordan River to the Mediterranean Sea. Though it appears that *Al-Arabi*'s claim that its interview with Husseini was the "last" before his death in June is false, the veracity of its substance should not be doubted; Husseini made similar statements in a meeting with Lebanese lawyers in Beirut last March.

In a private conversation I held about two years ago in Gaza with the head of one of the dozen or so Palestinian security services established by Arafat, I was offered a benign vision of that dream of Israel's demise: "This land is too small to sustain two states," explained the commander. "When the refugees return, there won't be enough resources and we will be forced to create one state—a beautiful country that will show the world how Muslims and Jews can coexist, just like in the days of Muslim Spain." That historical model, of course, is based on a Muslim sovereign majority and a dependent Jewish minority.

It is hardly coincidence, too, that the model most invoked by Arafat for the resolution of the Israeli-Palestinian conflict is South Africa. Israeli left-wingers misinterpreted that constant reference to South Africa as proof that the PLO leadership had embraced peaceful reconciliation. In fact, what most appeals to Palestinian leaders in the South African precedent is the transition from minority to majority rule. Though the Jews constitute a slim majority in the whole of Israel/Palestine and an overwhelming majority within the pre-1967 borders, Palestinian leaders believe that this is a temporary aberration. When the refugees begin returning (and Jews begin leaving), the "natural" majority will reemerge, and the Jewish minority, like the white South African minority, will then be compelled to negotiate the terms of its own surrender. This is why Nabil Sha'ath, the PA minister of planning and international cooperation, told a Washington audience on June 21 that the January 2001 Taba negotiations "witnessed significant progress." Of what did that progress consist? "A conceptual breakthrough on the issue of refugees and the right of return," said Sha'ath, who described Israeli negotiators as acknowledging that "Israel was responsible for the initiation of the refugee problem" and as agreeing that "the Palestinians had a right to return to both Israel and Palestine" (quoted from a rapporteur's summary of Sha'ath's remarks to a policy forum of the Washington Institute for Near East Policy, June 21, 2001).

Israel after Oslo

There certainly exist Palestinians capable of accommodating the Israeli narrative into their understanding of the conflict. Some of them are my friends and colleagues—a Palestinian Israeli academic who welcomes Israel's existence as essential for Middle Eastern evolution, a West Bank sheykh who believes it is God's will that the Jews returned to this land, a former leader of the first intifada who has come to realize that Zionism "wasn't just a form of colonialism but the return of a people home." Understandably, it is easiest for Palestinian citizens of Israel to reconcile with Israel, more difficult for Palestinians in the territories, and more difficult still for Palestinian refugees in the diaspora. The tragedy of the Oslo Accords was to impose on West Bank Palestinians—with whom Israel's conflict is potentially territorial rather than existential—the revolutionary leadership of the diaspora, which represents the Palestinian grievance of 1948; that is, the very existence of a Jewish state. The effect has been to suppress those Palestinian voices advocating genuine reconciliation. Even much of the Israeli Left today concedes that Israel gambled on the wrong man in mortgaging the peace process to Yasser Arafat. Many other Israelis would extend that critique to include the entire PLO-Tunis leadership. Israel has empowered a Palestinian leadership that is unwilling to revise its morally exclusionist view of the conflict. Genuine peace is impossible when one partner considers the other's very existence illegitimate.

The growing tendency among Palestinians and Arabs generally to view the Middle East conflict as a battle between good and evil has led to an outbreak of crude Jew-hatred, on both the official and mass levels, unprecedented since Europe in the early 1940s. By insisting that Israel's very founding is immoral, much of the Arab world inevitably finds itself aligned with classical anti-Semitism, which considered Jewish existence itself a crime. The state-controlled Egyptian media has revived the medieval blood libel and the Protocols of the Elders of Zion. Official newspapers in Syria, Lebanon, and in the Palestinian Authority deny that the Holocaust happened; indeed, Arab countries are the only places in the world where Holocaust denial enjoys mainstream credibility. Ahmad Ragab, a columnist for the Egyptian government-sponsored newspaper, *Al-Akhbar,* disagreed with the growing Holocaust revisionism: he noted that the Holocaust did indeed happen, and he expressed his gratitude to Hitler—"although we do have a complaint against him, for his revenge on [the Jews] was not enough." A recent hit on Egyptian radio was called "I Hate Israel"—and the state censor boasted that he inserted the title line into the song.

Though largely ignored by the international community, this growing chorus of hatred has reinforced the tendency of the Israeli mainstream to once again view the Arab world as genocidally minded. Holocaust terminology has seeped back into Israeli discourse, emerging from unlikely sources. In a recent letter of political contrition written by former left-wing activist Edna Shabbtai to her friend, right-wing activist Geula Cohen, Shabbtai invoked the Holocaust in her call for a war against the Palestinian Authority: "We need to read again the poster that [partisan leader] Abba Kovner directed at the Jews of Lithuania in 1942: 'Jews! Don't go like sheep to the slaughter.'"

Despite the growing sense among Israelis that we have slipped back into the pathology of Jewish history, Israeli society has not reverted to a simplistic moral understanding of the roots of the Middle East conflict. Most Israelis still perceive the conflict as being fought between two legitimate national movements; if a majority were convinced that a credible partner had emerged on the other side, they would opt, even now, for partition. While sympathy for the settlers under attack has grown, there has been no increase in political support for their annexationist agenda. Israel has repudiated the illusions of the Left, but it has hardly returned to the equally fantastic alternative of the annexationist Right. Indeed, most Israelis would probably agree that, together, both ideological camps share responsibility for the disaster—the Right, by inserting armed Jewish fanatics into Palestinian population centers; the Left, by empowering a Palestinian terrorist army on the border of Jewish population centers. Together, Right and Left have created the conditions for apocalypse in the territories.

In this atmosphere, the option that increasingly appeals to Israelis is unilateral withdrawal—itself an expression of despair in both greater Israel and a negotiated peace. The advantages of unilateral withdrawal would be to extricate us from a pathological process that ties us to a partner whose goal is our destruction, and to allow us to build a fence along borders we ourselves determine as essential for Israel's security. Unilateral withdrawal would grant the Palestinians sovereignty over most of the territories, but preserve Israeli rule over areas of dense settlement, the strategically vital Jordan Valley and, most crucially, over united Jerusalem. The notion of "sharing" Jerusalem with a violent and expansionist Palestinian Authority is now seen by most Israelis—even by many who in principle are prepared to share sovereignty—as an intolerable security risk that would almost certainly lead to the dismemberment of the city. The main disadvantage of unilateral withdrawal would be to magnify the impression created by Israel's hasty retreat from Lebanon—signaling the Arab world and especially the Palestinians that Israel is on the run, thereby inviting further violence and increasing the possibility of regional war.

In theory, only a national unity government—enjoying overwhelming public support and headed by Ariel Sharon, who built most of the settlements—could dare implement a unilateral withdrawal, necessitating the traumatic uprooting of dozens of Jewish communities embedded deep in the West Bank and populated by the most ideologically committed settlers. In practice, though, Sharon has repeatedly vowed not to initiate any move requiring the massive uprooting of Jews from their homes, and he should be taken at his word. True, there is the Yamit precedent—when Sharon, as minister of agriculture in Menachem Begin's government in 1982, bulldozed the Sinai town of Yamit as part of Israel's withdrawal from Sinai. But Sinai's historical, religious, and especially strategic significance for Israelis cannot be compared to that of Judea and Samaria. Yamit existed for barely eight years; by contrast, the West Bank settlements have already produced a second generation of native Judeans and Samarians.

Moreover, Sharon has repeatedly dismissed separation as an illusion: Jews and Arabs, he believes, are too economically and even geographically entwined. Finally, Sharon has since expressed regret for destroying Yamit: during a pre-election interview I conducted with him, he noted that Israel should have withdrawn to the international border in Sinai only in exchange for genuine peace, while in practice it received only an extended cease-fire. He will almost certainly continue to reject the notion of unilateral withdrawal from Judea and Samaria without a negotiated peace—inconceivable in the foreseeable future.

Still, if the current conflict with the Palestinians deepens and widens into regional war, pressure from within Israeli society and especially the army could induce Sharon to invoke the precedent of 1948, when some isolated and besieged settlements were evacuated. As hatred and self-righteousness increasingly determine the Arab agenda, the ground is being prepared for that scenario.

JUST AND JEWISH WARFARE

Michael Gross

PURITY OF ARMS—the unflinching commitment to humanitarian warfare—
is dogma in Israel. Jewish soldiers shield innocent civilians, do not mistreat
prisoners, fight honorably and with restraint, and raise their arms only in
self-defense. These are the rules every young conscript, fortified by images
of the Holocaust, learns to uphold. Why then are such rules so blatantly
disregarded as Israel wages its war with the Palestinians by torture, assassination, and blackmail?

Torture

In September 1999, the Israeli Supreme Court convened to hear the case of
Palestinian detainees who petitioned the court to prohibit torture. This was
not the first time that torture had seized public attention. Following earlier
complaints raised by the press, the courts, and human rights organizations,
the Landau Commission (a state commission of inquiry) had reviewed the
use of torture by the General Security Service (GSS) in 1987. The very establishment of a public body to study torture is probably unprecedented,
and throughout its deliberations the committee showed extraordinary sensitivity to the complexity of its mission. While acknowledging that torture
might be necessary to elicit information in extreme situations, commission
members were keenly aware that a democratic state, not to mention a Jewish democratic state, has a prima facie obligation to stand fast against the
use of torture in any form.

The Landau Commission struggled with this question by formulating three options, each of which rested on the unexamined assumption that torture was necessary to meet the existential threat that terrorism posed. This assumption would be examined later but stood as given at the time. First, the commission raised and then rejected the hypocrisy of some democratic nations like France who practiced torture but simply pretended that they didn't. Similarly, the commission rejected any effort to carve out a special niche for the General Security Service (GSS) by placing it beyond the law; doing so they thought characteristic only of less enlightened states. Instead, the commission formulated a new "Jewish-democratic" approach; in defiance of all international norms, they suggested that Israel could set standards and establish a regulatory mechanism to oversee the use of "moderate physical pressure."

Unfortunately, the details of the commission's report were kept secret, so it was not until the Supreme Court ruled on torture in 1999 that the public came to understand what had been done. It was not pretty. Taking its cue from the British and their long running troubles with the Irish, the Landau Commission took heart from an international court ruling in 1976 that saw the British government unsuccessfully defend the use of torture to interrogate suspected IRA terrorists.

At that 1976 hearing, sufficient evidence was presented for the European Court of Human Rights to conclude that the combined use of five techniques constituted inhuman treatment and torture. The five techniques included the seemingly innocuous practices of hooding (covering a suspect's head with a filthy, opaque sack), wall standing (forcing a suspect to stand spread eagle against a wall for an extended time), noise (excessively loud music played throughout the day and night), as well as sleep deprivation and starvation. The Landau Commission took special note of the term "combined use," concluding that individually employed techniques of lesser or equal savagery might constitute degradation but not torture. With this caveat, they gave the green light to the GSS. That is how the situation stood until 1999.

In the intervening years, mounting evidence indicated that the GSS was not content with the five techniques. B'Tselem, Amnesty International, and the Public Committee Against Torture in Israel published numerous reports of Palestinian detainees who were killed, beaten, crippled, and driven nearly insane by the combined use of an improved Jewish version of the techniques made famous by the British. In its 1999 ruling the Supreme Court vividly describes the interrogation techniques then in practice. These included "physical means" (beating and slapping), "shaking" ("forceful shaking of the upper torso, back and forth, in a manner that causes the neck and head to dangle and vacillate rapidly"), excessive tightening of hand-cuffs, the "frog crouch" ("consecutive, periodical crouches on the tips of one's toes, each lasting for five-minute intervals"), and, finally, interrogation in the "Shabach position" (seating a suspect on a "small, low chair, whose seat is tilted forward, towards the ground. One hand is tied behind the suspect's back, and placed between the chair's seat and back support, the second hand is tied behind the chair, against the back support"). Hooding and "powerfully loud music" were also used in conjunction with most of these techniques.

The Supreme Court was no longer impressed with the existential argument against terrorism: while they acknowledged that a democracy had to fight "with one hand tied behind its back," they pointed out that terrorism alone would not bring down the state of Israel. Nor was the court moved by the "ticking bomb" argument, the demand to torture a recalcitrant suspect who would not otherwise reveal information about an impending terrorist attack. The "ticking bomb" argument only holds if we know with certainty that others besides the suspect will not intervene to move the bomb to another time or place, or to change the detonating mechanism. This is rarely, if ever, the case in Israel. There are no lone, Timothy McVeigh–like terrorists among the Palestinians, whose networks are sufficiently organized to keep on ticking with or without one captured member or another. The ticking-bomb argument could not underwrite a sweeping policy of torture, the court ruled, and so moderate physical pressure was prohibited, absent more definitive legislation.

The Supreme Court decision vindicated years of anti-torture activism in Israel. But the ruling left the door ajar for the legislature to approve torture provided that a law infringing upon a suspect's liberty would be "befitting the values of the state of Israel, enacted for a proper purpose, and to an extent no greater than is required." A daunting task, to say the least. Nevertheless, this did not dissuade some legislators from trying to enact a torture law.

In the waning days of the Barak administration, forty-three opposition members, including the current prime minister, Ariel Sharon, and most members of his cabinet, drafted a law allowing the GSS to torture suspects. The law is couched in secrecy. No techniques are described, only "special measures" and "physical pressure." These may be employed with written permission from the director of the GSS for a period limited to forty-eight hours but renewable. If the director is unavailable and the situation urgent, an investigator may use special measures for a period of not more than two hours! While the GSS and the prime minister must periodically review the guidelines and report to the Knesset every six months, no publicly published accounting is required.

This law is probably unique in the annals of democratic legislation and, should it pass, there is every reason to believe that torture will quickly regain its status as the interrogative method of choice. It takes no imagination whatsoever to see what danger this kind of law poses to a democratically fragile nation like Israel. At this writing, the law remains suspended in committee, but the GSS approached the Justice Ministry as recently as February 2001, complaining that while it was abiding by the Supreme Court's ban, its work is hindered by lack of interrogation tools. This is not entirely correct. While there is no renewed indication of widespread torture, complaints of abuse are again increasing, particularly as the current conflict intensifies. Recent events also have occasioned a more menacing form of deviant warfare: assassination.

Assassination

Trying to quell the current round of violence that began following the collapse of Clinton's peace initiative in October 2000, Israel has been publicly "liquidating" Palestinian militia leaders. Palestinians have been assassinated before (most famously those who perpetrated the attack on Israeli athletes in Munich in 1972), but the sheer number of recent assassinations—more than twenty in ten months—is unprecedented. In response, international human rights organizations have strongly condemned Israel's policy of "extralegal" executions. Israel has replied in the language of a just war: the Palestinians are participants in an armed conflict. Assassination, therefore, is not a result of wayward law enforcement but the legitimate, preemptive actions of a nation at war.

It cannot be denied that assassination has a great deal of intuitive appeal. It satisfies the need to strike back and to exact just punishment, long overdue and unattainable in any other way. Assassination is a source of pride, demonstrating Jewish military prowess as targets are picked off by the most imaginative means possible: booby-trapped cell phones, rigged automobiles, and rocket and tank attacks executed with almost pinpoint accuracy. Many claim that assassination prevents imminent terror attacks and serves as a powerful deterrent, giving potential terrorists pause while convincing Palestinian locals to distance themselves from terrorists. Finally, it is said, assassination accomplishes all this with minimal civilian casualties.

Assassination sounds like the perfect military tactic—and it would be, but for the fact that all these assumptions are naive, wrong, and entirely misguided. Assassination instead erodes the basis for any future peace negotiations, deters no one, and precipitates a violent, vicious, and almost insane desire for revenge.

When terrorist bombings are viewed through the prism of ordinary criminal activity, it is—or it should be—obvious that terrorists cannot be punished without the due process afforded by the criminal justice system. No one advocates summarily executing even the most heinous common criminals. The potential damage to the rule of law is simply too profound should law enforcement officers become judge, jury, and executioner. Recently, Israel was stung by fierce international condemnation as Amnesty International, B'Tselem, and the U.S. State Department denounced assassination as an act of extralegal execution entirely proscribed by international law and common morality.

In an effort to deflect this international criticism, the Israeli government took the unusual step in February 2001 of unilaterally redefining the conflict with the Palestinians from one of "belligerent occupation" to one of "armed conflict." By redefining Palestinians as combatants, Israel abandoned the pretext that assassinations were a form of punishment or law enforcement and claimed instead that they were legitimate, preemptive strikes. In the context of armed conflict, enemy soldiers are fair game. This seemed to offer military planners a way out, reopening the door not to punish Palestinians but to assassinate them in order to preempt planned attacks and to deter others from similar designs.

Israelis are proud of their ability to preempt armed attacks. Used successfully to justify the Six-Day War, the argument is often resurrected to explain all kinds of incursions. In this case, however, assassination in the guise of preemption can be dismissed if three points are kept in mind.

First, a preemptive strike is an act of war and must conform to the law of war. No one questions the right of any nation to repel an actual or imminent attack, but when armed attacks devolve to threats, the situation becomes much more complex. Despite the horror of terrorist attacks, they do not pose a threat to national existence, and this severely limits Israel's right to strike prior to acts of open aggression.

Second, a preemptive attack must be proportionate to the death and damage one seeks to avoid. Excessive civilian casualties make an act disproportionate. The ratio of civilian casualties to assassinated (suspected) Palestinian terrorists is now about one to two. Is this disproportionate? Probably so. More to the point, however, is the question whether these deaths have brought any military benefit whatsoever. It seems to many people that terror attacks only increase after an assassination. At the very least the burden of proof must be on the authorities. Have attacks been foiled? No one knows. No evidence has ever been offered either to the public or to an independent commission to support assassinations. An act without visible benefit defies the test of proportionality.

Finally, nations cannot fight by illegal means. Another anachronism perhaps, but one that binds us. The laws of war are meant to limit suffering and protect civilians, and it is no accident that recruiting collaborators, for instance, is banned absolutely. But assassination won't work without local informers. This in and of itself should be sufficient to understand the ban on assassination.

Collaboration

Assassination is banned for many reasons. Most obviously, it invites retaliation unless, of course, the other side is conveniently unable to respond in kind. More importantly, assassination is condemned because it is "treacherous" and "perfidious." These are archaic concepts, gleaned from old and obscure sources, but speak directly to the ethics of Jewish warfare.

Treachery and perfidy are violations of trust and, while there is precious little trust during wartime, some is needed if conflicts are ever to end. When soldiers hoist a white flag, they invite trust. Neither prisoners nor captors are expected to shoot one another. To do so abuses the unsteady, temporary peace and undermines the entire practice of surrender. Next time there will be no prisoners. Peace negotiations work the same way. In olden days, military leaders were sometimes lured to their deaths by false promises of safe passage ostensibly offered to negotiate peace. In fact, this recently happened in Israel when soldiers attacked Mohammed Dahlan, chief of Palestinian security. After returning from a negotiating session in April 2001, Dahlan's car was fired upon by Israeli troops. Israel immediately apologized, but a cartoon the next day summed up perceptions on both sides. Dahlan is depicted next to his bullet-riddled car complaining loudly to Israeli defense minister Ben Eliezar that he almost got killed. Ben Eliezar replies, "I'll check to see why the operation failed."

These are deliberate acts of treachery and are roundly condemned. But the assassinations of Palestinians are not usually treacherous in this obvious way. They are treacherous simply because they depend on traitors and cannot be accomplished without collaborators.

By all accounts, Ibrahim Bani Odeh, a Palestinian bomb maker, was decapitated when the headrest of the car he borrowed from his cousin, a known collaborator, exploded. Fatah leader Hussein Abayyat was assassinated after being fingered by four informers, and Yahiya Ayyash, the famous "engineer" assassinated in Gaza in 1996 when his cell phone blew up, was set up by a colleague's relative turned collaborator. One can easily see how the assassination of such contemptible individuals meets with little outrage. But there is a price to pay. It comes immediately in the form of vicious retaliatory raids and in the long term through the pernicious effects of collaboration on Palestinian society.

Collaboration is the mainstay of Israeli intelligence in the territories. While seemingly innocuous compared to torture and assassination, any attempt to compel "protected persons" (an occupied people is supposed to be protected) to serve in the armed forces of an occupying power is a "grave" breach of the Geneva Conventions and tantamount to a war crime. Presumably one would have little to say if Palestinians were to enlist of their own free will in the GSS, but all the evidence compiled by B'Tselem points to heavy-handed extortion and blackmail. In return for collaboration, Palestinians are offered cash, goods, and/or reduced prison sentences, while those who refuse to cooperate are threatened with loss of work permits and blocked access to medical care. No long-term sociological study is required to imagine the effects that collaborators, spies, and informers must have on any close-knit, traditional society. When even close friends and relatives are suspect, normal social intercourse must be impossible. Just as the trust, friendship, and loyalty that are so necessary for any normal society to function are severely undermined, so are law and order constantly subverted as Palestinian vigilantes execute collaborators along with their own political enemies and the socially undesirable.

Once used, collaboration and assassination provoke blind fury, radicalize moderates, and strengthen collective solidarity. Who is going to be deterred in the face of torture, assassination, and blackmail? Who is being punished when death can be glorified so easily? The answer, simply, is no one. It's an old lesson; we just haven't learned it yet.

Learning Our Lesson

One would think that Israel might have learned a thing or two from the British, French, and Americans about attempts to quell national liberation movements through torture, assassination, collaboration, and assorted mayhem. Assassination and collective punishment are not new tactics, and they generated intense criticism when adopted by the United States in Vietnam. They did not win the war or deny the insurgents sanctuary. They only destroyed the infrastructure of rural Vietnam.

The French experience in Algeria is equally instructive. "The Mediterranean runs through France as the Seine runs through Paris" was a popular saying in France in the 1950s. When war broke out, the French settlers were convinced it would be short-lived if only everyone would back off and "let the army win." The war was not short-lived and the army quickly turned from conventional warfare to torture and assassination to fight mounting terrorism. Ultimately, the French, like the Americans, decided it was best to declare victory and leave. In 1963, leading French intellectual Pierre Vidal-Naquet decried torture as the "cancer of democracy," and the French continue to pick at their scabs until this very day.

In Israel, torture and assassination—both used with disastrous results to fight guerillas just a few years ago in Lebanon—now join a litany of similar policies including siege, collective punishment, and the limited destruction of infrastructure designed, in the words of senior officials, to "unbalance" the Palestinians, "weaken their morale," and "drive a wedge between civilians and the Palestinian Authority." One stares with disbelief when Raanan Gissin, the spokesman for Prime Minister Sharon, readily admits to reporters, as he did in February, that Israeli tactics are "out of the past" and then hastens to add, "but we think they can work here." The tactics are out of the past, and they can't work here any more than they have worked anywhere else.

Why Do We Do It?

Torture, assassination, blackmail, extortion, and collective punishment. Why do we do it? Has Israel lost its moral balance? Or is there just something about our war with the Palestinians that somehow justifies extreme measures?

The second argument is the easiest to make. The war on terror is a war of national survival and supreme emergency. "Necessity knows no law." But this has always been a dangerous argument and remains so. The fact is that we continue to fight by the blackest means imaginable to a democratic nation because we forget our strengths. We forget, or have not yet noticed, that the existential fight for the Jewish state is won and over. But the images that sustained that fight, most frighteningly the Holocaust, the War of Independence, the Six-Day War, and the Yom Kippur War continue to haunt many who feel compelled to inculcate their children with the same angst and trepidation. While these recurrent images were essential to forge a national identity and instill a fighting spirit, they are laced with fear and loathing.

Today, Jews fear the Arabs in the same way many white Americans feared the blacks during the race riots of the 1960s. Many recall how suburban whites, and not a few Jews, nervously brandished pistols to fend off the blacks should they make their way from the inner-city ghettos to the suburbs. But the pistols didn't help, for the blacks came the very next day, ready to clean our houses and collect our garbage as they usually did. There is the pervasive feeling that the Palestinians are equally intent on slaughtering Jews when in fact many would probably be very grateful just to clean our houses and collect our garbage. If Israelis can no longer lay claim to underdog status, they have not ceased to think they can. This myopia, fueled by a constant preoccupation with survival and an incessant fear of another pogrom, makes it impossible to come to grips with Palestinian national aspirations.

Unlike blacks, Palestinians have done a lot to feed these fears. The abominable acts of terror against civilians tar their entire cause and it's outrageous that more Palestinian intellectuals have not repudiated them. Not every Palestinian under arms is a terrorist, not every attack is a terrorist attack, but instead of seizing on this distinction and condemning attacks on civilians, Palestinians too often have followed the Israeli lead of trying to justify abhorrent practices by redefining the terms. Just as assassination is for an Israeli "preemption" and torture is "moderate physical pressure," so terror is for a Palestinian "national liberation," and Jewish civilians are but "potential combatants." But the argument does not wash and very few people buy it.

These two factors, Jewish fear of extermination and Palestinian terror, make it easy to ignore the humanitarian rules of war. But if this recognition makes it easy to turn around and seize the moral high ground, we must avoid getting trapped up there, unable to confront reality. Israelis are experiencing a level of personal insecurity unmatched since the founding of the state. Israeli officials, by the same token, are almost helpless. This helplessness breeds the final resort to pariah warfare and the subsequent spiral of reprisal and violence. And it leaves us in a quandary: "Suppose a bomb explodes in Tel Aviv," asked one Israeli official earlier this year, "and I knew who was planning it. I could not arrest him because he is in the PA [Palestinian Authority] and cannot eliminate him because it's not 'nice.' What shall I say to the families of the people who are ripped to pieces by that bomb?"

Following the suicide attack that killed more than twenty youngsters at a Tel Aviv nightclub in June 2001, opposition leader Yossi Sarid declared that we should gauge our response by a very simple criterion that might be called "Jewish utilitarianism": any action that saves more Israeli lives than it takes is good; any action that costs more Israeli lives than it saves is bad. In this sense, responding to terror with torture, assassination, blackmail, and collective punishment is bad. But it is important to understand why. More Jewish lives are lost because the means used to preserve them are morally odious from our perspective, from the Palestinian perspective, and indeed from any perspective. Ultimately, we are fighting a war in order to make peace, and the peace we make must be able to survive the way we practice war. Without just war, there will be no just peace.

Periodically we hear that the rules of just war are but a relic of European history, wholly inapplicable to local conflicts rooted in fierce ethnic enmities. But if true, what remains of any humanitarian law between nations? Is humanitarian law only an issue when the West is involved? If not, then those locked in regional rivalries face an abiding challenge to police themselves. Israel has an opportunity to show how a Jewish war might be just—how humanitarian law might apply in the kind of wars now in vogue, not international armed conflict but local hostilities confounded by an asymmetry of arms, terrorism, incongruent cultures, and the general indifference of most of the world. The tragedies of Jewish history were instrumental in bringing humanitarian law to the fore; it would be ironic if the Jews were the agents of its demise.

CLEARING UP THE
RIGHT-OF-RETURN CONFUSION

Jerome M. Segal

A FEW WEEKS PRIOR TO THE FEBRUARY ELECTION, some of the best minds on the Israeli left (Amos Oz, A. B. Yehoshua, David Grossman, and so on) issued, in the Israeli press, a letter to the Palestinian leadership. After noting that they have struggled for over thirty years for the two-state solution, the signers forcefully stated that they shall never be able to agree to the return of the refugees to within the borders of Israel. Instead they affirmed that "the refugees will have the right to return to their homeland, Palestine, and settle there." For the best minds, this was not their best thinking. By introducing "the right to return to their homeland, Palestine," the signers appear to be rejecting the key Palestinian demand for recognition of their right to return to their homes in Israel. In doing this, they reinforced the conflation of two quite different matters: the Palestinian *right to return* and the *actual return* of the Palestinians. Rather than merging these two, it is important to sharpen an awareness of the distinction.

Unfortunately, by addressing their message to the Palestinian leadership, the signers of the statement have perpetuated a dangerous misunderstanding of the deadlock in the negotiations. The Palestinian leadership seeks some formal recognition of Palestinian rights. They are not seeking the return of millions of refugees to Israel. This, they understand, is quite impossible. They are seeking a choice-based approach that will provide the refugees with a variety of structured options, of incentives and disincentives, such that only a small percentage will actually choose to return to Israel.

The problem with the statement is that it represents the Palestinians as seeking to overwhelm Israel with refugees. As such they are portrayed as seeking Israel's destruction. This portrayal can serve only as the basis for concluding that the Palestinians have no real interest in a negotiated solution and that diplomacy has exhausted its potential. But if diplomacy has exhausted its potential, then what need is there for a prime minister committed to the peace process? The stage is set for a military response, under the leadership of Ariel Sharon.

Rather than trying to get the Palestinians to embrace a "right to return to their homeland, Palestine," the yet-to-be-completed task of negotiations needs to be identified: finding a way to accommodate a Palestinian *right* of return to Israel, while avoiding any *actual* return that threatens Israel's Jewish character. This is a complex and subtle task, yet it is the future of the peace process, a major uncompleted task that requires further time and thought—a continuing peace process. Some think this an impossible effort to square the circle, but that view is quite mistaken.

Distinguishing Palestinian Objectives

Palestinians have sought all of the following objectives:

- That Israel would accept responsibility for the refugee problem
- That Israel would recognize "in principle" a right of return for Palestinian refugees
- That Israel would accept Resolution 194
- That returning to Israel would be one of the options available to refugees

Each of these formulations is subject to multiple interpretations. All of them can be distinguished from actual outcomes (for example, that one hundred thousand Palestinians will return; that one million Palestinians will return). What is truly striking about the gaps between the two sides in the negotiations is that they are about conceptualization rather than outcomes. The Israeli government is prepared, as an *outcome,* to allow certain numbers of refugees to return, but it wants them to be returning not by right, but as a matter of Israeli humanitarian policy.

In this, the negotiations over the refugees are quite different from those over Jerusalem or territorial withdrawal. In those areas Israel was pressured to make major compromises over outcomes: to agree that it would withdraw from 95 percent of the West Bank rather than 75 percent; to agree that Palestinians would gain sovereignty over neighborhoods within Jerusalem, not just over Abu Dis. And on these tangible matters, the Barak government made major concessions. Yet when it comes to refugees, where the Palestinians are not pushing for the return of five hundred thousand, one million, or two million—on this issue there was a logjam.

One would have thought that Israel could afford to be gracious in its victory. Possibly it is not, because it takes that victory totally for granted. Yet it is worth remembering that under the Partition Resolution of 1947 (Res. 181) the Jewish state that was created in 1948 was itself almost 50 percent Palestinian. As a result of the 1948 war, Israel gained control over much of the intended Palestinian state, which was 100 percent Palestinian. Thus pre-1967 Israel consisted of a territory that up until 1948 had a clear Palestinian majority. In other words, had the refugee exodus never occurred, pre-1967 Israel could never have existed as a Jewish state. Even with the vast immigration of Jews to Israel over the last 50 years, if there had been no refugee exodus, Israel today would be 50 percent Palestinian. The fact that it is possible to end the conflict, hold onto lands captured during the 1948 war, retain Jewish Jerusalem, and yet prevent 95 percent of the refugees from ever returning is a tremendous victory for Israel. It should be prepared to go to extraordinary lengths to give the Palestinians whatever conceptualization makes their defeat most bearable. Focusing on each of the Palestinian issues of conceptualization, there is much that Israel can indeed provide.

Moral Responsibility

Here a distinction needs to be made between overall responsibility for the creation of refugees and responsibility for specific acts that caused specific populations to become refugees. With respect to the latter, there is no doubt that during the 1948 war there were instances, perhaps numerous ones, in which Palestinian villages were forcibly evacuated without justification. This is well known to historians and to some extent is already part of Israel's high school curriculum. There is no reason to deny this in the negotiations. Indeed, Israel's ability to carry out the difficult processes of peace building that will follow any successful negotiations will be enhanced by fuller awareness of the tragedy that befell the Palestinians. If the Palestinians want to see a Truth Commission emerge from the negotiations, so as to finally bring to light their individual experiences, Israel should agree.

The question of overall responsibility for the refugee problem is quite a different matter. Here Israelis can reasonably maintain that there would have been no refugee problem at all if the Arab world had accepted partition, if war had not been launched against the newly created Israel, or if there had not been broad Palestinian support for such efforts. Moreover, it is a reasonable assumption that, had Israel lost the 1948 war, the entire Jewish population would have become refugees, if they had survived at all.

As important as these issues of moral responsibility are, many have feared to deal honestly with them because it is thought that they are directly relevant to the right of return. This is a point of confusion. The issues are quite distinct. Whatever right of return Palestinian refugees have, it does not rest upon showing that they were forcibly evacuated. A refugee who leaves a war zone out of fear or mere prudence has a generally recognized right to return once hostilities have ceased. The issue of responsibility for his exodus has nothing to do with it.

A Right of Return for Palestinian Refugees

Here it is useful to distinguish between recognizing a right that preexists and shapes the negotiations as opposed to rights established as a result of the negotiations. With respect to the latter, this is a quite reasonable goal. Israel should emphasize that the negotiations will result in the refugees having specific mutually agreed-upon rights. The contested issue, of course, is what rights refugees should have as a result of the negotiations, but the idea that the negotiations might establish certain rights for the refugees, or classes of them, makes eminent sense and would be a productive focus for future negotiations.

A preexisting right of return is a distinct and different matter. What rights do refugees carry with them into the negotiations? The Palestinian position is that all of the refugees (and their descendants) possess a right to return to their homes within present-day Israel.

The first matter to dispose of is the issue of homes. In most cases, the homes no longer exist. They were bulldozed as part of a systematic effort to wipe evacuated Palestinian villages off the map. Palestinian researchers have identified over four hundred such villages. In other instances, homes exist but have been occupied for fifty years by Israelis, often by those who have bought them from other Israelis who sold them under titles legitimized in Israeli eyes by Israeli law. While Palestinians have legitimate claims to compensation for their homes, it is hardly worth pursuing whether they have a right to return to them. Rather, the issue is whether they have a right to return to the areas from which they came or, perhaps more generally, a right to live anywhere in Israel and even a right to become Israeli citizens.

Part of the difficulty of sorting through such issues emerges from a confusion about "rights talk." An example might help. It makes perfect sense to say to a group of people: "Each of you has a right to do X" and at the same time insist that it is legitimate to regulate and limit the exercise or implementation of those same rights. For instance, consider a ferryboat with the capacity to carry two hundred people on its once-a-day route. The company sells one thousand annual passes giving holders the right to use the boat whenever they please. As a rule, no more than fifty pass-holders show up on any given day. One day all thousand passholders show up. Each has a right to use the ferry, yet it is quite appropriate to enforce the rule that says no more than two hundred are allowed at a time. *To insist on the legitimacy of rules for the collective exercise of individual rights does not imply any denial of the existence of those rights for each individual.* Indeed, it is hard to imagine any rights of individuals that under some circumstances would not be subject to appropriate restriction.

When considering governments with responsibility for protecting the common good, one can speak of the legitimacy of rules of implementation. When considering the bearer of the rights, one speaks of limitations of the right itself. Thus, one might say, "Yes, you have a right to take the ferry, but that doesn't give you the right to board if it is already at full capacity. You have to wait even if it is a long wait, even if it means missing your only opportunity. Of course, if you don't go, you get compensation."

There are no perfect analogies, but conceptualizing the issue in this way, Israelis can reasonably say to Palestinian refugees, "Yes, we recognize a right of return, but it is not an absolute right. It is conditioned as well by our right to self-determination. Because Israel has a right to exist as a Jewish state, and because your population has grown so massively, we insist on the legitimacy of a framework for regulating the exercise of the right of refugees to return." Saying this to the Palestinians does not constitute a great concession. Such rights are universally recognized for all refugees. Yet this allows Israel to accept a right of return "in principle."

Israelis may further say to the Palestinians, "You have repeatedly embraced UN resolutions as constituting the basis in international law for the rights of Palestinians, yet the Partition Resolution of 1947 (UNGA Res. 181) explicitly called for the creation of two states, 'one Arab and one Jewish.' This means that Israel has a right under international law to choose to remain a Jewish state." Israel can offer mutuality: it will recognize a

Palestinian right of return, provided that the Palestinians recognize Israeli rights that legitimize regulation of the implementation of return.

Could Palestinians accept this? Could they accept that international law provides a basis for regulating the implementation of the right of return? It is a possibility that needs further exploration. Here is an interesting fact. In 1988, meeting in Algiers, the PLO issued the Palestinian Declaration of Independence, one of the foundational documents of Palestinian nationalism. Within this declaration they for the first time recognized Resolution 181 as an element of international law. Indeed, it is cited as a basis in international law for establishing, without Israeli permission, a Palestinian state. Most strikingly, within their Declaration of Independence the Palestinians explicitly characterized Resolution 181 as having called for "two states, one Arab and one Jewish." This was an implicit acceptance of the fact that Israel's Jewishness is enshrined in international law. Thus it is quite possible that the Palestinians could enter into a mutual exchange of rights recognition. Israel would recognize a right of return, and Palestinians would recognize that Israel has a right to choose to remain a Jewish state, and thus a right to regulate the implementation of the right of return.

Regardless of whether or not the Palestinians go this far, this is the position that Israel should affirm: that because Israel has a right to choose to remain a Jewish state until such time as it decides otherwise, the implementation of the right of return is appropriately subject to regulation. Retaining its right to remain a Jewish state should not, however, be used by Israel as a hammer to deny Palestinian rights, but rather to structure a principled position with respect to how to approach and understand Palestinian rights.

Resolution 194

Israeli negotiators have refused to accede to Palestinian demands that they recognize the legitimacy of UN General Assembly Resolution 194, enacted in 1948. For the Palestinians, acceptance of 194 appears fundamental to settling the refugee problem. Here, too, Israeli negotiators should be flexible.

The key sentence in Resolution 194 reads: "The refugees wishing to live at peace with their neighbors should be allowed to return to their homes at the earliest practicable date." Several points are worth noting:

• The resolution does not use "rights language," saying only that the refugees should be allowed to return to their homes. It neither affirms nor denies that this is a matter of right.

- The resolution when enacted referred to the 1948 refugees. While international law recognizes the rights of descendants as well, the issue of practicability cited in the resolution is considerably transformed by the vast growth of the refugee population. The existing 1948 refugees constitute perhaps 10 percent of today's refugee population.
- The resolution carries within itself a critical condition. It speaks of refugees "wishing to live at peace with their neighbors." Thus Resolution 194 does not support a totally unconditional return. Implicit here is the notion that in order to return, the refugee must be willing to live at peace. Interpreting such a condition is not a simple matter. From an Israeli point of view, this does not mean a desire for peace in the abstract. It means a commitment to lawfulness under very uncertain conditions in the future, conditions that could even include war between Israel and one or more Arab states, including the future state of Palestine.

Given the fissure that exists between Israel's Jewish and Arab citizens, which has deepened in recent months, no one can guarantee how large numbers of returning Palestinian refugees would act in a crisis. The "wishing to live at peace" condition in 194 suggests that a person-by-person determination needs to be made. Yet this is hardly possible. While some particularly militant refugees might be excluded for obvious security reasons, there is no way of knowing about the future behavior of most refugees in unpredictable and trying circumstances. Indeed, it is possible to argue that the logic of the "wishing to live at peace" clause in Resolution 194 suggests that the extent of permitted return could be linked to the evolution of conditions of true peace. If peace proves to be genuine and resilient, then it becomes credible to say that 194 supports a large return; if lasting peace is uncertain, then a large return will itself undermine a willingness to live at peace.

The main point is that the scope and force of resolution 194 is open to wide interpretation. For the purposes of the negotiations, the key issue is that whatever is agreed upon by way of implementation of 194 must be affirmed to be adequate fulfillment of Resolution 194. If such an "adequate fulfillment" clause is part of the agreement, it would be highly desirable to affirm that the agreement was based on mutual acceptance of 194. Thus Israel should not treat mention of Resolution 194 as anathema.

The Option of Returning

The option to actually return is the central issue. For Palestinian leaders, the key is meaningful choice. They need to be able to turn to their people and say, "Yes, you have an opportunity to return to Israel, but you also have a variety of other options. Some of them are quite attractive. You decide." Israel and the Palestinians might wisely put aside the question of the basis on which such options to return are grounded. Indeed, as suggested above, such options can themselves be viewed as a right to choose from a particular menu, a right that will be *constituted* by the negotiated agreement itself.

The key question is, what return options can Israel live with? Here the leftists who announced that they will never agree to the return of Palestinian refugees (except for limited numbers based on humanitarian grounds) are mistaken. They and other Israelis can in fact agree to much more without any risk of being overwhelmed by refugees. A variety of tools to do this are available.

Establishing a Rate of Return

Ideally the Palestinian leadership would like to avoid any regulation of the option to return to Israel. Their idea is to offer the refugees a menu of alternative options sufficiently attractive so as to avoid any need to restrict implementation. Ideally, then, it would just work out that 95 percent of the refugees would decide to accept compensation and resettlement elsewhere rather than returning to Israel.

Israel, of course, can't put itself in a situation in which there are no guarantees that it won't be overwhelmed by Palestinian refugees deciding that, all things considered, they would like to become Israelis. So from an Israeli point of view, something more is required. The temptation is to impose a cap, to say, for instance, that only one hundred thousand or two hundred thousand refugees can ever return (two hundred thousand is roughly the decline in the number of Palestinians who would be under Israeli sovereignty if Jerusalem were divided). The problem here, however, is that a fixed cap seems to fly in the face of giving all refugees some option of returning.

As an alternative to any total cap, it is possible to say that the rate of returning refugees must not alter the character of Israel as a Jewish state. There could be a fixed rate (for example, ten thousand a year) or a negotiated formula. Many different kinds of formulas might be possible. For instance, the rate might be set at a certain percentage of the population (say, 0.2 percent of the population) or as a percentage of the previous year's population growth (such as 5 percent of the growth) or perhaps even a percentage of the Jewish annual immigration under the Law of Return for Jews (perhaps one-fifth of the previous year's Jewish immigration). Palestinians would, of course, argue for more permissive formulas.

The existence of a regulated rate of return means that if more Palestinians seek to return than this number allows, they have to wait in a queue. The more who seek to return, the longer the queue and thus the longer the wait. This in turn means that choosing the option of returning to Israel becomes less and less attractive compared to resettlement elsewhere accompanied by immediate access to a major financial package for assistance and compensation. Faced with waiting ten years to return to Israel or getting money, new homes, and land elsewhere, most would choose the latter. In any event, the actual numbers entering would be proportional to existing demographics.

The 1948 Refugees

From an Israeli point of view, the return of some refugees is more threatening than the return of others. The least threatening are the actual 1948 refugees, as opposed to their adult children and grandchildren. A child of fifteen in 1948 is sixty-eight years old today. This elderly and dwindling population is well past childbearing age. Their return, accompanied by minor children in the rare cases where they exist, poses no long-term impact on Israeli demographics. Similarly they pose no security threat. Yet surely as a matter of justice, priority should go to these elderly refugees. Moreover, the total number of living 1948 refugees is quite limited. Of the three hundred thousand or so in Lebanon, not more than thirty thousand fall into this category. *Subject to some regulation of the rate of return, Israel can extend an option to all of the actual 1948 refugees to return.* This return "by right" could be accompanied by a family reunification and visitation policy that would ease the hardship these elderly refugees would encounter in separation from adult children and grandchildren. But this secondary return could be controlled by Israel as a "humanitarian policy" under its discretion.

Location of Return

The refugees will have lots of options to return to places other than Israel. For those seeking to become citizens of Israel with the right to live where they please, only a very limited number could be accommodated each year.

But there are ways to give large numbers of Palestinian refugees a genuine option of returning to land that is today the state of Israel. The idea of land swaps was part of the negotiations. In exchange for territory that Israel seeks to annex to accommodate settlements in the West Bank, it will swap areas adjacent to the Gaza Strip. Since these areas will become part of the Palestinian state, large numbers of refugees can be settled there. This is a powerful solution. It allows the leadership to say that refugees are able to return to what is *today* part of Israel.

Unfortunately it does not seem that this idea is having the powerful effect that some had expected. In part, this is because Palestinians still cling to the idea of returning to their homes. In part, it is because being in refugee resettlement areas adjacent to Gaza sounds awfully like being in new refugee camps, and, in part, because "returning to Israeli land that becomes Palestinian" may feel like a bit of a shell game.

It is possible, however, to modify the "land swap" idea in ways that will make it more meaningful for refugees. The key here is to maintain one principle: the refugees returning to these areas will be citizens of the state of Palestine, and any children born to them will also be Palestinian citizens. Within this framework, there is considerable room for creative ideas. One option is to not press ahead with an exchange of sovereignty. Rather, Israel could *lease* certain areas to the state of Palestine and, similarly, lease from the Palestinians settlement areas in the West Bank (thus giving the Palestinians sovereignty over a larger percentage of the West Bank). Secondly, such areas need not be limited to territories adjacent to Gaza. If it was thought that ultimately all the leased territories would become sovereign areas, they should be adjacent to either Gaza or the West Bank. Along the Green Line, such areas need not be extensive. In fact, there might be a number of quite small pocket-villages, designed specifically not to resemble vast refugee camps. It might even be possible for some leased areas to be in interior regions of Israel, parallel to isolated settlement areas leased within the West Bank, far from the Green Line. Just as the Jewish settlers would not be Palestinian citizens, so too these Palestinians would not be Israeli citizens. Such options do not have to be of a large magnitude, they could be limited to a few thousand. The idea, however, is to offer to the refugees a wide variety of possibilities, an offer that is not easily categorized—or dismissed—while at the same time protecting Israel.

Binational Zones

An even more powerful idea would be the creation of binational zones, areas in which both Israeli and Palestinian citizens live. To appreciate this, it must be realized that the areas of the West Bank that Israel proposes to annex in order to accommodate Jewish settlers contain substantial numbers of Palestinians. On some proposals, upwards of fifty thousand Palestinians now living in the West Bank would find themselves suddenly living in what has become Israeli sovereign territory. Oddly, the demographic implication of this inclusion within Israel of a significant Palestinian population goes largely unexamined by many Israelis who say no to any return of Palestinian refugees.

Rather than simply annexing these areas to Israel, these areas could be designated "binational zones" in which both Israelis and Palestinians would live, each group maintaining citizenship in its national state. To these binational zones taken from West Bank territory would be added territories within Israel that would similarly become binational zones. Within these zones, areas would be developed for the return of specified numbers of refugees.

The question of sovereignty over the binational zones offers a variety of possibilities. They could come under the undivided joint sovereignty of the two states (condominium). Alternatively, it is possible for those binational zones falling within the Green Line to remain under Israeli sovereignty and those beyond the Green Line to fall under Palestinian sovereignty. Or this could be reversed, with those beyond the Green Line going to Israeli sovereignty and those within the Green Line to Palestinian sovereignty. Another option would be for the entire issue of sovereignty over these zones to be deferred until they have been in existence for ten years.

Their basic characteristic is not their sovereignty, but rather their binational character. These would be areas in which both Israeli and Palestinian citizens could live, with each group having citizenship only in their national state, thus without affecting the demographics of citizenship within either state.

Conclusion

These tools—regulating the rate of return, focusing on the 1948 refugees, using land swaps, and establishing binational zones—would operate within the larger context of compensation and resettlement alternatives outside Israel, whether in the Palestinian state, Arab countries, Europe, or the United States. Thus, a rich menu of choices can be devised, accompanied by some regulatory structure that safeguards Israel. From a political point of view, a choice-based approach of this sort has major advantages. For the Palestinian leadership, it allows them to avoid charges of having abandoned the right of return. Rather, it gives them the opportunity to deliver to the refugees a variety of attractive alternatives.

Such a choice-based approach is also best for Israel. Other approaches might wrest from the PLO a verbal statement affirming that the refugee claims have been satisfied. But this is unlikely to be accepted by the refugees themselves and their descendants. Other organizations (such as Hamas) would undoubtedly take up the cause, charging that the PLO had sold out the right of return. To truly end the conflict, it will be necessary for millions of Palestinians to actually feel that they themselves have made a decision about return, resettlement, and compensation. Only then will the refugee issue be finally resolved, a necessary condition for truly ending the conflict.

A STORY ABOUT A BOMB

Jonathan Tel

A STORY ABOUT A BOMB IS NOT A BOMB. However artfully constructed the plot, however incendiary the theme, although the topic may be volatile and the implications explosive, however dangerous the sentiments may be—a story will not in fact abolish itself in a blinding flash, scattering shrapnel within a radius of forty meters and shredding passersby. Despite our best efforts.

Several years ago I browsed through an anthology of Palestinian literature. It had been lent by an Israeli acquaintance of mine (the translator, in fact, of some of my own stories) and I had to return it before leaving the country—so I am telling you about it from memory, with the aid of jottings in my notebook. It was one of those plump, poorly printed, catchall UNESCO jobs—comprising poetry, stories, and autobiographical fragments. As a rule, the poems did not survive translation, and the prose was highly variable in quality. There was, however, one story that struck me as remarkable at the time, and that has stayed with me since, burning in my memory. Its title was *The Red Button*. It concerned a Hamas terrorist (or freedom fighter, if you prefer) who was on the point of blowing himself up, along with as many Israelis as possible. He was shifting from leg to leg in Jerusalem, near where the new city meets the old, across from Jaffa Gate, on the wrong side of the highway.

It was eight o'clock in the morning on the hottest Friday in August. He had come from a refugee camp in Gaza, and had spent the previous night praying with some comrades near Bethlehem. He had just been dropped off by a Toyota. He was wearing a long padded overcoat, buttoned up to conceal the bands of dynamite around his abdomen. He was sweating and shivering. His instructions were to cross the road (looking carefully to right and left first; it wouldn't do to be knocked down by a speeding vehicle before he had a chance to press the button on the detonator) to the bus stop on the far side. With any luck, there would be many Israelis waiting there. He would simply have to stand among them, mutter *Allahu Akbar,* and the next thing he knew he would be marching into Paradise, a pair of dark-eyed houris eager to kiss his bleeding wounds. In reality, of course, it was not as simple as all that.

The stones of the city wall were solid blocks of white sun. Every bone in his body ached. (He had had to crouch on the back floor of the Toyota, concealed under a carpet, for what had seemed like generations. The car had passed through checkpoint after checkpoint and had then been forced to idle in commuter traffic.) He smelled his own sweat. (No, worse. His wise comrades had insisted he swallow a hefty dose of Diocalm before his mission, to seal him up. It would hardly do to enter Paradise stinking from one's own shit. *On the Day of Resurrection,* it is written, *the wounds of the martyr shall be perfumed like musk.*) The bus stop in question was within view. He could see would-be passengers waiting there, more or less patiently. Women, children, old men, also about ten soldiers, perhaps on weekend leave. The ideal target. Yet he had to wait. The traffic was atrocious. He stepped into the road—and a great red Coca-Cola truck went roaring past. He retreated. He strode forth. A Subaru blurted its horn at him. A police car swept by. He hobbled back to the safety of the curb. Finally the road was empty. On the far side, a number 23 bus was halted at the stop. By the time he arrived there, the bus had departed, taking all the Israelis with it. If he reached into his pocket and jabbed down on the button now, he would explode nobody but himself. He could have wept with frustration.

Well, he couldn't just stand there. He was sure he looked suspicious. He walked down Hativat Yerushalayim, as far as where the wall bends by the Armenian Quarter. He walked up again to Jaffa Gate. He returned to the crossing. He recrossed the highway. And down the street to the point where he had begun. By now a dozen new Israelis had assembled at the bus stop opposite. Once again he tried to cross the road. Once again he had to reckon with the traffic. The horrible fumes . . .

He kept the vision of Paradise clear in front of him. As it is written, *that Allah may know those who believe, and take martyrs from among you.* Two houris would come dancing toward him. They would cloak him in the precious *hulla* robe. They would say, *May Allah put dust on the face of those who put dust on your face!* An acrid aroma; a clammy feeling around the groin. He had got beyond the trembling stage. He was on an exalted level of anguish. Now the twitching was intense, as if he were being banged like a saltcellar on a humid day. There was a gap in the traffic. He darted between a taxi and a Honda motorcycle. Once again he reached the bus stop. Once again a bus, the 13 Aleph, had just accelerated away, taking his almost-victims with it.

Once again he circled down Hativat Yerushalayim and back to the beginning. Once again the frustration. Once again the shuffling at the curbside—bare feet in basic polyurethane sandals. Once again the mumbling of prayers and quotes. The agony in his guts. The unscratchable itching underneath the load of high explosives. And then (as anybody who knows anything about the structure of fairy tales knows) it was on the third try that the pattern was broken.

Now at last the future seemed revealed. Now a fresh selection of Israelis had appeared at the stop. Now there was a hiatus in the traffic—no vehicles to delay him, no bus to carry away his victims. And then, just as he was about to scurry across the expanse of asphalt, to leap forward into his destiny, to switch on the detonator. . . .

A middle-aged couple approached the terrorist. They stood beside the curb, blocking his way. The man had thin sandy hair whirled over a bald spot. He was wearing baggy green shorts. An oversize map was sprouting from his shirt pocket. He was waving his yellow Holyland Tours baseball cap to attract the terrorist's attention. The woman, blonde, had on an identical cap; she was also in shorts, blue ones, matching her varicose veins. The two of them were addressing him in what he reasonably believed to be English.

Since he evidently did not understand, the tourists resorted to sign language. The man was holding up a camera—it was suspended from a strap around his neck—he was hoisting it free. The woman was pointing to it. Much dumbshow ensued, involving grasping and lifting the Olympus, gesturing at elements of it (automatic focus; you just have to aim the thing and shoot), peering through the viewfinder, and saying *cheese.* (And all the while, Hativat Yerushalayim remained free of traffic, the ignorant Israelis were unmoving—how simple and easy to blow them and himself up, the exemplary conclusion—if only those damn foreigners would just get out of his way!)

But what could he do? If he tried to escape from them, let alone grapple with them, he would only draw attention to himself. The Israelis would just run off, or one of them might draw a gun and kill him before he'd be able to complete his mission. No, the only hope was to go through with what the foreigners wanted, and then they would leave him in peace.

The tourists posed on the curbside. The husband put his arm around his wife's shoulder. They smiled as if they were genuinely happy. As if simply to be in Jerusalem was to be blessed. The terrorist stepped back, arranging their faces within the rectangle of the viewfinder. As a backdrop—the road. Travelers in cars, and pedestrians. An old woman, carrying a basket of oranges. Arab workmen, their pickaxes over their shoulders, en route to a building site. Soldiers waiting. Two Hassidim on bicycles, going by. Children playing hide-and-seek behind the bus shelter. And beyond that, the magnificent ancient wall of the Old City. He motioned the couple with his left hand, to lean their heads closer together; to step a little *this* way— so he could catch them with Jaffa Gate behind, for extra picturesqueness. Somehow, miraculously, as he squinted through the viewfinder, all his quaverings and uncertainties had ceased. He was aware of nothing except this instant. As for the tourists, they would look at the snapshot and remember their trip to the Holy Land for the rest of their lives. Ah, perfect now. The tip of an index finger pressed down on a red button—and the story ended.

Of course my summary of the story doesn't capture the magic of the original. How could it? The author (a certain Ahmed Fishawi) took great pains to bring us inside the mind and body of the central character. His name is S——. We are borne along on his stream of consciousness. His thoughts focus on the here and now (precise physical description) along with memories and ponderings concerning his childhood in the refugee camp: his mother who is suffering from breast cancer, his elder brother who had been arrested five times during the Intifada, his uncle who had been shot in the leg at a roadblock near Gush Katzir, and, interspersed with these, theological reflection.

Elements of this last aspect—a discussion of the role of the martyr in a jihad—I copied into my notebook. (You will excuse any erroneous spellings, mistaken attributions, and misquotations on my part.) At the Battle of Uhud, "Abd Allah b. Jahish cried out, 'Let me meet my enemy face to face! Let him cut off my nose and ear! So that when I meet Thee, O Allah, and Thou ask of me, "For whose sake were thy nose and ear cut off?" I may answer, 'for Thy sake and for the sake of Thy Prophet!'". . . And did not al-Ghazzali describe martyrdom as "the most wondrous of delights"? A martyr, according to a tradition going back to the Prophet, "may live in any part of Paradise he chooses." Also, "when the first drop of blood falls, he is granted forgiveness for all his sins." A martyr, alone among men, is not washed or shrouded after death, "that his bloody clothing may speak for him on the Day of Judgment. . . ." At the Battle of Badr, Umar b. al-Humam b. al-Jamuh al-Ansari was about to eat a date. He threw it away. "If I live to eat another date again, I shall have lived too long a life! . . ." And the Prophet informed Zayd b. Suhan that part of his body would precede him into Paradise. His arm was cut off in battle; subsequently, in the Battle of the Camel, he was fatally wounded. He declared, "Lo, I see my hand in Heaven, beckoning me to follow! . . ." On the other hand, suicide, generally speaking, is a horrible sin. Is it not written (Sura 2: 195): "and live in the way of Allah, and do not cast yourselves by your own hands into destruction"? Lots more similar stuff, besides.

On first read-through, I think I was unconsciously taking in the story (printed as it was amid essays, memoirs, and confessional poems) as if it were factual—a window into the experience of Palestinians. And so I was moved. The second time I read it, I became aware of the technical expertise of the author. And the third time, I was disturbed.

What exactly was the author, this Mr. Fishawi, trying to say? Was he drawing an analogy between terrorist and tourist? Just as the former regards innocent victims as items that serve a function in a theologico-political calculation—so the latter sees Jerusalem, complete with inhabitants, merely as a setting for a holiday. Each in his or her own way is an exploiter. But this is absurd! It's one thing to put outsiders in an album, quite another to rip them apart.

Furthermore, as the years have gone by, as this story has lived on in my head, I have come to wonder. Perhaps the author was *too* good a writer. He has taken us *too* much inside the mind of a terrorist. Of course that is the author's job. (A fiction writer can go places no journalist could ever venture.) But if we are brought to—more than understand—to *sympathize* with the terrorist, then are we not, in some sense, colluding with him? Far be it from me to criticize another author on these grounds, let alone call for censorship. I only wish to draw attention to my feelings of discomfort. The grander questions I leave open.

Naturally, over the years whenever I have encountered Arab intellectuals, I have mentioned this story. None of them had read *The Red Button* or heard of Ahmed Fishawi. Well, that's how it is on occasion; it happens that an individual—who normally never writes fiction at all, or badly—will pen one luminous story (as a rule, deriving from his own experience). Nothing he had ever done before or will ever do again is remotely comparable. I thought of contacting my Hebrew translator and getting him to fax me a copy, so I could show it around to friends and colleagues and associates, but in truth I wasn't at all sure I ever wanted to deal with the story again.

Until the other day, when I was at a party in Tel Aviv. It was taking place in a penthouse suite at the top of what by local standards qualifies as a skyscraper. The apartment belonged to a children's book illustrator (heiress to a real estate fortune, hence the setting) and her husband, a writer of techno-thrillers. The guests were mostly connected to the world of books—poets, journalists, a scattering of fictioneers. I had been brought here by my Israeli publisher. The view was amazing—a nighttime panorama of the city and the Mediterranean beyond. The air conditioning was intense. (We had been warned not to open the windows, lest a gull swoop in and snatch a slice of goat-cheese focaccia from our fingers. "Greedy bastards!" the techno-thriller author had remarked.) As usual in Israel, the guests were arguing about politics. I say "arguing"—for certainly voices were raised, fists were being shaken, everybody was fiercely interrupting everybody else—yet, as far as I could tell, the guests were pretty much in agreement. We all were in favor of peace, were we not? Normalization, human rights, an equitable settlement with the Palestinians? Now, happy as I was to sip my gracious host and hostess's Tishbi cabernet sauvignon, to listen in on these good people reciting draft versions of editorials to be appearing soon enough in the peacenik Israeli press, I did yearn for meatier conversation. I noticed a man standing by himself to one side, saying nothing. His hands were opening and shutting like lobster claws. He had buttoned himself into a tan summer suit that he did not seem to belong in, as if handed down from an elder brother. His short black hair did not so much sprout from his skull as cling to it, like a colony of barnacles; sunglasses were growing on top of his head.

I managed to trap him between a floor lamp and a high glass tabletop. A bookcase was at my side; on top of it a white china bowl brimful with pomegranates. I introduced myself. "What do you think of all this?" I asked him.

He stuffed a strip of pita dunked in taramosalata in his mouth and washed it down with Kinley soda—thus avoiding having to respond.

I asked next, "What's your connection with this party?"

He made a dismissive gesture with a bowl of guacamole.

But eventually, when he was satisfied nobody was overhearing our conversation, he loosened up.

"Fucking liberal losers," he said. "What do they know? The only Arabs they ever see are the guys who pick up their garbage. Believe you me, 99 percent of the Palestinians support Hamas—whether they admit it or not. The only way we'll have peace is if the Arabs know there's a gun pointing at their head."

"That's an interesting point of view," I said. "Can you pass the pistachios?"

"Sure."

"What kind of writing do you do?"

He seemed startled by my question. "I use an IBM-compatible laptop. How about you?"

I think we talked about computers, and food and drink, and the weather for a while.

And then, since we were fast running out of conversational topics, I alluded to *The Red Button*.

To my surprise, the man gave a broad grin.

"I know that piece. Yes, J——. I know it very well."

"Really? Where did you come across it?"

"I didn't have to come across it. The author's a good friend of mine. We go back a long way."

"You know Ahmed Fishawi?"

"Of course. But it's not his real name. It's his," in an atrocious French accent, "*nom de plume, nom de guerre.*"

He refilled his own glass with Kinley and mine with Tishbi.

I murmured some literary criticism of a conventional sort, praising the author's talent in drawing us into his fictional world.

The man ignored me. He raised his glass as if about to deliver a toast.

"As a matter of fact, I am Ahmed Fishawi."

Since in my astonishment I had not raised my glass, he "clinked" his against empty air. "*L'Chaim!*" Then he swigged the glass of soda in one gulp.

He added, "And by the way, don't keep calling it fiction. Fiction shmiction! *The Red Button* is true, every word of it. The events described took place on the morning of August 8, 1999. I know, because I was there."

"You're Ahmed Fishawi?" I said, stunned.

"That's what I keep telling you."

"Now wait a minute," I said. "I can just about believe that you wrote the story and published it under a pseudonym in an anthology of Palestinian literature. But you are not seriously telling me that you personally are a Palestinian terrorist! So what other character could you have been? I know you're not a foreign tourist with a camera. And even if you had been waiting at the bus stop, you wouldn't have known what was going on."

"All the same," he said, "I was there. Do you believe everything you read in books, J——? Do you believe it's not just the truth, but the whole truth? I was there all along, standing just out of frame. And the real story goes on after the story on the page ends. Do you want to know what actually happened? Or are you one of those post-fucking-modernists?"

"I want to know the truth."

"I was there. I was leaning against a lamppost, fascinated by the sports pages in *Ma'ariv*. On the other side of the terrorist, a couple of lovers were kissing. So the terrorist pressed the red button on the camera. At that moment—when we knew for sure he wouldn't have a free hand to operate the detonator—I came running up from behind and I slammed into his back. The 'lovers' seized his arms between them. And the male 'tourist' put on the handcuffs while the female 'tourist' kicked him in the balls."

The man laughed.

"My real name's E——. I'm in counter-terrorism—Shimshon Unit. Have you heard of us? We'd been following the poor bastard ever since he left Gaza. We eliminated his entire cell."

The man laughed louder. His shoulder knocked against the floor lamp, and set it vibrating, its bulb flashing on and off.

"I almost killed myself! And everybody else too! You know that? See, when I ran into him, somehow the detonator started up. It shouldn't have— maybe it was a faulty electrical connection, I don't know. By a miracle it didn't set the bomb off. So all that happened was that the bastard got third-degree burns on his belly, and I screwed up my arm."

He rolled up his right sleeve. Just above the wrist, a patch of skin was distorted, thickly ridged—as if the flesh had melted like wax and refrozen.

I took the opportunity to tell him my full name and what I was doing in Israel.

"Yes, yes," he said with a show of uninterest. "I know all about you."

He stared past my shoulder.

"So then we took him back to HQ. We put him in the medical unit for a while—intensive care—until we knew he wasn't going to die on us, and he was out of pain. Then we could torture him. Don't look so shocked, J——. We call it torture but it's not what you think of as torture, it's the gentle art of persuasion. We're not in Argentina, you know. We use the official methods. *Shabah*—making him sit in one position for hours, in a child-size chair. *Tiltulim*—shaking him till he rattles. Those softies over there," pointing with an asparagus tip at a group of giggling novelists, "they think I'm naughty—but it's toughies like me who stop the Arabs blowing up the kindergartens!"

He made himself a rough-and-ready sandwich of cherry tomatoes, asparagus tips, and baba ganoush wrapped in pita bread and lowered it into his mouth.

When he had chewed most of it, he went on.

"Of course we didn't have to torture him, hardly at all. Not in his case. He knew he'd be spending years in an Israeli prison, instead of partying with houris in Paradise. He didn't want to be alive. We stood beside the hospital bed, and we shouted at him. So he told us the names and addresses. Everything we wanted to know. Most of it we knew already, actually. Who his commander was, the location of his safe house. The basic facts. Not that we can do fuck-all about it if it's in the Palestinian Authority area. And then we locked him up, and that was the end of that."

I was silent.

I wondered if he was trying to fool me or fooling himself as well.

The man reached past me and took a pomegranate. He bit it open. He started sucking its juice, and spitting pith and seeds onto the carpet, as if daring me to challenge him.

I tried to respond indirectly.

"I think you underestimate yourself," I said. "You say you're not a fiction writer—and maybe the outline of your story is based on truth—but how on earth did you get inside the man's head? Those interior monologues. I can't believe this is your first story!"

"Oh I've published a few children's books. This is my first adult fiction—and I'm not going to do another ever again. It's hard work."

He pulled down his sunglasses, blocking out his eyes.

"I asked the bastard to help me. That's how I know. Not too bad a fellow, the terrorist, once you get to be friends with him. I gave him a Marlboro. I played the nice guy. I said, if you tell me every little thing that went through your head, I'll let you read the Quran, and I'll give you the cutest little prayer mat to keep you company. And then when he'd told me everything he could think of, I used the other method to jog his memory."

"What other method?" I said.

I literally felt the hairs stand up on my neck—a sensation I'd only ever read about in books that I'd always supposed to be fictional. An excitement like that a hunter feels, I imagine, when the object of the chase is within sight or like that of a writer who has at last found a way to construct his narrative, uniting form and content.

"What method do you think?" he said. "The usual. What a man like you would call background research. I went down to his cell and I tied a blanket soaked in piss over his head. Then I hit him in the kidneys with the butt of my rifle. It took seventy-two hours before he broke. He answered all my questions."

I took a pack of Winstons from my pocket, shook it out, and offered him one.

He ignored my offer.

"I don't need to tell *you* what he said. Every little detail and more besides. His childhood. His grandmother. His uncle. His religious beliefs. What he felt and what he smelled. And it was worth it. A chance in a lifetime. *The Red Button*'s a great story—you told me so yourself."

Then, suddenly, without warning, he charged past, pushing me out of his way.

He had vanished.

I gazed through the picture window. Stars, part of a moon, city lights diffusing eerily into photochemical smog, searchlights over the Mediterranean, destroyers on the horizon. Somewhere behind me, my Israeli publisher and my American publisher were murmuring lovingly together; elsewhere, poets were swapping malicious gossip, loud whispers in ferocious Hebrew. It was chilly. My hands were plunged in my pockets. Meanwhile I let my thoughts roam back again and again, analyzing and questioning the version in the book and his version, considering what use I could make of this knowledge.

I was jolted from my reverie by a voice close to my left ear.

"I've given it up. A bad habit. Don't mind if you do."

I looked straight at E——. I saw fractions of myself mirrored in his sunglasses.

He shrugged.

"So what are you going to do now, J——? Are you going to put me in one of your stories—me along with S——? It's up to you. I can't stop you. It's *your* story now."

PRAISE

FOR YEHUDA AMICHAI

Stanley Moss

1

Snow clouds shadow the bay, on the ice the odd fallen gull.
I try to keep my friend from dying by remembering
His childhood of praise to God, who needs us all. Wurzburg:
The grownups are inside saying prayers for the dead,
The children are sent out to play—their laughter
More sacred than prayer. After dark his father
Blesses and kisses him *Guttenacht*. He wakes
To go to school with children who stayed behind
And were murdered before promotion.

Now his wife lies beside him.
He may die with her head on his pillow.
He sings in his sleep:
Her breasts are white sheep that appear on the mountain,
Her belly is like a heap of wheat set about with lilies.
Awake, he says, as if telling me a secret:
When metaphor and reality come together, death occurs.
His life is a light, fresh snow blowing across the bay.

2

A year later in Jerusalem, he carries a fallen soldier
on his back, himself. The text for the day begins:

He slew a lion in the pit in a time of snow.
Seconds, minutes, hours, are flesh,
he tells me he is being cut to pieces—
if they had not made him turn in his rifle. . . .
He sees I can not bear more of that.
Yet a little sleep, a little slumber, a little folding
of hands in sleep and we drink to *life.*
Chilled in desert heat, what keeps him alive:
soldiers—his wife, his son, and daughter,
Perhaps the ashes of a girl he loved in childhood.
Outside their window
a Sun Bird and Dead Sea Sparrow fly
from everlasting to everlasting
Later he covers my head with his hands, blessing me,
later unable to walk alone he holds onto my hand
with so much strength he comforts me.

On Being
a Mensch
and Healing a
Troubled World

THE TASKS OF EMBODIED LOVE

ETHICS, RELIGION, DISABILITY

Roger S. Gottlieb

MY YOUNGER DAUGHTER, Esther, is fourteen. She is developmentally "delayed"—though I think her train is really on another track rather than simply slow to arrive at this one. She also has multiple physical problems, the most serious of which is a generalized muscular weakness leading to a severe scoliosis. Her other disabilities include a seizure disorder, an anxiety disorder, leg braces for the world's most pronated feet, easily dislocatable joints, bad knees, allergic asthma, mild to moderate hearing loss, and digestive problems. On a given day she takes six medications and ten to twelve supplements. In a given week she has six therapy appointments. In a given year she might have forty doctor appointments. However, she also loves pop music and Julia Roberts movies, will talk your ear off if you give her half a chance, had a bat mitzvah, and is often the most emotionally direct and spiritually advanced soul I know. Forgetting the precise word, she once called marshmallows "fire ice cream," and she is the only person I've ever met who has totally mastered the Buddhist virtue of sympathetic joy, of really taking complete delight in the happiness of others.

On the scale of special needs Esther fits somewhere in the middle. She is not in a wheelchair, she can talk, and she can relate to others, she continues to develop intellectually. Other cases are easier, and others are much, much harder.

I am describing Esther because I think that her life, and that of her parents as her primary caretakers, constitute a challenge to many of the ways we have thought about justice, morality, and spiritual life.

Rooted in the concept of the autonomous individual, secular moral theory has little place for persons in need of constant physical help and cognitive support or for those who provide care for them. Religious ethics, on the other hand, while much more keyed to the natural frailty and interdependence of all human beings, has had comparatively little to say about the *particular* situation of the disabled and their caretakers. Judaism in particular has rich resources in Moses' speech impediment ("I am slow of speech," he tells God, trying to evade God's command to confront Pharaoh) and in the way Jacob had to wrestle with an angel and become lame before he could carry on the covenant. Yet despite the occasional lovely folk tale about people praying to God by playing the flute because they are unable to read, disabilities are not given much attention or concern in the Jewish community. And the culturally Jewish emphasis on conventional forms of intelligence is particularly hard on individuals or families facing developmental issues.

As Esther's father—and someone who has spent his professional life writing and teaching about modern social theory, ethics, and spiritual life—I have found these gaping holes intellectually embarrassing and personally alienating.

This essay will continue recent efforts to redress this inadequacy by exploring some of the theoretically and personally vexing problems that come from the condition of serious disability, both from the point of view of the disabled child and from that of the child's caretakers. I will offer many more questions than answers. Indeed if there is any certainty in what I say, it is that the life *of* and life *with* a special needs child is centered on questions that are both inescapable and unanswerable.

As a preface, however, I invite the reader to reflect on why it has taken so long for moral, political, and spiritual thinkers—who have written so much about so many things—to think deeply about disability issues.

Here are two reasons I think are important.

First, those who do the thinking and writing about moral life are not the people who take care of children or the dependent. Thus they are not aware of the effects on our lives of having severe disabilities or of caring for those who do.

Even when those who care for the dependent—usually women—are socially liberated enough to take their place among those who write about ethics, they do comparatively little thinking about the disabled and those who care for them. This may be because insofar as they are able to write about ethics, other people are taking care of their children.

It is, I suspect, only when those who do the caretaking can also do the writing that this issue seriously comes to the fore. Further, it is under the pressure of a disability rights movement that the ethical issues involved are taken seriously by a widening circle. (This is another example of the dependence of abstract normative thought on historical and political change.)

Justice and Disability

Who is the typical moral subject? Western philosophy possesses at least five dominant moral traditions, each with a distinctive answer. There is the Greek emphasis on natural development and fulfillment, the rights tradition based on rational autonomy, the Marxist tradition based on the collective liberation and fulfillment of the working class, the feminist emphasis on mutuality and empathic connection, and the Judeo-Christian tradition based on submission to God stemming from a free moral choice.

These traditions, as different as they are in many respects, share two premises:

They first presuppose that all moral subjects are *capable* of entering into moral life: that they are healthy, or rational, or capable of empathic mutuality, or possess the ability for committed moral choice, or for participating in democratic processes.

Second, they agree that all moral subjects are equally *free* to enter into moral life. That is, that people's life responsibilities are roughly equal or, at least, apportioned to their abilities and station. If they are not equally free, then it is our historical task to make them so. Those who are not allowed to own property, vote, receive an education, or become the head of philosophy departments fail to do so only because they are unfairly prevented. Only history holds them back.

Why are disability issues a problem for these moral theories? Because for the disabled, and for their caretakers, it may be too physically or intellectually demanding to take part in the processes of deliberation, self-representation, emotional connection, or ethical self-development that these models require.

Consider first the problem of political participation. As Eva Kittay argues brilliantly in *Love's Labor*, formal political equality will not produce a just society as long as the labor of dependency, itself requiring a unique blend of personal involvement and moral commitment, is *culturally* assigned to women; and *economically* assigned to poor and nonwhite women. Will women who can vote, own property, and become brain surgeons be truly equal if they are expected to take primary responsibility for caring for their own children, their aging parents, their paraplegic sister?

In a society in which political rights are assigned to—and lived out by—autonomous individuals, caring for a disabled child puts caretakers at an extreme disadvantage. One comes to public affairs with half a mind, unable often to think beyond the next doctor's appointment, medical crisis, or need to deal with some caregiver who is not doing a good job. This dilemma is similar to the more widespread phenomenon of women taking a disproportionate amount of responsibility for childrearing and housework. However, in the small nuclear family the period of childhood dependence is contracting, and a good deal of it can be commodified. The much more extreme dependence of those with disabilities goes on forever, cannot be commodified to anything like the extent to that of normal children, and is much more extreme in any case.

Similar problems arise for other moral frameworks. For instance, access to the collective processes of workplace democracy or community control of local economic affairs in socialist or Marxist schemas is restricted by a life of care. If socialism is impossible because, as someone once said, it requires too many meetings, the caregivers of the disabled are typically too physically, emotionally, and intellectually drained to take part in those meetings.

In feminist models of morality, which often invoke mutually empathic relationships rather than the collective administration of justice as the key to moral life, there are also problems. The ability to have a truly mutual friendship when you are devoting so much time, energy, and emotion to a child is seriously compromised. At the end of a day filled with anxiety and frustration, I often find myself emotionally drained, too filled with my own feelings to listen very well to those of another, or to reach out across a divide in which I literally feel like I live in another country. Our family has often lived at the edge of emotional and physical (not to mention financial) collapse. (As one acquaintance put it, "You remind me of Job." Why was I not comforted by the remark?) Those friends who have stuck with my family have been people who find it rewarding *despite* a frequent lack of full mutuality.

Similarly, at times my marriage has seemed more like one long exercise in collective medical management than romance or emotional bonding. For a while, as my wife put it, it seemed I had married Esther, so much of myself was given to her care. And my wife, for her part, seemed married to the telephone, through which she engaged in an endless round of making, rescheduling, canceling, and checking on appointments, finding new healers, instructing old ones, getting more information, dealing with teachers and therapists—many of whom *themselves* had to be taught, handled, instructed, coddled, or challenged. Also many of the disabled themselves, for instance those with autism, are moral subjects but cannot enter into mutual relations to a full degree. They do not give back as they are given to.

As to the Greek model, the melancholy truth is that disability and the care for disability limit our capacity to understand and to act in the world. Simply, disability constitutes a kind of ill health. It can often keep us from fulfilling the model good of our species and from reaching a characteristically human fulfillment. Caretakers often cannot develop many virtues that we should. At other times we are called on to develop other virtues— like looking on the bright side of things or putting up with endless rounds of frustration—to an extreme degree. If the disabled are to be included as full subjects in this framework, a radically different model of health will need to be presupposed.

How then will the disabled and those who care for them even be thought of as having moral worth, since they cannot take part equally in the activities that define one as a moral subject?

Infinite Worth and Finite Triage

One answer to this problem of the exclusion or second-rate status of the disabled and their caretakers is to rework our conception of moral life in spiritual terms. I actually have great hope for this framework, and I believe that you cannot confront disability without spiritual resources, not if you are to avoid slipping into bitterness, despair, envy, or numbness.

In a spiritual perspective we concentrate on gratitude instead of entitlement, on devotion rather than publicly measurable achievements, on serving without limit rather than making sure we get full value for every bit we do. Instead of secular moralities based in (individual or collective) self-representation or personal fulfillment, on strict calculations of justice where (God forbid) we never fail to get the least thing we deserve, we offer submission to the will of God and the recognition of the infinite worth of each soul. Like Arjuna in the *Bagavat Gita,* we learn to act without expecting to control the outcome. Like the characters in the Elijah folk tales of Jewish tradition, we think that our child might be a great prophet whose every gesture carries a hidden meaning. Or as Mother Teresa said when asked how she could get so close to a leper, "He's just Christ in one of his more distressing disguises." We make the best of what we have. And try to find its hidden treasure.

However. Let us keep in mind that disabled children require a disproportionate amount of time, energy, and money. Conventional ethical and religious platitudes about the "infinite worth of the soul" (just like the secular version of "to each according to his or her needs") are not particularly helpful when a child needs a hundred doctor visits a year, three to four hours of direct help for activities of daily living, and between fifteen and twenty hours of indirect help per week for phone calls to doctors, therapists, HMOs, and schools and for strategizing by parents.

Of course if we presuppose a spiritual calculation of the infinite value of each soul, then the enormous care given to the child who has disabilities could be justified—but *only if* that child were the only thing the parents had to do in their lives. However, typically, or at least often, this is not the case. There are other children, and there is the rest of our lives. Given the level of care that some children with disabilities require, what's to become of the parents' *other* ethical obligations?

For a start, how are parents of the disabled to fulfill their responsibilities to the disabled child's siblings? When your emotional resources are drained with the disabled child, when you want the "normal" child to make up for what the child with disabilities cannot, when you want *something* not to be difficult? Many answers are offered here: try to find some "special" time to be with the "normal" sibling; explain to them what's going on; give them space to express their feelings; generate resources from extended family, friends, community; remember that love is all that matters. All these are true. But they do not eliminate the haunting sense of guilt, confusion, and self-doubt that arises—bit by bit or all at once— as you see the effects on the other sibling(s) of what you've given to the disabled one. There is a permanent sense of inadequacy: a sense that requires—certainly—therapeutic intervention; but which is *moral* as well as *emotional*.

It is in fact a *moral* question to ask: How much should I give, as a father, to each of my children? When do I say: "I've done enough for Esther; now it's Anna's turn"? Does the fact that Esther's problems are more serious and that her disappointments are less capable of being assuaged by some substitute gratification mean that I can at times turn my back on Anna's needs? Is Anna's heartbreak, even if only of the normal adolescent type, but one made worse by our "special family" status, always to be less pressing than Esther's? And if it is not, then when does the normal child get precedence?

As I've suggested, I wouldn't for a moment deny that there is a strong undercurrent of neurotic angst in these questions, but I would insist that there is something of interest to moral theory as well. Who receives, in this emergency room of family life, the benefits of triage? This is a moral as well as a psychological question. As someone who makes a living responding to moral questions, I ask myself: to which moral theorists— secular or religious—would I turn for help in answering these questions? Consider these stellar names from the canon: Plato, Aristotle, John Locke, Immanuel Kant, Moses, Buddha, Jean-Paul Sartre, John Stuart Mill, Karl

Marx, John Rawls, Richard Rorty, Carol Gilligan, Iris Young, Michael Walzer, Cornel West, Michel Foucault, Jacques Derrida, Jurgen Habermas. Who among them has directly addressed such matters?

Let's draw the circle wider still. Does the "proximity" of the disabled child necessitate or justify the parents' abandonment of their ethical obligations in the wider society? Is their moral horizon to be contracted to one person? Talking about "infinite" worth is comforting in some respects. As the Talmud teaches, to save one life is like saving the whole world. But how should we respond when we face a whole range of "infinitely worthy" lives and find that we're equipped with considerably less than infinite resources. If there are philosophical resources here, they must come from Søren Kierkegaard's account of the Tragic Hero, caught between the pincers of conflicting ethical obligations. Or, perhaps, from Job.

People will say, and it is comforting when they do: "You've done wonders for her. You should really feel proud." And at times I do feel that way, marveling at what one acquaintance called our "masterpiece child." But when I think of how I have pretty much abandoned the activist, in the street politics of my youth and early middle age, let countless opportunities to enrich the university where I teach pass by (or even learn most of my students' names), and failed to reach out to friends, that sense of pride can wither somewhat.

Finally, under what conditions—and in what ways—may parents simply give up the struggle to sustain their disabled child's quality of life? This question is usually cast as the quandary of euthanasia: Do we abort the damaged fetus, disconnect the feeding tubes, refuse "extraordinary" measures, avoid another "necessary" yet excruciating surgery? Such dilemmas, as important as they are, do not exhaust the range of personal and moral difficulties. Few special needs parents choose death for their children. From my own experience, and that of other special needs parents I know, the questions are at once less dramatic but more—much more—persistent.

Consider Esther again. There is, for instance, a renowned expert of craniosacral therapy in Hartford, Connecticut, a two-hour drive from my house. Sometimes extraordinary healers give extraordinary results—often it's time and money and effort down the drain. We're already taking Esther an hour away for a once-a-week treatment by a leading physical therapy office, hoping to handle her potentially life-threatening scoliosis without potentially life-threatening surgery. This takes about four hours of driving and treatment, and costs $100 out of pocket. But perhaps the craniosacral (CS) person is worth it. Or perhaps the CS plus the physical therapy would have spectacular results, enabling Esther to develop that sense of her body's position in space to straighten her own spine. Can we afford the extra $120 a week, the extra five hours of driving and treatment? If we can't afford it now, should we make enough changes so that we can? How about a new supplement that will cost, say $15 a week, but which (some people say) really makes a difference in terms of energy and resistance to colds? We already spend around $1,500 year for supplements, but is that enough? And what will happen to our budget for other things, not to mention our ability to donate to environmental or feminist or human rights causes if we do so?

A life of triage is morally demanding because there always seems to be so much at stake, so much dependent on the instrumental and moral correctness of what one does. The spiritual view of infinite worth does not solve these questions. There is simply too much infinite worth to go around.

The Responsive Community

One thing that has been established in writing about disability is that the concept is to some extent socially constructed. Whether or not someone is disabled is partly a function of what resources are available at a given time, what conveniences are "standard" in a society, and how we expect people to behave. Those of us who wear eyeglasses, suffer from asthma, couldn't survive a New England winter without central heating, or use orthotics will have some idea what I mean. The nature of paraplegia will be changed when wheelchair ramps are as standard as elevators.

Similarly, the question arises: What changes are to be made—the institutional equivalents of wheelchair ramps—in equalizing the participation of caretakers of the disabled to make our society more just?

The most important single move here would be to socialize the care of the dependent, with a collective realization that the disabled, their caretakers, the caretaker's extended family, friends, colleagues, and the larger community are all practically and morally connected. This sounds fine in the abstract. (Actually, it sounds pretty good in the concrete as well.) However, we should realize that making the requisite institutional changes so that dependency needs could be met without destroying or crippling the caregiver's own life would require massive alterations in our social priorities.

For instance, before my department criticizes me for missing committee meetings, I could be asked whether my absence has something to do with the hundred or so medical appointments to which I take Esther each year. Once this fact (and several others) registers, it might be necessary to alter my workload accordingly. If extra help is needed to educate a delayed or hyperactive child in a religious school, perhaps what's necessary is for the budget, curriculum, and structure of the entire school to be rethought, rather than to be told: "We're short of funds for an aide this year; you'd better go somewhere else. Or perhaps you could help out in the classroom."

Responding inclusively to such situations would require a massive rethinking of social goals. Am I to be excused from faculty meetings and departmental committees because of my responsibilities for Esther's care? If I am not, is my workplace unjustly relegating issues of dependent care to the private sphere with the attendant negative and unjust consequences? If my workload is to be adjusted, then to compensate for my limited participation others will have to take up the slack. The department, and the university, might have to state (and mean) that equitable caring for my disabled daughter is one of their central goals, and that satisfied students, lots of publications, and top rankings in *U.S. News and World Report* do not always outweigh what Eva Kittay calls the "nested dependencies" presented by Esther, myself, and the surrounding community. Institutional and personal "success" would have to be redefined. This would be hard enough at my nonprofit university. Imagine a similar situation arising in a law firm, a software company, or the military.

In the modern world, where money, power, commodities, and pleasure have substituted for community, it seems hard to see how this transition might come about. Supporting the disabled and their caretakers in a loving and equitable way may well be the just and virtuous thing to do, but in our present society it seems a very distant goal.

Many of us offer as an alternative a society organized around need rather than autonomous individuality and the marketplace. As much as I long for such a society, and as much as I feel healed when I'm in a setting where even a little of it takes places, there is a problem here. And this problem links my particular situation to what may be the critical question for contemporary social philosophy.

It is this: traditional communities governed by ties of need and connection rather than autonomous individualism and commodities not only integrated their members and cared for them in ways modern society does not, they were *also* rooted in hierarchy and tradition. Everyone felt at home, but as in most homes authority and privilege were neither equally shared nor democratically allocated. If you think of gender relations among orthodox Jews or the Amish, for instance, communities where the dependents are typically quite well cared for, you get some idea of what I mean. The questions therefore arise: What would social morality *be* if it were not based on equality, reciprocity, and autonomy? How can a need-based social morality function in a modern society? How can we have community without hierarchy defined by rigid tradition? How can we have the freedom and equality of modernity and still respond to people's dependency?

Further, in a modern society in which needs are created by strategic social engineering, how are we to define what real needs are? Could we even envision a society in which people are able to distinguish between real needs and false needs, needs and wants, healthy desires, unhealthy desires, and plain old addiction? And this question necessarily leads to the question of what people deserve. The family triage questions get writ large. How much should we spend on special education, on aides in the classroom, on special exams or curriculum, on helping the disabled work or live like other people? Are we willing to cut the military budget in half to take care of our disabled children? To give retarded adults a decent place in the community? To love our senile elders?

At the very least, when will moral philosophers and theologians bring such questions into the center of what they write and teach?

Self-Representation

While Esther can express her feelings and preferences, she cannot fully comprehend the consequences of life choices or assess the effects of her actions on her own future experience. A good deal of the time, when she is allowed to choose her decisions are greatly affected by how choices are presented to her. At other times, my wife and I must straight out speak *for* her.

How do we know when we're doing it right? What norms and virtues are called into play in determining when the way we speak for her is legitimate?

There are no fixed answers here, and certainly no talk of Esther's "rights" will solve the myriad complicated questions. Do we, for instance, allow her to play on the basketball team at her special needs school, knowing that even in this setting of the disabled she is at serious risk of falling and breaking a bone, throwing off months of work to strengthen her spine? Esther has seen her sister play varsity basketball for years. Now, she thought, it would finally be her turn. Do we let her know why we are forbidding it, in the hope that she will mature in her understanding of her own bodily needs? Or do we simply lie and say that she is too young and could play perhaps next year? Or that the coach—who actually left the decision to us—said she would not be safe?

No ethic of rights or justice or greatest happiness can begin to touch such questions. Rather, what is needed is close attention to a range of virtues that must be developed. I have had to work very hard to develop two of these. The first is the ability to look without flinching, denial, avoidance, or false hope at exactly what my child's disabilities are. What can she do, what can't she do? Where is she safe and where is she in too much danger? When is *my* emotional need to see her have some fun to be put aside in favor of *her* need to be safe? The point is that I will not be able to judge what needs to be forbidden (even though trying it would give her great pleasure) and know what is worth the risk *unless* I first have the courage and honesty to see who she actually is.

The second virtue may be the emotional foundation of the first. It is a kind of acceptance that says, "Yes, my child is disabled. And may die from it. And will certainly be limited by it. And my life, and hers, can still be of value nevertheless." This might have been harder for us than for some others, just because Esther has never had a diagnosis and thus for many years lacked any clear prognosis as well. It requires a kind of surrender in the midst of never-ending labor. A kind of realization that the desperate effort to fix is both a great virtue and a great vice; that it can accomplish what look like miracles and also cause us to ignore the beauties that we do have. Combining dedicated effort with detachment is, I believe, something we all need to help us face the vicissitudes of life. In this, my situation is no different from that of someone not caring for a child with disabilities, except that perhaps in mine the issues stand out more clearly.

Rage, Acceptance, Love

While there is a kind of psychological acceptance that is necessary if we are to see our children clearly and hear them even if they cannot speak, spiritual acceptance is a different matter. As I witness my child's undeserved pain, when is rage at God a justified spiritual response? Are familiar spiritual values of submission to God's will or acceptance of our lack of control over life always the preferred response?

Further, when disability is socially caused—for example, traceable to environmental pollution or poverty—what do religious ethics have to tell us about the proper mix of anger and acceptance as I confront my child's fate?

I do not think there is much of value about this question in most religious traditions, though perhaps that is only because I haven't looked very hard. I have been told by folks much more knowledgeable than myself that traditional Judaism has spoken very little about the issue. And in *The Art of Happiness*, the Dalai Lama, when asked about the moral choice between abortion and raising a profoundly disabled child, had remarkably little to offer. This might take us back to a point made earlier. Religions, just like political philosophy, are typically created by people who do not care for the disabled.

My own thoughts here are scattered and incomplete, a work in progress.

One thing I'm sure of is that it is a mistake to personalize a social problem. Environmental pollution is responsible, I'm sure, for a significant percentage of genetic problems that cause disabilities. Esther's mysterious neuromotor problem may well be the result of some environmental toxin that affected my wife during pregnancy. In this way, many disabilities are *social* problems, not personal tragedies. To those readers who have, or know someone who has, breast cancer, the same lesson applies. The disabled need their rights not only after they are born with problems. We also need to exercise the right to an environment that does not damage us to begin with.

As for God? I know that for a start, anger at God is a legitimate aspect of spiritual life. To be angry at God is just as much a part of prayer as is love or devotion, awe or repentance. In all those states of mind, feeling, and soul, we are confirming that moral laws bind the universe as a whole, just as they bind us as moral agents within it.

That's why I think I'm entitled to rage at God when I witness Esther's pain, her limitations and disappointments. When I think that "normal" love relationships and opportunities will simply never be hers. As she herself said when I told her that because of her special needs she could not return to her beloved day camp as a counselor, "Now's the time to scream at God."

Yet I also believe that spiritual life need not be bound by any one moral posture—neither anger at the unfairness of life nor gratitude for the blessings we do enjoy. I believe I can thank God for the simple purity of Esther's soul, for the emotional support she gives to our family and her friends, for the glinting light of pure happiness she finds in simple pleasures—other people's as well as her own. I am, like others who suffer unjustly in this life, entitled to rage at God for the unjust pain I feel or witness—if I *also* praise Her for the beauties and joys I've received—gifts that I deserve, really, no more than I deserve the pain.

And Esther, what of her rage, acceptance, and love? Despite her pain, Esther knows that life is beautiful. And when asked at age twelve what the meaning of life was, she answered without hesitation, "to love people." (Later she added, "and dogs and cats!")

At her bat mitzvah she commented on a passage in Numbers 20 about yet another time when the Jews lost confidence in their journey. "I think this story basically means that you should not complain because it only makes the journey harder. You should just keep going and try hard and not complain. Just do what you have to do to get where you're going.

When the Jews were losing confidence, I think they should have breathed and said to themselves 'It's okay, we'll make it.'" Her own life, she went on to say, is that way too.

Another time, as part of a talk she gave to five hundred people at a Friday night service to mark our temple's commitment to inclusion, she said:

> To parents that have kids with special needs, you need to learn to be patient because it's not your fault that your kid was born like this. If your child is having a hard time, you can give them a hug and say, "Everything's going to be okay" and put your arms around them and be loving to them. . . . Having special needs, I have been able to deal with it in a way that has been calming most of the time. For me, I have been able to be closer to God because of having special needs.

On the other hand, Esther is perceptive enough to see the differences between herself and her able-bodied sister, the other kids on the street, or the teenagers in the sitcoms she watches. And, amazingly, she is wise enough to know how to voice her disappointments not only to her parents or friends but to God as well. "God, why did you give me this body? Why did you give me special needs?" she will cry out sometimes, in the middle of shooting baskets in our driveway. And then, having demanded an accounting from the Source of Meaning, she will shoot another layup.

In her wisdom there lies a great lesson for ethicists and spiritual teachers alike: to acknowledge the pain, to love and care for each other as best we can, and to carry on. But this task will evade us unless we make sure that our moral insights, political struggles, and prayers include the Esthers of the world along with everyone else.

RECIPROCITY

David Abram

The Lessons of Salmon

My first encounter with spawning salmon gleams with a cool, moonlit radiance in my memory. I'd grown up on the suburban East Coast and knew nothing of this wild fish and its ways. The year was 1987 and I was kayaking in the Prince William Sound twenty months before the taut, ever-shifting surface of that life-filled sea was generously layered with a glistening blanket of oil by the Exxon Corporation. We had beached our kayaks on one of the larger islands for the night, and after a simple meal I went walking off along the coast as the sun slipped down toward the horizon, drinking the salt air and listening to the lapping of the small waves and the wind in the needles. After some time I came to the edge of a surging stream about twelve feet across, whose surface was rippling and splashing in the fading light. Without paying much attention, I sat down on a mossy rock a ways back from the stream's edge just to bask in the rushing speech of those waters, and to gaze out into the oncoming night. I remember I lost myself in some reverie or other, until my awareness was brought back to the place by a pale glow beginning to spread into the sky from the rocks on the far side of the stream. The glow got steadily more intense until, as I watched, the full moon was hatched from those rocks, huge and round as a ripe peach, pouring its radiance across the stony beach and the gleaming waves and the rustling spruce needles and generally casting a kind of spell over the whole place.

Now, I have never, of course, seen a cow jump over the moon. But that night I did see a fish jump over the moon. A great streamlined silhouette, its tail flapping, arced right over the full moon, and splashed back into the water. Whaa?! I couldn't believe what I'd just seen, and so was still staring at the afterimage—and then another silhouette leapt right over the moon!

I got up and walked over to the water's edge: the stream was thick with salmon, boiling with salmon, all jostling and surging against the current in fits and starts—it was as if the stream was made of salmon! I gazed and gazed for a couple hours. Then went back to my tent and tried to sleep, but couldn't. So I came back in the middle of the night and stood staring into that moon-illuminated river of fish, then waded out into that mass of silvery, sparkling muscles all surging and lunging against the current. In the middle of the stream I was up to my knees in salmon, but they didn't care—didn't even notice; they bumped into my legs and then plunged on past with a single-minded determination I'd never encountered before, nosing aside their dead or dying siblings and cousins as they floated back downstream on their sides, their mottled skin beginning to fall off; the earnest salmon around me just nudged them aside, hardly noticing, intent on one thing and one thing alone—getting upstream to their spawning place, depositing their eggs and fertilizing those eggs, before they too began to fall apart and die. I'd never imagined such intensity, such single-mindedness. Their total focus on getting upstream to create new life, their utter obliviousness to everything else—to their dead or dying relatives, to other species who might prey upon them (to me, for instance, my own legs shivering among them), to everything other than the impulse to procreate.

There seemed something strangely familiar about this apparent readiness to multiply at all costs and this consequent obliviousness to all other beings and species. It seemed so similar to . . . so much like, like—well yes, of course, so much like us, us humans!—our own species, Homo sapiens, steadily multiplying and multiplying these last several centuries without much noticing anything else, seemingly deaf and blind to the presence of all the other species with whom we share this wild world. And so, right then and there, I began to wonder if our own species was not caught in a kind of spawn, if we were not, indeed, spawning. I mean, this would explain our apparent obliviousness to everything other than ourselves, our willingness to shove aside not only other species in our rather reckless rush to multiply and fill the earth, but to nudge aside also all those humans who are falling apart and dying as a result of the steady swelling of our numbers and the steady surge of technological progress. And it would imply that those who wish to spark a new awareness and recognition of other species—of other animals, plants, and forests—must also work to awaken us from this steady, many-centuries-long spawning behavior that seems to hold us in its grip.

But I mean no disrespect to the salmon. I have no wish to insult them or offend them in any way, and so I must straightaway apologize to them— apologize to the wild Sockeye and the Chinook, to the Pink and the Chum and the Coho, for this admittedly awkward comparison. For if we humans are in a spawn, it is hardly that seasonal, cyclical replenishment that the salmon practice; rather, it is a steady, unending surge, a procreation and proliferation without bounds—after all, we've more than tripled the human population of this wild planet in the course of the last sixty years. The amount of increase in the 1990s alone exceeded the size of the entire human population that was alive in the year 1600! Moreover, if spawning salmon seem oblivious to all else as they surge up the rivers and streams, their relentless self-sacrifice on behalf of new life actually nourishes countless other species. After they spawn, their spawned-out bodies provide food for bears, river otters, raccoons, coyotes, skunks, bobcats, and squirrels, food for eagles and red-tailed hawks and winter wrens, and for all the local corvids—ravens and crows and Steller's jays and gray jays—and thus the salmons' spirit filters into and nourishes the whole of these forests. If the steady growth of the human population leads us to clearcut these mountainsides, the spawning salmon vitalize and invigorate these forested slopes, gifting them with wild nutrients.

So let me try to correct whatever offense I might have committed with my clumsy comparison by praising the salmon, this most amazing of earthly mysteries, this graceful intelligence that joins the land to the sea and the sea to the land, this bright intermediary binding matter and spirit whose life feeds both our bodies and our imaginations and whose loss impoverishes human culture no less than it impoverishes the vitality of the land and the forests. Is not salmon the real genius of these coastal forests? All who live and work in these forests, sheltered from the drenching rains by hemlocks and cedars and firs, harvesting wood from these trees, planting soils fed by these mountain rivers—or even poring through books plucked from the library stacks at the universities or toiling away in front of computer terminals up on the Microsoft campus—all who live here in the coastal Northwest are under the influence of salmon, our minds inevitably informed by this collective anadromous intelligence whose patterns and rhythms provided the living template for the earliest patterns of human settlement in this terrain, the infrastructure for the rhythms of human culture in this watery realm.

The strange ways of the salmon are a key and unifying component of this ecosystem, as integral to the mind of this land as is the monsoon to the mind of the Himalayas. As we become conscious of their influence, as we watch them and eat them and ponder their ways, we learn so much from them. They teach us wonder, of course, and humility—since these fish carry secrets that we simply cannot fathom with all our analytical tools. How do the wild salmon find their way back to their home stream after swimming thousands of miles out across the vast Pacific? We simply do not know. After several years out at sea, do they simply retrace their strokes to get home? No! Indeed, it is clear that the salmon commonly return by a different route than that by which they left. From Freeman House's splendid book, *Totem Salmon,* I learn that a single stock of wild sockeye that were marked and later observed spread out across twenty-three hundred miles of ocean (sighted off the Aleutian Islands, off the Kamchatka Peninsula, and along the coast of Japan) all turned up at the mouth of their natal stream within three days of one another.

How? By what magic do they find their way back not just to the right river mouth, or the right tributary of that river, but to the precise little stream where they once hatched? By what kind of deep somatic attunement—feeling their way between faint electromagnetic anomalies, riding a particular angle of the sun as it filters down through the rippled surface above, dreaming their way through gradients of scent and taste toward the lost beloved—how do they find their way to that source, that particular place inseparable from their being? Each genetically distinct population of wild salmon is perfectly tuned, it would seem, to the geological character, the climatic variables, the disturbance regimes, and the flow patterns of its native stream, an attunement born from thousands of years of intimate adaptation to that one stretch of water and rock and shadow, each fish (according to naturalist Tim McNulty) a perfect expression of the evolutionary wisdom of its particular watershed. And so, besides teaching us a new capacity for astonishment, the salmon also instruct us about the primordial primacy of place. It is a primacy long forgotten by our steadily globalizing civilization, with its spreading malls and video outlets, this culture where the highways heading into town—lined with Taco Bells, video outlets, Jiffy Lubes, Sizzler steakhouses, and Barnes & Noble superstores—look just like the highways leading into every other town, and so the stream of cars we're swimming in might just as well be carrying us into Eureka or Eugene or Ukiah (or, for that matter, into Bellingham or Birmingham or Billings) because when we finally reach the headwaters of our highway and head inside our office building, the computer terminal we'll gaze at when we finally get to work will gaze back at us with the same blank stare no matter where we're pushing the buttons. The place doesn't really make any difference for us, at least not as long as we consider the land to be merely a backdrop against which human history unfolds or a stockpile of resources for the global spread of our human monoculture.

But doesn't the place where we are actually make some difference to who we are? Clearly that is what the salmon teach us. As we try to compensate for the dwindling salmon runs with hatchery-reared fish whose eggs have been plucked from other, far-off, watersheds, those confused and dumbed-down hatchery salmon make it clear to us that real places are not interchangeable—at least not for wild, earth-born beings—and that wild, sustainable (or self-replenishing) culture is indissolubly place-specific.

However, the greatest and most profound lesson that the salmon teach us is the power and the magic of reciprocity. Reciprocity! The two-way flow, the reciprocal exchange between realms. The gift of the mountains and the forests to the vast ocean and, later, the return of that gift, now offered from the sea to the land, to these forests and mountain valleys, which ensures that the gift will be reborn afresh from a clump of luminous eggs buried beneath a layer of pebbles, so that it can be given once again to the salty depths of the sea. This circulation, this systole and diastole, is one of the signs that the earth is alive, this rhythmic pulse of finned and flashing fish spreading out through various arteries into the wide body of the ocean, circulating there, growing there, only to return by various veins to the beating heart of the forest, gravid with new life.

Or maybe it's best to think of this seasonal reciprocity as a kind of breathing, as an exhalation of thousands, of hundreds of thousands, of young salmon from the land out into the sea to mingle there with whales and algal blooms, and then the great inhalation, the breathing back in of all that vital nourishment from the oceans into the mouths of rivers, flowing up those rivers into tributaries, and from there into the branching streams that filter into the green forests, the living lungs of this earthly world. Or else it is the ocean that is breathing, inhaling these finned nutrients down from the forested slopes, sucking them down over rocks and through rapids and hydroelectric dams, past settlements and cities and out into its vast cycling currents and tides, circulating this silvery life within itself before breathing it back up into the valleys and the mountain forests.

Reciprocity, the ceaseless give and take, the flow that moves in two directions—this is the real teaching of the salmon. It is the foundation of any real ethic: give unto others as you would have them give unto you. But this is not the golden rule; this is, rather, the silver rule, the lesson taught by silvery fish scales glinting in the moonlight: if you wish to receive sustenance from the land then you must offer sustenance to the land in return. If you wish to draw nourishment from the waters and the winds, then you must honor and shelter those waters and winds. Most specifically, never take more from the living land than you need, and indeed never take more from the land than you return to the land—not only with nourishing offerings and propitiations, but also with prayers and praises—gifting the breathing earth with our eloquence, honoring the sensuous and sentient surroundings with the heartfelt gratitude of our songs and our dances, feeding the more-than-human world with our grateful attention. The First Salmon ceremonies that once resounded up and down the Northwest coast every year were filled with such eloquence, with such prayers and praise songs honoring the salmon and the rivers and the abundant, animate earth.

The City Walls

In so many ways our culture has forgotten the wild teaching of reciprocity. Our civilization does not consider the land around us as an animate, living matrix but as a set of determinate processes that we describe in entirely mechanomorphic terms. We define nature not as a community of living subjects held together by an intricate gift economy—wherein each being, each life, is nourished by a host of others and then gives of its life in return—rather, we speak of the nature around us as an almost random concatenation of passive things, a conglomeration of objects and automatic processes, void of all interiority, lacking all spontaneity, without any active agency—merely a stockpile of resources waiting to be requisitioned by us.

But how can one practice reciprocity with an inert or determinate object? How can one enter into relationship with something that has no life, no interiority, no active agency of its own? The only active agents in this world, the only real subjects among this concatenation of passive objects, are us humans. And so, indeed, reciprocity is cultivated between human persons, and ethics emerges as the practice of right relationship within human society. The rest of nature, presumably, cannot reciprocate our attentions.

For over two millennia, Western, alphabetic civilization has defined itself in opposition to the wild, as a realm apart from earthly nature. Our philosophers have played a key role in establishing and certifying this opposition. In one of Plato's most brilliant and scintillating dialogues, Socrates is asked by Phaedrus why he almost never ventures out beyond the walls of Athens to wander in the open countryside. Socrates answers him with these words: "Look Phaedrus: I'm a lover of learning, and trees and open country won't teach me anything, whereas men in the town will." There's nothing I can learn outside the city walls. Trees and other animals have nothing to teach; only from other people can I really learn anything. Right there, at the very origin of our philosophical tradition in Athens, is already erected this apparent bifurcation—this wall—between the intelligent world of humans and the ostensibly mute world of nature. Two thousand years later, the same wall is patched up and renovated by Descartes, with his neat distinction between thinking substance, or mind— which is the special province of humankind—and extended substance, or matter—which is everything else. You still see that old wall, not quite between the city and the country now, but between the human mind, which is one thing, and material nature, which is another thing. Material nature is a kind of pure exterior, the human mind a kind of pure interior. Many thinkers have tried to breach this wall in the course of the twentieth century, but it has proved surprisingly resilient. The barrier has been well preserved in the academic distinction between the sciences, which study the objective, readily quantifiable world of external nature, and the humanities, which get to deal with the subjective interior—with that more qualitative domain that is, presumably, the special haunt of humankind.

But my main point here is that reciprocity—and hence, ethics—is simply not possible in such a situation, when the entities to be related do not partake of the same world, when they have no commonality, no common ground on which to meet and make contact. It is simply not possible to enter into a living relationship, much less a reciprocal relationship, with an inert object. It is not possible to reciprocate a purely passive or mechanical or insentient conglomeration of objects.

Reciprocity is only possible if there is some common ground, some common medium through which a mutual exchange can unfold. But how shall we locate or establish a common ground between ourselves and the rest of nature? Shall we say (in the manner of biologist Edward O. Wilson) that we humans, too, are entirely a part of the objective, quantifiable, determinate world of nature that we see automatically doing its thing all around us—that our actions, our emotions, and even our thoughts are nothing but a set of genetically programmed automatisms that will soon be mapped out and measured? Perhaps, but then we rob ourselves of our own active agency, our own ability to willfully act, to respond, to reciprocate another being.

Maybe, then, we should try to breach the wall from the other side, like many postmodern theorists who assert that nature itself is largely a social construction. These thinkers claim that our experience of other-than-human phenomena is always already structured by the dynamic play of social forces—by the polarizations, distributions, and dissimulations of power in which we are culturally situated. Numerous deconstructive analyses stress the extent to which the natural world we seem to experience is thoroughly "constructed" by the particular culture that enfolds us.

Yet such theorists tend to perpetuate in postmodern guise the most spurious of all modern presumptions—the presumption that humankind is the sole creative (or constructive) agency in the earthly world. Their analyses all too easily become merely a new justification for the manipulation and alteration of other-than-human realities for our own, exclusively human purposes. They risk being taken up, for instance, by those who wish to justify the biogenetic engineering of other organisms for purely human benefit: since nature is already a social construction, then why not continue to "construct" the nature around us as we see fit?

But what if we were to supplement the warranted assertion that our experience of nonhuman nature is largely structured by human culture, with an acknowledgement that human culture is itself structured and informed in countless ways by the wider-than-human matrix of powers in which humankind is embedded? Why not acknowledge that while our notions of the world may be structured by our particular culture, cultures are themselves structured by the interplay of gravity, winds, waters, and sunlight, by the migratory movements of particular animals and the nutritional and medicinal powers of the local plants. Why not admit that human culture is itself influenced, organized, and mediated by many agencies that are not human or of human artifice?

By acknowledging the direct material influence of these nonhuman agencies, we do not pin human reality to a static or determinate order of essences. For by affirming the canyons, the wind, the moon, and the forest as actors, as animate agents like ourselves, we simultaneously acknowledge their formative influence and their otherness (their wild indeterminacy, their existence not as fathomable objects but as inscrutable entities with whom we stand in a living relation). Of course the world we experience is not an objective and determinate reality—there is no doubt that it is a social creation! But the "society" that constructs this indeterminate world is much vaster than any merely human society—it includes spiders and swallows and subterranean seepages along with us two-leggeds. Surely it is time to outgrow this most tenacious of modernist presumptions: for all our craftiness and creative ferment, we humans are by no means the sole, or even the primary, agents of the world's construction.

As soon as we acknowledge the active influence of these other beings and elements, we find ourselves negotiating relationships with every aspect of the sensuous terrain that surrounds us. And reciprocity—the simple practice of mutual respect—becomes an imperative.

In other words, reciprocity, the deep lesson of the salmon, only becomes possible when the rest of nature is experienced as something that can reciprocate us, only if nature is recognized not as a concatenation of objects but as a community of living subjects, a complexly intertwined society of beings who, like us, are active, animate agencies. But also only if we humans are recognized not as disembodied minds but as material, bodily subjects, as animals in our own right, and thus as participants in the same world that the salmon inhabit, characters in the same vast story.

Among many of the First Nations peoples who fished and hunted along the Northwest coast, it was common knowledge that the salmon, when they were not visiting us in the rivers and streams of the forest, were off living in their own camps and villages, under the sea, or beyond the horizon, where they would take off their silvery skins and walk around in human form. When, for example, in the nineteenth century several Skagit Indians accompanied a white expedition back to the East Coast and saw the abundance of pale, pink-skinned people living there, they reported back to their tribe that they had been to salmon country and had seen the salmon walking around as human beings! To most moderns today, this seems like an amazing flight of fancy. But what if such a notion—of humans and salmon sharing a common flesh, indeed as relatives, as members of a common family—is a basic prerequisite for reciprocity, for the establishment of a right and respectful relation between the people of this terrain and the fish that sustain them? Does contemporary American culture today maintain such a respectful relation to the salmon? Not at all: salmon populations have been dwindling and going extinct since we began manipulating salmon runs for our own purposes in the nineteenth century. Perhaps then there is something to be learned from these curious beliefs and ways of speaking.

At the First Salmon ceremonies people paid homage to the fish and spoke to them, addressing them by such honorific titles as Noble One or Lightning Following One Another, Two Gills on Back, Quartz Nose, Three Leaps, Noble Chief, or Chief Spring Salmon. The salmon, in other words, were treated as royalty—as, in Jonathan Raban's words, "the lords and ladies of the sea." And they were addressed, spoken to. But really, now: why speak to a fish in this exalted manner? Why even speak to these fish at all? Surely they cannot understand our words, if they can even hear us. Clearly, it is another flight of fancy. Unless the very act of addressing these strange, water-born beings is the simplest, most elegant way of turning our awareness toward them, unless speaking to the salmon and then listening or watching for their reply is a powerful way to tune our human senses to these other shapes of sentience—to bind our own attention to these other embodied intelligences—and so to let ourselves be instructed and informed by their ways. Another way of ensuring and of enacting reciprocity.

The Many-Voiced Earth

What role then does language play in the practice of reciprocity? In the mainstream, dominant culture, we spend a great deal of time talking about nature, about other animals, about "the environment." But many indigenous, oral peoples seem to spend just as much time talking to the world—speaking to the salmon, to the forest, to the land itself—and listening for its replies.

The modern, civilized assumption is that language is precisely that which distinguishes and separates us two-leggeds from all the other animals, since humans alone possess the capacity for meaningful speech. Language, for us moderns, is an exclusively human property. Traditional oral cultures commonly hold a much more expansive view of language, one which includes verbal language, of course, but which also includes the communicative power of bodily expressions and gestures (like a scowl or a shrug or the tail-between-the-legs gesture made by a submissive young wolf) as well as the expressive, evocative potency of many nonverbal sounds (laughter, for instance, or the honking of a flock of geese veeing south for the winter or the distant rumble of thunder or even the whoosh of the wind in the high grasses). For a majority of indigenous cultures, language—or meaningful speech—is not an exclusively human property, but is rather a property of the surrounding earth itself in which we humans participate. The commonality of this belief is remarkable, given the tremendous differences between indigenous peoples worldwide. Nevertheless, whether one consults the Haida people of the island Northwest or the Hopi people of the Southwest desert, whether one asks among the Huarani of the Amazon basin or the Pintupi and Pitjantjarra of Australia, the most articulate members of the culture will insist that the coherence of their spoken language is inseparable from the coherence of the local ecology—from the expressive vitality of the more-than-human terrain. For such indigenous, oral peoples, it is the animate earth that speaks; human speech is just one part of that much wider conversation.

From an indigenous perspective, in other words, everything speaks. And so we humans must take care with our own speaking, since many other beings are listening and can hear us. Here, for example, are some observations made by a member of the Mattole Indians—a California tribe that has vanished from the world. Recorded in an interview half a century ago, his words describe the proper way to behave around water and waves.

The water watches you and has a definite attitude, favorable or otherwise, toward you. Do not speak just before a wave breaks. Do not speak to passing rough water in a stream. Do not look at water very long for any one time, unless you have been to this spot ten times or more. Then the water there is used to you and does not mind if you're looking at it. Older men can talk in the presence of the water because they have been around so long that the water knows them. Until the water at any spot does know you, however, it becomes very rough if you talk in its presence or look at it too long [G. W. Hewes, quoted in Alfred Kroeber and Samuel Barrett, *Fishing Among the Indians of Northwest California*].

What a curious kind of etiquette! And how odd it sounds to many of us today. And yet it is a striking example of reciprocity—the felt mutuality and exchange between people and water. And it functions to keep the members of a coastal fishing culture exquisitely attentive and attuned to the fluid ways of the water, to the shifting eddies along the river, the pattern of waves along the coast. Such an etiquette toward the fluid element inculcates a steady respect and ensures that the culture will not readily violate the health of those waters or the vitality of the watershed.

Of Whales and Wild Culture

The Makah Indians are a culture profoundly informed by the whale—a society whose traditions have been defined by the hunting of gray and humpback whales and by the intimate knowledge of the whales that such hunting requires. For at least two thousand years (and very probably more like four thousand years), the ancestors of the Makah have lived in settlements around the Northwestern tip of the Olympic Peninsula—the westernmost point of land in what is now the contiguous United States—close to the migratory routes of whales and other sea mammals. Archeological evidence unearthed over the last forty years confirms the deep record preserved in the Makah oral traditions and demonstrates that theirs was a complex and highly organized hunting and fishing society. It is clear from both the oral stories and the material evidence that the Makah traditionally fished not only in the streams but offshore and that they hunted fur seals and other sea mammals in long cedar canoes. It is also abundantly clear that the most formidable and awe-filled event, which radiated its intensity into all areas of the culture, was the whale hunt. That is, the engagement most laden with spiritual power and significance was the life-and-death encounter with this entity who comes to meet us humans from the depths of a fluid world we can barely penetrate, this mysterious intelligence so much larger than our own, the confrontation with whom startles us, willy-nilly, into our most attentive and wakeful mode of being. The whale was the primary source of sustenance—both physical and spiritual—for the Makah people, and as the gift of its flesh was shared among all members of the community, a kind of nourishment spread not just into their limbs and muscles, but into their minds as well. The vast life and the inscrutable sentience of the whale became a part of their own collective being, binding them into a common spirit, ensuring the rich cohesion of their culture. These were a people made of whale.

The Makah are the only tribe whose right to hunt the whale was written into the treaties that they signed with the U.S. government in 1855. They knew the habits of the whale as well as anyone, and when the numbers of gray whales were plummeting as a result of overhunting around the planet by American and European commercial whaling ships, the Makah recognized it early and voluntarily gave up hunting whales in the 1920s, fully a decade or more before the United States issued a ban on the taking of gray whales. What a painful decision this must have been, to voluntarily turn away from this encounter, this exchange with a wild Other that lay at the heart of their cultural life. So much of daily life, from mundane practices like the fashioning of tools and the preparation and cooking of food to their ceremonial traditions—their stories and songs and dances, the initiation of the young into the secret societies that carried the ritual lore of the tribe—were all structured by their interchange with the whale.

Today the gray whales—blessed be!—seem to have rebounded somewhat from the brink of extinction. Thanks no doubt to the moratorium on commercial whaling, perhaps some twenty-five thousand of them are now pursuing their nomadic life in the Pacific Ocean, migrating between their winter breeding grounds off the Mexican coast and their summer feeding areas in the Bering and Beaufort Seas. And in May 1999 the Makah people—or, more specifically, seven Makah whalers paddling a dugout cedar canoe and using a handthrust harpoon to initiate the kill—hunted and killed a gray whale for the first time in seven decades, reviving a tradition that dates back at least two millennia. For this they have been reviled in the media, they have been called murderers by environmental groups, and they have been laughed at and ridiculed because their technique was not perfect—because, that is, it wasn't entirely easy for them to resuscitate traditional techniques that have been slumbering for some seventy-five years.

It is a conundrum, this killing of a whale. Many of my environmental comrades are outraged—indeed, almost the entire environmental community seems to be scandalized that anyone, much less a Native American community, would hunt or willfully kill such a unique and mysterious being. Why cannot the Makah renew their cultural traditions by simply pretending to hunt the whale or by a symbolic hunt? Instead of harpooning the whale, why couldn't they just dart it with a radio-transmitter so we could more accurately track the whale's migratory route? In this manner they could contribute to the rational, scientific assessment of whale behavior. Or else, if the Makah are hoping to revitalize their economy, why can't they do it by taking people out on whale-watching tours like everyone else? Why do they have to kill the whale?

Such arguments from the environmental community arise from a perspective all too similar to the one I wrote of above, the view that considers nature to be something entirely different from human culture. Culture, with Socrates, exists on this side of the city wall; nature and the whales exist on the other side. Nature is something that we humans look at from outside, not something that we are in and of. The whales are a remarkable spectacle to see, so let's peer at them from the rail of the boat, or better yet let's fit them with radio transmitters so we can track them on our screens, as we now track the wolves through Yellowstone, but let us take care not to ever imagine that we ourselves are really inside the same world that those whales inhabit! Our relation to nature must remain that of spectators looking at a spectacle or perhaps that of managers overseeing a very complicated set of processes, but we are never to participate in those processes.

If our sense of standing outside of or apart from nature once led us to manipulate and mine the living land with little consideration for anything other than our own benefit, today that same sense of separation leads us continually to try to monitor and manage nature from outside, as though we were not entirely embedded in the very matrix we seek to control. Lord knows it is a difficult and scary thing to give up one's sense of control and so to accept one's vulnerability. Yet reciprocity is simply not possible in such a one-sided situation—where one entity is always the manager and the other is the managed; or where one species is the spectator and the other the spectacle.

What is most disturbing and most astonishing about the possible renewal of the whale hunt by an indigenous nation like the Makah is that it marks a potential site where the managerial ethos that currently holds sway between humankind and the rest of nature is beginning to dissolve in the face of a new, more participatory ethic of vulnerability and reciprocity.

Would the whales prefer that the Makah give up hunting and leave their harpoons in the museum? Not being a whale, of course, I don't know. I'm fairly sure that the whales would prefer it if industrial whaling came to an end, if the commercial whaling fleets of Japan and Norway backed off and shut themselves down. And maybe they'd even prefer it if the indigenous whalers in Alaska and Russia, who are permitted to hunt them under the "aboriginal clause" of the International Whaling Commission, would also back off from their easy reliance on motorboats and high-powered rifles and harpoon cannons and radio transmitters and airplanes and even helicopters in their pursuit of so-called "subsistence whaling." But I'm not sure that the whales much prefer those folks who chase them around in whale-watching motorboats just to gawk and stare at them. (After all, whales have an exquisitely refined auditory sense underwater: can we imagine what it would feel like to hear these whale-watching boats following us around all the time? "Whiiiirrr.") I'm not sure that the whales don't crave a more direct way to teach us, a way less encumbered by tech-nology and yet more motivated by the practicalities of our own mam-malian life—I'm not sure that they don't desire a more straightforward way to instruct us, to lead our canoes around on risky chases, to trans-form our lives with astonishment, to enliven our communities, and to shape our cultures.

Of course those like me who are members of the dominant culture can hardly tell the Makah that they should not avail themselves of the tech-nologies that the dominant culture uses whenever it wants (motorboats and helicopters and harpoon cannons). But we can admit to the Makah that our own overdependence upon such technologies is slowly killing us, that our overreliance upon many technologies is destroying our health and wreaking havoc on our society—that we desperately need to learn how to live and work without depending so much upon all these machinic mediations. We can say to the Makah: "Your culture, your traditions still carry knowledge of how to live a life relatively unmediated by such high-speed technologies, which seem to undermine any prospect of reciprocity not only with other animals, but with our human neighbors as well. As you now find and rejuvenate those traditions, might you please teach us something of those skills?"

For the Makah, it seems to me, are not only resuscitating their own tra-ditions. If they are sincere in their wish to revive their traditional, labor-intensive hunting practices, and if they persist in this careful and difficult craft, then they are also opening a channel for the whales to begin to in-form human culture again—not as quaint, aesthetic symbols to put on posters, but as magnanimous and dangerous powers with whom we find our lives entwined.

Humility in a More-Than-Human World

Of course the whales would not be the only species to break through our contemporary hubris and to draw us back into relation. Other species are already beckoning to us, trying to lure us back inside the world. Indeed, the salmon, it seems, are at last beginning to get through to us. If and when we finally do breach those dams on the lower Snake River, it will be a remarkable moment in the human story. It would be an event quite different from merely being forced by the Endangered Species Act to back off from overfishing or from overhunting a particular animal; something very different from deciding not to clearcut another swath of old-growth forest or not to develop a particular plot of land that turns out to be prime habitat for a rare critter. It would be different because in this case we would not only be halting our projected plans or interrupting progress, but actually undoing what has already been done, reversing our ostensible progress. We'd be acknowledging that a mistake was made and acting to undo it—even at the cost of certain arrangements that have come to be taken for granted by various citizens. And perhaps at some real economic cost as well, at least in the short term. In this instance, in other words, we would be acting not just to limit ourselves, but to reverse ourselves on behalf of another species.

Such a reversal would indeed mark a wondrous moment in the human story—the moment when modern humankind, so drunk on our apparently unlimited technological capacity, begins to recognize and accept that we do have limits after all, and that we have overstepped those limits and must take a little step back in order to correct things. Breaching those dams would be like, well, like collective humankind drinking a full glass of humility. It would be one of our finest moments—an act to stand in stark contrast to other contemporary activities glaring with unexamined hubris, like our steady plunge into biotechnology (our gleeful rush to alter the genome of other animals and plants to serve our own, exclusively human, purposes).

And what, after all, would have induced us to take down the dams, to reverse ourselves in this manner? Some might say that it was the Endangered Species Act that forced the breaching of the dams. Or maybe it was the native tribes—the Umatilla, the Warm Springs, the Yakima, and the Nez Perce—these peoples who are struggling to keep alive their own old cultural traditions so deeply intertwined with the wild salmon runs (fishing traditions that stretch back some two or three hundred generations) and that are now threatening to sue the federal government if those dams are not breached. Or maybe it was the economic interests, like the Alaska fishing industry or the Bonneville Power Administration, that began to realize that it might be cheaper to lose a little of their generating capacity than to continue spending hundreds of millions of dollars every year on elaborate, Rube Goldberg–like salmon-recovery schemes that simply don't work. Or perhaps some would say that it was simply the steady rise of environmental and ecological awareness in the minds of more and more citizens throughout the Northwest. But while each of these factors will have made a difference, when we finally breach the dams, it will be ultimately because the salmon themselves induced us to do so. Because we got tired finally of the endless arguing among ourselves, exhausted by the constant call for further studies and the interminable bickering between our various human factions and so decided to let another voice, another shape of intelligence, in on the conversation. It is an intelligence that speaks to us not in words, but in an eloquent language of metamorphosis and grace and reciprocity. A fluid voice that, once we allowed it into the conversation, could not help but begin to heal the various rifts within our communities.

It is the salmon, in their sad, eloquent way, that are instructing us to take down the dams, and we would do well to acknowledge their active influence in all this. For our own health, I suspect, we need to accept that there are other animate forces in the world besides ourselves and our own creations. We need to acknowledge that humans are not the only active agents in the world—that there are other kinds, other shapes, other styles of active agency.

And, in truth, the glinting speech of the salmon is not unfamiliar to us. Not only because our cultures have long been influenced and informed by these finned and fluid folks, but because their collective style of sentience stirs an echo in the very depths of our flesh, a kind of memory in the bones. For of course we too are a gift from the ocean to the land. It is a truth readily evidenced by the salt in our tears and the saltiness of our blood: we still carry the sea within us—we are ocean-born beings!—swimmers who once crawled out of the brine and grew legs and began wandering up the river valleys. And so we owe it to allow magic to move in the other direction as well and not to impede the flow of life from the mountains and the forests back to the wombish world of the sea.

ROSES

Gerald Stern

There was a rose called *Guy de Maupassant,*
a carmine pink that smelled like a Granny Smith
and there was another from the seventeenth century
that wept too much and wilted when you looked;
and one that caused tuberculosis, doctors
dug them up, they wore white masks and posted
warnings in the windows. One wet day
it started to hail and pellets the size of snowballs
fell on the roses. It's hard for me to look at
a *Duchess of Windsor,* it was worn by Franco
and Mussolini, it stabbed Jews; yesterday I bought
six roses from a Haitian on Lower Broadway;
he wrapped them in blue tissue paper, it was
starting to snow and both of us had on the wrong shoes,
though it was wind, he said, not snow that ruined
roses and all you had to do was hold them
against your chest. He had a ring on his pinky
the size of a grape and half his teeth were gone.
So I loved him and spoke to him in false Creole
for which he hugged me and enveloped me
in his camel hair coat with most of the buttons missing,
and we were brothers for life, we swore it in French.

THE MORAL DIMENSIONS OF GLOBAL ENVIRONMENTAL PROTECTION

Paul Wapner

WE ARE USED TO THINKING of the Sabbath as time. It is a moment in the week when we stop doing all the things we do and just be. The Torah tells us to do no work on the Sabbath and to keep it holy. We pause from all our efforts to create and change the world and simply appreciate the way things are. The Sabbath, as such, is a type of withdrawal. It is a moment, a hiatus, in the otherwise endless stream of acting in the world. It is a time to refrain from laboring and, to use Heidegger's awkward phrase, to let "Being be."

What if the Sabbath could be not only a time but also a place? What if the Sabbath could be not simply a pause in our day-to-day lives but also a space on the planet devoid of our presence and even our crossings? What if there could be places on earth unetched with human design, unmarked by the human footprint, untouched by our efforts to create and change the world? What if there could be a Sabbath of place, where we withhold our labors and let the other-than-humans just be?

The idea is not so farfetched. The practice of *shemitah,* where farmers let their fields rest every seven years, aims to bring the concept of Sabbath to the earth. Shemitah means to drop; it refers to the practice of letting fruit, vegetables, and stalks fall to the ground, unpicked and unutilized by people. Crops go uncultivated for a year; the soil finds rejuvenation; the land becomes a place where humans withdraw. Shemitah is a time when humans let the land rest and take a break from its productivity. It represents one form of a Sabbath of place.

We can imagine another kind. Instead of giving the land a year off, we can choose to withhold our labor from the land permanently and create special places to harbor the gift of the Sabbath. Here the idea would be to cordon off part of the land to let the extra-human world express and experience itself free from constant human presence and intervention. This idea is also not so farfetched. In many ways, officially designated wilderness areas and wildlife refuges are "land-Sabbaths." According to the 1964 Wilderness Act, wilderness areas are places where "the earth and its community of life are untrammeled by man, where man himself is a visitor and does not remain." Refuges are similarly protected areas designated specifically for protecting wildlife and habitat in perpetuity. In both cases, the idea is to demarcate places where the nonhuman world is supposed to reign supreme, places where other beings live out their lives free from extensive human interference.

It makes some sense to think about a Sabbath of place in the current controversy over the Arctic National Wildlife Refuge (ANWR). ANWR is the crown jewel of the National Wildlife Refuge System. It protects 19 million acres of land from development and permanent human presence. According to the Department of Interior's official Website, ANWR is "among the most complete, pristine and undisturbed ecosystems on earth." It is often referred to as America's Serengeti. The refuge supports numerous plants and animals, including polar bears, whales, snow geese, and wolves, who have lived in the region since time immemorial. The spring migration of 129,000 porcupine caribou across the refuge to birthing places in the northern coastal plain is supposed to be one of the grandest displays on earth of nature's dynamic patterns. It has been taking place uninterrupted since at least the last ice age. The Bush Administration wants to drill for oil in the northern coastal plain of ANWR. An estimated 1.9 billion gallons of commercially recoverable oil are locked under ANWR's majestic landscape, and we are told that the U.S. needs that oil to keep the economy going. We should be critical of such proposals. While the administration claims that it can drill for oil without disturbing the fragile ecosystem, the record of extracting and transporting oil in the Arctic provides indisputable evidence that oil drilling irreparably damages the delicate tundra and wildlife. Moreover, oil from ANWR would do little to meet our current and future energy needs. The administration points to California's current energy crisis to justify the search for more oil, claiming that California presages what is in store for the rest of the country. The administration fails to explain, however, that California does not use oil for electricity and that its current fiasco stems more from botched deregulation schemes and possible price gouging than from a lack of supply. Furthermore, even the most optimistic estimates claim that ANWR will provide only six months' worth of oil for the U.S.—hardly a dent in our long-term energy needs and certainly questionable in terms of ecological costs. Bush's proposal threatens to spoil a national and, indeed, global treasure in exchange for greater profits for the oil industry. The plan should be stopped dead in its tracks for these reasons alone.

But, there are other deeper reasons to oppose the plan. At a higher level of abstraction, the issue is not simply how carefully we can remove the oil or how many days the ANWR supply will last. It also has to do with the meaning of our intrusion. The Bush proposal asks us to relinquish the value we place on setting aside land for other beings. It asks us to give up on the notion that there is more to human life than endless enterprise, industry, and activity. The authors of the Wilderness Act sought to express our humanity by establishing places free from human doings. Although they did not use the language, they sought to create Sabbaths of place, areas of rest, spaces free from human activity. To the degree that the Sabbath protects our lives from being consumed by the daily work of our hands and the enslavement of our minds by our day-to-day exertions, the plan to drill for oil in ANWR is in many ways a desecration of its principles.

The idea of the Sabbath finds its biblical sources in two places. In Exodus (20:8) the Torah tells us that the Sabbath commemorates creation itself. God, we are told, created the world in six days and on the seventh rested from the work. Imagine what that repose must have been like! Having just created the heavens, earth, human beings, and all other living creatures—each with its own infinite complexity and held together in ever more complicated sets of mutualities—God sits back and takes in the fruits of divine labor and appreciates (if one could use that word) the magnificence of the newly created universe.

Deuteronomy (5:15) explains that the Sabbath also honors Israel's redemption from Egypt. The Israelites were slaves in Egypt, bound to labor in the servitude of other's desires. When God brought them out of Egypt "with mighty hand and outstretched arm" the Jews were finally able to feel the openness of freedom. That must have been quite a moment. Apparently, the authors of Leviticus thought so, insofar as the book commands Jews to observe the Sabbath as a way of keeping the liberating moment alive in one's heart and soul.

ANWR, as a Sabbath of place, celebrates creation. It preserves the magnificence of nature's bounty and stands as an instance of the world basically untouched by human hands. It is a place not of our making nor of our tinkering but of the earth's expression. By preserving it as a Sabbath—and thus cordoning it off from human activity—we keep it holy, as it were. We keep it as a reminder of the world's creation—something well beyond ourselves and our powers.

ANWR also stands as a place of liberation. Human beings are obviously wonderful creatures. It just so happens, however, that in our quest for deeper experience and as a consequence of our numbers, affluence, and technological capability, we spread ourselves across the planet and fold increasing parts of the earth into our domain. In this way we increasingly master the natural world and bind it to our needs and desires. Existing apart from human enterprise, the other-than-human world of ANWR is still free from human mastery. It enjoys a type of liberation that has analogies in the Exodus and Leviticus stories.

Imagining a Sabbath of place and connecting it with the ANWR may be a stretch. But what else is there to meaningful engagement with the world? Human beings are creatures that make meaning. The Torah is, according to some, a set of narratives that expand human experience by connecting our individual and collective lives to larger, transhistorical stories about the human condition. The idea of the Sabbath is a story within a story (within a story). Many of us find it helpful for appreciating the various dimensions of life and making sense of what it means to be human.

As we struggle for ecological sanity, we must mine our traditions for meaningful metaphors and wise counsel. We must also be willing to unleash our political and spiritual imaginations to gain insight into what is meaningful to us today and to understand why this is the case. There is something enduring about the ancient idea of Sabbath; there is wisdom in the idea of pausing from our doings and experiencing a moment of being. It is like a distant echo that reverberates through the ages, telling us that time spent resting, reflecting, contemplating, rejoicing, and simply withdrawing from the world of enterprise is worthwhile. As the Buddhists say, "Don't just do something, sit there!"

We can learn much from withdrawing. As the Bush Administration tries to pillage one of the last pristine places on earth, we should remember the commandment to observe the Sabbath and keep it holy. Protecting ANWR as a Sabbath of place represents an opportunity to withhold our power and let the world do its thing. Ironically, working to protect ANWR may be one of the best and most basic ways of doing our thing.

THE PLEASURES OF
JEWISH CULTURE

FIRST THINGS TO HAND

Robert Pinsky

In the skull kept on the desk.
In the spider pod in the dust.

Or nowhere. In milkmaids, in loaves,
Or nowhere. And if Socrates leaves

His house in the morning,
When he returns in the evening

He will find Socrates waiting
On the doorstep, Buddha the stick

You use to clear the path,
And Buddha the dog-doo you flick

Away with it nowhere or in each
Several thing you touch:

The dollar bill, the button
That works the television.

FROM OLD MEN AT MIDNIGHT

Chaim Potok

The War Doctor

I grew up in a religious home in the Ukraine, and during the First World War the army of the tsar put me into a labor battalion. Probably because I was a Jew and those in command didn't trust us to be proper combat soldiers. That was all right with me; I wasn't eager to be in the front lines fighting the Germans. We loaded boxes of artillery shells onto wagons, and for a while I even drove one of the clattering wagons—it was always heavily laden and had a team of four strong horses—back and forth between the loading area and the front through marshland and along dirt roads. In a bad rain the horses slipped and strained and sometimes our wagons sank to their axles in the mud. One morning the Germans shelled us as we raced through a bog, and when the barrage lifted, only eighteen men were left. I was among them.

All around me in the marshy terrain lay pieces of soldiers and horses. I sat in shallow water leaning against the head of a wiry black mare and met the gaze of its dead eyes. There was a ringing in my ears and a trembling in my arms and legs. Through the ringing I thought I could hear the wailing of the wounded, though it may have been the cold autumn wind blowing past my ears. It made me sad to see our ammunition wagons in ruins, with shells spilled everywhere. Many of the boxes containing English artillery shells had exploded in the barrage, which is why so many were killed. I felt bad because there was a shortage of ammunition in the three lines of our trenches. Later that day the division retreated and I thought we were to blame for that and they would say it was the fault of the cowardly Yids.

They then made me an officers' orderly in a quarter-master battalion and I tended to their boots and uniforms and brought them lunches and suppers and sometimes cared for their horses. The officers used the foulest language, cursed their men, and were often drunk. Sometimes they beat the men with their swagger sticks and even with the knout, calling them lazy and stupid and wishing them dead. Nights they spent with women of the village where we were billeted. One morning many of the officers rode off to a division meeting and later we heard the rumbling of a distant thunder and some of the officers came galloping back in a sweat and we quickly packed up everything and joined a big retreat.

Retreating along dusty roads and barren fields, I heard men muttering to each other that the Yids were the reason for the success of the German army in Poland. I tried to find out-of-the-way places where I could put on my tefillin and pray the morning service, but some days I couldn't. We kept marching or waiting for hours on end; there was a confusion of jammed roads and lost units. We heard that the Germans had taken the city of Vilna.

One day we forded a shallow river and I saw two villages burned to the ground and along a road dozens of men hanging by the neck from trees, and an old toothless peasant standing by the side of the road, his hat in his hand, told us they were Jews who had been spying for the Germans. I think that was near the border of the part of Poland called Galicia.

We came to a region of low hills and rolling fields and dirt roads and there we dug lines of trenches and the Germans attacked and our soldiers drove them back and then we attacked and afterward all I could see in the fields were bodies. Amid the poppies and birch groves and flower-covered slopes—a rich harvest of torn bodies.

They gave me a shovel then and told me to help with the digging of graves. We dug them more than six feet deep and very long and wide and filled them nearly to the top with the bodies of our soldiers. For days we dug and filled graves. Bodies in odd positions stiff as wood, and gasses and eerie sounds coming from the wounds. We tried to keep their faces covered. The dead, the dust, the flies. Sometimes I saw from a partially naked body that it was a Jew I was tossing into a mass grave and I quietly said a psalm.

We were retreating again. Then my platoon leader told me to run forward with the others and if one was killed I was to take his weapon. I pulled a rifle from the hands of a headless soldier and ran alongside another soldier and fired when he fired, stopped when he stopped, fell when he fell. I saw he was dead and followed another soldier. For a while artillery was landing just behind us and I thought our own batteries must be firing on us to drive us forward into the attack. But I really could not figure out what was happening. Whining shells and erupting earth and the dry, distant rattle of machine-gun fire and lines of men falling and terrifying noises and the smell of gunpowder and blood. I had no idea where I was going and did what those around me were doing, running toward a forest. I kept slipping in blood and stumbling over parts of bodies and falling into dust and dry grass and getting to my feet. Abruptly, everyone stopped heading toward the forest and turned and ran back, and I with them. No one seemed to know where to go. Then I remember swamps, frost, icy winds. And many dead lying in strange positions everywhere. During all that time I was not seriously hurt—some cuts, a badly bruised foot, a wrenched back, lice, blisters, rotting skin between my toes, but never truly hurt—though on occasion I never slept without bad dreams and there was little to eat. We built fires in the open and in trenches and scoured the fields for vegetables and sometimes I ate the meat of pigs but never of horses.

Early one morning I turned a corner in my trench to be alone so I could put on my tefillin and pray the morning service. I was wrapping the tefillin around the fingers of my left hand when an artillery shell landed where I had stood minutes earlier and blew to pieces everyone there, six men. I stood amid the blood and pieces of flesh, and trembled and vomited.

Can you believe that for some weeks I was a machine gunner and killed many German soldiers? Then they found that I could ride a horse and they gave me the chestnut mare of a cossack who had been killed and suddenly, feeling the eyes of the battalion upon me and insane with reckless courage and heeding the orders of an officer, I raced ahead into a forest where we lost most of our men but routed the enemy and they made me a platoon leader because there were almost no noncommissioned officers left after that attack.

All the time I followed orders and did what those around me said to do. One day I heard my men cursing the tsar—my men, peasants mostly, actually cursing their own tsar. Soon afterward there were new soldiers in our regiment. They looked like students—pale, thin, wearing eyeglasses and crimson caps. They handed out leaflets and talked about an end to this cursed war. One pushed a leaflet into my hands and said the country would soon belong to the workers.

That summer we took Lvov. But then we retreated again. Really it was a rout—I had lost most of my platoon and rode exhausted in a long cart with about a dozen others, pulled by four half-starved horses. We were in a dusty column of troops and vehicles that stretched ahead and behind as far as we could see. In late September the Germans attacked again and we withdrew through forests and marshes. I think we were moving back toward Riga and Petrograd.

I had been given a new platoon and overheard some of the men talking about being led by a Yid—Kalik the Yid, they called me—and that night two deserted. One day in the fall an officer informed us that there was a new government in Petrograd and it would make peace with the Germans. He then announced that he was going off to get drunk. I went out to a nearby field to pray the afternoon service and to thank the Almighty for bringing an end to the war. Standing in tall dry grass, I heard a whisper of air go past my left ear and felt the small stir of a shock wave followed by a thin distant crack and knew that someone was shooting at me. Were my men firing at their Yid leader? There were two more shots from behind me, from my own unit. I ducked down and began to run. Something struck my left arm below the elbow. I looked and saw the sleeve of the gray uniform torn and awash in blood, and then I was clubbed across the head.

I emerged from the darkness and opened my eyes. "Don't move your head," a woman's voice said into my ear. But I moved it anyway. A stab of pain rammed through my head and down my spinal column into the back of my legs.

I lay still as a nurse tended to my head. She brushed something into my forehead that burned briefly, and put on a new bandage. Then she went away, taking with her the enameled pan into which she had tossed the old bandage and some swabs and a pair of scissors.

Slowly, I turned my head and saw I was in a large room with tall windows through which pale sunlight shone. A field hospital. The floor was strewn with straw. Three rows of men lay beneath blankets on the floor. Two attendants and a nurse moved among the men. Dust-filled air and the stench of urine and blood and the whining of the wounded.

At the head of the middle row close to the far wall stood a man with a long white beard and white hair. His face was ghostly in the pale light. He wore a long dark robe and a small dark skullcap. In his left hand he held a book and in his right a large cross.

A priest!

He was chanting from the book, blessing the wounded and the dying. Should I tell them I was a Jew and the priest's blessing could cause me harm? He was using the name of their god.

I lifted my head off the straw and instantly felt a wave of nausea. A terror fell upon me.

The priest stood chanting from his book under the raised cross.

I fell back into the darkness.

FIVE POEMS ENTITLED "QUESTIONS"

Gail Mazur

QUESTIONS

What is my purpose in life
if not to peer into the glazed bowl
Of silence and fill it for myself
with words? How shall I do it?
The way a disobedient child sings
to herself to keep out the punishing
night, not knowing that her brother
and sister, hearing the song,
shift in their cots of demons
and are solaced into sleep?

QUESTIONS

What is my purpose in life
if not to feed myself
with vegetables and herbs
and climb a step machine to nowhere
and breathe deeply to calm myself
and avoid loud noises
and the simmering noon sun?

Isn't there more,
more even than turning to you,
remembering what drew us together,
wondering what will tear us apart?
Does it matter if I tell
my one story again and then again,
changing only a tracing of light,
a bit of fabric, a piece of
laughter, a closed cafeteria—
if I add a detail almost every day
of my life, what will I have done?
Who will I give my collections to,
who would want to use them?
Don't answer, don't make me
hang my head
in gratitude or shame.

QUESTIONS

What is my purpose in life
if not, when there is nothing to say,
to control myself and say nothing?

What could wisdom be if not
a mastery of waiting and listening?
is it my purpose to become wise?

What is wisdom? Isn't it a pose,
the will refusing realms of confusion?
How would I approach it, unless

I learned to love the absence of speech,
even the implication of language,
so violently I'd remind myself

of a friend who detests the mimes
who gesticulate on Sundays in the park,
and has begun a postcard campaign

to Silence the Silent. She knows
gestures, too, are a part of speech.
Would it have enough meaning for me,

to watch and listen, to touch
the warm fur of animals and the sandy dunes,
to drop handfuls of fine gravel

into the graves of the newly dead,
to learn grief from the mourners' tears
and courage from their squared shoulders

as they return, each one alone
to the limousines? What gives anyone
the daring to adore paradoxical life?

Won't I always yearn for and fear an answer?
Will I someday have the one thing to say
that contradicts and clarifies itself,

and without falseness or sorrow,
without strutting or stumbling,
will I know to say it?

QUESTIONS

What is my purpose in life
if not to practice goodness
I know isn't graphed in my genes
the way designs are programmed
in the cells of a butterfly's wing?
How can I pretend
that the modest beauty of self-
lessness is not a false glory?
Why hope altruism is part of me,
set into the elegant machinery
by which form and temperament
are generated? The saints are boring
and fictional, their great acts
accidents of a moment, reactions
to cataclysm. What is goodness?
Haven't I tried long enough,
stepped on my own heart, broken
my hands trying to pry it open?
Haven't I lain awake, my head

aching with the chronic dementia
of the would-be virtuous? Haven't I
settled on my right to be harmless,
nothing better? Didn't I fail
at sacrificing, wasn't the last time
it worked when my son and daughter
still slept in their own messy beds?
Who did they think mothered them,
without rage or tears, with no ideas
of escape? Now they are thrilling
voices on the phone, they're at home
in the world, they have discrete selves,
there are layers to them, they are like
poems. What will I do from sunrise
to midnight now they don't use me,
why should I take on anyone's pain?
How will I live if I won't care
for anything in this world again
more than I care for myself?

QUESTIONS

What is my purpose in life
now that it's too late for regret,

now that I've apologized
to the murdered dead and the ones

who went with tubes & needles
on ungiving rubberized beds

and the ones who left glowing,
lovers holding their thin cold hands,

compassionate angels hovering
in the sweetish light of candles,

snow folding itself gently outside
over the dry summer gardens,

soothing the streetlights
and the angular cars, and hydrants?

What can I want now but to be
solitary in a white cell,

with only a mattress and table,
my soul simplifying as Thoreau

advised? I know I'll want one thing
on my wall, a framed poem of LiPo's,

the Chinese characters say the moon
is making him homesick, drunk and lonely,

I'll want 5 things on my table:
a block of woven paper; a brush;

a stone brushrest in the shape
of the 4 sacred mountains;

I'll want to look at a Chinese rock,
small and violent like my soul,

mountainous as the landscape
of Guilin, vertical *jade hairpins;*

and then, a gold and red pagoda,
a ceramic music box—

when I wind a key, it will play
a folk song I've heard only once

on ancient instruments years ago
as I sat on a carved bench

watching huge golden carp
swimming madly in the miniature lake

of a scholar's garden in Suzhou;
it will play in perfect time

for a while until it winds slowly
down, and then the dying song

will pull me mercifully back
to my calm, impenitent room.

POEM ENDING WITH A PHRASE
FROM THE PSALMS

Grace Schulman

Here where loss spins the hickory's dry leaves,
Rolls miles under wheels, and bleaches reeds
that shone wine-red, I invoke a rose
still rising like a choir, past its prime
on spindly bush that bore scarce blooms,
as I wake to hear a jay screech like a gate
swung open, and see your hand enfolding mine
on linen: *teach us to number our days.*

FROM THE SAME SEA

Amos Oz

All of a Sudden

Early next evening Dita turned up. Light-footed, out of breath, unannounced she rang his doorbell, waited. No use, he's not in, just my luck.

When she had given up and was on her way downstairs she met him coming up, carrying a string bag full of shopping. She grabbed one handle and so, embarrassed, hands touching, they stood on the stairs. At first he was a little startled when she tried to take the bag away from him:

For a moment he didn't recognize her, with her short hair, and her cheeky skirt that almost wasn't there. The reason I came is that I got a postcard this morning.

He sat her down in the living room. He told her at once that he too had had a postcard from Tibet. She showed him.

He showed her. They compared. Then she followed him into the kitchen.

Helped him unload the shopping, and put it away. Mr. Danon put the kettle on. While they waited they sat facing one another at the kitchen table. One knee over the other, in her orange skirt, she seemed almost naked. But she's so young. Still a child. Quickly he averted his gaze. He had trouble asking her whether she and Rico were still or no longer. He chose his words carefully, tactfully evasive. Dita laughed: I'm not his, I never was, and he isn't mine, and anyway, you see, those are just labels. Everyone for themselves. I'm allergic to anything permanently fixed. It's better to just let everything flow. Trouble is, that's a kind of fixed notion too. As soon as you define, it's a mess. Look, the kettle's boiling. Don't get up, Albert, let me see to it. Coffee or tea?

She stood up, sat down, and saw he was blushing. She found it sweet. She crossed her legs again, straightened her skirt, more or less. By the way, I need your advice as a tax consultant. It's like this: I've written a screenplay, it's going into production, and I've some papers to sign. Don't be mad at me for taking the opportunity to ask you, just like that. You mustn't feel obliged. On the contrary, I'll be delighted.

He started to give her a detailed explanation, not as to a client, more to a daughter. As he clarified things from various angles, his docile body began suddenly to strain at the bit.

Refuge

Dita is at the door. On her slender back a mountain of backpack with another bundle tied to it, clutching some plastic bags and a handbag: she is seeking refuge, for a couple, a week at most, if it's not an imposition. She's ended up with no flat and no money, all her savings and everything gone; she found some kind of producer, got taken for a ride. But why are you standing in the doorway? You'll fall over. Come inside. Then you can tell me all about it. We'll have a think. We'll get you out of this mess.

She gulped down a soft drink. Undressed. Took a shower. For a moment she embarrassed him when she emerged wrapped in a towel from mid-breast to thigh. She stood in front of him in the kitchen and told him in detail how she had got stung.

And her parents were abroad and their flat was let, she had simply nowhere to turn. It was no good his staring down at the floor: the sight of her naked feet sets his heart at odds with his body.

Rico's room is yours from now on. It's empty anyway. Here is the bedding. That's the air-conditioning. His wardrobe isn't too tidy, but there's some room. I'll bring you a cold drink in a minute.

Lie down. Get some rest. We'll talk later. If you need me for anything just say Albert and I'll be right there. Don't be shy. Or simply come to my office. It's through there. I'll just be sitting finishing off some accounts.

You're no trouble at all. On the contrary: for some time now—

He stopped himself. Under the towel her hips made a whispering sound and he was blushing as though he had been caught red-handed.

IN THE LIGHT-GROPING DARKNESS

A widowed father with an honest name
Lies wide awake in the night consumed with shame:
A sleeping woman the cause of his pain.

She's there alone—his eyes are open wide—
Next door she's lying naked, on her side.
So young. A child. My daughter, my bride!

He switches on the bedside light and blinks
At his son and wife on the sideboard. He thinks
For a while. Then pads to the kitchen and drinks.

He sits down at this desk and begins to dream
Heavy thoughts: his shadow stares back from the screen.
What a difficult summer, he types, this has been.

From the garden outside where nothing has stirred
In the light-groping darkness, a single bird:
Narimi, narimi. Yes, I heard.

Restless he stands: how he longs to spread
A blanket on her, and stroke her head.
He stifles these feelings, and goes back to bed.

He turns and tosses. Of sleep there's no sign.
He turns on the light and checks the time:
It's five o'clock here—so in Tibet it's nine.

EXCAVATING THE PAST

LOOKING INTO JEWISH STORIES

Shelly R. Fredman

I LOVE JEWISH SHORT STORIES. I read them for the same reason I read other short stories—for the exhilaration, for the suspense, for the thrill of sparks flying between reader and writer. I read them because they take me far away from where I live, and in Jewish short stories in particular, because they take me closer to home. As Philip Roth has said, the Jewish quality of books doesn't really reside in their subject matter. "It's a kind of sensibility: the nervousness, the excitability, the arguing, the obsessiveness, above all, the talking. It isn't what it's talking about that makes a book Jewish—it's that the book won't shut up."

Perhaps it's that "not shutting up" quality that draws me in so deeply. That relentlessness, that refusal to let go, which seems to be Jewish at its core. An obsession with the past is one of the central concerns of Jewish writers; in fact, Jewish sensibility often emerges out of the possibility of tying oneself to the experiences of earlier Jews.

As a teacher of short-story writing, I am sometimes tempted to tell my students, most of whom are not Jewish—to look for that *Ma nish ta na* moment. Why is this night, this day, this moment different from all other moments? Out of that kind of moment, drama and suspense begin. Change occurs. A story is born. Jewish short-story writers tend to locate that moment at some junction with their past. A Jewish short story often harks back to a previous time, place, person, or way of life. What less can we expect from a people who are constantly being told by their history, their literature, their liturgy—*zachor*. Remember.

343

And so, perusing a sampling of some of the finest short stories—some, not all—we find one character after another attempting to bridge the distance between the self and the tradition, attempting to link up with a past, be it literary, historical, communal, or familial. Jewish writers ride the coattails of their ancestors, and their stories often seem to hang as if suspended in time, energized by the ever-forward thrust of plot on the one hand, and this instinct to reach back on the other.

Take, for instance, Jonathan, in E. L. Doctorow's *The Writer in the Family*. Jonathan is a teenage boy who finds himself in the precarious position of impersonating his dead father, writing letters to his grandmother in a nursing home. The boy's aunts have cooked up this scheme, afraid the shock of her son's death might kill the old woman. "He can't even die when he wants to!" Jonathan's mother laments, "Even death comes second to Mama!" As aunts and mother battle for the boy's allegiance, a battle that even death cannot dull the edge of, Doctorow reveals the fictions and lies that sustain us, the preemptive power of family. Urged on by his Aunt Frances, forced to write from his father's perspective, Jonathan discovers a chink through which he gazes into the man's soul. At the end of the story, still posing, he writes the most honest letter of all: "As for the nature of my ailment, the doctors haven't told me what it is, but I know that I am simply dying of the wrong life."

Good stories, like all good writing, percolate with questions. They ask more than they answer. The questions bubbling beneath this story concern the ways in which our lives get sidetracked, become the property of others, veer off into directions we had no intention of taking. Doctorow raises questions about our own failure to express what is most precious to us, the essential identity hidden at the base of our being. In this story, the young boy's lack of knowledge of his own father's inner life doesn't even surface until after the man dies.

Alongside that theme, there are profound fissures dividing this family. The joustings for power occur at such a deep level, one may be reminded of yet another Jewish family—Jacob and Esau's. In that story, too, it isn't until Jacob is persuaded to don the mask of Esau, until he lives in the skin of the other, that he discovers the hidden parts of himself. Until Jacob opens to the possibility of incorporating his brother's traits into his being, taking on the opposite's mantle—he cannot leave his father's house. He cannot carry out his destiny on the other side of the Jordan. In both stories, it is the fiction, the masquerade, that makes our heroes whole.

In "Zagrowsky Tells," Grace Paley takes on the "isms"—racism, feminism, even Nazism. Beyond all these, as her character suggests, "Life is going on. You have an opinion. I have an opinion. Life don't have no opinion." The suggestion is that beyond the world of the story, a larger world exists and now and then it will leak into the story, giving the story a context, a dimension beyond itself. The technique adds depth and fullness, and it also allows Paley to register the world's indifference to our private struggles, while at the same time acknowledging just how important those private endeavors are. Like the best writers, Paley is comfortable dwelling within the paradox—we both hardly matter—our "little disturbances" barely register on the Great Screen of life, and yet there is nothing more important than the telling of one man's story.

Furthermore, Paley plops her characters down right between two realms—the political and the personal. Zagrowsky is an aged pharmacist who meets up with Faith, one of his former customers in the park—he's never forgiven her for staging a picket line in front of his drugstore, decrying his racist policies. The story turns on an irony: as the two rehash their past, a small boy with a long Jewish name, Emanuel, Zagrowsky's black grandson, clutches his hand.

Instead of a simplistic good-versus-evil dichotomy, we witness the complications of these characters; their traits allow us to love and hate them at the same time. Zagrowsky himself is crotchety and thick-headed, but he is also wise—too wise for us to dismiss. "Thank God for the head," he tells us. "Inside the head is the only place you got to be young when the usual place gets used up." The old man invokes the power of the imagination, the ways it invigorates memory and infuses present moments. And though he is a racist, he is also the one who recognizes the redemptive power of story-telling. In the midst of a rebuke of Faith, he tells himself: "Calm down, Zagrowsky. Because for a fact I didn't want her to leave, because, since I already began to tell, I have to tell the whole story. Tell! That opens the congestion a little—the lungs are for breathing, not secrets."

Telling, in fact, is at the heart of Jewish experience. Not only are we inheritors of a rich oral tradition, but the tradition itself exhorts us to tell and tell again. Not only do we, as a people, recount the exodus journey from slavery to redemption year after year at a Passover seder, but every evening, the central Jewish prayer, the Shema, is traditionally recited. It is a review of the day's efforts, a confession, a version of telling in which the "listener" is none other than the Divine.

Whether or not Zagrowsky is aware of the tradition doesn't really matter. When he tells, this is the ancestral ground, the foundation upon which he stands. In addition, we have Faith playing a God-like role here. She "tests" Zagrowsky four times before exacting her punishment—staging the protest in front of his pharmacy. And the writer's almost biblical sense of justice spares no one, not even Faith herself. "Then this lady Queen of

Right makes a small lecture," the old druggist says. And Faith's lecture reveals just how selective her memory is. She has forgotten Zagrowsky's nervous daughter Cissy and her plunge into madness, but remembers his remarks about a racially mixed couple. The scales bear down again, this time on Zagrowsky's side. The Jewish obsession with the past is invoked in this story, but here it is an imperfection of memory the writer describes, the way we compile our histories, invent as well as receive our pasts.

All the while, the park's noise—music playing, balls juggling, people talking—crescendos. As one telling follows another, the ever-present, incessant conversation of a people builds, and voices of the past—they even speak of Isaac and Ishmael at one point—mingle with those of the present. There is the redemptive quality of language in this New York City meeting place, and also the chaos. Jews, still a stiff-necked and wandering people, are a people that find their way in talk.

Bernard Malamud's "The Silver Crown" is the story of Albert Gans, a self-proclaimed "non-mystic" who nonetheless enlists the help of one Jonas Lipschitz, a rabbi with a business card, to construct a silver crown that will magically save his dying father. Albert is another character trafficking in the world of his ancestors, and the story describes the odd collisions of one landscape with another—past and present, religious and secular, faith and reason, magic and miracle. Albert is a high school biology teacher, but it is as if he has entered another universe—his father's perhaps—when he reaches the rabbi's home. It is adjacent to a "battered synagogue in a store, Congregation Theodore Herzl." In the rabbi's apartment, "the shades resembled faded maps of ancient lands" and "an old gray-bearded man with thickened left eyelid, wearing a yarmulke, sat heavily asleep, a book in his lap." That he would seek out such a healer underscores the dire condition of Albert's father; it also reveals the bleak atmosphere prevailing between father and son.

Albert asks if the crown will work even if he's a nonbeliever, and the rabbi answers, "Doubts we all got. We doubt God and God doubts us. This is natural on account of the nature of existence. Of this kind doubts I am not afraid so long as you love your father." In the modern, post-Holocaust era, the kind of faith that once buttressed the lives of Jews is gone. Doubt has become part of the religious language. Whereas the theologian Abraham Joshua Heschel was able to claim, "All of human history as described in the Bible may be summarized in one phrase: God is in search of man," Malamud portrays a world in which it is not the struggle to know the Divine that is reflexive, but doubt. We have fashioned a doubting God; we have projected our anxiety onto Heaven.

The rabbi then offers blessings and two prices. We seem to have entered a cockeyed universe, where the holy and mundane rub shoulders. In the past, places like synagogues and rabbi's studies once at least pretended to be sanctuaries, attempted to distinguish themselves from the secular. In our current universe, the two sit rather uncomfortably side by side. The rabbi poses mystical questions, yet he operates like a salesman. He owns holy books, but he kicks them under chairs instead of kissing them. And yet he is the one who teaches Albert, "For those who believe there is no magic," which is perhaps the "truest" statement in a story filled with veils and mirrors. Magic is the work of sorcerers and wizards, a realm Judaism has always disavowed. The kind of faith the rabbi espouses, charlatan that he may be, transcends the physical. It is no sleight-of-hand experience, a trick involving vanishing rabbits, or silver crowns, for that matter. It is a realm those like Albert, empiricists who need their theories proven before they believe, cannot enter. Magic is physical, but faith is divine.

In the end, Albert's efforts earn him nothing but the revelation of his true feelings—his hatred for his father—and a "massive, spike-laden headache," the silver crown he went seeking in the first place. It is a stark and brutal conclusion. The ending suggests the world we inhabit will never exceed the bounds of our vision. The Alberts of the world are diminished by their inability to imagine, their refusal to eke out "a measure of astonishment at the nature of life," as Malamud himself described the dilemma in his memoir.

Redemption becomes possible only when we are willing to pay the highest of prices, only if we are willing to suspend our disbelief, to stare long and hard into the mirror of the self, to excavate identity, as one would unearth a buried Temple.

"Enchantment," by Daphne Merkin, is an excavation that moves through successive layers of a daughter's psyche as she tries to uncover the mystery of her mother. Merkin's heroine admits she has a tendency to lose things yet she also characterizes herself as "the most intractable of hoarders." She holds onto a near-empty tube of toothpaste that's been lying in various medicine cabinets, untouched, for several years. When her friend tells her to throw it out, she does, only to retrieve it later, restoring it to its "place." Merkin has me laughing with recognition, yet I can't help wondering if this isn't a form of behavior born out of a people's collective experience of being shifted from place to place for thousands of years. Given that kind of archetypal experience, is it any wonder we cling to unnecessary objects?

The weight of the past is physical as well as psychological. It sits there on the narrator's bookcase, where a photograph of her Orthodox grandfather, who read Thomas Mann and bore a resemblance to Sigmund Freud, sits. His religious ambivalence manifests itself in absurd predicaments in the third generation. Our heroine finds herself stranded at a train station (yet another evocative locale for a Jew), having missed the last train out to her parent's house before Shabbat. At a nearby pay phone, distraught, as she dials her mother she realizes: "When I pictured my life as an adult, it never resembled this: I sit on the beach and watch other people's families, all the pails and shovels, and the husbands standing, talking to other husbands."

The gap between the imagined life and the real one echoes the biblical one, the gulf between God's promise and the reality the families of Abraham have been living out ever since. And whereas biblical figures like Moses are described as having known God *panim al panim*, face to face, the best we postmodern Jews can hope for is to know our mother's face. As a biblical people, Jews once aspired to know God. Abraham, Jacob, Moses, and the women, too, if you read between the lines—Hagar after her flight from Sarah's tent, Rebecca in her bewilderment at the warring twins in her womb, Hannah in her prayer, all sought redemption through a higher Force or Power. They turned to God. Now we struggle to know our parents. Merkin ends with a close-up of the mother as the story, and the life, circles back on itself: "the straight line of her mouth, which makes me think of a child's drawing. I know her face by heart. Sometimes I think nothing will break her spell." Like God, mother is a kind of Mystery we cannot enter.

Great short stories portray characters in crises. And the more tsuris a character has, the better. Suffering makes for great story telling. In the best stories, though, there may also be an affirmation—a gesture, a remark, a sign—some signal that rises out of the suffering, takes its breath from the ashes, like a phoenix with tarnished wings. Out of the narrow straits, there is a will that surfaces, a character that says—yes.

Ira is adrift at a Jewish wedding in Los Angeles, in the story "S Angel" by Michael Chabon. Set amidst the Persian carpets, French doors, and sparkling pool of a Pasadena hotel, most of the people don't seem to want to be at this wedding, including the bride! Chabon characterizes the synagogue congregation as "dour and Conservative," with a capital C. He writes, "As the service dragged on, Ira found himself awash in a nostalgic tedium, and he fell to wishing for irretrievable things."

It's a "nostalgic tedium," a boredom tinged with longing. For how many weddings have Jews like Ira sat at, longing to be struck by the miraculous, tethered to their seats with the hope, at least, that somewhere amidst the pageantry and ceremony wherein one human being binds her life to another's, the humanity will break through, the recognition of the potential for transcendence, for transformation.

One of those "irretrievable things" arrives in the form of Carmen, a young girl who "spews a huge nervous chaos of smoke," and yet strikes Ira as hiding a "wise and tormented soul." Carmen is portrayed as a smidgen Reb Nachman, a smidgen Hollywood starlet. At one point in the story, she rises to her feet in what seems to be an evocation of the "kadosh, kadosh, kadosh" moment in traditional prayer, when congregants rise on their toes in imitation of angels. "Having risen to her feet rather dramatically, she now seemed uncertain what to do next and stood wavering a little on her blue spike heels," Chabon writes. This is no angel with a mission, as biblical literature portrays celestial beings. Carmen, in fact, is mission-less, and perhaps that is the root of her problem. Angels in Pasadena, Chabon may be suggesting, no longer aspire to Heaven. They traverse more earthly realms, dealing in love and real estate. Whereas in classic Jewish works like S. Ansky's *The Dybbuk* angels are depicted as messengers given the task of uniting souls destined to be together, here they arrive only to proclaim the death of romantic love. At the end of the story, Ira is poised on the hotel balcony not unchastely kissing his cousin, the bride.

Again, the connection our protagonist was seeking has failed to occur. Or has it? The affirmation is there in the fact that he and the girl are holding hands. But we, and Ira, end up in a nether land halfway between earth and heaven, suspended on the balcony. It seems to me a prototypical American-Jewish experience, this balcony hovering, imposed by our spiritual longing on the one hand, and on the other, our need, still, to integrate the values of American culture—individualism, materialism, success.

Consider the story "Bloodshed," by Cynthia Ozick. The story begins as Bleilip sets off to visit his cousin Toby in "the town of the Hasidim." He carries in his pocket what turns out to be a loaded gun and a picture of Toby taken nine years before, on the grass at Brooklyn College, in the days when "she used to say she would be the first lady Jewish President." Now Toby wears a bandanna, a hairpiece, and a dress "outlandishly long." Lest we think Ozick is writing simply to explore the phenomenon of the newly religious, she carries the story several degrees beyond. Ozick is less interested in what may cause the ba'al teshuva to return than in the complicated ways that Jewishness, being a Jew, courses through all of us.

Bleilip concludes that Toby "almost passed for some sort of peasant." It turns out the peasant image resides as deeply, perhaps more so, in Bleilip's consciousness as it does in his cousin's physical garb. Later, the secularist watches his cousin's boys sliding down the snowy hill of the yeshiva. "Bleilip could smell through the cold something different from the smell of winter," Ozick writes, "a deep pineyness that moved him: he had a sense of . . . farness, clarity, other lands, displaced seasons, the brooks of a village, a foreign bird piercing." The tumbling children have taken him to another era. Eventually, Bleilip sees also ghosts of children and his (dead) grandfather sailing down the hill, a child with an old man's nose. He sees camps and trains and showers of poison and Buchenwald and eventually he sees the kohen gadol and the Temple and the Holy of Holies.

Though Bleilip has come to condemn these Hasidim in their nameless town, their rebbe forces him to look beyond their payes and tzitzit, beyond the outer garments. As readers, we are forced to examine the naivete of our judgements, our own inability to see into the true nature of things. Ozick presses Bleilip's nose, and ours, too, to the glass. Bleilip later attends a prayer service with the men of the town. He had wanted "only what he needed, a certain piece of truth, not too big to swallow," Ozick writes. But in the midst of the prayers he experiences a dream of the ancient sacrifices at the Temple, complete with High Priest and holy garb. And the Hasidic rabbi refuses to let him go without a confrontation. The rabbi recognizes what Bleilip's cousin and the others cannot. Bleilip is no mere observer; in fact he has brought a "gun." He is here to condemn. At the end, as in the Malamud story, the rabbi's accusation comes in words about vision. "Who are you not to look?" he asks. There are no visitors in these realms, Ozick seems to be saying. There are no partial forays into this territory, no easy switchbacks on the trail. Just as the Nazis were all-inclusive when it came to the question of who is a Jew, so the mantle of Jewish identity cannot be easily shaken. As carriers of, if nothing else, the genes of tribes that involved themselves in animal sacrifice—there always will be blood on our hands.

That enveloping sense of guilt, of implication—of being implicated is at the heart of many contemporary Jewish stories. It is there in the character of T. Gertler's Harold Stein in the wonderful story "In Case of Survival." Burdened with his "endless, enduring helplessness," late one night Stein composes a letter to the families of victims of an air crash, a plane he himself was scheduled to fly on, but refused to board. "An accident is an accident," he writes, "but what do you call an accident that gives a preview?"

Stein is a kind of modern-day prophet with no tribe behind him. The only one interested in his "vision" is Dr. Ira Bloom at the local university, who wants to "evaluate his paranormality, or ESP." And instead of following him, as a desert people once might have, his buddies Frank Merwitz and Mac Lishinsky refuse to play their weekly game of gin with him, accusing Stein of being able to "see" what cards are in their hands.

In what must serve as resolution, our hero makes a final gesture at the end of the story. He couldn't save the victims of the air crash, but perhaps he can do something for his daughter, Edith, whose depression takes the form of imagining a lion on her roof, waiting, pacing, ever-present. Gertler writes, "Helplessness settled on Harold with the steam from reheated potatoes. . . . After dinner, if he took his bath quickly, he would have enough time before the ten o'clock news to make a neat copy of his letter to the air-crash survivors and the victims' families. Even if he never sent it to them, it was something, at last, that he could send to Edith." Again, it is only a gesture, but it is a gesture that says, yes.

In his introduction to the 1980 edition of *The Best American Short Stories*, which includes Gertler's story and perhaps a disproportionate amount of other stories by Jewish writers, Stanley Elkin says that endings of short stories tend to be wonderful, carrying as they do "something summary and terribly final about the concluding rhetoric—the ringing long-range view of language. We are dealing with solace, the idea of solace, art's and language's consolation prize. It's something a bit beyond the conventional notion of epiphany, inasmuch as epiphany is usually some sudden, fell-swoop blast of insight. This is epiphany that sticks to the ribs."

At the end of Philip Roth's "The Conversion of the Jews," the young Ozzie Freedman is poised on the edge of a roof, about to jump, with all of Rabbi Marvin Binder's Hebrew school class, as well as his mother and the fire department gazing up at him, their "necks stretched backwards, faces up, as though he were the ceiling of the Hayden Planetarium." Ozzie refuses to come down until they all kneel and admit that Jesus was a Jew. Ozzie, and perhaps Roth, too, wants the Rabbi Binders of the world to crank open their windows, to take off the "blinders" through which they gaze at the world, to open to a universality waiting beyond the Hebrew school walls. Ozzie evokes Icarus, or perhaps even Isaac at the sacrificial moment. He knows the only way to redeem Rabbi Binder (and his mother, too!) is to place his head on the stone, to offer up his life.

Or there is Rosellen Brown's Joey, at the end of "A Good Deal," waiting for his father to come home: "Steam coming out of his mouth as he turned the corner from the hilly avenue and headed toward me where I sat in front of the apartment house, in exactly the same place every day, even preposterously (and to my mother's irritation) in the dead heart of winter. It was my challenge to myself, my hardship, my fifty-pound weights, my four-minute mile, my swan dive, to sit with my corduroy knees drawn up in the three-quarter dark, tears of cold in my eyes, my gloveless hands jammed in my pockets, waiting for him, knowing it was only my secret endurance that made him come." Brown, too, evokes the image of flight. Both she and Roth capture the short-story character's willingness to launch himself into thin air, to die in order to live.

It is a place we know all too well—that precarious place suspended midway between one world and another. It is a place made up of memory and mischief, marked by the imagination. It is a place where the past infuses the present and creates yet another layer through which we must trudge. To look back is to look forward also, to realize that what you're schlepping along—crowns and peasants, photographs and grandfathers, a lost cousin, a vision, a dream—holds you down and also buoys you up. It has made you who you are. You are indebted to it. It owns you.

Jewish short-story writers bear witness—to the past—and to the humor and complication and light and squalor that are our lives. There is an old Yiddish expression, "What is truer than the truth? The story."

OCTOBER 1

Susan Hahn

(*MORNING*)

Mother, two days ago he left
with another woman
for a tour of Jerusalem.
Together they'll visit the Old City,
including Mount Zion and the tunnel
excavations under the Wall; arrive
at the Jewish Quarter and the Citadel Museum;
walk along the Cardo, the underground
Roman Street; be driven to the Masada
and ascend the rock fortress where the Zealots
made their last stand, then took their own
lives. *He is not a Zealot, but I*
believe in suicide. Then, they'll swim in the Dead

Sea and enjoy the mud
baths. *It rained here yesterday*
on your grave and the grass over
it was so sparse and soft—the ground
a sponge. If I would have chosen, could I have dug
down to you? Tomorrow or the day after

they go to Mount Nebo, the burial place
of Moses. *How many Commandments*
can anyone handle? Will he think of you
before *that* grave? Those long months
of your dying, when he'd disappear—
was it to be with her? And when he visits

the "rose red city" of Petra—carved
out of solid rock, surrounded by soaring
temples and elaborate tombs—will he
think of the empty red suit that your bones are dressed in?
The healthy fleece covered by an oily
substance that protects the sheep
from the rain, forever dried out.

(*AFTERNOON*)

I wished him a good trip—was polite—
and can only imagine
what it would be like to be at
Vad Va'Shem—the memorial to the six million—
and what the synagogue with the Chagall stained
windows might look like when the sun hits
the glass at high noon. *Here, the sun hit*
your plaque, creating a wet, golden maple leaf
effect that you would have liked.
Your favorite season has arrived
without you and he's gone

to Old Jaffa, Tel Aviv, the Diaspora
Museum. Soon, we'll all be scattered
relics beneath the ground, waiting only
for some archeologist to dig up
and examine. *Let him go,*
I said to my hand, my closed palm.
His last trip to the holy
land, that's what he said. A place
I've never been and probably never
will be, my eyes just left to absorb the *angered*

red I see over
and over. Is that the reason—your fury

over dying, *over him*—why you insisted
on a suit of rage, slowly becoming invisible,
outside the margin of what we could possibly see?

(*NIGHT*)

My brain can no longer organize
the nerve signals and my green thoughts
are a jumble—
hardly the complement to what
you are shredded in.
I have stumbled through the spectrum
of emotion—gone full circle
on the wheel, spun
from yellow to orange to purple,
have ground through all the blues
and always come back
from my inward travels to you—
undone by what is done—
to leave only the sun-
flowers on your autumn grave—forever
the honeybee hovering near home
for any hope of pollen.

THE GREATEST JEW
IN THE WORLD

Leo Haber

MY GRANDFATHER WAS A TALMUDIC SCHOLAR of the first rank, knowledgeable in every abstruse argument found in that sacred legal tome of the Jewish people, but in the year 1999, the simple notion of the upcoming millennial year on January 1, 2000, and its projected Y2K computer problem defeated him utterly. My friends on the job at that time at the scientific laboratories at Brookhaven, who had met my grandfather on the rare occasion that he came by to visit me during a Sunday afternoon cookout for my colleagues, were amazed and incredulous.

"Go on," one of them said to me that October. "The old man's a genius. He can rival St. Thomas Aquinas in philosophy and all that esoteric stuff. Don't tell me he can't understand a simple matter of a two-thousand year date and computers that aren't programmed to surmount the new number."

I assured him and my other friends that this was so. What I could not tell them, not yet, was the real reason why. In fact, I came to that knowledge very belatedly myself, and only by a rare combination of unforeseen circumstances.

Both my mother and father had died young, victims of various forms of cancer. This was devastating not only to me but also to my grandfather, who had lost an only son and a daughter-in-law. He grieved, but it did not change his attitude about Godly service and transcendental things in the least. He continued studying the Talmud on a daily basis and writing intricately reasoned monographs on Jewish religious law that so many others would consider hair-splitting legalisms of no major import. To him, they were life itself, or more accurately, the pulsing bloodstream of the good life. These articles of his were sometimes published in a Hebrew weekly, and when he felt like it, he translated his own work into English and published it in a learned journal with a circulation, at best, of five hundred souls. He could not live on these occasional publications, which often paid him in copies of the magazine instead of real money that could buy him a meal or another book for his bulging library in a small apartment on Fourteenth Street in Manhattan. But he didn't really have to worry about surviving hunger and thirst and paying the rent. I took care of that, unbeknownst to my wife.

Not that he welcomed me all the time with my shopping bags filled with food. "You again? Cluttering up my apartment?" he would growl in impeccable English with hardly the trace of an accent, even though he had come to America as an adult after the war and after his surviving the Holocaust. "Not on bread alone does man subsist, it says in the Torah. So why are you trying to stuff me with food? You have a wife and children who need to eat. Bring it to them. I have no room for so much food."

He really didn't. Every inch of table space and even pantry space was filled with books. And piles of them teetered right and left on the floor, leaving very little room to walk in. It was a veritable maze, and you could almost kill yourself if you tried to zip through the apartment on the way to the bathroom without negotiating the obstacle course very carefully.

He was a short skinny old man who always wore a broad-brimmed fedora out in the street. One would think that an aged scholar of this type would not look after himself, but the truth is the opposite. He was very nicely groomed at all times, beautifully dressed in clothes he could not afford, and he could easily give the impression of being a dapper "dirty old man" about town to those who did not know him well.

My wife did not like him. She never actually said so; she wouldn't hurt me in this way. But I could easily see that she saved her smiles and her giddy, expansive behavior for others in the family, not for him. To her, he was a religious "fanatic," a word or words flippantly used by a good many people to characterize those who live in a world of belief in divinity they cannot fathom. It was not my world either, but unlike my wife, I had come from this world, had witnessed it at first hand, and knew the consolations provided by such beliefs even though I could not share them myself. She didn't like his beard, even though it was neat and in fact very becoming. She did not like the fact that when he did come to visit we had to provide him with paper plates, plastic utensils, and a separate menu of "Glatt Kosher" foods for him to consume on another table away from the treyfe stuff that graced our dining room or the cookout in our suburban backyard.

Most of all, she did not like his conversation, which consistently unnerved her. She never explained it fully to me, but I think that there were two aspects of it that miffed her—his frequent use of biblical quotations, even in English, and his frequent reliance on Yiddish and Hebrew expressions that were Greek to her. Another friend suggested that one could be put off by his blasé references to poets and philosophers whose work hardly anyone in our crowd, including my wife, had ever read—Hegel said this and Spengler said that and Eliezer ha-Kallir wrote this beautiful piyyut and Robert Browning, though a goy, wrote that marvelous poem about a Jewish scholar. I don't actually think that my wife was as much offended by his constant barrage of information on almost everything the way my professional friends were. But then again, maybe she was. My grandfather, without a vain bone in his body, could easily make people feel stupid without his realizing it.

I say "almost everything" in reference to his encyclopedic learning, because I finally found out that there were things he did not know. But before I could find this out, I had to observe once again the awesome extent of what he did know, which astonished even me, his doting grandson, who apparently knew very little indeed.

After the year of mourning the passing of my father, it was time to return to music. The wacky idea came to me to take my grandfather to a classical concert and introduce him to another world. I decided to begin with blockbusters and arranged for the three of us to go to an all-Beethoven concert at the Philharmonic, featuring Yefim Bronfman playing the master's Third Piano Concerto and also his Choral Fantasy that included a chorus, vocal soloists, the pianist, and the orchestra. The program began with one of the Leonore Overtures (not number three, I'm sure) and Beethoven's First Symphony, whose last movement I particularly liked. My wife was also a Beethoven fan, so I expected the evening to go swimmingly.

It didn't. My grandfather yawned during the overture and almost fell asleep during the symphony. At intermission, he eased out of his seat carefully, wandered out to the lobby, and then to the balcony for a breath of fresh air. I followed him, and so did my wife. I was stupid enough to try to make small talk with him.

"What's the matter, Grandpa? You finally found something intellectual that you haven't mastered?"

The old man shrugged his shoulders. "Even the Fidelio Overture is better than the first Leonore that they played," he said. For a moment I didn't get his drift. He continued: "No wonder Beethoven had to write the Leonore Overture three times to get it right. The first one is a total failure. As for the symphony, nu, if I want Mozart, I go to Mozart. If I go to Beethoven, I want real Beethoven, like the Eroica, that means the symphonies from three to nine. I suppose the maestro didn't want to put all the greatest works on one program tonight. Otherwise nobody would come to the next all-Beethoven. Well, danken Got, at least we didn't hear Wellington's Victory, and other schlock like that. I'm looking forward to the Choral Fantasy that a lot of people think is also schlock, maybe kitsch, because it sounds a little like the last movement of Beethoven's Ninth, except not so good. But I like it immensely. It has a piano and a chamber quartet, and a theme and variations, and soloists and chorus that yell at the top of their lungs. Hafoch baw va-hafoch bawo d'cholaw vaw. Turn it over and turn it over because everything is in it, lehavdil. Well, not exactly everything. It doesn't have Schiller's poetry like the Ninth, which is meleetzish geredt, gorgeous words, but you can't have everything. God gives and God takes away. Don't I know that."

I almost toppled over the balcony. I did not know that he knew music, any music except cantorial prayers, let alone classical music. I know it's unbelievable that a grandson regularly in touch with his grandparent would not know of such an activity that has to take up a substantial portion of a person's time, but I honestly did not know. My grandfather didn't own a radio or a TV, I never saw a single LP record or CD or even an ancient 78 rpm set in his apartment, and I'm sure he never could afford to go to a concert on his own. So where did he learn all this stuff? From books? Couldn't be, because on the way back to our seats, he sang the main theme from the Choral Fantasy for us, then the theme in the last movement of the Ninth, and finally the theme in the last movement of Brahms's First Symphony, in order to show us the similarities and differences between these three themes. Could he read music? Were there scores of music hidden in his junkyard apartment? Impossible. I refused to believe it. So where did all this knowledge come from?

My wife didn't care to know. All she knew was that his blather was insufferable and that she could not tolerate more pedagogical instruction from the old man that made her feel like an idiot. She sat through the Third Piano Concerto and the Choral Fantasy with a look on her face that would have stopped Beethoven in his tracks. But I was thrilled with my grandfather's virtuosic display of a wayward field of knowledge. That is, until I suddenly heard after the concert what it was that he didn't know at all.

"Hey Gramps," I said to him. "Who else do you like? Schubert?"

"For sure," he said, "even though he was a feygele and got himself maybe syphilis that caused him to die young at thirty-one. But his last symphony is a masterpiece, better than the unfinished."

I couldn't help smiling. "You like Bach?"

"Which Bach?" he asked.

"Johann Sebastian," I said impatiently. "I wouldn't be asking you about his minor-league sons."

"I never heard of him," my grandfather said.

"You never heard of him? C'mon, quit kidding me. You know everything about Beethoven and Schubert and Mozart, and you never heard of Johann Sebastian Bach?"

"Never."

"Come to think of it," I said, "his music wasn't well-known at all for about eighty years after his death until Felix Mendelssohn revived interest in Bach by conducting his St. Matthew Passion in Leipzig for the first time." Now I was showing off.

"Never heard of him either," my grandfather said.

"Never heard of who?"

"Him. That Mendelssohn."

"That's not exactly true, Grandpa," I snapped. "I've heard you orate countless times on the philosophy of Moses Mendelssohn, Felix Mendelssohn's grandfather."

"The grandfather I know. The grandson, nyet."

My wife tugged at my sleeve. She was at the end of her patience. Beethoven had not been fulfilling for her in the company of the old man. I could not get angry with her because I had to concede that the old guy could sometimes be very annoying.

A month later, another shock. This time I got the bright idea to take my grandfather to a museum. I was going to expand his horizons beyond the limited four cubits of the law that he inhabited. I would show him what emancipation and enlightenment had done for his grandson's generation.

At first, my wife refused to come along. I sat down with her to talk things out as I always did when we had an argument. After all, the least our generation had learned was to let it all out, to discuss things, to express feelings, not to keep boiling inside until it explodes, to get to know the other person as I didn't know my own grandfather.

"C'mon, hon," I said. "Nothing to be afraid of at the Met. Very religious Jews don't know a goddam thing about art. It's making images, and that's against the Ten Commandments. You're safe."

"He's impossible," she wailed. "I don't give two hoots about him showing off with all his book learning. It's another thing entirely."

"Another thing? What thing?"

"He hates us."

I was stopped in my tracks. "Hates us? C'mon, you're kidding."

"Hates us. That's what."

"No way," I said. "He can't hate anybody except a Hitler."

"He hates us because we've given up the religion. We're fancy assimilated Jews. That's his term for us. He hates us because we've left his tiny constricted world for the secular Christian world outside."

I must admit that I was a little surprised by my wife's intensity and even more by her analysis. I hadn't thought of it that way. But I couldn't really agree.

"He never said a word to us about our way of living," I mused.

"It's in his eyes. It's in his gut. It's in his soul."

"How do you know?"

"I know, I know. I know things too."

But she went with us to the Met, the three of us a strange group in a glorious milieu. My grandfather at first surprised her by hardly saying anything in the rooms with French nineteenth-century art from Delacroix to the Impressionists. He stood for a long time in front of a giant portrait of Napoleon and his army by the painter David. He even spent time in front of a rural scene by Monet without moving forward and backward as others did to see how the impressionist blobs coalesced into a real scene.

I sensed that there would be some trouble when we came to a Pissarro and the old man turned to us to say that Pissarro was Jewish. We didn't respond, and he remained silent for a moment. He moved to a Van Gogh and suddenly spoke up again.

"The foolish man cut off his ear. Self-mutilation is against Jewish law, as is suicide. Nowadays, freedom means that you have the right to put tattoos on your body, rings into your nose, and to kill yourself, if you feel like it. Modigliani was also Jewish. Nobody knows that. They know Chagall and some even know Soutine because his first name was Chaim, but they don't know Modigliani with his skinny women instead of zoftik Jewish daughters with a little meat on them."

I sighed. My wife scowled. We marched through doors and corridors and came to Italian Renaissance art. I stopped in front of a Raphael

Madonna and child. My grandfather walked right past the painting, out through another door, and disappeared.

My wife saw him leave, but she didn't chase after him. When I turned around and saw that he was gone, I motioned to her to follow, almost assured that he had gone to a men's room. We spent more than half an hour looking for him in every corner of that floor to no avail. I was getting nervous. I even had him paged, but he didn't show up. We waited at the entrance to the museum, on the long expanse of steps, for another half hour. It was a fruitless waste of time.

"We're going to his apartment," I said emphatically.

"Call him," my wife said.

"I don't want to call," I responded. "I have things to say to him face-to-face."

When we got to his apartment above a store on Fourteenth Street, we found the door open and no one inside. The open door didn't shock me. Another relative would have frozen to find the door ajar, expecting to see my grandfather's bloody body stretched out on the floor among the piles of books. But I knew that he had always refused to lock his door in the face of modern infamy. "Who would come to an old man's apartment who doesn't have a cent to his name?" When I remonstrated with him and insisted that his vaunted sense of logic was deficient in this case, since robbers and killers expect to find tons of money hidden in the mattress by senile senior citizens, he shrugged. "You should be happy if they rob me. Maybe they'll take away all the piles of books and sell them to Strand's Bookshop. Then your intellectual generation will be able to say that their grandfather had a nice, clean apartment without a book in it."

We found him in Union Square Park studying the laws of charity in the Mishneh Torah of Maimonides. He looked up at us, nodded two or three times as if to say, I think I know you people, and continued reading. I blew my stack.

"Enough already. We've had enough. We were supposed to go home and relieve the babysitter."

"So go."

"Why did you disappear all of a sudden?"

"Disappear is a relative term. I didn't disappear. I appeared somewhere else."

"Stop the shtick, Grandpa. You're driving me nuts. You disappeared when we were both standing in front of the Raphael painting."

"Who is Raphael?"

I couldn't take it anymore. I began screaming in a public park, unaware of others seated on nearby benches, unconcerned about their possible reaction. "Who is Raphael? Who is Leonardo da Vinci? Who is Michelangelo?"

"Him I know. He did a nice statue of David, even though he showed him with the gesheft in droysen. You know what I mean—exposed, the whole business showing. My wife, may she rest in peace, your grandma, would have been embarrassed."

"So you finally know somebody," I screamed. "So you finally know Michelangelo, the sculptor and painter. Geloybt is Got!" I had begun talking just like him with my "praise God" in Yiddish.

"A painter? I don't know Michelangelo a painter, only a sculptor."

"The Sistine Chapel ceiling, Grandpa. You know, in the Vatican."

"Where is that, may I ask?"

"In Rome, in Rome. Where the hell do you think it is? Where the Pope lives."

"The Pope?"

I finally decided that the smartass old man, my own flesh and blood, was pulling my leg, leading me on, giving me a royal screwing—whatever the metaphor. He didn't mean a word he was saying. I was sure of that now. My wife, for the very first time in his presence, had a smile on her face, a Mona Lisa smile. She was finally enjoying the sight of her grandfather-in-law baiting her husband to the point of no return.

Then came a comment from me that let it all hang out. "So you don't know who the Pope is. Next thing you'll be telling me is that you never heard of Jesus, that you don't know he was born on Christmas, circumcised on New Year's Day, and that we're now approaching the year 2000, the close of the second millennium of the Christian era, although the actual beginning of the third millennium should be in 2001, and that if all the banks in the world don't shape up on the Y2K computer problem, we'll all be screwed and every cent in our savings accounts and money-market funds and stocks and bonds will be down the drain, and you'll be the richest man in America with all your money tied up in the mattress."

"The year is 5760. What's with this 2000!" my grandfather said, as if he hadn't heard a word of my harangue.

"The coming year is 2000," I yelled.

"You're mistaken. 5760. We have 260 years to go to the next millennium. I may not live that long to see it. Maybe the moshiach, the messiah, will come then."

My wife burst out laughing for the first time in her life in the presence of her nemesis. She leaned over and said to the old man, "Grass will grow on all our heads before the messiah comes. You can bet on that, Pops."

It had been a very tardy Indian summer lingering into midfall, and the leaves in the city were turning much later than usual. A cluster of golden brown leaves fluttered to the ground beside us as if ordered at that moment to cover the heads of the living and the dead in deference to my wife's prophetic statement. The leaves wafted noiselessly this way and that, but if one listened, one could hear them struggling against the shifting winds. From the distance came the cries of sellers and buyers at some outdoor fair, the hubbub of commerce piercing the cold air of a limited patch of countryside within the giant city like arrows vaulting a castle wall to find their destiny. The sun was going down.

"Why do you lie all the time and make out you don't know things?" I asked softly.

The sudden wail of an ambulance in competition with the human cries of commerce could be heard on the far side of the park. It came as a surprise, as if nobody on this halcyon day, the last reminder of glorious fall, could possibly be taken sick. It was comforting that all things had to be as they are, as it was unsettling.

"I don't lie," my grandfather said. "All my life and in all the life of my parents and grandparents over there, we made order of the world through the terms of our sacred history. Someone was born two days before Purim, not on the date of the goyim. Someone died on the intermediary days of Passover. It is cold now because we live in the month of Cheshvan, which some call Marcheshvan because it is the beginning of bitterness, and mar means bitter. The previous year ended with Rosh ha-Shonoh, and the New Year began with it, not on the first of January. If the world insists on telling me that Columbus discovered America in 1492, then just as the American Indians refuse to think of the intruder as a discoverer of unoccupied land where they didn't exist, so do I refuse to think of Columbus's year. That was 507 years ago. That means that it took place in the year 5253 since Creation, this year's 5760 minus 507. What can be simpler? I refuse to know about second millenniums and third millenniums counting since who knows when. My own history is meaningful to me. It was everything to my father. It means less and less to you and you and you, and the children after you may not even know who they are."

His last "you" with a wave of the hand encompassed the park benches, the tall buildings surrounding the park, the giant skyscrapers in the near distance, the world now, and the world later.

"Did you ever read the Sherlock Holmes stories by Mr. Doyle?" he suddenly asked my wife in a conspiratorial whisper, leaning over to catch her ear. She did not get annoyed. She shook her head to mean yes even though she probably had no idea what he was driving at.

"When Dr. Watson meets the great detective Holmes, who has a university education, he is shocked to find out that Holmes does not seem to know that the earth revolves around the sun. Everybody knows that these days. But not Holmes. The detective explains to the amazed doctor that long ago he had decided to be the world's greatest detective and that he would devote all his energies to that end. This meant that he must learn chemistry and geology and other sciences that would allow him to track criminals through the streets of London. And so, to make room for all this knowledge in his limited brain, he conveniently decided to forget any fact or statement that was of no use to him in his profession and might crowd out a more important idea from his mind.

"I decided to do what the greatest detective in the world did. I would hear about madonnas and Christmas and millenniums and Y2Ks and I would make a rational decision to dismiss the newly learned information from my mind to make room for my Jewish history. When all my children are doing the very opposite, I would stand fast against the stream. How do you say it? I would hold the fort. I shouldn't mix metaphors. I would keep my finger in the dike. Perhaps the water will break through another hole, but at least I tried my best. That's the least I can do."

At that moment, a little black boy, perhaps five, perhaps six, strolled by, stopped to look at my grandfather, and sidled up to his knees without any fear or discomfort. I could see the parents three or four benches away, who were engrossed with another child in a carriage and who had not noticed the itinerary of their straying elder son.

"You look like Santa Claus," the little boy said to my grandfather, putting his elbows squarely on the old man's knees and his hands on his own chocolate cheeks cupping his chin. "You got a white beard."

"But I'm not dressed in red," my grandfather said.

"It ain't Christmas yet," the boy responded, unfazed. "Red is your working suit only when you go to houses."

"I'm too skinny," my grandfather said.

"You ain't asleep yet in the North Pole like bears, so you still didn't get fat."

The mother of the child looked up for a moment and panicked. She didn't see her son. "Uriah," she screamed. "Uriah, come here, child!"

The boy paid no attention. "Where are your reindeer?" he asked.

My grandfather probably didn't hear the mother's screams. Or maybe he didn't want to hear. "They already went to sleep with the bears to gain weight and strength for the trip with me. They're not as strong as I am, so they need more sleep."

"Show me your muscles," the boy demanded.

"Uriah!"

My grandfather got up from his seat, bared his arm, and flexed his muscle. The whole arm was thin as a rail and bony, and the invisible bicep never moved.

"Boy, you're strong."

"Uriah, stop bothering the man. Come here this instant!" The mother had caught sight of her son. When the boy would not budge from my grandfather's side, the mother whispered to her husband who held on to the carriage while she came quickly to our bench.

"I'm sorry the boy bothered you. He likes to talk to everybody. That's dangerous. I'm sorry." The woman was dressed from crown to toe, sleeves down to her fingers, no scrawny biceps showing, with a colorful bandana-like linen covering her head. She looked like an African queen.

"He thought I was Santa Claus."

"You're gonna bring me a present soon?" the boy asked.

"Don't pay any attention to him. We're Muslims, but he still thinks we're Christians. It's so hard weaning kids away from outside influences."

"I want a jet airplane with a thousand seats for all my friends at my birthday party."

My grandfather noticed the look of despair on the mother's face. He patted the child on his head.

"Santa Claus was born long before there were airplanes. He doesn't know about all the new inventions. He doesn't even know about computers. And Y2K. He's an am ho-orets. But he knows what good little boys should really like. He'll bring you something good, even if it isn't Christmas in your house. Maybe he'll bring you a magic carpet, and you can take all your friends to Mecca for a big party and to say your prayers there."

The mother, unsmiling, whisked the child away quickly. Perhaps she thought that my grandfather's response to her son wasn't very helpful. My grandfather did not sit down. He stood there motionless, his skinny old arm still bared to the cold winds of late fall, his eyes following the retreating couple, mother and child, madonna and child, Pharaoh's daughter and the child in her charge, an exotic painting in black and white, in a local city park of brown and gold.

Grandfather spoke to the winds. "His name, Uriah, means *God is my light*."

My wife stood up and put her arm around the old man's hunched shoulder. He was short, and she was taller than the average woman. I remained rooted to my seat on the bench, seeing only the protruding shoulder blades of my two, not seeing their eyes or their mouths or their hearts.

"Don't worry, Grandpa," my wife said. "The Y2K problem will be solved, one big world will continue to wait patiently for the Second Coming long after the year 2000, and the other little world will wait for the messiah long after the year 5760, and we will survive. God lets people who love little children survive."

Then all three of us went back home and to our separate lives together, perhaps to await the new millennium, perhaps not, but nevertheless to savor revelation. And I—I had a story to tell my learned coworkers at the local mecca of contemporary scientific research that they would not believe.

THE EDITOR

Rabbi Michael Lerner is editor of *TIKKUN: A Bimonthly Jewish Critique of Culture, Politics and Society* and the author of *Jewish Renewal: A Path to Healing and Transformation* and of *Spirit Matters: Global Healing and the Wisdom of the Soul.* He is rabbi of Beyt Tikkun synagogue in San Francisco. He welcomes your suggestions for poetry, fiction, and essays published in 2002 to be highlighted in the next volume, *Best Jewish Writing 2003* (RabbiLerner@Tikkun.org). He invites you to join the Tikkun Community at www.tikkun.org or by writing to him at 2107 Van Ness Ave., San Francisco, CA 94109.

THE CONTRIBUTORS

DAVID ABRAM, PH.D., is an ecologist, anthropologist, and philosopher, and the author of *The Spell of the Sensuous: Perception and Language in a More-Than-Human World* (Vintage, 1997), for which he was awarded the Lannan Literary Award for Nonfiction. An accomplished sleight-of-hand magician who has lived and traded magic with indigenous sorcerors in Indonesia, Nepal, and the Americas, David lectures and teaches widely on several continents.

ALLAN APPEL is a novelist, poet, teacher, and playwright whose books include, in addition to *Club Revelation, The Rabbi of Casino Boulevard* (National Jewish Book Award finalist), High Holiday Sutra (Barnes & Noble Discover Great New Writers Award), and the anthology *A Portable Apocalypse: A Quotable Companion to the End of the World.* His work has appeared in the *National Jewish Monthly* and the *Progressive.* He lives in New York City and New Haven.

URI AVNERY is a journalist, peace activist, former member of the Knesset, and leader of Gush Shalom, the most militant part of the Israeli peace movement. He was the first Israeli to meet Yasser Arafat (during the siege of Beirut, July 1982).

MICHAEL J. BADER, DMH, is a practicing psychologist and psychoanalyst, a member of the editorial board of *TIKKUN,* and the author of *Arousal: The Secret Logic of Sexual Fantasies* (Thomas Dunne Books, 2002).

NILTON BONDER was trained at the Jewish Theological Seminary in New York City and lectures regularly in the United States. Born in Brazil, he is a best-selling author of eleven books in Latin America. He leads one of Brazil's largest congregations and is also active in civil rights and ecological causes.

ARYEH COHEN is associate professor of Rabbinic literature and chair of Rabbinic studies at the Ziegler School of Rabbinic Studies at the University of Judaism. He is most recently the editor, with Shaul Magid, of *Beginning/Again: Toward a Hermeneutics of Jewish Texts* (New York: Seven Bridges Press, 2001).

DAVID A. COOPER is author of *God Is a Verb: Kabbalah and the Practice of Mystical Judaism* (Riverhead) and *Handbook of Jewish Meditation* (Jewish Lights). He and his wife, Shoshana, lead Jewish meditation retreats.

LEONARD FELDER, PH.D., is a licensed psychologist in West Los Angeles. His new book is *Seven Prayers That Can Change Your Life: How to Use Jewish Spiritual Wisdom for Enhancing Your Health, Relationships, and Daily Effectiveness* (Andrews-McMeel).

SYLVIA BARACK FISHMAN is associate professor of contemporary Jewish life and codirector of the Hadassah International Research Institute on Jewish Studies, both at Brandeis University.

SHELLY R. FREDMAN teaches writing at the University of Missouri-St. Louis and Jewish literature at the Central Agency for Jewish Education. She earned an MFA from Washington University. Her fiction and essays have appeared in a number of journals, including the *Chicago Tribune Magazine, Hadassah, Lilith,* and the *Sagarin Review.* She has recently completed her first novel.

ROGER S. GOTTLIEB is professor of philosophy at Worcester Polytechnic Institute and "Reading Spirit" columnist for *TIKKUN.* He is the author or editor of eleven books on political theory, the Holocaust, contemporary spirituality, and environmentalism; his most recent works are *Joining Hands: Religion and Politics Together for Social Change* (Westview) and *A Spirituality of Resistance: Finding a Peaceful Heart and Protecting the Earth* (Crossroad).

MICHAEL GROSS teaches in the department of international relations at the University of Haifa. He is the author of *Ethics and Activism* (Cambridge University Press, 1997) and is currently writing a book on the ethics of Jewish warfare.

LEO HABER is editor of the monthly journal *Midstream.* His first novel, *The Red Heifer,* was published in 2001 by Syracuse University Press. He taught English at the City College of New York; Hebrew at Baruch College and Hebrew Union College; and English, Hebrew, and Latin at Lawrence High School (Cedarhurst, New York) where he also served as chairman of the Department of Foreign Languages.

BONNA DEVORA HABERMAN is a lecturer at Brandeis University, where she is also director of Mistabra, the Institute for Jewish Textual Activism.

SUSAN HAHN is a poet, playwright, and the editor of *TriQuarterly* literary magazine. She has published five books of petry, most recently *Holiday* (2001) and *Mother in Summer (2002).*

YOSSI KLEIN HALEVI is the Israel correspondent for the *New Republic* and a senior writer for the *Jerusalem Report.* His new book, just published by William Morrow, is called *At the Entrance to the Garden of Eden: A Jew's Search for God with Christians and Muslims in the Holy Land.*

JILL HAMMER works at Malyan, the Jewish Women's Project, at the JCC in Manhattan, as the editor of *Journey* and a coordinator of community outreach. She was ordained as a rabbi by the Jewish Theological Seminary in 2001 and holds a Ph.D. in social psychology from the University of Connecticut. She is a poet and author. Her first book (JPS, 2001) is entitled *Sisters at Sinai: New Tales of Biblical Women.*

SUSANNAH HESCHEL is the Eli Black Associate Professor of Jewish Studies at Dartmouth College and chair of the Jewish Studies Program. She is the author of *Abraham Geiger and the Jewish Jesus,* a study of modern Jewish attitudes toward Christianity. She has also edited several books, including *On Being a Jewish Feminist* and, with David Biale and Michael Galchinsky, *Insider/Outsider: American Jews and Multiculturalism.*

LOOLWA KHAZZOOM has been a ground-breaking Jewish multicultural educator for over a decade. She is director of the Jewish Multicultural Curriculum Project and editor of the forthcoming anthology, *Behind the Veil of Silence: North African and Middle Eastern Jewish Women Speak Out.* She offers Jewish multicultural workshops for children and adults of all ages (www.loolwa.com).

MICHAEL KIMMEL is the author of *Manhood in America* and, most recently, *The Gendered Society* (Oxford University Press, 2000). He teaches sociology at State University of New York at Stony Brook.

BINNIE KIRSHENBAUM is an adjunct professor in the writing division of the Columbia University School of the Arts. She received the Critics' Choice Award for fiction in 1996 and was a regional winner of *Granta's* Best Young American Novelists Award. She lives in New York City.

PHILIP LEVINE is the author of sixteen books of poetry. He has received the Ruth Lilly Poetry Prize, the Harriet Monroe Memorial Prize for Poetry, the Frank O'Hara Prize, and two Guggenheim Foundation fellowships. For two years he served as chair of the literature panel of the National Endowment for the Arts; he was elected as chancellor of the Academy of American Poets in 2000.

JONATHAN MARK is associate editor of the *New York Jewish Week*. He was twice named writer of the year by the New York State Press Association.

GAIL MAZUR teaches in the Graduate Writing Program at Emerson College. She is the author of four books of poems. *They Can't Take That Away From Me* was a National Book Award Finalist, 2001. She lives in Cambridge and Provincetown, Massachusetts.

STANLEY MOSS is a poet. His new book, *A History of Color,* will be published in 2002 (Seven Stories Press).

JACQUELINE OSHEROW is the author of four books of poetry. She's been awarded fellowships by the Guggenheim Foundation, the National Endowment for the Arts, and the Ingrain Merrily Foundation, and the Wittier Bynner Prize from the American Academy and Institute of Arts and Letters.

ALICIA OSTRIKER is a prizewinning poet and midrashist, and author of *The Nakedness of the Fathers: Biblical Visions and Revisions.* Her most recent books of poems are *The Little Space* and *The Volcano Sequence.* Ostriker's work appears in many anthologies and has been translated into many languages, including Hebrew and Arabic.

AMOS OZ is a highly regarded author of numerous works of fiction and collections of essays. He has received several international awards, including the Prix Femina, the Israel Prize, and the Frankfurt Peace Prize. He lives in Israel.

ROBERT PINSKY'S most recent book of poems is *Jersey Rain.* He teaches in the Creative Writing Department at Boston University.

JUDITH PLASKOW is professor of religious studies at Manhattan College and author of many books and articles on feminist theology.

LETTY COTTIN POGREBIN is the author of eight books, most recently *Getting Over Getting Older*. Her first novel, *Three Daughters*, is being published in 2002 by Farrar, Straus and Giroux.

CHAIM POTOK trained as a rabbi and an editor, became an international success with his beloved first novel, *The Chosen*, and over the following thirty-odd years has given us many other memorable works, both fiction and nonfiction. He lives outside Philadelphia.

TANYA REINHART is a professor of linguistics and cultural studies at Tel Aviv University and the University of Utrecht in the Netherlands. In 1994, following the Oslo agreements, which she viewed as a painful deception of the Palestinian people and the setting of a sophisticated apartheid regime, she turned to political writing. Her political writings appear regularly in *Yediot Aharonot*.

ADRIENNE RICH'S most recent books of poetry are *Dark Fields of the Republic* (Poems 1991–1995), *Midnight Salvage* (Poems 1995–1998), and *FOX* (Poems 1998–2000). Her most recent selection of essays is *Arts of the Possible: Essays and Conversation*. She has received the Dorothea Tanning Prize and the Lannan Foundation Lifetime Achievement Award. She lives in California.

JONATHAN ROSEN is the author of the novel *Eve's Apple*, published by Random House in 1997. His latest book, *The Talmud and the Internet: A Journey Between Worlds* (Farrar, Straus and Giroux, 2000), was chosen as a *New York Times* Notable Book of the Year in 2000, was published in paperback in 2001, and is being translated into six languages. His essays have appeared in the *New York Times Magazine*, the *New York Times Book Review*, the *New Yorker*, the *American Scholar*, and several anthologies.

DANYA RUTTENBERG is the editor of *Yentl's Revenge: The Next Wave of Jewish Feminism* (Seal Press) and a contributing editor at *Lilith: The Independent Jewish Women's Magazine*. Her work has appeared in numerous anthologies and magazines, including the *San Francisco Chronicle*, *TIKKUN*, *Bitch*, and *Salon*. She lectures nationwide about religion, spirituality, and culture.

GRACE SCHULMAN'S latest poetry collections are *Days of Wonder: New and Selected Poems* (2002) and *The Paintings of Our Lives* (2001), both published by Houghton Mifflin.

RICHARD H. SCHWARTZ, PH.D., is the author of *Judaism and Vegetarianism, Judaism and Global Survival,* and *Mathematics and Global Survival.* He has more than one hundred articles on the Internet at jewishveg. com/schwartz and frequently speaks and contributes articles on environmental, health, and other current issues. He is professor emeritus of mathematics at the College of Staten Island.

JEROME M. SEGAL is a research scholar at the Institute for Philosophy and Public Policy at the University of Maryland and president of the Jewish Peace Lobby. He is coauthor of *Negotiating Jerusalem* (SUNY Press, 2000).

RAMI SHAPIRO is president and senior rabbi of Metivta, a center for contemplative Judaism in Los Angeles, and author of *Minyan, Wisdom of the Jewish Sage, The Way of Solomon,* and *Proverbs.*

GERALD STERN has received many awards, including the National Book Award, the Lamont Prize, a Guggenheim, three NEA awards, a fellowship from The Academy of Arts and Letters, and the Ruth Lilly Prize. He taught at the Writer's Workshop in Iowa City and at many universities, including Columbia University, New York University, Sarah Lawrence College and the University of Pittsburgh.

DAVID SUISSA is founder and CEO of Suissa Miller, Inc., a $300 million advertising agency in Los Angeles. He is founder, publisher, and editor of *Olam* magazine, with more than three million readers and a mission of spreading global spirituality and Jewish unity. He was named one of the top fifty Jewish leaders in 2001 by the newspaper *Forward.*

JONATHAN TEL was educated in the United States and Britain and studied cosmology with Stephen Hawking. He has worked as an elementary particle physicist and lived and traveled in many countries. Currently he divides his time between New York, London, and Jerusalem.

TOVA is a Jewish working-class lesbian feminist. Her writing has appeared in numerous journals and anthologies, including *Bridges: A Journal for Jewish Feminists and Our Friends, Jewish Currents,* and *Nice Jewish Girls.* She recently received a grant from Brandeis to work on a book about poor, working-class Jewish women. She lives near Eugene, Oregon, with her partner, their beautiful seven year old, and two other families.

GALINA VROMEN spent ten years as a foreign correspondent for Reuters News Agency in Israel, the Netherlands, and Britain before settling down with her family in Israel, where she is a staff translator and copyeditor for the English edition of the daily *Ha'aretz* newspaper. Her fiction has appeared in a number of publications, including *American Way, Reform Judaism,* and the *Jerusalem Review,* and has been anthologized in *With Signs and Wonders: An International Anthology of Jewish Fabulist Fiction* (Invisible Cities Press, 2001). *The Secret Diary of a Bat Mitzva Girl* was second-place winner of the Fourth Annual Dora Teitelboim Center for Yiddish Culture Writing Contest and was subsequently published in the secular, progressive monthly *Jewish Currents* in June 2001.

PAUL WAPNER is associate professor and director of the Environmental Policy Program at American University. His most recent publication is *Principled World Politics: The Challenge of Normative International Relations* (Rowman and Littlefield, 2000).

ARTHUR WASKOW has, since 1969, been one of the leading creators of theory, practice, and institutions for the movement for Jewish renewal. He is the Tikkun Olam Fellow of ALEPH: Alliance for Jewish Renewal. He founded and directs The Shalom Center (www.shalomctr.org), a division of ALEPH that focuses on Jewish thought and practice to seek peace, pursue justice, heal the earth, and build community.

Among his seminal works in Jewish renewal are *The Freedom Seder, Godwrestling* (1978) and *Godwrestling—Round 2* (1996, recipient of the Benjamin Franklin Award), *Seasons of Our Joy,* and *Down-to-Earth Judaism: Food, Money, Sex, and the Rest of Life.* With Phyllis Berman, he has written *A Time for Every Purpose Under Heaven: The Jewish Life-Spiral as a Spiritual Path.*

Waskow has been a leader in the shaping of Jewish theology and practice committed to the protection and healing of the earth. He was the managing coeditor of *Trees, Earth, & Torah: A Tu B'Shvat Anthology* and the editor of *Torah of the Earth: Exploring 4,000 Years of Ecology in Jewish Thought.*

Waskow was ordained as rabbi in 1995. In 1996, he was named by the United Nations a "Wisdom Keeper"—one among forty religious and intellectual leaders from around the world who met in connection with the Habitat II conference in Istanbul. In 2001, he was presented with the Abraham Joshua Heschel Award by the Jewish Peace Fellowship.

WENDY WASSERSTEIN is the author of numerous plays, including "The Sisters Rosensweig" and "The Heidi Chronicles" (for which she received a Tony Award and the 1989 Pulitzer Prize).

JOSHUA WEINER is the author of *The World's Room* (Chicago, 2001). He teaches in the MFA program in writing at the University of Maryland and lives in Washington, D.C.

C. K. WILLIAMS'S most recent book of poetry, *Repair,* won the Pulitzer Prize. He teaches in the writing program at Princeton University.

ABRAHAM B. YEHOSHUA is one of Israel's greatest living writers. His literary achievements have long been recognized throughout the world, and he has been awarded literary prizes in Israel and the United States.

ERIC H. YOFFIE is president of the Union of American Hebrew Congregations, the synagogue arm of the Reform Movement of North America, which represents more than nine hundred congregations in the United States and Canada.

DAVID ZASLOW was ordained in 1995 by Rabbi Zalman Schachter-Shalomi and is the spiritual leader of Havurah Shir Hadash. He leads men's retreats and Shabbat weekends nationwide and can be reached at shalomrav@aol.com.

CREDITS

Jewish Response to September 11

ARTHUR WASKOW   "The Sukkah and the Towers" by Rabbi Arthur Waskow, director of the Shalom Center (www.shalomctr.org) and author of *Godwrestling—Round 2*. Copyright © 2001 by Arthur Waskow.

SYLVIA BARACK FISHMAN   "Flaws in 'Blame America' Arguments" by Sylvia Barack Fishman. Originally printed in the *New York Jewish Week*, Nov. 2, 2001. Used by permission.

C. K. WILLIAMS   "War." Originally published in the *New Yorker*, Nov. 5, 2001.

JONATHAN MARK   "E-mails from the End of the World." First appeared in the *New York Jewish Week*, Dec. 2001.

MICHAEL J. BADER   "Posttraumatic Love Syndrome." Reprinted from *TIKKUN*, Jan./Feb. 2002, vol. 17, number 1.

MICHAEL LERNER   "Should Scared Jews Become Tough Jews?" by Michael Lerner.

DANYA RUTTENBERG   "Red, White, and Gold: On the Numbing of a Nation" by Danya Ruttenberg. Copyright © 2001.

The Many Identities of a Jew

JOSHUA WEINER   "Psalm." From *The World's Room*, pp. 1–3, University of Chicago Press, 2001. Reprinted by permission.

ARYEH COHEN   "Permeable Boundaries." Reprinted from *Conservative Judaism*, vol. 54, no. 1, Fall 2001, pp. 53–59, with permission. Copyright © by the Rabbinical Assembly.

Reclaiming the Spirit in Judaism

RICHARD H. SCHWARTZ "Vegetarianism: A Global and Spiritual Imperative." Reprinted with permission.

PHILIP LEVINE "My Fathers, the Baltic." Copyright © 2001 Philip Levine. First appeared in *Ploughshares,* Fall 2001.

DAVID A. COOPER "Bringing Messianic Consciousness." Originally published as "Seventh Millennium Judaism." Reprinted from *TIKKUN,* Jan./Feb. 2001, vol. 16, no. 1.

LEONARD FELDER "Prayer as Rebellion." Reprinted from *TIKKUN,* Nov./Dec. 2001, vol. 16, no 6.

ERIC H. YOFFIE "The Worship Revolution." Reprinted by permission of *Reform Judaism* magazine, published by the Union of American Hebrew Congregations. This article is adapted from his Presidential Address to the UAHC General Assembly in Orlando, Florida, on December 18, 1999.

JACQUELINE OSHEROW "Psalm 37 at Auschwitz." Reprinted from *Dead Man's Praise.* Copyright © 1999 by Jacqueline Osherow. Used by permission of Grove/Atlantic, Inc.

DAVID SUISSA "The Curse of Being Right" by David Suissa. First published in the Spring 1999 issue of *Farbrengen* magazine.

ALICIA OSTRIKER "Zohar." Originally published as "The Yearning" in *The Volcano Sequence* (University of Pittsburgh Press, 2002).

ABRAHAM B. YEHOSHUA "The Biblical Story of Cain and Abel, Genesis 4." Selected from *The Terrible Power of a Minor Guilt,* pp. 3–16. Copyright © 2000 Abraham B. Yehoshua, Syracuse University Press.

JUDITH PLASKOW "Authority, Resistance, and Transformation: Jewish Feminist Reflections on Good Sex." From *Good Sex: Feminist Perspectives on the World's Religions,* edited by Patricia Beattie Jung, Mary E. Hunt, and Radhika Balakrishnan. Copyright © 2001 by Judith Plaskow. Reprinted by permission of Rutgers University Press.

NILTON BONDER Selections from *Our Immoral Soul* by Rabbi Nilton Bonder. Copyright © 2001 by Nilton Bonder. Reprinted by arrangement with Shambhala Publications, Inc., Boston, www.shambhala.com.

JILL HAMMER "The Tenth Plague." Reprinted from *Sisters at Sinai.* Copyright © 2002 by the Jewish Publication Society. Used by permission.

Israel in Conflict

On Being a Mensch and Healing a Troubled World

The Pleasures of Jewish Culture

ROBERT PINSKY "First Things to Hand." First published in the *New Yorker,* Nov. 19, 2001. Copyright © 2001 Robert Pinsky.

CHAIM POTOK Excerpt from "Old Men at Midnight" by Chaim Potok, copyright © 2001 Chaim Potok. Used by permission of Alfred A. Knopf, a division of Random House, Inc.

GAIL MAZUR Five Poems Entitled "Questions." Reprinted from *They Can't Take That Away from Me,* copyright © 2001 University of Chicago Press. Used by permission.

GRACE SCHULMAN "Poem Ending with a Phrase from the Psalms." Reprinted from *The Paintings of Our Lives,* Houghton Mifflin, 2001.

AMOS OZ "The Same Sea." Excerpted from THE SAME SEA by Amos Oz. Copyright © 1999 by Amos Oz and Keter Publishing House Ltd. Translation copyright © 2001 by Nicholas de Lange. This is a translation of OTO HA-YAM. Published by Harcourt, Inc.

SHELLY R. FREDMAN "Excavating the Past: Looking into Jewish Stories." Previously unpublished.

SUSAN HAHN "October 1." Reprinted from *Holiday* (University of Chicago Press, 2001). Copyright © 2001 Susan Hahn.

LEO HABER "The Greatest Jew in the World." First appeared in *Midstream,* Apr. 2001, vol. 47, no. 3.

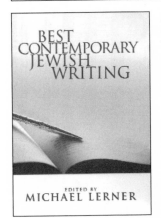

Best Contemporary Jewish Writing

Edited by Michael Lerner

$16.95 Paper   ISBN: 0787959367
$27.50 Hardcover   ISBN: 0787959723

"This volume is the first in a series that is planned to come out each year. It is clearly an auspicious beginning."—*LA Times*

"The message that the world could be healed and transformed was revolutionary when first articulated by Jewish writers of the past, and it remains radical even today. . . . Cruelty is not destiny. Jewish writing helps us understand that the pain of the past can be transcended."—From the Introduction by Michael Lerner.

Between the covers of this book is a treasure trove of great fiction, poetry, social analysis, and spiritual insight by renowned contributors such as Philip Roth, Marge Piercy, Senator Joseph I. Lieberman, Naomi Wolf, Norman Podhoretz, Jonathan Rosen, Robert Pinsky, Yehuda Amichai, Rachel Adler, Nathan Englander, Daniel Boyarin, Adrienne Rich, Arthur Waskow, William Safire, Zalman M. Schachter-Shalomi, and many others. Included are famous writers, young and upcoming writers, writers with politics ranging from liberal/progressive to neoconservative. Despite their disparate opinions and points of view, these writers have been chosen by Michael Lerner because they transcend the cynicism and narcissistic self-indulgence of contemporary culture and contribute to the Kabbalistic vision of a world that has been shattered, but can be healed. The first volume in a planned series of annual publications, *Best Contemporary Jewish Writing* is an essential tool for understanding contemporary culture and social reality.

You don't have to be Jewish to be moved and to learn from these authors. The poetry, fiction, memories, and essays in this book are provocative and engaging, entertaining and inspiring, irreverent, and filled with awe.

MICHAEL LERNER is the editor of *TIKKUN* magazine and rabbi of the neo-Hasidic Beyt Tikkun Jewish Renewal synagogue in San Francisco. One of his most recent books, *Spirit Matters: Global Healing and the Wisdom of the Soul*, was selected as "one of the most significant books of 2000" by the Los Angeles Times Book Review and won a PEN award. Rabbi Lerner was designated by *Utne Reader* as one of America's 100 Most Important Visionaries. He holds Ph.D.s in philosophy and clinical psychology.

[Price subject to change]